Working With Kids Who Bully

This book is dedicated to all of YOU who are working hard to improve the lives of the children, families, and communities with whom you work. So often your work is unrecognized and underappreciated. Let that not be the case in this instance. Thank you.

Working With Kids Who Bully

New Perspectives on Prevention and Intervention

Walter B. Roberts, Jr.

CORWIN
A SAGE Publishing Company

CORWIN
A SAGE Publishing Company

FOR INFORMATION:

Corwin
A SAGE Company
2455 Teller Road
Thousand Oaks, California 91320
(800) 233-9936
www.corwin.com

SAGE Publications Ltd.
1 Oliver's Yard
55 City Road
London EC1Y 1SP
United Kingdom

SAGE Publications India Pvt. Ltd.
B 1/I 1 Mohan Cooperative Industrial Area
Mathura Road, New Delhi 110 044
India

SAGE Publications Asia-Pacific Pte. Ltd.
3 Church Street
#10-04 Samsung Hub
Singapore 049483

Senior Acquisitions Editor: Jessica Allan
Senior Associate Editor: Kimberly Greenberg
Editorial Assistant: Katie Crilley
Production Editor: Libby Larson
Copy Editor: Amy Harris
Typesetter: C&M Digitals (P) Ltd.
Proofreader: Sally Jaskold
Indexer: Kathy Paparchontis
Cover Designer: Scott Van Atta
Marketing Manager: Jill S. Margulies

Library of Congress Cataloging-in-Publication Data

Names: Roberts, Walter B., author.

Title: Working with kids who bully : new perspectives on prevention and intervention / Walter B. Roberts, Jr.

Description: Thousand Oaks, California : Corwin/A SAGE Company, 2016. | Includes bibliographical references and index.

Identifiers: LCCN 2016007887 | ISBN 978-1-5063-3387-8 (pbk.)

Subjects: LCSH: Bullying in schools—Prevention. | Counseling in elementary education. | Counseling in middle school education.

Classification: LCC LB3013.3 R634 2016 | DDC 371.5/8—dc23
LC record available at http://lccn.loc.gov/2016007887

16 17 18 19 20 10 9 8 7 6 5 4 3 2 1

Contents

Acknowledgments vii

About the Author x

PART I. CURRENT AND NEW PERSPECTIVES ON BULLYING BEHAVIORS 1

Chapter 1. Why a Book on Those Who Bully? 2

Chapter 2. Understanding Those Who Bully 8

Chapter 3. What Exactly *Is* Bullying Today? 20

Chapter 4. Relational Aggression 39

Chapter 5. The Law and Bullying Behaviors 48

PART II. WORKING WITH THOSE WHO ENGAGE IN BULLYING BEHAVIORS 71

Chapter 6. Will This Stuff Work? 72

Chapter 7. Essential Skills for Interveners 75

Chapter 8. Making the Communication and Relational Connection 90

Chapter 9. Forced Apologies and Mediations 98

Chapter 10. Applying Elements of Restorative Justice Techniques With Those Who Engage in Bullying Behaviors 102

Chapter 11. Building Empathy Within Those Who Bully 112

Chapter 12. Thought Before Action: Slowing Down Impulsive Behaviors 135

Chapter 13. Morality as a Component of Bullying Prevention 151

Chapter 14. Dealing With the Demon That Is Anger 158

Chapter 15. When Bullies Live in Space 172

Chapter 16. Bystanders or Upstanders? 191

Chapter 17. Engaging the Parent 200

Chapter 18. Documentation 217

Chapter 19. Bibliomedia Therapy 232

Chapter 20. When All Else Fails 243

Chapter 21. Potholes, Gravel, and Road Tar 250

Resources for Consideration 253

References 258

Index 285

Acknowledgments

This is another piece in a lifetime of research and advocacy on behalf of helping schools and communities be safe places for all students. It is also the last "installment" of a "trilogy" of efforts to look at how bullying behaviors impact kids, families, and the communities in which they live.

Through three decades, I have examined bullying behaviors and helped communities develop prevention and intervention techniques and strategies to address them. These approaches have not followed traditional pathways. In 2006, we started the journey with *Bullying From Both Sides: Strategic Interventions for Working With Bullies and Victims.* That book was one of the first efforts to emphasize the reality that there are two parties involved in the bullying dynamic—one who creates the problem and one to whom the problematic behavior is directed. Where approaches to that date had focused primarily on those who were targeted for bullying behaviors, *Bullying From Both Sides* began the discussion of how to also approach and better understand the instigators.

In 2008, we turned our focus again to another nontraditional and overlooked group who plays a pivotal role in helping reduce bullying behaviors—parents. *Working With Parents of Bullies and Victims* was an effort to encourage educators and others in supervisory positions to see the value in bringing parents into the problem-solving equation. Parents, by and large, to that date had been excluded from the helping process. The truth is that without parental involvement our efforts are likely destined to be far less successful and long-term than desired.

The next eight years were devoted to intensive advocacy on behalf of safe schools and bullying prevention efforts. These efforts involved public testimony at both the legislative and judicial levels, along with exhaustive efforts to pass legislation in one of the last states in the country to have viable statewide equitable bullying prevention protection in place for K–12 children. I have met the most remarkable people through professional conferences, school and community workshops, and consultations—dedicated professionals, parents, and kids, always the kids. Their experiences and stories helped shape the direction of this book, educated me about their needs, and reminded me of the original mission I devoted myself to in the beginning—to look at the problem of bullying from different angles in an effort to help the kids and those engaged with them to develop the "best-fit" approaches to solving the issue.

There are many people to thank for this most recent part of the journey. First, I want to thank the editorial staff at Corwin over the last ten-plus years that I have had the honor of working with and who have helped me learn the business of writing professional trade books. Jessica Allan has stuck with me since her first day on the job and believed me all the times I told her, "Yeah, yeah, yeah. Next year. I promise. I'll start on that one next year." I also owe a great debt of gratitude to Stacy Wagner-Kinnear, who, during her time at Corwin years ago, started me on *The Trilogy*, as we came to call them, and who sent me an e-mail before a national conference where I was doing a workshop on bullying prevention and inquired about my interest in possibly writing something on the subject. If it had not been for her, perhaps none of these books would have been written.

I also want to thank the reviewers of the various drafts of this book on whom Corwin depends for publication decisions. Your reviews were kind, complimentary, and helpful. Likewise, I am grateful for the hard work of the copy editors and related Corwin staff who helped turn the draft manuscripts into the final product. I learn so much from reviewers and editors every trip down the book publishing highway.

We have dedicated graduate students at the master's and doctoral levels at Minnesota State University, Mankato. They have helped me ferret out resources over the two years this book was in process, collate the massive amount of resources consulted for the final version, and vet references. Those students include Dharshini Goonetilleke, Becca Thompson, and Lauren Solenek.

I had the privilege of cochairing a select task force created by Governor Mark Dayton here in Minnesota to address the problems directly associated with bullying and the negative conditions that help create them. That group, the Task Force on the Prevention of School Bullying, was composed of some of the hardest working educational, medical, legal, and community members I have ever met, all committed to ending bullying in the state's schools. We took testimony from hundreds of parents and students across the state. The recommendations of that task force, along with that testimony, resulted in the historic Safe and Supportive Schools Act of 2014. The work with this group further motivated me to move forward in addressing the unmet needs of those who create the problem in the first place, as well as helped me realize that a major paradigm shift was needed to move us away from all that goes with the stereotypical label of *bully*. Underneath the behavior is a child in need of assistance. Labels help us forget that.

Last, but certainly not least, are the two furry friends found in my photo accompanying this book. Murphy and Prairie are two golden retrievers who came into our lives as rescues from abusive situations. Both are certified therapy dogs. They have been by my side the entire trip while working on the manuscript and its various iterations. They are lounging beside me as I write this very page. They are role models for kindness and forgiveness, and I use their stories in my work with people every day.

We need more kindness and forgiveness in the world. I hope that in some small way this book will enable you to help provide just that for the kids—and adults—with whom you work.

PUBLISHER'S ACKNOWLEDGMENTS

Corwin gratefully acknowledges the contributions of the following reviewers:

Cindy Corlett
Administrator
Douglas County School District
Parker, CO

Regine Dejean
School Counselor
New York City Department of Education
Jamaica, NY

Julie Duford
Fifth-Grade Teacher
Polson Middle School
Polson, MT

Susan N. Imamura
Principal, Staff Developer
Hawaii State Department of Education
Honolulu, HI

Susan Kunz
School Psychologist, LEP
Conejo Valley Unified School District
Thousand Oaks, CA

Angela M. Mosley
Principal
Essex County Public Schools
Tappahannock, VA

Dr. Tricia Peña
Education Consultant
E.C.H.O.360 Education Consulting
Vail, AZ

Brigitte Tennis
Headmistress and Eighth-Grade Teacher
Stella Schola Middle School
Redmond, WA

Dana Salles Trevethan
Interim Superintendent
Turlock Unified School District
Turlock, CA

About the Author

Photo by John Cross

Dr. Walter B. Roberts, Jr. is a professor of counselor education at Minnesota State University, Mankato, whose research and advocacy are in the areas of bullying prevention, school safety, and mental health. He began his career as a classroom teacher in 1978 and later served as a school counselor before moving to higher education in 1993.

In addition to being licensed for private practice, he has extensive public policy experience, consults and testifies with legislators and the judicial system as an expert witness, and is a frequent source with the media on counseling-related issues. Along with his nationwide speaking engagements and university responsibilities, he has authored two books on the subject of bullying prevention, *Bullying From Both Sides* in 2006 and *Talking With Parents of Bullies and Victims* in 2008. From 2012 through 2014, he served as cochair of the governor of Minnesota's select task force on the prevention of school bullying, which resulted in the passage of the state's Safe and Supportive Schools Act of 2014. His research has expanded into the arena of animal-assisted therapy. He and his certified therapy dogs, Murphy and Prairie, visit a wide array of facilities by request.

PART I

Current and New Perspectives on Bullying Behaviors

1

Why a Book on Those Who Bully?

This is the third book I've written on the subject of bullying prevention and intervention. The first book was *Bullying From Both Sides: Strategic Interventions for Working With Bullies and Victims* (2006). It was followed in 2008 by *Working With Parents of Bullies and Victims*. The purpose of this final book in the trilogy is to focus on the group of individuals who participate in the ***bully–target continuum*** that are, in many respects, the most important of the relationship—those who create and generate the problem.

Traditional terminologies and stereotypical labels are about to be challenged. That is one purpose of this book. First up—the conceptualization of a ***bully–target dyad.*** A dyad implies two people or two positions. It has been traditional to refer to the interaction between those who bully and those who receive the bullying behavior as if the behavior is easily and neatly identifiable between the two parties. That is too simplistic a way to view the relationship although it is one that even I have used in previous writings, consultations, and presentations.

It is more effective to view the behaviors associated between those who bully and those who are impacted by it along a ***continuum***, or sliding scale, with varying levels of intensity between the two parties (Espelage, 2003; Espelage & Swearer, 2003; Rigby, 2005). In essence, some individuals bully in ways that are easily identifiable to anyone and everyone who would observe or read a description of the behavior. Others, not so much. It is the same with those who are on the receiving end of the misbehavior: Some are more negatively impacted by it than others; the behavior is intended for some, but not others, yet they may also be impacted by it; some are aware of the behavior, are not in the crosshairs of it, yet choose to remain uninvolved; and still others are either completely oblivious to, immune to, or unaffected by what happens to others. Viewing bullying behaviors along a continuum allows for "students [having] different bullying and victimization profiles" (Espelage, p. 87).

Of all the literature and media attention given to the subject of bullying and its aftereffects, very little attention has actually been given to those who are at the heart of the interaction—the ones we have traditionally labeled the *bully*. This book is an effort to start the conversation and process of plugging that interventional gap and to enable those who choose to "go upstream" to find the causes of why it is that some children choose to intimidate their peers, while others do not.

This is an unusual effort. It has been the tradition of educators and pundits to ignore the thought processes of those whom we have deemed problematic. We tend to be reactionary as opposed to proactive in dealing with interpersonal situations because even though it can be more cost effective in the long run (just ask the medical community the whole idea behind preventive medicine), it is also hard work to practice prevention when dealing with human behavior. We humans are wiggly creatures. In our efforts to change behaviors, it is often unclear the direct links between cause and effect. There are too many "extraneous factors" impacting the direction of input to output. *It will require a paradigm shift to change the belief and realization that if we are willing to truly address the issue of bullying prevention and intervention, it is always more difficult to clean up the fallout from an incident of physical and psychological aggression than it is to prevent it.*

Case in point: A school district received repeated indications that certain groups of students within that district were targeted with discriminatory behaviors. These behaviors were not only manifested among the student body in clearly identifiable patterns but even among some of the teaching staff. Complaints from students and parents to school district personnel were met with denials and rebuttals. While admitting that such incidents may have occurred, the district saw no need to do anything any differently from what it was currently doing; that it was adequately addressing those incidents of which there had been complaints; that those who were doing the complaining were making much ado about nothing. The district even used its public relations machinery to target critics who expressed concerns about what was occurring. In sum, the district expended great energies and money designed to stonewall and refute evidence being brought to its attention on a regular basis in hopes that the "problem" would go away. However, the problem in this instance was defined by district administrators and the school board as the parents, students, and community members who were concerned about the treatment of students within the district, not the actual behaviors which were clearly discriminatory and harmful.

The school district continued to engage in this systematic refusal to address the bullying behaviors within the district even when students who had been targeted began self-injurious behaviors, inclusive of suicide attempts and completions. No amount of public relations and denials, however, could refute what was becoming more obvious by the day—the district was, de facto, inadequately addressing the bullying behaviors which had, in essence, become institutionalized by the district's refusal to address the real problem.

Only after a protracted legal battle did the district move toward solution. Intervention at the federal court level forced its hand. In this instance, the bullying behavior had become institutionalized within the entire district, from the children and adolescents who tormented their peers, all the way up through some (but, mercifully, not all) of the teachers, administration, and school board who fought tooth and nail to avoid addressing the issue.

As is so often the case, bullying behaviors occur in an environment where they are either encouraged or allowed to happen as a result of neglect. This is one of the embarrassing truths as to why bullying still occurs. In large part, we *allow* it to happen. We wait until something has occurred before we deem it worthy of a response. But children and adolescents—and adults—don't live in a vacuum. In the absence of guidance from mentors or positive role models, kids stretch the limits of what they can get away with until acted upon by a greater force. That greater force sometimes ends up being the consequences imposed upon those who neglect and abuse the bounds of respectful, civic, and legal behaviors.

SO WHAT WILL YOU GET FROM THIS BOOK?

Want a short and honest answer to that question? Nothing if you only read it. *Knowledge means nothing if not applied.* We *know* and have *ample evidence* that bullying behaviors are detrimental to the development of children, adolescents, adults, and society. We *know* and have *ample evidence* that bullying behaviors cause insufferable harm to those on the receiving end. We *know* and have *ample evidence* that some of those individuals are so tormented by the agents of bullying that they make decisions to harm themselves or others out of deep desperation. And we *know* and have *ample evidence* that *someone* ought to *do something* to stop bullying behaviors before the problem gets "any worse."

So if we know all of these things, if we have all of this evidence, why aren't we able to solve the problem? And who is that "someone" who is supposed to do that "something" to help put a stop to it?

Look in the mirror.

The answer is you. The answer is me.

Think about it. While there is only one of "me" in the world, there are lots of "yous." You and me. Us. Together. But nothing will improve if we don't *act* toward solutions. Nothing will improve if all we do is provide lip service to a problem that is soaking up a tremendous amount of our creative energies in our educational institutions. That is where our failure lies in addressing the problem of bullying behaviors—we have failed to act *collectively* and *effectively* to solve the problem. In many instances, we have benignly neglected or refused to act at all. In the worst cases, we have tacitly approved or actively encouraged it to continue. Like the school district discussed earlier, we have tried to wish, ignore, or deny the problem away or claim it doesn't exist. That may work for a while until we are thrown into another reaction phase because another bullying act has occurred and another child is brought to our attention in a way that we cannot ignore.

It is the same with working with the causes of the ***aggressor–target interaction.*** We have chosen to avoid dealing with the principle actors who create the mayhem of bullying because they have historically been cast into the purgatory of "problem children" who are to be dealt with through discipline and punishment. To a certain extent, there is a ring of truth to that—those who harm others should be held accountable for their actions. But the traditional stereotypical views of those who bully are not as relevant as they once were, and a one-size-fits-all response does not work. The causes and logic behind bullying behaviors have changed since the turn of the century, as we shall see in Chapter 2.

GETTING SMARTER AND GETTING STARTED

Just as the motivations and modus operandi of those who bully have changed, so must our approach to addressing the challenges. This book takes two blunt positions: (a) Unless we address the children and adolescents who cause bullying—the "centerpiece" of the puzzle of the bully–target continuum—we will never solve the problem, and (b) until we address the children and adolescents who engage in bullying, current and traditional methods used to address the problem are doomed to mediocre results at best, failure at worst.

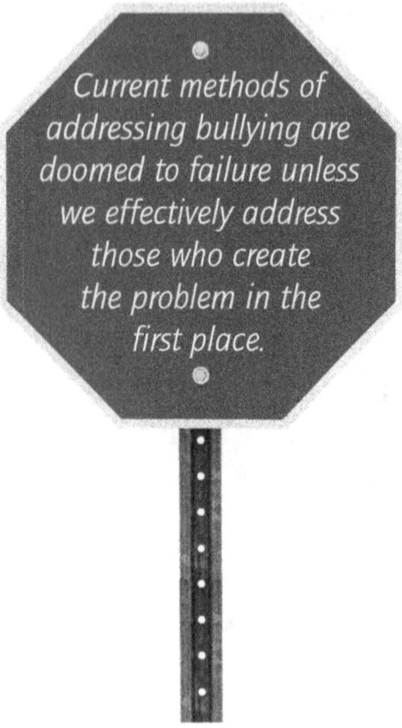

This book hopes to be a part of the solution in helping us work with those who are the first piece of the puzzle. It is designed to be useful to the practitioner to offer both practical considerations and applications of strategies and tactics for helping those who engage in bullying behaviors to pull back, and hopefully, cease their behaviors. Additionally, it is hoped that this effort will begin to encourage a new generation of additional creative ideas. What happens from this chapter forward depends on the "me" and "yous" taking the material within and applying it to the real world.

May we be successful in our endeavors.

WANT TO LEARN MORE?

Those interested in learning about one example of how a school district's recalcitrance to acknowledge and address bullying behaviors negatively impacted the community and the ultimate fallout that followed can consult the following resources:

Emily Bazelon. (2012, March 7). A big win: The landmark settlement in a Minnesota bullying case and how it could help gay students everywhere. Slate.com. Retrieved from http://www.slate.com/articles/news_and_politics/bulle/2012/03/the_anoka_hennepin_settlement_a_big_win_in_the_fight_against_gay_bashing_bullies_.html.

Sabrina Rubin Erdely. (2012, February 16). One town's war on gay teens. *Rolling Stone,* 1150, pp. 50–57, 68.

Laura Yuen. (2009, September 2). Teachers put on leave after bullying supposed gay student. MPR News. Retrieved from http://www.mprnews.org/story/2009/09/02/teachers-accused-of-mocking-student-on-leave.

2

Understanding Those Who Bully

©iStockphoto.com/monkeybusine

The reader will notice immediately that I have specifically avoided the use of the term *bully* to address children and adolescents who engage in those behaviors. That has not always been the case. Why the change?

First, we never should have been using the label in the first place for that very reason—it stereotypes those who engage in any number of behaviors that can be classified as bullying, but as with all labels, it does not do justice to the full attributes of the person or the behavior. Using a behavioral attribute as a simple descriptor tends to encourage us to see only the stereotypical and historical attributes of those who have in the past been called bullies. While some individuals may, indeed, subscribe to those stereotypical characteristics, not all do and that has always been the case. What we have tended to do is lump all of them together since the dawn of time and assume that those who engage in the behavior were all the same.

This is even more important today and is one of the central themes of this book. The characteristics and rationale of those who bully have changed with the advent and increase of social media communication. They will continue to evolve toward behaviors we have yet to imagine.

SOME INTERCHANGEABLE TERMINOLOGIES

In this book, the terms ***children*** or ***individual*** and their variants will be used as all-inclusive for both children and adolescents. It is clear that a "child" and an "adolescent" are chronologically and developmentally different, but it is felt that for the purpose of our discussion and in order to streamline the text, the terms *child, children,* and *individual* will suffice. If the term *adolescent* or *adult* is used, then that will be indicative of specific relevance to those age groups.

Likewise, the terms ***bully*** and ***bullying*** will be used as global terms for all aspects of the behavior, be it technically or legally defined intimidation, harassment, stalking, or hazing. The point of using the term is to indicate behaviors that encompass any variety of actions designed to belittle, demean, injure, or deny rights to others. If a specific type of bullying behavior needs to be noted (e.g., in a discussion of the legal aspects of what constitutes "harassment"), then that specific term will be used. Similarly, ***cyberbullying*** will refer to all the types of bullying that occur through electronic devices.

This book is intended for use in any setting in which bullying behaviors might occur among children and adolescents. It tries to avoid using references exclusive to the school setting whenever possible. As such, while many of the situations and examples used take place in the school setting, the reader should think "outside the school box" to other settings where bullying occurs—community activity centers, after-school programs, off-campus athletic facilities. When possible, the term ***institution*** or ***organization*** is used to expand our thinking beyond that aforementioned box. The reality is that any place where young people gather in numbers greater than one—be it a church basement, a parking lot, a field of dirt, or cyberspace—bullying can occur.

Whenever possible, the term ***supervisory personnel*** is used as an all-encompassing term for any adult in a supervisory position with children. That not only means those in school systems—principals, teachers, school counselors, and related support staff—but also those in paraprofessional and volunteer positions or supervisors of community programs. Readers should feel free to take the examples used in the text and bend and shape them to fit the relevant situations of their interaction and involvement with children.

RELEVANT AND LESS RELEVANT CHARACTERISTICS OF TRADITIONAL AND STEREOTYPICAL BULLYING BEHAVIORS

The professional literature is filled with attributes of bullying behaviors. Let us examine characteristics previously identified by Hazler (1996) that remain relevant today, as well as those that may not be as relevant as they once were.

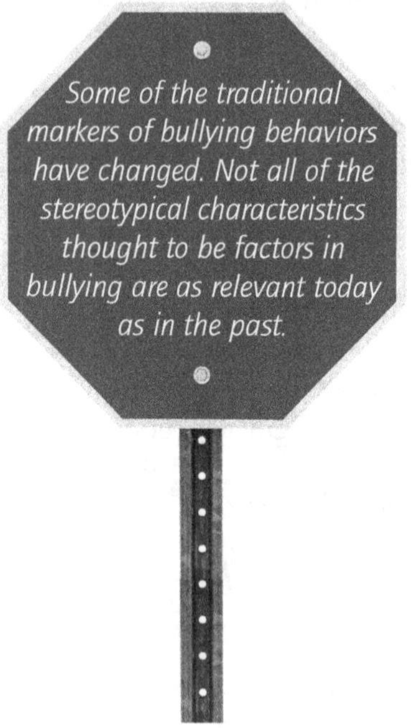

Relevant Behaviors Associated With Bullying

Those who engage in bullying behaviors are involved in the ***exercise of power*** (Mendler, 1992). While the literature has traditionally focused on the use of that power as a method of avoiding the aggressor's sense of inadequacy, recent trends in bullying behaviors indicate changes in motivation.

Those who act aggressively today are even more likely to be engaging in—practicing, if you will—***behaviors that are learned***. Succinctly, "aggression is considered a learned behavior" (Casebeer, 2012, p. 167). This is likely one of the most important characteristics that has remained constant throughout the study of bullying behaviors (Bandura, 1973; Hoover & Hazler, 1991). Still today, we measure correlational evidence between exposure to television and the increased likelihood of verbal or physical bullying behaviors (Kuntsche et al., 2006). Increased exposure to violent and relationally aggressive themes, such as is the foundation of most reality television today, does nothing but increase the likelihood that children will view conflict and domination as the way to solve problems among peers.

Children who bully today are more likely to be observed in engaging in ***verbal and psychological intimidation*** than overt physical violence, particularly girls. This a direct result of increased school security efforts, which are more likely to spot overt physical behaviors, as well as the increased use of violence and bully prevention programs in schools over the last decade that have sensitized both children and adults to recognize and report physical instances of bullying. As such, those who bully today often have more advanced social communication skills than traditionally noted in the early literature (Dodge, Murphy, & Buchsbaum, 1984; Hazler, Hoover, & Oliver, 1992; Trawick-Smith, 1988). In essence, the agents of bullying are smarter and better adept about hiding their intimidation than in the past.

The ***lack of empathy*** and ***objectification*** (Caravita, Di Blasio, & Salmivalli, 2010; Gini, Albiero, Benelli, & Altoe, 2007) toward those who are targeted remains a key factor in the thought processes of those who bully: "Bullies tend to see . . . victims primarily as objects rather than as human beings" (Hazler, 1996, p. 193). One of the earlier markers of the rationalization of those who bully, this characteristic has increased in direct proportion to the use of social media as a tool of intimidation.

Behaviors Not as Relevant Today Previously Associated With Bullying

Many of the factors in the past thought to be a reason behind why individuals choose to bully others have changed or are not as relevant as they were just a decade ago. The factors cited in this section still have merit but are less influential in the reasoning given by children as to why they choose to engage in bullying behaviors.

While previous literature has indicated that those who instigate bullying are victims themselves of ***low self-esteem*** or ***insecurities*** (Greenbaum, 1989; Mendler, 1992; Robinson, Rotter, Fey, & Vogel, 1992), recent history suggests that not only do those factors continue to contribute to the psychology of aggression toward others, but that, for many others, the aggression is undertaken by those whose self-esteem is wholly intact. In fact, many who report engaging in bullying behaviors today come from backgrounds of higher social and peer status and secure family settings. The act of intimidating others is viewed as a dominance and maintenance behavior of that social status.

The characterization of the schoolyard bully as being one ***physically larger*** and ***older than those they victimize*** (Elliott, 1991; Greenbaum, 1989; Olweus, 1978) is not always true today, particularly when cyberbullying is involved. Because bullying is much more covert and psychological than in the early days of measurement of the phenomena, size is less important than it used to be. Case in point: The technological "geeks" of yesterday can be today's master cyberbully when they use veiled and anonymous technological means to harass others. Technology has leveled the playing field of intimidation. Second case in point: Research into the world of relational aggression among girls has shown the high levels of astuteness involved in the deployment of such psychological torment (Crick, 1996, 1997; Crick & Bigbee, 1998; Crick, Casas, & Mosher, 1997; Crick & Dodge, 1996; Crick & Grotpeter, 1995; Crick, Grotpeter, & Bigbee, 2002).

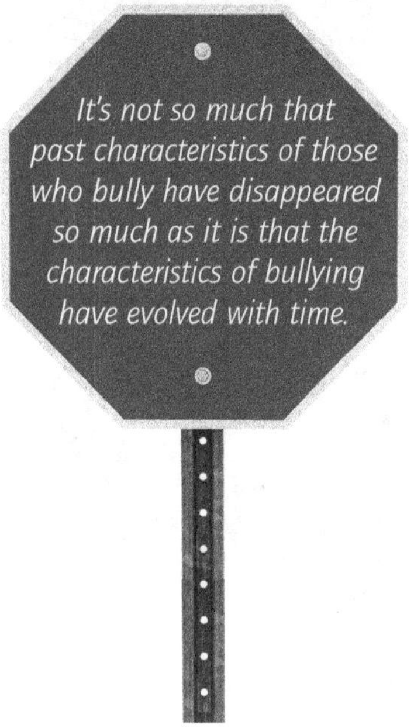

Where ***intellectual and academic problems*** along with a ***poor attitude toward school*** were once considered in tandem with physical size as likely markers of those who bully, there is less evidence that such is the case today (Lagerspetz, Björkqvist, Berts, & King, 1982). Bullying behaviors are observed being instigated today by those all across the academic spectrum—the honor student is just as likely to be involved in an incident of bullying behavior as those students who find school unworthy of their time, except, perhaps, for the social interactions they find within.

Will today's children and adolescents who engage in bullying ultimately be ***more likely to run afoul of the law*** as they mature (Huesmann, Eron, Lefkowitz, & Walder, 1984)? While the verdict may still be out on this one, it is difficult to assume, with the broadening of the spectrum of who participates in bullying, that all of them will end up with legal problems as adults. We do know that there is a link between aggressive children who are not intervened with successfully and later aggressive behaviors as adults,[1] but we do not have enough evidence to say affirmatively or concretely that those who bully for sport as youth will continue to do so in adulthood.

---

1. Espelage and De La Rue (2012) remind us that bullying "is a multi-faceted issue . . . best understood in the larger social context. . . . Individual characteristics of students contribute to bullying involvement when students have families that promote violence, teachers that ignore or dismiss bullying, schools that have negative climates and students who socialize with friends who bully" (p. 3).

Some of the biggest stereotypes of those who bully are that they come from a ***dysfunctional family life***, that they are often ***unsupervised or undisciplined by adults***, and that they may well be ***subject to physical or emotional abuse*** themselves (Edmondson, 1988; Greenbaum, 1989; Hunt, 1993; Oliver, Oaks, & Hoover, 1994). These factors certainly contribute to unhappy childhood experiences, but many of those who bully today come from homes that are secure and from parents who do not advocate violence or bullying behaviors among their children. Since bullying and cyberbullying seem to be *peer activities* today, not to engage in them may well place children at risk of being targeted themselves.

THE NEW BULLYING BEHAVIOR: THE PSYCHOLOGY OF DOMINATION

Bullying during the past decade has changed in some ways, none of which are for the betterment of any of us as a society. In addition to the increase in the use of psychological tactics by those who bully, particularly through the use of social media, those who engage in bullying today are more likely to do it not for the historical and stereotypical factors discussed in the previous section, but simply because they want to do it, they can get away with it, and the domination of others through bullying behaviors has become normed and entrenched within the popular culture. Call it the ***psychology of domination.***

While it has been documented that those who have received bullying behaviors sometimes seek others to "practice on" as they get older or become more emboldened, today we see children and adolescents engaging in dominating behaviors from the logic of practicing what they see role modeled in popular media and greater society.

A case study: As part of preparation for this book, I had the opportunity to visit and interact with hundreds of children, adolescents, and adults in seeking their opinions and solutions as to what encourages kids to bully and what can be done to stop it. Here are some of the themes that emerged from those conversations.

Kids Bully Others Because They See Examples in Role Models

No matter how hard we try to encourage positive role models in schools, many children and adolescents are still more easily influenced by what they see portrayed on television and across the Internet. This is particularly true when it comes to the role of reality television. Some memorable comments:

"I know kids who pick on others just because they think it's what's supposed to happen to somebody else. They've seen it on television. They've seen it on YouTube. They think that's just what you're supposed to do to others if you want to hang with the hot kids."

"They watch [reality television shows named] because they can find new ways of doing things to people they don't like that they hadn't thought of before."

"If you don't dominate, you're not a player."

"I've had things done to me at school that were shown the night before on [reality television show named]. Some days, I don't want to go to school after [reality television show named] because I know they're going to play tricks on me that they learned from it."

Kids Bully Others Because They Can Get Away With It

In spite of all our frenetic efforts to stop bullying, kids tell us that they sometimes bully others simply because they can and not get caught:

"Sometimes people bully others because adults don't have a clue what we do and how we do it. They're clueless about technology and they don't know what goes on between classes in the hallways, who says what to who, who gives the I'm-going-to-get-you look to somebody else."

"When it comes to cyberbullying, kids generally have their parents and teachers at a disadvantage. About the time that adults figure out what we're doing, we've stopped using that kind of technology and moved on to whatever's the latest. They never catch up. I kind of feel sorry for them."

"We do stuff at school where the teachers don't think we're doing it—right under their noses, in class, while class is going on. I know one kid who constantly picks on this other kid in science class. The kid whose getting it doesn't say anything and so it goes on and on day after day. The teacher has no clue what's going on. I don't know if she doesn't actually know or if she just doesn't care."

Kids Bully as a Display of Power in a School Climate Where Others Don't Feel Safe

One way to increase the chances of one who is not to be messed with is to create the aura of "badness." In essence, one's ability to dominate others sends a message to potential victimizers that they should "back off" or suffer the same fate. This is one example of ***vicarious victimization***, which has been speculated to negatively impact far more than just those in the bully–target spectrum (Smokowski & Kopasz, 2005).[2] While this preemptive strike strategy may work in some instances, it may well encourage others to see how quickly they can "dominate the dominator" in order to send a message within their sphere of influence that they, too, are not to be intimidated and the cycle of domination is perpetuated:

> *"I watched one little guy always pick on others who he thought he could get away with it just so he could try to keep some of the other bullies away from him. In a way it worked because one day the bigger bullies took him under their wing and made him sort of like their mascot."*
>
> *"This one girl makes it a habit of doing this in-your-face stuff with any new girl who comes into the school just to show the new girls who's boss. And she spreads gossip, too. She has this [social media] account under an alias where she talks all this smack about people. Nobody does anything and her power just grows and grows."*
>
> *"One kid acts tough all the time and picks on little kids because he knows it's just a matter of time before somebody else gets around to nailing him. That's what we all kind of have to do in our school, protect ourselves. You do it to somebody before they do it to you. None of the teachers are going to protect you."*

BULLYING TODAY IS MORE PSYCHOLOGICAL THAN EVER BEFORE

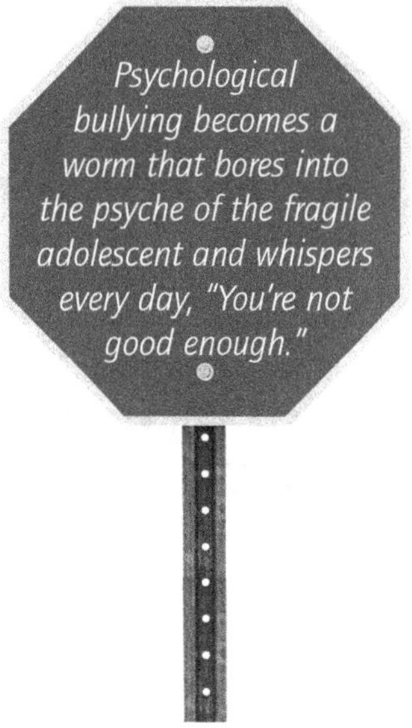

Ironically, because of the very successes of the public awareness campaigns directed toward bullying prevention and intervention, those who engage in the behaviors have had to be more creative and covert in practicing their craft. Because overt acts of physical interactions between students are easier to observe and are viewed with a different lens today—more as an act of school violence than an act of "kids will be kids"—and because school personnel deal with such physical instances more harshly and generically (usually via suspension under a "zero tolerance" mantra), those who choose to engage in bullying behaviors have had to find less observable methods of intimidation. Bullying has moved farther into the depths of the psychological than ever before.

---

2. Smokowski & Kopasz (2005) have even gone so far as to term those afflicted vicariously by bullying behaviors a "silent majority" (p. 108).

Let us be clear that bullying that is physical is also psychological. The target of bullying behaviors who is physically assaulted is also psychologically assaulted. One's sense of personal safety is violated and weakened.

Bullying does not, however, always involve physical contact. It can well be invisible via the spoken word, by way of an electronic Facebook, Twitter, Ask.fm, After School, or Yik Yak account post, through the encroachment of a target's physical space, or by a menacing glance. It becomes a destructive psychological worm, boring into the self-esteem of an individual with the same basic message—"You're not good enough."

The adolescent psyche is a fragile thing. Full of wonderment and natural self-doubt, adolescents depend upon peer feedback for validation of the world around them. If the ***groupthink*** of the peer group says something is OK ("Everybody's doing it!"), then it is OK. If the groupthink says that something is not OK ("That's messed up!"), then it's not. And while the safety of the peer group and its groupthink is a powerful experience to bolster the confidence of the group itself—think about how many times adolescents believe things contrary to the way adults view the same phenomenon—it can also be just as powerful a weapon when turned and laser-beamed onto the hapless target of a ***peer group attack.***[3]

Kids today understand that the worst type of bullying is the kind that stays in the mind all day and all night, that from which there is no respite, no switch available to turn off the worm of self-doubt as it whispers its message of inadequacy day in and day out. Such psychological torment serves as the best terror that can be delivered to a target of intimidation. Rejection by the peer group is death in Kid World. The individual who controls the mind of the target is the truest of dominators, as the individual who dishes out the effective dose of psychological torment truly owns the victim. The worst part is that the tormentor does not have to continually add to the harassment—although to do so certainly embeds the worm even deeper—because the individual who has been infected by the attack continues to fuel the intimidation by his or her own self-doubts and insecurities. In the worst-case scenario, the agony can overwhelm the target and encourage the individual to make self-harming decisions.

CAN THOSE WHO BULLY MAKE OTHERS COMMIT SUICIDE OR ACT OUT REVENGE FANTASIES?

Are those who bully the "cause" of their targets' decisions to engage in self-harming behaviors or take actions directed toward others in revenge? In a word, no. But it's not as simple as just a one-word answer.

3. This was traditionally termed ***mobbing*** (Olweus, 1993, p. 8) in the earlier literature that emerged from Europe.

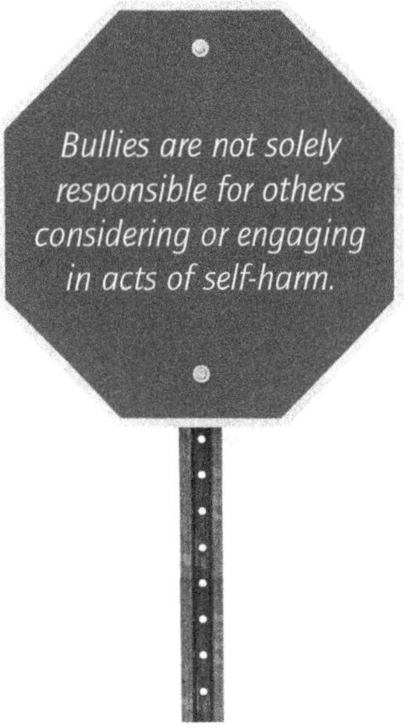

Do those who bully contribute to the deteriorating logic of their targets so that they consider suicide, self-harm, or ***retaliatory aggression*** (i.e., harm to others; Corvo & deLara, 2010, p. 186) in an effort to end the suffering or exact revenge?

Yes. But in saying so, it is important to focus on the key word *contribute* and phrase *deteriorating logic*.

The decision to engage in self-injurious behaviors or to lash out at others is process oriented. A ***process-oriented decision*** is one that evolves over a period of time and after exposure to a series of situations that leads an individual to believe that engaging in the specific behavior is a rational response to the circumstances. The logic of individuals who choose to turn the psychological pain inward or outward believe that to do so is the only option available to them. From their viewpoint, they are engaging in a rational act.

To purposefully harm oneself or others as a result of being bullied is not considered a rational act by accepted social or legal standards. It is, however, the result of distorted thinking on the part of individuals who have been subjected to intense or constant abuse from peers. Because peer acceptance is so critical, particularly during adolescence, the loss of such peer support can be devastating. Exposure to public humiliation in person or via social media on a 24/7/365 basis only intensifies the feelings of isolation on the part of the target.

Case in point: A sixteen-year-old high school junior became the target of vicious social media attacks for no apparent reason. Messages posted in various electronic formats included, "Go cut yourself until you bleed to death," "You're a whore, a stupid bitch, a horrible person," and "You deserve to die."

The impact on the teen was profound: "I didn't tell anybody about it. I didn't want to talk about it, usually. I didn't know where it was coming from, or why, and I deleted most of it. But after a while, I started believing it myself." She received treatment for depression during the cyberattacks. "Cyberbullying influenced that," she stated.

Notice what this young woman said—cyberbullying "influenced" her depression. This is incredibly insightful since our behavior is always greatly influenced by the feedback we receive from those we consider significant in our lives, but unless those same individuals physically force us to do harm to ourselves or others, ultimately *we* are responsible for our actions.

I need to make crystal clear the true nature of my opinion and experiences in dealing with bullying and school violence during four decades—others' actions toward targets of bullying and intimidation do have ***strings of culpability*** attached to them, especially when those actions are willful

and malicious. The hurtful messages and actions directed toward victims help create a ***sense of helplessness*** within the targets, the impression that no one is there to help them, that they are powerless to end the abuse that consistently comes their way. This is, of course, exactly the psychology of domination and what the perpetrator of the aggression wants.

Those strings of culpability *do* make the agents of bullying behaviors accountable for their actions. They *do* make them a part of the process-oriented decision that can lead an individual to make the poor choices to act against oneself or others. They *are* a part of the end result that we too often only see after the fact.

But they are not *directly* responsible. Should they be held accountable for their actions? Absolutely. But what type of accountability—moral, civil, criminal? By the standards of morality based in almost all civilized cultures, there should be a moral sense of outrage directed at those who participate in the intentional malicious destruction of others. While case law in this area is murky, there may well be civil penalties attached to the behavior of those who make efforts to willfully hurt others. It is more difficult to find an aggressor guilty of a criminal act unless statutes exist within a state specifying exactly what constitutes behaviors that can be penalized. Such is the problem of attempting to statutorily define what bullying and intimidation are. Assault and battery is more easily identified by law—but when is an action or behavior, difficult to define, enough to be considered a violation of someone else's rights?[4]

4. Opponents of antibullying legislation use the very argument that because bullying is often difficult to define and can include many different venues and aspects of interpretation, by creating a definition "everything then becomes bullying." It is not lost on those who have spent decades advocating on behalf of bullying legislation and increased protection against bullying behaviors that those who sometimes oppose such efforts are concerned about having their own behaviors questioned.

WANT TO LEARN MORE?

For those who are interested in the relationship between being a target of bullying behaviors and the potential for self-harm, readers are directed to the longitudinal study by Fisher et al. (2012), which indicated that children who were bullied were, indeed, more likely to engage in acts of self-harm than nonbullied peers, but such acts were likely the result of complicating additional variables negatively impacting the child, such as a "family history of attempted [or] completed suicide, concurrent mental health problems, and a history of maltreatment by an adult," all contributing to heightened levels of "distress" within the child (p. 1). Likewise, Klomek, Marrocco, Kleinman, Schonfeld, and Gould (2007) found higher rates of self-harm among targets of bullying behaviors and that "frequent exposure to victimization or bullying others was related to high risks of depression, ideation, and suicide attempts" (p. 40).

To fully understand the pernicious impact of cyberbullying on the self-esteem and self-harmful behaviors of one young woman, see Paul Levy, "Cyberbullied: As Online Bullying and 'Sextortion' Spread, Schools and Parents Face an Ever-Changing Evil," Minneapolis (MN) *Star Tribune*, October 6, 2013, pp. B1, B10.

How do we teach others to feel helpless to solve problems, particularly when it comes to conflict in interpersonal relations? The sense of helplessness is a combination of self-doubt and what one learns about the ability or inability to escape physically or emotionally painful situations—for example, ***learned helplessness.*** It was first postulated by Martin E. P. Seligman and his colleagues. For the history and background on the development of learned helplessness theory, see Abramson, Seligman, and Teasdale (1978), Overmier (2002), and Seligman and Maier (1967).

What are some of the ramifications of attempting to criminalize bullying behaviors that have contributed to self-harmful behaviors of its targets? An in-depth look at a highly publicized case was investigated by Stephanie Allen, "More Laws Needed? Proposed Bullying Legislation Spurs Debate," Lakeland (FL) *Ledger*, March 12, 2014, at http://www.ledgerdata.com/bullying/#day-four.

3

What Exactly Is *Bullying Today?*

It has become somewhat of a not-so-funny joke within the bullying prevention world that before we can solve the problem, we have to be able to know what it is. While most of us "know it when we see it," when we try and specifically define bullying so that we can more effectively address it, we tend to stumble all over ourselves. Bullying means different things to different people (Espelage & Swearer, 2003; Ross & Horner, 2009). There exists a "diversity of characteristics attributed . . . to bullies and victims" (Ross, 2002, p. 106). The same problem comes into play with efforts to try and measure its frequency or the effectiveness of programs designed to intervene and prevent—how do we measure that which we cannot adequately define (Cornell, Sheras, & Cole, 2006)? It also has cultural connotations. Hong and Espelage (2012) noted that the term "'bullying' has been commonly used in English speaking countries" and that "when one tries to translate 'bullying' from English to other languages, there is no single word that captures the exact, precise meaning" (p. 312). When you start trying to tie specific behaviors to statutorily defined parameters wherein a child could be held criminally or civilly accountable by the courts, it gets even more difficult. A definition suddenly becomes a matter of potential penalties and denial of access to educational opportunities.

In this chapter, we will focus on some basics and conceptualizations of what bullying is and, perhaps more importantly, what it is not.

WHAT BULLYING IS NOT

It may seem peculiar to start this chapter with a discussion of what bullying is not. However, it helps to get some things off the table so as not to get distracted by them before we begin to talk about what constitutes bullying behaviors.

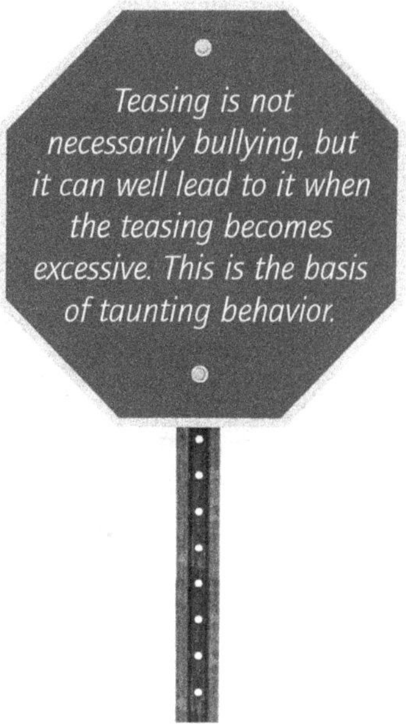

People sometimes have a misconception about what bullying actually is. The tendency of individuals to try and identify behaviors as bullying when they are not is called ***bullycreep***. Sometimes that occurs because we are unclear on the concept. Other times it happens when people overzealously try to make a point about the rude behavior of another and confuse boorishness for bullying. Still other times it happens intentionally when people attempt to create a justification in which individuals or someone under their care is involved in a negative interaction with another. That third example occurs quite frequently, with parents justifying the bullying behavior of their own child. If we see it everywhere, then our ability to distinguish it when it actually occurs is marred. Like Aesop's fable of the

"Boy Who Cried Wolf" (Perry, 1952), if we cry "I've been bullied!" or "That's bullying!" to every difficult interpersonal interaction, when it actually occurs, no one will believe us. With that in mind, here are a few examples of what bullying is not.

Bullying Is Not Teasing

Teasing is usually carried out in a verbal manner. It often involves making fun of a certain characteristic of another individual. Teasing can lead to bullying, but in its most innocuous form, teasing can be a playful interaction between parties when both of them understand the ground rules and are at par with one another on the power spectrum (Kruger, Gordon, & Kuban, 2006). Teasing can be used as a form of flattery and flirtation and is often learned within one's family of origin as a communication tool to show endearment (Keltner, Capps, Kring, Young, & Heerey, 2001). A key component to the understanding of a nonaggressive teasing communication is the ability of the target of the tease to ***decode the purpose*** of the message. It is used frequently as a method of romance (Eder, 1993). Teasing was originally termed a "joking relationship" (Radcliffe-Brown, 1940, p. 195) and has sometimes been referred to as "mock aggression," "rough and tumble play," or "jostling" (Doll & Swearer, 2006, p. 184), but the basic markers of the interaction remained the same—the target of the tease understood the unwritten rules that "no offence" [sic] (Radcliffe-Brown, p. 195) was intended and that equivalent responses from the target of the same nature might well be a part of the equation.

Teasing becomes more of a problem when it is unaccepted by the target of the interaction or when there is a power inequity between them. When the agent of the behavior continues the teasing in the absence of acceptance by the target, this becomes ***taunting***. Taunting is not based on equivalent power between the parties. One of the key markers of taunting is that the agent continues to say or do things to aggravate or embarrass the target in spite of requests, protests, or other indicators by the victim to stop the behavior.[1] Individuals intent on increasing their domination on the power spectrum continue to harass and taunt as the target withdraws or refuses to indicate disapproval. At some point, teasing becomes taunting, and taunting can become bullying.

So can teasing be construed by observers as bullying? Yes. Is it necessarily so? No. One way to determine what is what is to look at the ***power inequity*** between the agents and the targets of bullying, gauge the responses of the targets to the behaviors directed toward them, and ask the targets privately about their thoughts on how they are being treated by the ones doing the teasing.

---

1. There is one more important consideration to these descriptors of taunting. If the target is incapable of indicating a preference that the taunting stop (e.g., if the individual has a physical, mental, or developmental impairment or disability of some type), then it is incumbent upon supervisory personnel to determine if the behavior is malicious.

Bullying Is Not Abnormal Developmental Behavior

It is normal for children and adolescents to test the boundaries of the world around them. That is how they learn limits, especially with what they can get away with in the Adult World. Children and adolescents are designed to push the envelope of their current existence. This is especially true of adolescents—just ask their parents.

One aspect of discovering who kids are among their peer group is via testing the waters of where they fall on the ***power spectrum***. They do this by pushing the limits of being verbal and physical to both adults and peers, and they are particularly adept at pushing those boundaries with peers when there is a lack of adult supervision.

This ***"push-until-pushed-back" behavior*** is designed to discover where one falls on the power spectrum, and the Petri dish to tests these limits is anywhere that children and adolescents congregate. While this is most frequently within the school environment, it is important to remember that schools are just the most convenient places where kids can practice behaviors among their peers. This exploration could just as easily occur in those church basements or unsupervised parking lots mentioned in Chapter 2

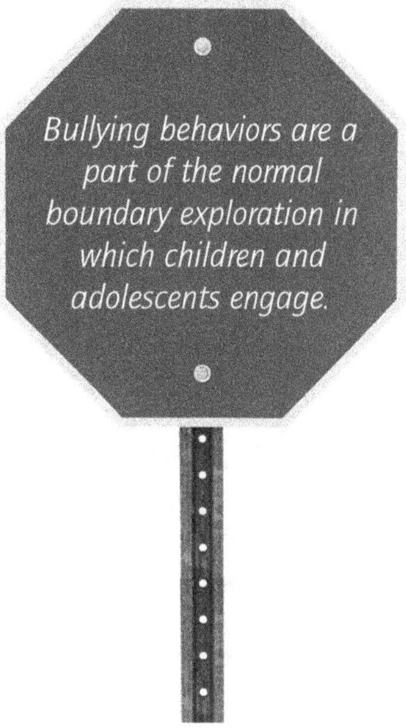

What do they do? Just watch kids from a distance when they think they are not being supervised. They push. They shove. They engage in physical horseplay. They insult one another. They laugh at each other's imperfections, sometimes with brutal honesty and sometimes just brutally. It's not always designed to be harmful, but it is designed to see how far they can go during the interaction. And if they are truly unsupervised, the behavior will always usually spin out of control until someone is injured in some fashion, either physically or emotionally, or until something happens to get the entire group into trouble, usually when the responsible adult shows up. This is particularly true of elementary children who often truly do not know the limits of their power and stumble upon it quite accidently.

Don't believe me? Watch young children on the playground when there is no adult in the vicinity to provide guidance and intervention. This is what you will likely see if they are unsupervised long enough: The play among the parties will escalate. It gets more vigorous and physical until one of two things happens—the kids either exhaust themselves or they get into some kind of mischief because one (usually the less aggressive one) gets hurt or the rest realize they have violated some kind of rule that is big enough to get all of them into trouble (e.g., a rock gets thrown through a window, a toy is broken). Again, this is often not because of intent. It's just that the universe of Kid Play expands until it either flames out or it flames into another problem.

Bullying Is Not a Psychological Illness

Do some kids who engage in bullying behaviors do so because they have a diagnostic mental illness? Yes—but very few fit this criteria. Children and adolescents who display symptomatology for a diagnosis of conduct disorder as described by the *Diagnostic and Statistical Manual of Mental Disorders* (5th ed.; American Psychiatric Association, 2013) may well engage in persistent aggressive behaviors toward others so as to meet the definition of bullying. But that is rarely the cause behind such behaviors in the vast majority of instances. A more likely interpretation is that children who engage in uninterrupted long-term bullying behaviors—either as a ***primary agent***[2] (one who instigates and engages in bullying behaviors consistently), a ***secondary agent*** (one who follows the lead of a primary agent and joins in the behavior), or as a ***target-agent***[2] (one who is typically targeted for bullying behaviors from others and then who, in turn, bullies others)—are likely to carry those behaviors into adolescence and adulthood (Copeland, Wolke, Angold, & Costello, 2013; Huesmann et al., 1984; Kumpulainen & Rasanen, 2000). It is a serious error, however, to assume that all child and adolescent misbehaviors are predictive of "deviance" later in life. At best, the debate over the persistence of child and adolescent behaviors being indicative of later adult psychopathology is "contentious" (Dolan, 2004, p. 467).

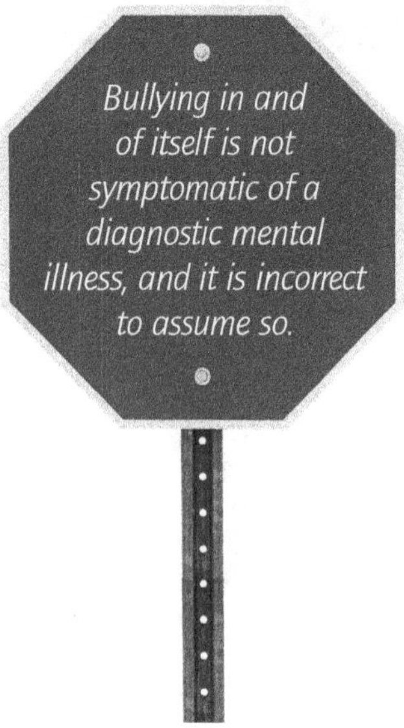

It is improper to view bullying behaviors under a clinically diagnostic and pathological lens. While we read about bullying behaviors to be of "epidemic proportions" in the media, such descriptions are far more metaphorical than actual medical reality. Let us not disagree on the fact that there is, indeed, too much bullying mayhem in the world, but it is not effective to view what is often normal developmental exploration of one's place on the peer group power spectrum as some type of aberrant or deviant behavior among the species inhabiting Kid World.

Unfortunately, we live in a world where we want labels for everything. Labels make us feel good. They make us feel safe. They help us find order in chaos. We think that labels always help us understand behaviors better. In some instances, that may be true. However, labeling tends to make us lazy, and we really, really like our labels when it comes to explaining difficult behaviors that actually require more intensive and extensive study and refinement. Bullying occurs for a myriad of reasons, and one child or

---

2. Terminologies of these types of behaviors have historically labeled these individuals as the ***pure bully*** (Gudjonsson, Sigurdsson, & Sigfusdottir, 2010; Copeland et al., 2013) and the ***bully-victim*** (Veenstra et al., 2005), respectively.

adolescent's motivation is different from another's. Our task is to ferret out the reasons for those behaviors prior to enforcing or inflicting upon everyone a one-size-fits-all response.

Bullying Is Not Necessarily Disconnected Single-Incident Negative Interactions With Different Peers

As with labeling, one incident of bullying-like behavior does not a bully make. Sometimes, kids just get into a fight. Sometimes, they yell at each other. There are always other people that we just sometimes don't like. But when two kids have some kind of short-term negative interaction, does that mean that one of them is a bully?

Not necessarily. It all depends on context, and we won't understand the full basis of what caused a particular interaction unless we take the time to sit down and discuss what the parties involved view as the cause of their kerfuffle. We have to understand if the nature of the dispute was the result of longer-term negative interactions (i.e., a ***pattern***) or a temporary situation. That is most likely to occur when we ask the individuals involved how they view the situation that led up to the eventual negative behaviors.

Please note that we hedge a bit in this section by saying "not necessarily." Everything must be viewed in ***context***. It is entirely possible that a child has poor social skills and has sporadic negative interactions with others that are just that—spats of some type that are random and not based on intent but are just an outcome of the poor social skills that the individual employs toward others.

However, it is important for all involved in the supervisory loop to keep track of incidents of negative behaviors in order to better identify developing trends that may be occurring with certain individuals. We have to connect the dots. Not all instances of negative behavior are so random, sporadic, or spontaneous. If a pattern emerges wherein an individual is identified as the intentional instigator of negative behaviors in a repeated fashion, then that is information that is useful in determining the steps for intervention.

Bullying Is Not Having a Disagreement With Others

We are losing our ability to disagree with others in an agreeable fashion. We have to help our children learn those skills. That first step begins with those of us in our supervisory positions acting as the role models we have to be—whether we think we are or not.[3]

---

3. This is particularly important for young adults in supervisory positions to remember. I am mindful of my own sense of inadequacy during my first year of teaching in that, a few

We adults are not doing such a great job as role models these days. Case in point: The tone of political discourse that is demonstrated today is deplorable. It has all the hallmarks of bullying behaviors: name-calling, attempts to undermine credibility, and outright lying about the facts of the political issue de jour. While politics has always involved, to some degree, a modicum of intimidating characteristics—if not outright bullying—it was not always on display and as easily accessible in the past as in today's hyper news markets. The need for media outlets to feed the monster ensures that the sound bites and video clips of the most outrageous statements and behaviors will be replayed over and over in the echo chamber that is the 24/7 news cycle.

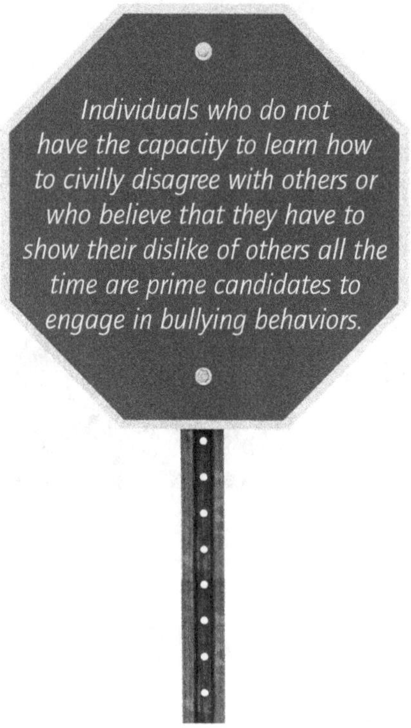

Add to this the exposure to what passes as dramatic reality television, which is, in fact, nothing more than conflict-driven and -fueled scenarios contrived specifically to titillate the audience and keep them wondering who will betray and backstab who in the next episode, and you have a toxic brew wherein young people get the impression that when they have disagreements, the way to solve them is to curse, pull hair, seduce, cheat, yell the loudest, or lie. Christensen (2013) observed, "In the end, being nice makes for dull entertainment."

Young people have to understand that disagreement with others is a major part of the human experience. There are over seven billion people on our planet, and the likelihood is pretty great that we will not all agree with each other all the time. That being said, we have to help our kids learn the skills to navigate the world of natural disagreements, of different opinions, of likes and dislikes.

In my consultations, I am often asked about bullying behaviors that are, in fact, not bullying behaviors at all. Some individuals—and I'm including adults here—have the belief that just because someone disagreed with them on an issue or topic, they have been bullied. Such is likely not the case, even if the disagreement manifested itself in a rude or inappropriate way. Some people are gruff, rude, blunt, and inappropriate, but their behaviors do not constitute bullying. Once again, the key to what determines bullying is always in the *behavior that is displayed*. I don't agree

---

month earlier, I was just another wild undergraduate with no real responsibilities in the world. To be suddenly cast as a role model was not a part of the job I had considered. Luckily, I accepted that responsibility quickly and, in all likelihood, being a teacher made me a better person all-around.

with people all the time, and they don't agree with me. Actually, that's fantastic. I've gained a lot of new insights and views from listening to people I disagreed with who challenged my worldview. Learning how to live with our disagreements and agree to disagree agreeably is the basis of ***civil discourse*** and ***civil behavior***. If that doesn't work, we can part company or limit our interactions to just those times that we have to accomplish a mutual goal. We often have to work with others that we disagree with, and those disagreements may make our work together more difficult, which is exactly the reason that we shouldn't pal around with them when the work day is done.

Bullying Is Not Disliking Another Person or Group

"She doesn't like me. I'm being bullied." How many times have you heard variations on this theme? This is particularly true among younger children who ***tattle***, the goal of which is to tell something about someone else to get the other party into trouble. It's not just kids who express such sentiments. Adults often seem to believe that we are supposed to like everyone all the time, including those we work with, and if we don't, we are somehow engaging in bullying behaviors. As with disagreements discussed earlier, the odds are pretty great that with seven billion people on the planet, we're likely not going to get along with all of them all the time, either.

What we think or feel about others is not bullying, even when those thoughts or feelings are vile. It is only when we *act* on them in the negative manner that we feel or think that those cognitions and affects become bullying. *Behavior is what turns bullying into reality*—the sending of the nasty e-mail or the pushing of someone who is not liked—that is, the *action* that takes bullying out of the privacy of the head and into the public venue. As long as an individual has the coping ability to interact with others in a fashion that does not disrupt the good of the order and keeps negative opinions to oneself, then only that individual knows of the disdain for another.

Unfortunately, we tend to act on our thoughts and feelings because their repression creates anxiety within us for resolution. When we do, if those thoughts and feelings are inclined to want harm or misfortune to another, then we may create a problem. And that leads us now to understanding and looking at the definitional parameters of what exactly bullying might be if the circumstances fit.

WHAT BULLYING IS

One of the basic issues behind determining exactly what constitutes bullying is the ability to identify its characteristics. We have to be able to adequately describe what is involved in creating an incident of bullying. Ross (as cited in Macklem, 2003) noted that there was "no clear consensus" (p. 1) regarding the definition of bullying up through the 1990s. Efforts to try and legislate definitional parameters into school rule or legal statute in order to hold individuals accountable have been unsatisfactory at best, abysmal failures at worst.

Common Definitions

Berger's (2007) definition of a bully is quite simple: "someone who repeatedly attacks another individual who does not fight back" (p. 96). Perhaps the best and most rock-solid definition is the one that we have come to commonly accept as the starting standard for determining bullying behaviors created by Olweus (1993, 2001, 2003) in his seminal works on the subject in the 1970s and 1980s:

> *Bullying is the exposure to long-term, repeated negative actions on the part of one or more persons.* (Olweus, 1993, p. 9)

Sounds great. We can all agree on this. But how do we ***operationalize*** it? In order to be able to respond to a problem, especially if we are going to hold someone accountable for objectionable behavior, we have to parse the particulars of a definition and twist them to and fro in order to consider all manner of possible interpretations. It helps to be a mind reader.

What exactly is a "negative action"? Certainly, physical violence falls into that category, but what about things that are said that carry a bite along with a sharp word—does that constitute bullying? What if the "negative action" was not intended on the part of the person who engaged in it, but the individual who is on the receiving end perceived it as such? And what about that perception? Whose perception is valid, especially when the behavior occurred outside of unbiased third-party observation? What constitutes "long-term"? Does one day's worth of repeated, intense bullying qualify, or does the behavior have to occur over multiple days in order to be considered as long-term?

Crick and Grotpeter (1995) defined bullying as "harming others through purposeful manipulation and damage of their peer relationships" (p. 711). This description expands the conceptualization of bullying and is the basis for the definition of ***relational aggression,*** which focuses on the destruction of interpersonal relationships, primarily among girls and women. Likewise, Haynie et al. (2001) and Macklem (2003) view bullying through a lens of ***power domination.*** Smith and Morita (as cited in Macklem, 2003) include the abuse of "normal social power" (p. 2) in their conceptualizations of what constitutes bullying behaviors. Sharp and Smith (2002) speak of the intent of individuals to "intimidate and dominate" (p. 1) their targets.

Leff, Power, and Goldstein (2004) add to the Olweus (1993) and Crick and Grotpeter (1995) definitions of bullying with the inclusion that the behavior also involves the Smith and Sharp (1994, p. 2) perspective of a "systematic abuse of power" in a "dynamic process that occurs within the context of a relationship." The agents of aggression act intentionally toward targets with the goal of injuring them in some fashion, either physically, socially, or psychologically.

So what are we to gain from this list of additional descriptors of bullying definitions? Four basic things:

1. Bullying has both physical and psychological components.
2. Bullying may also include attacks on the social fabric of relationships.
3. Bullying involves a power inequity between the parties.
4. Bullying typically involves efforts to do harm over a time period and is prolonged.

It is my contention that no matter however else we may attempt to describe bullying, these four components must be included in some fashion. Using this as the foundation for what is involved in bullying behavior, let's add the bells and whistles from additional examples and information as we move forward. Those bells and whistles, by the way, will become more important when we get into the legal aspects of attempts to define what exactly does, and does not, constitute bullying behavior.

It's Not Bullying Until It Manifests Itself in a Behavior

As previously mentioned, *bullying can only be expressed behaviorally.* This will likely stir the pot of controversy since most of us would like to believe that bullying can also occur in both thought and emotion, as well as behavior. Not so, and let us examine what makes it that way.

Ultimately, the only thing we can measure in human behavior is what is *observable*. Pause and think about that for a moment. We may *assume* that we know what another person is thinking. We may *assume* we know what another person is going to do. We might be right. We might also be wrong. In the end, there is only one thing we can be sure of when it comes to knowing precisely what an individual does, and that is through observing exactly what the individual is doing.[4]

4. Then again, behavior, too, can be misconstrued by misinterpretation. We often behave in a manner that was not intended to be perceived by others in the way that it was. How many times have we heard (or said) this: "But that's not what I meant!"

I am offering an additional dimension to all those definitions which has heretofore been overlooked or ignored. Bullying is a ***behavioral manifestation*** of what an individual thinks and feels about another person. It is not the cognition and affect themselves that are the bullying. While what I think and feel may be malicious, as long as I do not act in the manner in which I may want to, then I have not bullied anyone. Thoughts and emotions are certainly an underlying combustible catalyst for an individual's actions, but until those thoughts and emotions become overt and acted upon, then technically, they do not exist in such a fashion so as to be measureable.

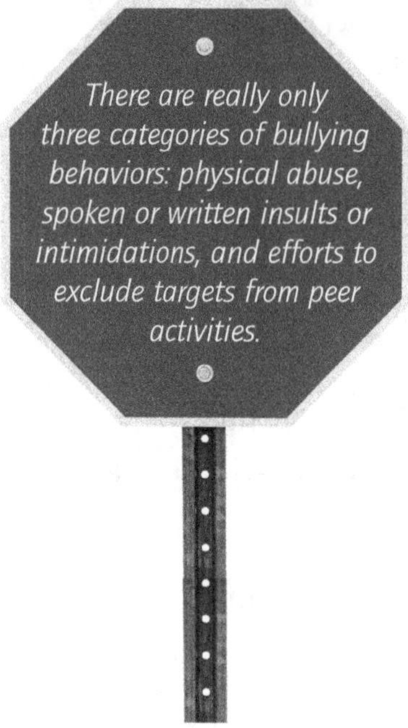

What, then, qualifies as a behavioral example of bullying? All of the things we associate with bullying, intimidation, and harassment—physical abuse of others, insults or intimidations which are spoken or written, and actively encouraging others to shun or exclude specific individuals from peer activities—are a few examples. When you think about it, those are the three major classifications of what we consider bullying behaviors. We either engage in some type of physical activity, we speak or write in a fashion that disturbs others, or we make efforts to prevent the targets of abuse from being able to participate fully in activities which they are entitled to do so. Of course, there are endless methods that can be used to accomplish these three goals, but basically, those are the only three things that one can do to another person in terms of endgames. Whatever tactic is employed is always a behavior—not a thought or a feeling. Those behaviors, of course, create thoughts and feelings in targets that influence their behaviors so as to either acquiesce to the aggressor's wishes or avoid situations wherein the target is likely to be exposed to continued behavioral intimidation.

Bullying Is Aggressive Behavior

Bullying is ***behavioralized aggression*** intended to exercise power over others for tangible or symbolic gain. A ***tangible gain*** usually includes something physical, such as property or, in extreme instances, sexual favors. A ***symbolic gain*** involves manipulating the relationship to gain dominance or social status within the peer group. The agent of aggression *always* gets something out of the dominance, usually the latter rather than the former, since taking property from others may constitute a criminal act and is much easier to prove than the theft of self-esteem, power, or position within the peer group. As Klein (2006) so aptly observed, "Students . . . vie to accrue ***cultural capitol***" (p. 55).

There are two types of aggressive behaviors: direct and indirect. ***Direct aggression*** is most easily observed. It is usually face-to-face and may involve physical contact of some type (Hyde, 1984; Maccoby & Jacklin, 1974; Card, Stucky, Sawalani, & Little, 2008). Boys and men are considered to engage in more direct aggression than females; however, this trend has been changing in the most recent decade because of role modeling of females involved in overt aggression in popular media. ***Indirect aggression*** is more covert and usually involves efforts to attack the social fabric of relationships through peer rejection or exclusion (Card et al., 2008; Feshbach, 1969). It is the classic "mean girl" persona as written about by Wiseman (2002) and has historically been attributed more to girls and women than men. That assumption remains true today. Boys and men remain predominantly more physical and women more verbal and social in their negative interpersonal interactions and relationships with others. But males *do* also engage in indirect aggression, so we should not stereotype indirect aggression solely to girls and women.

Whether direct or indirect, both forms of behaviors are aggressive in nature because they are designed to injure the targeted party in some fashion. There is nothing pacifistic or noble about bullying behavior. There are no social benefits to which bullying behaviors contribute. While it employs many strategies and tactics, it ultimately has one goal in mind—to obtain something of value to the aggressor. It is time we call bullying what it actually is—*aggression*. More specifically, it is ***interpersonal aggression*** (Felson, 2000), even though the use of that term should not confuse the gravity or seriousness of the methods used to inflict interpersonal harm on others. In sum, do not confuse interpersonal aggression as synonymous with relational aggression, which we discuss in more depth shortly. While relational aggression is certainly a form of interpersonal aggression employing indirect tactics, direct aggression involving physical harm, too, creates interpersonal harm with a peer group.

A PROPOSED NEW AND MORE COMPREHENSIVE DEFINITION OF BULLYING

Let's take what we know about the characteristics of bullying and try to make it both as operational and comprehensive as possible. Here is what I propose as a new definition of bullying incorporating others, previously cited, who have played a role in the evolution of the behavior:

> ***Bullying*** *is a negative behavior from one or more individuals who have power or status of a personal or social nature (called* ***agents*** *or* ***actors****) directed toward one or more other individuals (called* ***targets****) with the intent to lessen the power or status of the targeted individual(s). Bullying can be perpetrated in a manner in which the target is aware of the action (****overt/direct bullying****) or in a manner in which the target is not aware (****covert/indirect bullying****) of efforts to undermine one's status or credibility. It is also possible that observing the bullying of others negatively impacts an individual cognitively or affectively (****vicarious victimization****). An act of bullying can occur in the moment or across a more lengthy time period. There may or may not be a direct or long-term personal relationship between the agent and target. The interaction between the two parties, however, is considered an* ***interpersonal relationship*** *for the duration of the behavior. The goal of the bullying behavior is to maintain or increase the power or status of the actor. Bullying may occur in a variety of fashions, venues, and dimensions (e.g., an actual physical act, verbal abuse, or through intimidation in alternate formats, such as electronic media), but it ultimately is designed to psychologically dominate the target of the behavior through disruption or destruction of the personal and social fabric of the target's life (****relational aggression****).*

Now, let's parse this proposed new definition and see how it fits with past and present descriptions of bullying.

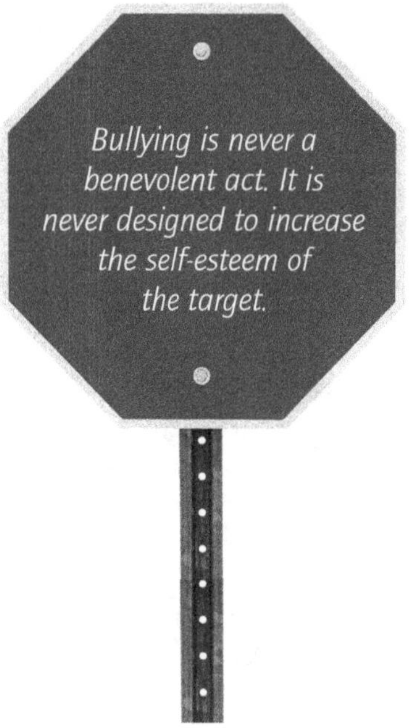

> ***Bullying*** *is a negative behavior from one or more individuals who have power or status of a personal or social nature (called* ***agents*** *or* ***actors****) directed toward one or more other individuals (called* ***targets****) with the intent to lessen the power or status of the targeted individual(s). . . .*

Bullying is not undertaken for benevolent reasons. It is not designed to increase the self-esteem of those on whom it is inflicted; therefore, it is considered to have negative intent. The individuals involved either want to maintain, obtain, or increase a position of social or personal rank within the relationship or within some peer group of importance to the actor. If the behavior is personal, then it is directed between the agent and target, usually in identifiably observable methods. If the behavior is social, the agent may or may not make the behavior known to the target (e.g., rumor and gossip), but the target's peer group is contacted by the agent with information or behaviors designed to weaken the influence of the target within the group. The power or status that is targeted by the agent of bullying is most likely designed to damage the interpersonal relationships of the target among the peer group.

It is also entirely possible for an individual who has been the target of bullying to engage in bullying behavior toward others—what has been traditionally labeled the ***bully-victim*** (Marini, Dane, Bosacki, & YLC-CURA, 2006).

*. . . Bullying can be perpetrated in a manner in which the target is aware of the action (**overt/direct bullying**) or in a manner in which the target is not aware (**covert/indirect bullying**) of efforts to undermine one's status or credibility. It is also possible that observing the bullying of others negatively impacts an individual cognitively or affectively (**vicarious victimization**). . . .*

The agents of bullying may or may not make their actions known to the target. If an individual does, then that is an example of what is termed *overt* or *direct bullying*. The concept of covert and direct bullying is the same as with direct aggression, except that this definition is more inclusive of verbal confrontation and less gender-stereotyped than what is typically considered with direct aggression.

Girls and women are more likely to engage in overt or direct bullying through verbal confrontation and less likely (less likely, but not totally!) to physically assault their targets, hence the greater utility of the term beyond the realm of the purely physical. Of course, any effort to harm another's social or personal being that is undertaken in a covert fashion would be an example of indirect bullying. Indirect bullying could also occur vicariously. Bystanders could be as psychologically impacted by what happens to another person and feel as if it happened to themselves. No matter how the direct or indirect bullying is conducted, it is always designed to negatively impact some form of the target's status or credibility within one or more peer group affiliations.

. . . An act of bullying can occur in the moment or across a more lengthy time period. . . .

Can bullying be a single instance? Yes. Does it usually occur in that fashion? No. But it can occur.

One of the constant questions posed when supervisory personnel are attempting to determine whether or not a behavior was or was not bullying has to do with the time period in which it occurred. This is a direct result of the original definition proffered by Olweus (1993, p. 9). The phrase *long-term, repeated negative actions* in the Olweus definition has prevented many an actor of bullying from being held accountable for bullying when the negative action directed toward a target was a one-time incident.

This new definition makes it clear: Bullying *can* occur in a single instance. It is entirely possible that a child or adolescent who engages in bullying behaviors does not do so in a documented fashion against the same target over any length of time. But it is also entirely possible that the individual engages in those behaviors in single instances with many different targets in such a random fashion that no pattern of bullying behavior is detected unless a concerted effort on the part of adults is made to connect the dots and reveal the overall picture.

It is also possible that an individual engages in a single-instance behavior that has racial or sexually discriminatory underpinnings. In that situation, not only may the individual have engaged in an instance of bullying, but she or he may have also crossed a line into harassment, intimidation, discrimination, hate speech, or hate crime as defined by legal statute.

> *. . . There may or may not be a direct or long-term personal relationship between the agent and target. The interaction between the two parties, however, is considered an* ***interpersonal relationship*** *for the duration of the behavior. . . .*

The parties involved in an act or series of bullying behaviors do not have to be involved in any type of personal relationship in which they know each other well, or even at all. Usually, however, it is the case that there is some type of personal knowledge of, acquaintance, or regular interaction between the agent and the target. However, no matter if the individuals "know" one another or not or have any type of association on a regular or irregular basis, once they are engaged in a bullying interaction, an interpersonal relationship has been created. It's not a pleasant or healthy interpersonal relationship, mind you, but it's a relationship nonetheless. Ironically, the interpersonal relationship may last much longer in the psyche of the targets than in the agents of bullying since the target is less likely to be able to forget the damaging interaction that occurred. The perpetrators of the mayhem go merrily on their way to find their next victim. The targets are left holding the emotional baggage.

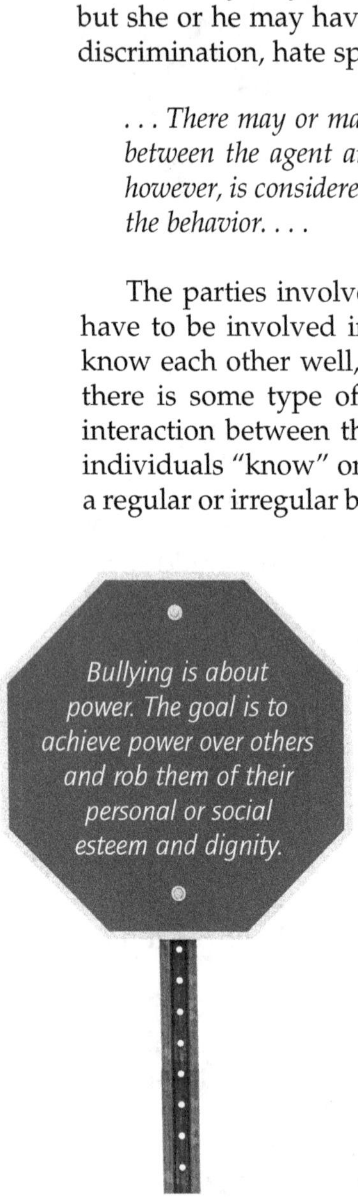

> *. . . The goal of the bullying behavior is to maintain or increase the power or status of the actor. . . .*

The goal of the instigators of bullying behaviors is the inverse of their goals for their targets. The bullying agents' sole intentions for their targets are to take power and status away from them. In doing so, the assumption is that their power is increased. This is usually the case. Those who bully, in addition to the injury they inflict upon their targets, send strong ***vicarious messages*** to the ***bystanders*** and ***observers***: "I can do this to *you* if I want to. Don't try me." This is especially true when there is no intervention by others within the setting taken toward stopping the agent from acting again.

Whether there is an existing power inequity or not is secondary to the power inequity that is created *after* an incident of bullying occurs. If a power inequity did not exist before, it will after an act of bullying. The entire purpose of the interaction is for one person to win (the agent or actor) and one person to lose (the target). Aggressors, in addition to any particular tangible gain they achieve (money, property), get the opportunity to climb the ladder of peer status within those peer groups in which bullying and intimidation are valued or allowed to happen without consequence. ***Benign neglect*** toward bullying behaviors on the part of adults in supervisory positions ("Kids will be kids" or "It's just something they have to go through and grow out of") has done as much to encourage bullying behaviors in schools and other places as have actual acts of bullying to attract onlookers into joining in or starting their own bullying behaviors.

> *. . . Bullying may occur in a variety of fashions, venues, and dimensions (e.g., an actual physical act, verbal abuse, or through intimidation in alternate formats, such as electronic media) but ultimately is designed to psychologically dominate the target of the behavior through disruption or destruction of the personal and social fabric of the target's life (**relational aggression**).*

No matter what method is employed, the end result of bullying is always the same. It is a psychological attack on the self-esteem of the target. Period. We need to start understanding that it is foolhardy and damaging to believe the old assumptions that a black eye will go away and an apology is all that is necessary to make acts of bullying "all better." It sends a message to the targets that all they have to do is forget what happened—or act like it—and that we really don't put much credence in their dilemma, while at the same time it emboldens the ones who create the mischief to act as if they are apologetic. For them, it's about the ability to escape accountability so that they can bully somebody else in another place, another day.

Psychological damage does not simply "go away." It embeds itself into the sense of safety and security of the individual victimized by the negative behavior. Older adolescents who inflict psychological punishment on others know exactly what they are doing. Younger adolescents and children, however, may or may not fully understand that their actions have deeper consequences to their targets than what appear on the surface. But they learn quickly—all the more reason to intervene as early as possible.

THE MISERY INDEX

There is no end to the different methods employed by those who bully to damage their targets. Contemporary research still identifies the physical, psychological, and psychosomatic misery experienced by those who are bullied (Bogart et al., 2014; Gini, 2008; Gini & Pozzoli, 2013). And any list of mayhem listed here would both be incomplete and out of date by the time this book sees its first printing. In the time it takes you to read this sentence, some kid, somewhere, will have created yet another method of physical or psychological intimidation to harass another kid. Much of the psychological bullying that takes place today comes in the form of verbal insults, put-downs, and intimidations, be it spoken or intimated quietly or plastered for all to see in cyberspace. A particularly pernicious aspect of bullying today is that it can be accomplished and perpetuated incessantly because of social communication venues, always present, always lurking. If it disappears or vanishes from cyberspace, the target knows that it can resurface at any time at the will of the actor. Such conditions create a sense of insecurity within the minds of those targeted. They are always on alert, perhaps even ***hypervigilant*** as they await the next attack. In the middle of the night while asleep, a vicious slam can be posted about two individuals on a social media site and two hundred kids will have seen it and added their own insults before the targets have even gotten to school the next day. By the time the targets arrive, they are already fodder for any or all of those social media posts of which they know nothing about until they turn on their cell phones, laptops, or computers and log into whatever social media site is hosting the insults de jour.

Take these concepts under consideration: a sense of isolation among the peer group; situations that create a sense of futility and learned helplessness; threats to one's safety, sense of security, friends, or family; withholding information; personal degradation and humiliation; deliberate attempts to diminish the personhood of the individual. These are just a partial list of what those who bully inflict upon their targets. Guess what? These are also characteristics of what can be considered ***psychological torture*** and ***emotional abuse*** as documented in domestically violent relationships (see Breiding, Basile, Smith, Black, & Mehendra, 2015; Ojeda, 2008). Psychological torture and emotional abuse in our schools and playgrounds? Isn't that an exaggeration? Talk to those who have been subjected to it. They may convince you otherwise:

> *"I felt so small and dirty. They were on me constantly about everything I did and that it was never right. I just wanted to crawl in a hole and die."*

> *"I was able to put up with most of what they did until they started throwing my stuff in the toilet and using the bathroom on it. I couldn't use any*

of what they threw in there and I lost some really important homework and clothes. The worst day was when they soaked the only pair of workout pants I had for gym in the toilet and then hit me in the face with them. Everybody was in there and they all saw it. Then I had to wear them for the rest of class. People kept laughing, saying, 'Who stinks?' all day."

"I remember this one kid in the eighth grade who was sort of effeminate and everybody called him a faggot and all the other stuff that goes with it. One day they put ketchup on a bunch of tampons and taped them to his locker. He was so embarrassed. The rest of the day people would toss a tampon his way when the teacher wasn't looking. It was really bad."

"The physical stuff I could handle. But the name calling, I couldn't. It was constant. I got it on [name of social media] and in the halls. They used to whisper it just low enough in class so that the teachers couldn't hear it. I just wanted to die."

We may argue about whether or not bullying behaviors constitute *psychological torture* in the strictest sense of the term, but I do not think that there is likely disagreement among those who have experienced such behaviors that it is, at the very least, emotionally abusive. And for many, I would argue that bullying behaviors do fit the criteria for psychological torture.

WANT TO LEARN MORE?

Does the child or adolescent who engages in bullying behavior continue to do so as an adult? There have been findings linking the long-term implications of bullying behaviors present in childhood and adolescence. In a classic longitudinal study, Huesmann et al. (1984) found an association between those children identified as aggressive in the third grade and their subsequent behavior over the next two decades. A Kumpulainen and Rasanen (2000) study in Finland found a continuance of behaviors in later years for those identified as agents and target-agents in childhood. Target-agents, in particular, were at higher risk of showing more problematic behaviors at later ages of development. Ragatz, Anderson, Fremouw, and Schwartz (2011) found that those students in postsecondary settings who self-identified their behaviors during the last two years of their high school years as falling into the study's operational definitions of *bully, victim, bully-victim*, or *uninvolved* scored higher in later years on incidences of "aggression, criminal thinking, and psychopathy" (p. 156), as well as being more proactive in the administration of their bullying behaviors.

(Continued)

(Continued)

Examples of bullycreep can be found in everyday media headlines. Here are just a few of the headlines from a cursory search of the web in March 2014: "Our Children Face a Bullying 'Epidemic'" (*USA Today*); "School Bullying Is Epidemic and Turning Deadly" (ABC News); "The Only Way to Combat America's Bullying Epidemic" (Fox News); "The Bullying Epidemic" (Black Entertainment Television); *The Bullying Epidemic: The Guide to Arm You for the Fight* (Kathleen Patel); "How to Beat America's Bullying 'Epidemic'" (Latitude News); "Fear of 'Blaming Victims' Perpetuates Bullying Epidemic" (*Psychology Today*); "The Bullying Epidemic" (*Ladies Home Journal*). Then, for good measure, let's throw in the website *Bullying Epidemic: Make Every Day Bullying Prevention Day* (bullyepidemic.com and on Facebook).

While incidences of bullying behaviors occur on a larger scale, to call the behavior "epidemic" might well be an exaggeration, which tends to provide critics of bullying prevention programs with the ammunition they need to declare that the problem is a media manifestation and not really as bad as it appears to be. See Jessica Bennett, "Is the 'Bullying Epidemic' a Media Myth," *Newsweek* online version, October 5, 2010, at http://www.newsweek.com/bullying-epidemic-media-myth-73847.

Truth be told, bullying behaviors better fit the medical definition of ***hyperendemic***—"persistent, high levels of disease occurrence," as defined by the US Centers for Disease Control and Prevention. See "Principles of Epidemiology in Public Practice, Third Edition at http://www.cdc.gov/osels/scientific_edu/ss1978/lesson1/section11.html for a full understanding of the difference between such terms.

For views on the impact of reality-driven media, see Jen Christiansen, "Our Unhealthy Love of Reality TV Bullying," CNN, February 28, 2013, at http://www.cnn.com/2013/02/28/health/reality-tv-bullies/; Eric Deggins, "Facing Up to Bullies, Everywhere but on Reality TV," National Public Radio, June 19, 2012, at http://www.npr.org/2012/06/20/155358188/facing-up-to-bullies-everywhere-but-on-reality-tv; Nicole Evatt, "Reality TV Causes Bullying? 'Real Housewives Star' Says Yes," *Huffington Post*, November 2, 2011, at http://www.huffingtonpost.com/2011/11/02/real-housewives-star-bullying_n_1071482.html; and Victoria Yancey, "Youth Are Turning Into Reality TV Bullies (RTVB)," February 13, 2012, at http://www.examiner.com/article/youth-are-turning-into-reality-tv-bullies-rtvb.

4

Relational Aggression

The emphasis on relational aggression is one that has gained traction since the books *Odd Girl Out: The Hidden Culture of Aggression in Girls* by Rachel Simmons (2002), Rosalind Wiseman's (2002) *Queen Bees and Wannabes: Helping Your Daughter Survive Cliques, Gossip, Boyfriends and Other Realities of Adolescence*, and the subsequent film, *Mean Girls* (2004), based on Wiseman's book. It's not that relational aggression was anything new. Simmons's and Wiseman's best-selling books and the movie that followed simply highlighted and stylized a phenomenon that was largely practiced among girls and women, not that relational aggression did not occur among all the sexes and genders. It is my contention, as well as my experience, study, and interviews, that relational aggression is at the heart of all bullying interactions since the goal of the agent is to dominate the social interactions and status of the target within respective peer groups. It is not as sex- or gender-specific as we have heretofore been led to believe (Espelage & Swearer, 2003). How the aggression is manifested in order to negatively impact those relationships, however, has been noted as having certain sex- and gender-specific characteristics.

DEFINITIONS OF RELATIONAL AGGRESSION AND THE CONCEPT OF REJECTION SENSITIVITY

Just what is ***relational aggression***? First and foremost, it is a form of intimidation designed to negatively impact or manipulate social interactions between individuals within their respective peer groups. Perhaps a synonym for relational aggression is ***masked aggression***, as the intimidation is often done in covert ways so as to go unnoticed by those in supervisory capacities. Relational aggression is less direct, physical, and more verbal in nature, particularly among girls and women, but overt and physical methods can also be used to implement the negative consequences. It is often difficult to detect to the outsider (i.e., adults; Strauss, 2012). The goal is to undercut the bonds of social connections between the target and the target's supporting peers. While relational aggression is stereotypically assumed to occur among early adolescents and adults, it has also been noted that preschool age children can display simple relationally aggressive behaviors in response to immediate provocations (e.g., "I won't be your friend unless you give me your crayon").

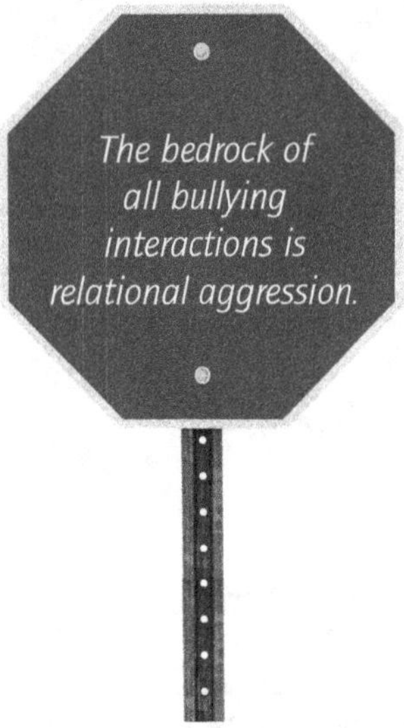

Relational aggression was first highlighted by the work of Crick and colleagues (Crick, 1996, 1997; Crick & Bigbee, 1998; Crick, Casas, & Mosher, 1997; Crick & Grotpeter, 1995; Crick, Grotpeter, & Bigbee, 2002) in the mid-1990s and includes aspects of Galen & Underwood's (1997) contention that the purpose is to "attack another's self-esteem or social status" (Geiger, Zimmer-Gembeck, & Crick, 2004, p. 30). Downey, Irwin, Ramsay, and Ayduk (2004) proposed a rejection sensitivity model based on the importance of "close relationships in women's lives" and that "maintaining harmonious intimate relationships is integral to women's self-concept" (p. 8). According to the concept of ***rejection sensitivity***, girls and women are acculturated to be more anxious, perceptive, and overreactive to changes in relationships or indications that hint to some type of rejection in a relationship. Some individuals are more prone to misinterpreting these signals than others and, as a method of protection of the self-concept, may "activate a defensive motivational system" (Downey et al., p. 9) in preparation to fend off the perceived pending rejection. Individuals who are hypervigilant about rejection or who have been driven to hypervigilance and anxiety as a result of being targeted may, ironically, act in ways to encourage or provoke the very rejection they fear—what has been termed the ***provocative victim*** (Smokowski & Kopasz, 2005, p. 105). This explanation provides credence as a potential rationale for those who are victimized, as well as those who target others—the previously mentioned bully-victim (Juvonen, Graham, & Schuster, 2003; Marini, Dane, Bosacki, & YLC-CURA, 2006; Smokowski & Kopasz, 2005; Swearer, Song, Cary, Eagle, & Mickelson, 2001; Vlachou et al., 2011).

It is safe to assume that some individuals are more rejection sensitive than others. Additionally, rejection sensitivity does not explain and is not the cause of every instance of relational aggression when it occurs. Likewise, poor relationships between children and adolescents should not be viewed solely through the lens of relational aggression. Relationships among children, adolescents, and adults sometimes just don't work. There may be times that ending a relationship is the best outcome for everyone involved.

One of the markers of relational aggression is that the goal of the negative interaction is generally not to end the relationship between the agent and the target. Quite to the contrary, the endgame is to perpetuate the dominance of the aggressor onto the target in order to keep the target in a one-down position within the relationship. *If the relationship ends, the aggressor has no power.* It is only in the continued one-up, one-down aspect of the toxic interaction that the agent maintains status as the dominant member of whatever peer group the individual is trying to impress or control. Mounts (1997) found that students who engaged in relational aggression are more likely to do so within their known and identified peer group, unlike those who physically bully who are equal-opportunity abusers and are not reticent about acting outside their circle of friends and associates (Macklem, 2003, p. 58).

RELATIONAL AGGRESSION AS A GENDER-NEUTRAL PHENOMENON

Males have long been considered the more aggressive of the sexes (Espelage, Mebane, & Swearer, 2004; Felson, 2000). This stereotypical viewpoint, of course, is directly related to what one defines as "aggression." Certainly from the viewpoint of physical aggression, males have historically been and remain far more likely to express aggression in this form than females. However, as previously noted, girls and women are becoming more physically aggressive. One explanation is that females are more likely to act out the role models they see in the media, particularly television shows marketed as reality television that derive their primary drama and plot lines from the conflict arising among participants. Another emerging consideration is that as society becomes more ***gender-neutral***, girls and women are increasingly engaging in less stereotypical modes of behavior as the differences in men's and women's lives become less gender specific (Eron, 2004).

It is fallacy, however, to assume that boys and men do not engage in relational aggression using many of the same tactics as their counterparts. While physical aggression off-campus and in venues unsupervised by personnel with authority continues, the increased emphasis on school and campus safety at the K–12 and postsecondary levels has forced many male agents of bullying to resort to less traditional methods of delivering abuse to their targets. Brute strength and unabashed force is far more likely to be seen and heard by others. They are also more likely than ever before to be addressed in some fashion by supervisors, even those who previously might have turned a blind eye to the interaction, due to the increased expectation of parents and society that bullying behaviors will not be tolerated as they have been in the past.

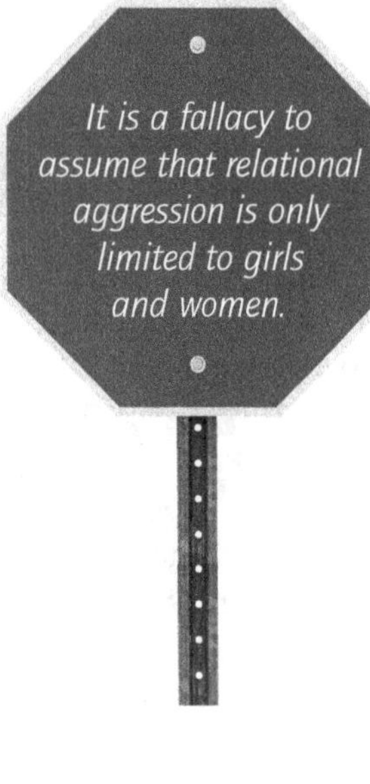

One of the most effective taunts or threats used by both sexes, particularly during adolescence, is one that impugns or questions the sexual identity of the target. A part of the success of this tactic is directly related to normal human development during the adolescent years. Adolescents doubt, question, and experiment sexually during this time. Additionally, adolescence is a time when both boys and girls are forced via social pressures to align themselves with one sex or another—in essence, to become "more a boy" or "more a girl" than perhaps they behaved previously in childhood. Children are, in many respects, quite androgynous toward a sexual identity. As such, it is not uncommon for them to engage in play behaviors as children that might be classified as cross-gender behavior during later adolescence. Adolescents frequently use their memories of sexually curious childhood peer interactions as weapons later during adolescence by sharing embarrassing tales of such experiences with others in efforts to gain dominance and power.

Case in point: A thirteen-year-old seventh-grade boy was hounded by his same-aged male peers for playing with dolls as a five-year-old. Never mind the fact that other members of his peer group did the same thing during their own childhood. Because of the particular vulnerability of the adolescent at that precise time and developmental place, his peers used this childhood behavior to spread rumors about his sexuality. Though tormented during his seventh-grade year, the young boy had enough resilience to survive the rumor campaign and be accepted back into his peer group the following year.

As stated at the outset of this chapter, it is my contention that all acts of bullying are designed to weaken, manipulate, control, or destroy the relationship of the target within a respective peer group. Peer relationships are the staff of life in Kid World. This is particularly true among adolescents who, by then, have the cognitive skills to "understand their peers' social and behavioral reputations" (Vlachou, Amndreou, Botsoglou, & Didaskalou, 2011, p. 334). They give support and validation to each other and form a cohesive defense against their arch enemies—usually adults. Right or wrong, the peer group is *die supergruppe* in a world where it's us against them, adults are clueless about what it's like to be a kid these days, and "your parents are so cool, mine are so strict and clueless."[1]

Destruction of the peer relationship, then, is the *bacio della morte* in Kid World. The act of bullying—either physical or psychological—helps unravel and dismantle the bonds of connectivity within this intricate and all-important support network of children and adolescents. It destroys the security of targets at a time when they are alienated from the very people they need most as they reject adults and try to shape their own independence by shying away from adult advice. Persistent efforts to isolate the individual from the peer group, ***shunning***, has long been used within society to send a message from the dominant group or power holders within a group that the behavior of the target is not acceptable. And because in Kid World everything is personal, efforts to prevent association by the target to the peer group becomes a de facto rejection of the individual.

---

1. For humorous validation of this behavior, read the comic strip *Zits* by Jerry Scott and Jim Borgman. On any given day, perpetual teenager Jeremy is mortified by his parents' inability to fathom his existence.

WHEN DOES RELATIONAL AGGRESSION OCCUR?

Relational aggression occurs when the dominant party cannot obtain the desired goals with a target by more overt means because more observable methods would likely draw attention to the aggressor by those in a supervisory capacity. The strategy is simple: Why use more effort than necessary to get what an individual wants if it can be obtained via an alternate, stealthier method? In addition, the use of relational aggression through unattributed rumor or innuendo decreases the likelihood of direct linkage with the source of the destructive falsehood or half-truth: "Have you heard . . . ?"

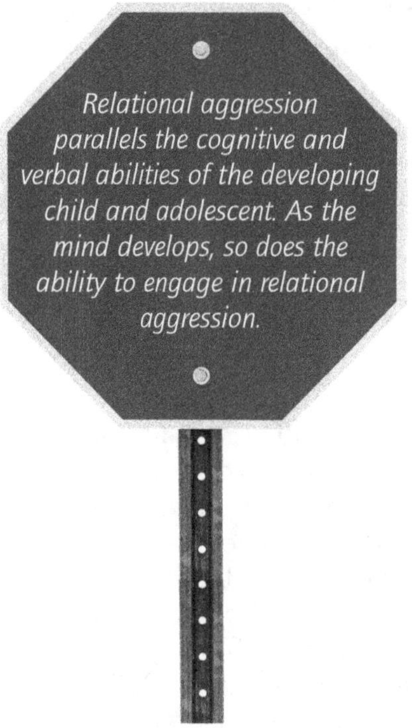

Case in point: A high school girl had a reputation for being physical within her peer group. It was not uncommon for her to pull hair or punch targets to get what she wanted. As she moved through the upper grades, the physicality of her approach became less necessary because her reputation as a bruiser preceded any request she might make within her peer group. When she was counseled about her behavior after being observed berating another girl, she responded rather matter-of-factly, "Hey, I don't *have* to hit anyone anymore. All I have to do is request something and it happens. People know me well enough to know that if I don't get what I need, I can make things happen with their friends so that they aren't their friends anymore."

There are human development aspects as to when relational aggression occurs. It generally does not occur until early childhood (Espelage, Mebane, & Swearer, 2004), though it can and has been observed in children as young as three to five (Alsaker & Vakanover, 2001; Vlachou et al., 2011). It usually begins to develop in later childhood when peer groups begin to crystallize and the child has developed enough cognitively to understand how to "manipulate the social environment" (Espelage et al., 2004, p. 30, who also direct the reader to review the work of Crick & Rose, 2001). Macklem (2003, p. 57) notes that verbal aggression increases in direct proportion to language development. It certainly occurs during the early teen years as cognitive abilities mature to a higher level of perception in understanding how social relationships work. Some of the most brutal relational aggression happens during the middle school years when friendships become increasingly important to the social and personal identity of the individual.

During the high school years, relational aggression continues, particularly during the grade transition years—after all, moving to a high school building is just three months removed from being in a middle school building, so not much has changed socioemotionally for the adolescent. Relational aggression is often the preferred tactic employed among girls and women during disputes involving romance (Linder, Crick, & Collins, 2002).

EXAMPLES OF RELATIONAL AGGRESSION

Though certainly not all-inclusive, Macklem (2003, pp. 58–59) compiled a sample list of relationally aggressive behaviors among middle childhood from the existing literature at the time. Those examples follow, updated as necessary to account for the passage of time, with additional resources and sourcing highlighted at the end of the chapter:

- Spreading lies and rumors about a targeted individual
- Starting, contributing to, or maintaining existing rumors
- Exclusions of targets from personal peer activities not related to the school day
- Ignoring or shunning the target
- Writing messages about individuals and passing them around in the school setting (or posting the same on electronic and social media)
- Giving the impression that the peer group is talking or whispering about the target, sometimes in the presence of the individual
- Scapegoating the target
- Making active efforts to turn classmates or peer group against the target
- Refusing to accept friendship
- Becoming a friend with someone just to make the target jealous
- Telling secrets on a target
- Laughing at someone's misfortune
- Damaging reputation among a target's peer group
- Withdrawing or withholding friendship as a domination tactic
- Distributing photos or photocopies with embarrassing or personal information (or posting the same on electronic and social media)
- Actively and publicly shunning (e.g., moving away from an individual in a public setting who is the target of exclusion)
- Using social or electronic media to send harassing or intimidating emails or messages
- Leaving negative comments or messages about the target in a location so that the individual finds them

The list, of course, is virtually endless. Much of relational aggression perpetrated today is spread via social media and e-mail (which, ironically, leaves an electronic signature that can be traced to its source). However, that does little to assuage the damage done to the self-esteem, well-being, or security of those targeted for peer isolation or abuse.

POISONING THE WELL

Interfering with the ability of a child to interact with one's peers is a true poisoning of the well of interpersonal development. Kids gain support and sustenance from the ability to learn from their peers—both the positive and the negative. One of the cruelest lessons that is often learned in childhood and adolescence is how to shred the social fabric of interpersonal relationships in order to control and dominate those peers within Kid World who either choose not to play by the rules of manipulation or who are unable to compete in the game.

Damaging the relationships of others tremendously damages the healthy interpersonal interactions needed for children during a critical developmental phase of their lives. For adolescents, in particular, who are "dependent on the approval of peers for a sense of self-acceptance, as well as group acceptance" (Corvo & deLara, 2010, p. 186), it creates doubts among targets about their value and worth, while at the same time emboldening those who intentionally set out to do the damage with a sense of unchecked power.

WANT TO LEARN MORE?

An excellent explanation of the *social cues of the individual viewed as a provocative victim* is found from the Colorado Trust's Bullying Prevention Initiative at http://www.bullyingprevention.org/repository/Best%20Practices%20PDFs/ProvocativeVictim.pdf.

Those who are targeted for bullying and who also bully—the *bully-victims*—are often at greatest risk for a host of academic and interpersonal problems. The Juvonen et al. (2003) study of sixth graders noted that this group was found to be the "most troubled group, displaying highest levels of conduct, school, and peer relationship problems" (p. 1231), as well as "by far the most socially ostracized by their peers . . . least engaged in school, and they . . . reported elevated levels of depression and loneliness" (p. 1233). Swearer et al. (2001) found, among middle school-aged students, both those who bully and those who were targets and who also bullied, to be "similar in terms of anxiety" (p. 114) and had a level of anxiety which may encourage them to "respond to bullying in an aggressive fashion" (pp. 114–115) or more reactionary than the more passive target of bullying.

The *societal and peer pressure to "grow up" and become the gender one is "supposed to"* can have tragic consequences. See Loris Grisham, "School Bans 9-Year-Old Boy's My Little Pony Backpack," *USA Today*, March 18, 2014, at http://www.usatoday.com/story/news/nation-now/2014/03/18/my-little-pony-backpack-banned-school-north-carolina/6565425/; Casey Blake, "School Will Allow Boy to Bring My Little Pony Backpack," *USA Today*, March 21, 2014, at http://www.usatoday.com/story/news/nation/2014/03/21/my-little-pony-backpack-banned-school-north-carolina/6685403/; and Michelle Hankerson, "Wake Sheriff's Office Still Investigating 11-Year-Old's Apparent Suicide Attempt," *Charlotte* (NC) *Observer*, March 14, 2014, at http://www.newsobserver.com/2014/03/14/3702347/wake-sheriffs-office-still-investigating.html.

For additional background, greater depth, and examples of *relational aggression*, see Boulton & Hawker (1997); Crick et al. (2001); French, Jansen, & Pidada (2002); Henington, Hughes, Cavell, & Thompson (1998); Lagerspetz & Bjorkqvest (1994); and Ross, 1996.

5

The Law and Bullying Behaviors

Now we enter the swamp. And it has lots of alligators.

One of the most frustrating aspects of attempts to address the issue of bullying is the legislative and judicial responses designed to solve the problem. The most cursory review of existing statutes, policies, and case law reveals a confusing array of proclamations, declarations, and proscribed solutions. There are two conclusions that might well be drawn from all of these efforts to stop bullying: Either there are many ways to solve the problem, or there are so many approaches floating around because we really have not yet figured out the most effective legal method to do so.

You would be right to pick either one, or both, of those two options.

THE PROBLEMS ASSOCIATED WITH EFFORTS TO LEGISLATE BULLYING PREVENTION

Efforts to deal with bullying from a legislative or legal perspective have proven contentious (Clark, 2013). The primary problem deals with the difficulty or inability of the jurisdictional bodies to determine exactly what behaviors constitute bullying from a legally definable and defensible standpoint.

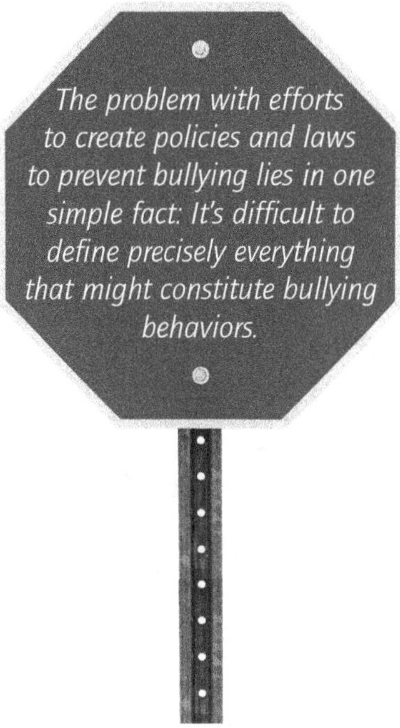

We must remember that no matter what is defined in statute, rule, or policy, if the definition is not actively or practically enforceable through the judicial system, then it neuters application. Only what the courts ultimately can uphold becomes relevant. One of the major problems is that the theoretical, conceptual, scientific definitions and characteristics of what constitute bullying behaviors often do not translate well into what is enforceable under the law. In sum, it is often through the operational definitions of a behavior by which laws and rules sink or swim.

Case in point: Look at the Olweus (1993, p. 9) definition of bullying. It is perhaps the simplest and most basic definition employed in school districts across the world:

> *Bullying is the exposure to long-term, repeated negative actions on the part of one or more persons.*

As we saw in Chapter 3, this simple definition, commonly understood by anyone who reads it, is fraught with unanswered legal practicalities. With law, these questions must have answers that are enforceable and fall within the boundaries of existing statutes, case law, or, if the law is new, what is likely to be allowed in the courts if challenged. A statute, rule, or policy which is not enforceable or cannot meet legal muster is in jeopardy of being overruled when challenged in the courts.

So taking the simplest of definitions of what constitutes bullying, here is what must be clarified and operationalized in order to make the Olweus (1993) definition enforceable according to a statute or rule:

- *Exposure* must be defined. Does exposure mean being acted upon by an individual who is *actively* bullying a target? What if a student *observes* bullying that occurs to someone else (vicarious bullying)? Does that constitute an act of bullying that must be addressed?
- *Long-term* must be defined. Exactly what constitutes the *length of time* that makes for a "long-term" exposure? Does a one-second malicious slur directed toward an individual qualify for action?
- *Repeated* must be defined. Repeated implies something that occurs *more than once*, but what if something that is ultimately defined as bullying only occurs once? Is a one-time incident of what seems to be bullying to a third-party observer not eligible to be addressed under this definition? Does "repeated" mean that the behavior must only be directed at a single person? What if an individual engages in multiple single-instance bullying with different targets each time?

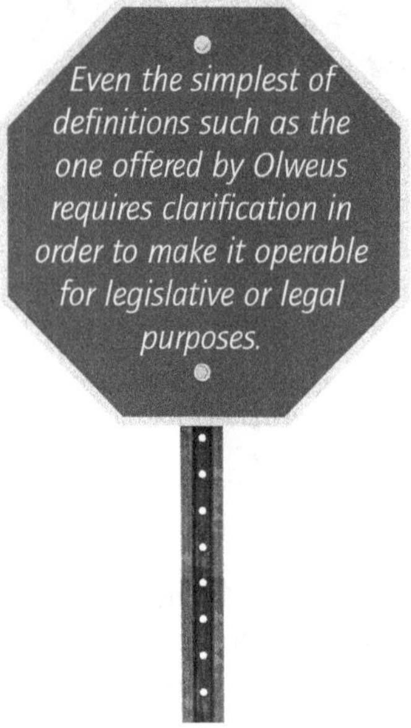

- *Negative action* must be defined. Clearly, *physical violence* is a negative action, but what about *verbal abuse*? And if a negative action includes verbal abuse, how does that fit with *free speech rights* of others to express an opinion? What if two people just disagree on an issue, but one person is more strident in expressing that opinion than the other? And does a "negative action" extend to *cyberspace communication*? At the time of the Olweus definition, the Internet and cyberspace were in their infancy, if a piece of the equation at all.
- *Part of* must be defined. Does this mean that a *bystander* who seems to be supportive (smiles or laughs) of the actions of the bully is a "part of" the bullying behavior and should be held accountable? If so, should the individual be held to the *same level of accountability* as the primary agent? What if five hundred kids knew that an act of bullying was going to occur the next day at school as a result of a posting on social media—are they all a "part of" the eventual act of bullying that takes place?

Out of a simple seventeen-word definition, three words and two phrases have to be clarified before we can begin to truly operationalize it. And here's what happens when we begin to parse those words and phrases: They involve additional words and phrases that, too, must be parsed and dissected so that those who are charged with enforcement will know exactly what they should look for and what they can and cannot do. Ultimately, the courts will interpret whether or not those who enforced the law did so properly within the confines of the words chosen to define the behavior.

Any wonder the 2011 analysis of state bullying laws and policies by the US Department of Education (US DoE) Office of Planning, Evaluation, and Policy Development (OPEPD) ran 182 pages (Stuart-Cassel, Bell, Springer, & EMT Associates, 2011)?

WORD GAMES: LEGAL DEFINITIONS OF WHAT CONSTITUTES BULLYING

Much of what has driven society to (finally) pay better attention to the needs of those who have been tormented in schools is related to high-profile incidents of school violence attributed, in some fashion, to the bullying that was received and viewed as insufferable on the part of targets and worthy of retaliatory violence to level the playing field. The ultimate influence, however, was the increasing number of lawsuits brought against school districts and supervisory personnel for failure to adequately intervene or prevent bullying from occurring in the first place, particularly the failure to protect students who identified themselves as gay, lesbian, bisexual, or transgendered. Part of this has been directly related to the legal definitions associated with what meets the threshold of harassment by federal definition.

By 2010, most states had legislation that identified the term(s) *bullying, bullying and harassment*, or *bullying, harassment, and intimidation* and requiring school district policies and practices to intervene if such behaviors were present (US DoE OPEPD, 2011, p. 15). Some states identified bullying differently from intimidation while others solely spoke of harassment without mentioning bullying. Each term has, if not different legal meanings, then certainly nuances which make them nonequivalent by varying degrees in the eyes of the law.

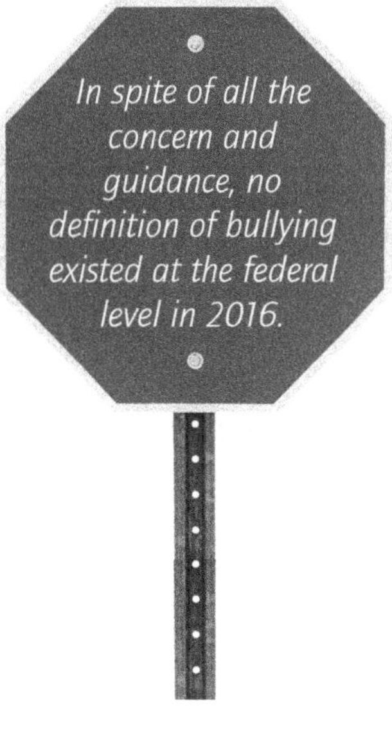

Ironically, as of 2016, there was still not a specific federal definition of bullying in statute that could be used as a template or guide. All definitions of the behaviors considered to be such were created at the state legislative levels. Cursory review of multiple state definitions shows a variety of behaviors considered to meet respective state criteria. However, the components of what constitutes those behaviors often cross into federal legal territory for consideration as violations of sexual, racial, or workplace (translate: school environment) harassment.

Some behaviors are operationalized by the federal government. The definition of ***harassment*** for the school environment refers to behaviors that are (1) severe, pervasive, and persistent; (2) create what can be considered to be a ***hostile environment*** (defined as behaviors which interfere with or prohibit a student from engaging in the activities and opportunities afforded to all others) in the school setting; and (3) are directed toward a target based on currently federally identified ***enumerated groups***: race, color, national origin (ethnicity), sex, disability, or religion.[1]

The federal government expects states to address behaviors that fall under the federal guidelines for harassment and work to prevent their reoccurrence. If states fail to do so, the federal government has the option to step in. However, school districts are only obligated to respond to harassment in schools if the behaviors trigger the federal standards, unless a state sets additional guidelines for what should be addressed in that state. In essence, the federal government establishes a baseline for harassment in a hostile environment for specifically identified enumerated groups. States can pass legislation with higher standards as long as those laws do not conflict with federal or state rights as granted under those respective constitutions.

THE CURIOUS CASE OF THE "REASONABLE PERSON"

What we see when we begin to analyze efforts to address bullying at the state and national levels is a ragged patchwork of efforts, all depending upon what that state's definition of bullying happens to be. Perhaps now is the time to introduce Mr. and Ms. Reasonable Person into the equation.

The ***reasonable person standard*** is a legal concept that is often used in courts to assist in the determination of what the "average person" would assume or do if presented with the same set of information or circumstances (Alexander & Alexander, 2009). Because law can be such a confusing element to the average person, especially when what is written into statutes, rules, and policies may not end up being exactly what was actually intended or may have ramifications beyond original intent—***unintended consequences***—courts and rule-making bodies often refer to a reasonable person clause in assisting them in interpretation and application. In sum, the questions to be answered are "What would a reasonable person do in this instance?" or "How do these laws/rules/practice impact the reasonable person?"

1. See "Federal Laws" at http://www.stopbullying.gov/laws/federal for a full explanation with examples, along with updates.

> The reasonable person has been described by different courts as a prudent person . . . a person of ordinary sense using ordinary care and skill . . . an ideal, a model of conduct, and a community standard. . . . [The] characteristics . . . [include] . . . the attributes of the persons involved and with the circumstances. (Alexander & Alexander, 2009, p. 646)

The reasonable person standard is important because laws are made to apply to everyone, not just a few.[2] This is particularly true in public educational settings which must adhere to federal laws and guidelines if they accept federal assistance of some type (usually fiscal). Private educational institutions that receive federal assistance must also adhere to federal standards in order to continue to receive the assistance. It is, however, entirely possible for a private educational entity that receives no federal assistance to avoid, but not totally be exempt from, having to follow many of the same rules of public institutions.

As of 2011, a US DoE OPEPD analysis of existing state laws on bullying prevention indicated that 15 states incorporated some form of reasonable person guidance in interpreting state policies.[3] Examples included the following:

- Delaware (Del. Code. Ann. Tit. 14, §4112D)
  "As used in this section, *bullying* means any intentional written, electronic, verbal or physical act or actions against another student, school volunteer or school employee that *a reasonable person under the circumstances should know* will have the effect of."
- Georgia (Ga. Code Ann. §20-2-751.4)
  "Any intentional written, verbal, or physical act which *a reasonable person would perceive as being* intended to threaten, harass, or intimidate."
- Mississippi (Miss. Code Ann. § 37-11-67)
  "For purposes of this section, *hostile environment* means that the victim subjectively views the conduct as bullying or harassing behavior and the conduct is objectively severe or pervasive enough that *a reasonable person would agree* that . . ."

---

2. While the reasonable person standard assumes "normal intelligence" (Alexander & Alexander, 2009, p. 646) on the part of the individual involved in the situation, it does not excuse the behaviors of those determined to have mental incapacities from being held responsible for their actions. While allowances may be made in specific circumstances, the "courts have traditionally held that a person with less mental ability than an average person must adjust and conform to the rules of society" (Alexander & Alexander, 2009, p. 646).

3. The reader should assume that these examples may have been amended in some fashion since the US DoE OPEPD analysis. Laws are in constant flux.

- Minnesota[4]
  "... require school employees who witness prohibited conduct or possess reliable information that would lead *a reasonable person to suspect that* a student is a target of ... "

The importance of reasonable person language in statutes or interpretation cannot be underestimated. The reasonable person standard allows for the likelihood of better implementation of bullying prevention policies due to the flexibility of possible interpretation on the part of those who must implement them, the likelihood that all instances will have particular aspects which are specific to the circumstances,[5] as well as greater acceptance on the part of the general public. The more precise and prescriptive a policy, the more onerous it may become to put into practice. On the other extreme are laws, such as the one in Minnesota until 2014, that were too broad and provided little guidance to school districts as to how to proceed:

> Each school board shall adopt a written policy prohibiting intimidation and bullying of any student. The policy shall address intimidation and bullying in all forms, including, but not limited to, electronic forms and forms involving Internet use. (Minn. Stat. 121.A 0695, 2013)

Critics of antibullying legislation who prefer to have weak state directives for the sake of "local control" by school boards, or who would rather not have any such protections at all, point to the revised New Jersey statute in 2011 (N.J. Stat. Ann. § 18A:37) as too burdensome and restrictive for implementation (Hu, 2011; Nash, 2012; "New Jersey's Anti-Bullying Law, Toughest in Country, Garners Praise and Criticism," 2011; Norgard, 2014).

THE US DEPARTMENT OF EDUCATION ANALYSIS OF CURRENT STATE STATUTES

The 2011 US DoE report on the status of state efforts to address bullying was issued primarily as a direct result of the mounting number of legal

4. The Minnesota bill to revise and strengthen existing bullying prevention policy (which at 37 words was the shortest such legislation in the country) passed the House but stalled in the Senate in 2013. It was ultimately passed and signed into law with the same language in 2014 as the Safe and Supportive Minnesota Schools Act.

5. Hence the absurdity of trying to enforce zero tolerance policies.

challenges directed toward school districts by families and related parties of legal standing who felt as if school boards and personnel were not providing adequate protection for children from preventable acts of bullying, intimidation, and harassment. Higdon (2011) compared the failure of American schools to adequately address bullying or protect its targets, particularly those who do not conform to gender stereotypes, as a modern-day lynching of children. Likewise, the US DoE report was issued in response to an increasing number of high-profile incidents of self-harm undertaken by students who were targeted for such behaviors.[6] The report revealed the hodgepodge of state efforts to address the problem, undertaken largely in the absence of any existing guidelines or model for what might be termed ***best practice legislation***. As a result, states cobbled legislation from a variety of sources and created a myriad of responses (Sacco, Silbaugh, Corredor, Casey, & Doherty, 2012), many designed with a focus on punitive measures toward the actors of bullying. Little focus or consideration was provided to remediative or restorative efforts that might be better suited for either the agent or target (Riestenberg, 2012).

Much of what states attempted to do to increase bullying prevention initiatives became a jumble of amendments to existing criminal legislation as a direct response to reports linking incidents of school violence to retaliation by the targets of bullying. Though similar incidents existed prior, it was not until the 1999 school shooting at Columbine High School in Littleton, Colorado, that state policy makers began to attempt to focus on bullying prevention efforts. In direct response to the Columbine shooting and an in-state high profile suicide with association to bullying, Georgia enacted the first bullying prevention legislation through the implementation of character education (US DoE OPEPD, 2011, p. xi). The years following saw a steady increase in legislative initiatives. Between 1999 and 2010, there were 120 legislative actions of some sort to either create or amend existing statutes to address some aspect of bullying behaviors. At the time of the specific data analysis (2010), only four states did not have legislation on the books—Hawaii, Michigan, Montana, and South Dakota. Since then, all have passed some form of bullying prevention legislation. Until 2015, Montana was the only state in the country without identifiable statutes directed specifically toward bullying (Clark,

6. The reader is encouraged to plug in the search phrases *list of students who killed themselves from bullying* or *list of students who died from bullycide* to Google to see an updated tragically long list of names of youth who died with bullying believed to be a contributing factor.

2013).[7] It is also important to note that this compilation does not include the states that have moved to address bullying that occurs via electronic means. As of 2015, not every state with statutes on bullying prevention also addressed bullying that occurred via e-mail, social media, or website (Hinduja & Patchin, 2015).

KEY FINDINGS OF THE US DEPARTMENT OF EDUCATION ANALYSIS

Key findings of the report indicated the following (DoE OPEPD, 2011, p. x):

- Almost every state (46)[8] had some kind of law related to bullying.
- Virtually all of the states with such statutes (45 of the 46) directed local school districts to "adopt bullying policies." It is unclear from this description if that meant that districts were to design and implement their own policies or adopt a recommended state model policy.
- Model bullying policies existed for use by school districts in 41 states.
- Cyberbullying through electronic means was addressed by statutes in 36 states.
- Only 13 states extended jurisdiction to schools to respond to electronic communications that created a "hostile school environment."
- There was a direct relationship between how expansive the local district policies were and how expansive state statutes were among the bullying prevention policies reviewed by the US DoE.

US DEPARTMENT OF EDUCATION RECOMMENDATIONS FOR EFFECTIVE LEGISLATION AND POLICIES ADDRESSING BULLYING PREVENTION

As expected, there was a tremendous amount of variation among exactly what was included in the 46 state statutes analyzed by the US DoE in 2011. Few of the states included all of what the US DoE considered essential components of effective bullying prevention law or policy (US DoE OPEPD,

7. A bill to address cyberbullying was introduced in the Montana House of Representatives on February 10, 2015 (Noon, 2015; Talwani, 2015), was ultimately passed, and signed into law. See also "Anti-Bullying Policies and Laws" at stopbullying.gov for the latest information and updates on bullying and cyberbullying statutes.

8. By 2015, this number had changed to 50. The reader is encouraged to check the most recent statistics regarding state policies, rules, and laws on the interactive map found at "Policies and Laws" at http://www.stopbullying.gov/laws/.

2011, p. xiii).[9] In an effort to provide guidance to states as they designed or amended their future legislation and policies, US DoE recommended 11 key components to be considered.[10] These included the following:

- *Prohibition of Conduct and Statement of Purpose.* Designed to provide a sort of preamble as to the need for such a policy in order to ensure for a safe learning environment, as well as make it clear that bullying behaviors are inappropriate and will not be tolerated.
- *Statement of Scope.* Designed to indicate that bullying behaviors are not prohibited exclusively to the school campus, but prohibitions apply to all school-related functions and locations in which the school is involved. Also extends the prohibition to the use of school property of any sort, such as school computers or even private electronic communications originating at a school function.
- *Specifying Prohibited Behaviors.* Provides for the definitions of exactly what bullying behaviors include that will hold an individual accountable. Also provides for the consideration of behaviors that encourage bullying as being subject to accountability.
- *Expansion of Protection to Enumerated Groups.* Indicates that bullying protection also extends to groups and classes of individuals who have historically been targeted for discrimination but is not exclusive to those classes as identified by federal law.
- *Describes How Local Policies Should Be Developed and Implemented.* Emphasizes that as local school districts move to translate statute into policy, various stakeholders should be consulted to increase community buy-in.
- *Local Policy Review.* Provides for the review of local policies on some type of timetable to ensure relevance and effectiveness.
- *Identifies Six Components to Be Included in Local Policies.* These components include the following:

  1. Provides definitions of bullying as identified by existing state statutes.
  2. Makes clear the mechanisms for reporting incidents of bullying to school personnel for students, faculty, staff, parents, and others.
  3. Outlines procedures for investigations of reports of bullying along with assurance that targets or reporters will be protected.

---

9. The report offered seemingly contradictory information regarding this. On p. xiii of the report, Exhibit C indicated that no state met all of the recommended US DoE criteria, yet in the text following the graph, it indicated that "Maryland and New Jersey are the only states that contains [sic] provisions covering all of the key components and school district policy subcomponents." The reader is encouraged to research and reconcile the two.

10. See *Exhibit 1: Description of 11 US Department of Education-Identified Key Components and School District Policy Subcomponents in State Bullying Legislation*, US DoE OPEPD, p. 6, for full details.

4. Assures that incidents of bullying will be documented with interventions conducted to address them.
5. Provides descriptions of potential interventions and accountability strategies for handling incidents of bullying.
6. Allows nondisciplinary options to handle bullying, inclusive of counseling or other mental health referrals, as necessary, for all involved in the actor–target interactions.

- *Communication of Bullying Policy to Stakeholders.* Identifies the methods of ensuring that policies and procedures will be distributed and made available to school and community.
- *Establishes Training and Prevention Initiatives.* Indicates that all school staff will be included in education and prevention efforts during inservice staffings.
- *Monitoring and Reporting.* Sets expectations that school districts will publicly report in some fashion data related to incidences of bullying and the efforts to address them.
- *Without Prejudice Clause.* Requires that all policies must inform those impacted that adherence to school policy in relationship to bullying does not preclude individual(s) from seeking additional relevant legal remedies.

PROTECTING ALL VERSUS PROTECTING ONLY A SELECT FEW: THE CONTROVERSY OF ENUMERATED GROUPS

The wags who complain about laws and policies designed to protect kids from bullying direct their harshest criticisms to the enumerated groups who have historically been targeted for just such behaviors both in schools and larger society. As previously noted, ***enumerated groups*** refer to those classes of individuals who are specifically identified in federal statutes (referred to as ***enumeration***) for additional consideration as groups *perhaps* needing protection. Enumeration does not provide these groups with additional protection; it merely recognizes the past history of abuse they have received as a result of simply being a member of those groups. Examples of enumerated classes include identification by the following characteristics:

- Race
- Ethnicity
- Color
- Religion
- Ancestry
- National origin
- Gender (actual)

- Gender identity (actual or exploring)
- Sex (actual)
- Sexual identity or orientation (actual or exploring)
- Mental, physical, developmental, or sensory difference or disability
- Socioeconomic status
- Academic status
- Association with a person who has or is perceived to have one or more of the characteristics considered to be in an enumerated group

While those who oppose bullying prevention legislation often do so for a variety of reasons, one of the primary arguments used is based on the philosophical or tangible disagreement over the designation of enumerated groups. Their rationale is a simple one and on the surface seems harmless enough: No one group of people should be more protected than others, and if we specifically mention certain groups, then we are, in essence, giving them greater protection. Particular targets of scorn in the 2000s are individuals who have different gender or sexual orientation.

Of course, we know the history of exclusionary and prejudicial behaviors in this country directed toward those deemed to be "out of the norm" (whatever that means by local standards). In 2012, the US Government Accountability Office (US GAO) issued a report to Congress on the efficacy of legal protection afforded to enumerated groups from bullying (US GAO, 2012). It offered somewhat confusing conclusions, as in the case of adequate protection available through existing federal and state civil rights actions:

> Federal and state civil rights laws offer some protections against bullying, but most vulnerable groups may not always be covered. . . . [The] nature and extent of protections available to them depend on the laws and policies of where they live or go to school. (US GAO, pp. 16, 26)

However, the report did not definitively identify enumerated groups to be at particular risk of bullying in its continued conclusion that "the prevalence of bullying of youths in certain vulnerable demographic groups is not known" (US GAO, p. 27). It concluded by calling for additional study of the demographics of those groups that may be more disparately impacted by and at risk for bullying.

What can be seen in a photograph that's not taken? The US GAO's findings are more likely the result of the lack of adequate measurement tools than a definitive conclusion that certain groups are not at greater risk for being targeted by bullying behaviors. One of the major criticisms from opponents to bullying policies is that data is always skewed toward favoring enumerated groups so as to show the need for their protection. That would not be the case according to the GAO report. But while the GAO may have indicated that the federal government did not have enough data in its 2012 report to be definitive about certain groups being more likely to

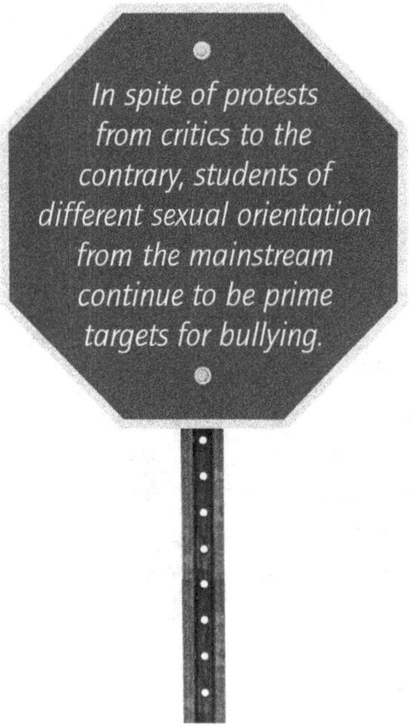

be targeted for abuse, snapshots taken by other cameras would seem to indicate otherwise:

- Twenty-seven percent of students report being harassed in some fashion for not being viewed by peers as fitting into traditional sexual stereotypes.[11]
- In New Jersey following the implementation of its comprehensive revised law in 2011, almost 11 percent of the 12,024 students who reported being bullied in the 2011 to 2012 school year indicated that they were targeted because of their sexual orientation; over 4 percent were abused due to gender identity or expression. Nearly 10 percent reported being bullied as a result of gender, and nearly an equal percentage said they were targeted due to mental, physical, or sensory difference or disability. Race or color as a reason for being targeted were reported over 8 percent and over 4 percent, respectively.[12]
- The US Centers for Disease Control and Prevention (CDC) indicated that in 2009, of seven thousand students who identified themselves as lesbian, gay, bisexual, or transgendered in middle and high school, 80 percent reported having been verbally harassed during the past year; 40 percent reported having been physically harassed; and 20 percent indicated that they had been physically assaulted.[13]
- A 2011 school climate survey reported that almost 85 percent of students who self-identified as lesbian, gay, bisexual, or transgendered heard biased remarks and language directed toward their sexual orientation; over 70 percent heard frequent use of derogatory language considered homophobic; and over 55 percent heard such remarks or language used by teachers or school staff. The rates of verbal and physical harassment were similar to the 2009 CDC report.[14]

---

11. American Psychological Association. (n.d.). Bullying: A module for teachers. Retrieved from http://www.apa.org/education/k12/bullying.aspx?item=1.

12. Calefati, J. (2012, October 3). Bullying in N.J. schools spikes over previous school year, new stats show. *Star Ledger* (NJ). Retrieved from http://www.nj.com/news/index.ssf/2012/10/bullying_in_nj_schools_spikes.html.

13. Kosciw, J. G., Greytak, E. A, Diaz, E. M., & Bartkiewicz, M. J. (2010). *The 2009 National School Climate Survey: The experiences of lesbian, gay, bisexual and transgender youth in our nation's schools*. Retrieved from http://www.cdc.gov/lgbthealth/youth.htm.

14. Kosciw, J. G., Greytak, E. A., Bartkiewicz, M. J., Boesen, M. J., & Palmer, N. A. (2012). *The 2011 National School Climate Survey: The experiences of lesbian, gay, bisexual, and transgender youth in our nation's schools*. Retrieved from www.glsen.org/research.

THE "TWO PS" OF SUCCESSFUL INTERVENTION

So what is one to make of all this legal wrangling and lawyer speak? There is quite a bit of it, all of which just seems to make intervention efforts more confusing. Let's see if we can't make common sense out of all of this mumbo jumbo. In order to do so, we have to focus on the "Two Ps"—***policy*** and ***practice***.

A policy is only as good as the ability to implement it. Policy in and of itself does nothing. It is just words on paper. Any policy that sits on a shelf, is unenforceable, or is impossible to turn into some semblance of reality is worthless. The corollary to that last sentence is this: No policy is likely to be 100 percent perfect. The key, then, is to have a policy that is as *practical* and *realistic* as possible. We also must not forget ***reasonableness***. Remember our discussion of the reasonable person standard? It certainly comes into play in designing policy. The more a policy is practical, realistic, and reasonable, the more likely it is to be implemented and enforceable, which brings us to the second of the Two Ps.

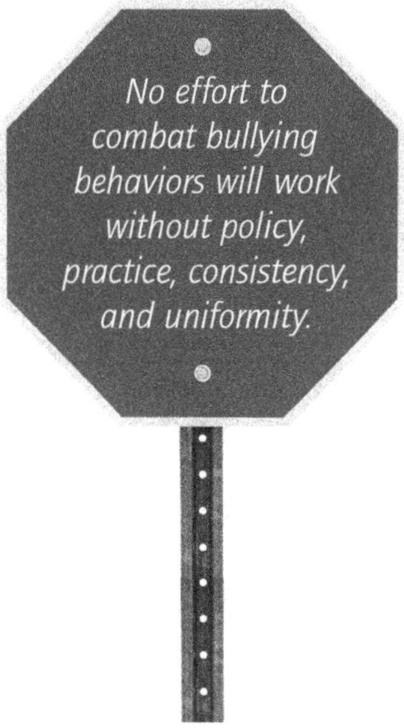

Policy must be practiced in order to be effective. The words on paper must be capable of being turned into a behavioral reality by those who are given the task of following them. Policy, then, becomes a set of instructions for how to construct an end product—in this case, effective bullying prevention and intervention actions. While practice may or may not make perfect, it certainly will increase the likelihood of some level of successful implementation as opposed to just having a policy "because we have to," the raison d'être for most of the paperwork that burdens the lives of educators these days.

Practice becomes the heart and soul of any bullying prevention statute, rule, or policy. And along with practice comes two subparts: ***consistency*** and ***uniformity***. A policy must be implemented as consistently as possible by all who enforce it. Children must see that the school policy regarding bullying prevention is applied with a high degree of similarity within the environment in which they happen to be operating. They have to know that bullying will not be tolerated throughout the entire system from the time they begin their experience within it until they leave the authority and supervision of that system—they are as safe on the bus as they are in math class, as they are in gym, as they are at an extracurricular event after school hours because the policy on bullying prevention is practiced consistently throughout the totality of the school environment.

Likewise, everyone who is in a position to prevent bullying must be willing to practice it uniformly. One of the biggest failures of efforts to combat bullying is in the haphazard and Swiss cheese manner in which policies are applied by personnel. Children have to know that not only is a policy practiced consistently throughout a system, but that the practice of enforcement is the same, or as close to the same, whenever supervisory personnel apply it. There are no weak links in the chain. Everyone holds those who engage in inappropriate behaviors accountable. There is no question among students about one member of the supervisory team allowing misbehavior under the specific code of conduct related to bullying. Everyone enforces the rules everywhere all the time, and as closely and equitably as is humanly possible. Additionally, the rules are enforced fairly to all within the student body. The ultimate goal is to incorporate an atmosphere of safety and security within the entire school, so children know that if they need to turn to an adult to discuss bullying behaviors, they can do so with any staff member and will be treated with the dignity, respect, and equity they deserve.

ABOUT THOSE "ZERO TOLERANCE" POLICIES

Let's be blunt: ***Zero tolerance policies*** *do not work as intended*. They are doomed to fail for a very simple reason—there is no such thing as "zero" in human behavior (unless the individual is dead, in which case, it becomes a moot point).

Humans as a species are active creatures, even more so as children than adults. If we are healthy and given the opportunity, we wiggle, we explore, we branch out, behaviors all designed to propel us forward toward some kind of personal goal or self-fulfillment. As a result of this innate drive to explore the limits of the world, children and adolescents, in particular, are not shy about pushing limits to see just exactly how far they can sail before they fall off the edge of whatever earth it is they happen to be navigating at the moment. All we have to do as adults is try to establish a limitation of zero in Kid World to see how fast that rule can be broken.

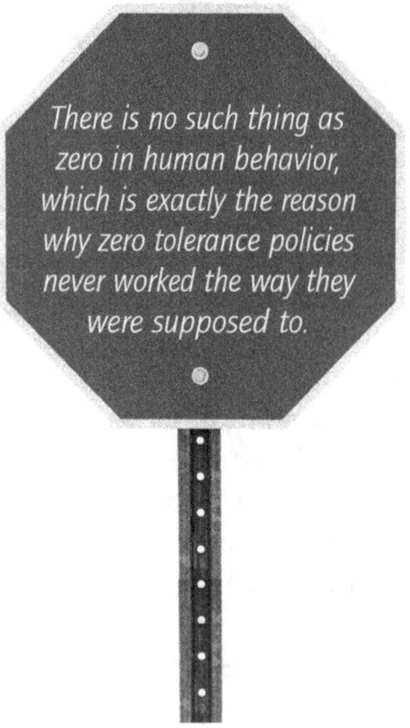

Zero tolerance sounds great and looks even better on paper. Who doesn't want an environment where we can banish all the evils lurking out there that bedevil our children under any instance or circumstance? Think about the absurdity of that for a moment in relation to what we know about real life—there *are always* and *always will be* exceptions that break the mold of a zero tolerance rule. Life is full of exceptions. Human beings are exceptional creatures. All of us strive to be the exception to the rule. We all want to be special. That specialness is at the heart of our individuality.

In the enforcement of zero tolerance policies, there is also no need to think, no need to determine true culpability, or look beyond the surface to the circumstances of the infraction. You break the rule, you get the penalty.

No sharp objects on campus? Done! But what about the scissors in the first aid kit necessary to cut athletic tape for the football team? And what about umbrellas on a rainy day? No drugs on campus? Done! But what about the Tylenol and other prescription medications that teachers bring with them on a daily basis?

OK, OK, this one we can do: No guns or violence-related images on campus? Done! But what about the kid in shop class in rural America who brings an antique shotgun to be sanded and reconditioned? And what about those fierce athletic team mascots designed to instill fear into the hearts of the opposing team? There aren't many football teams known as the Florence Nightingales or the Cheese Puffs.

While we certainly can likely agree in theory that we do not want weapons or drugs or guns or violence-related images on campus, the reality is that to decree that all of the instances cited previously and their surrounding kin are absolutes for banishment or punishment is, in practice, unfair and unenforceable. It is also foolish.

Here's what we know about the realities of zero tolerance policies between the 1980s and 2010s:[15]

- Zero tolerance policies emerged during the "Just Say No" drug prevention policies of the Reagan era of the 1980s and were put into overdrive during the Clinton administration's Gun-Free School Act of 1994, which made it mandatory that a student be expelled for one full year if found in possession of a firearm on school property.
- Schools found the zero tolerance approach a nifty way to address more than just drugs and weapons violations and expanded its use to truancy, fighting, or disputes with a teacher.
- Children have been disciplined by zero tolerance policies that defy reasonable person interpretations. For example, a kindergartener tells her seatmates that she is going to "shoot them" with a toy that makes soap bubbles; a first grader plays cops and robbers on the playground and shapes his fingers into the shape of a gun; a five-year-old points a self-made Legos creation at other students and makes gunfire sounds.

15. See "Kids' Suspensions Renew Debate Over Zero Tolerance" (2013); Shah (2013a, 2013b); Shah & McNeil (2014); and Teske (2011) for more details.

- Though not exclusive to zero tolerance policies, students who are non-White are far more likely to be suspended or expelled than their peers who are not (Shah, 2013a).[16]
- Students subject to denial of access to education through suspension or expulsion are at greater risk to become entrapped in the ***school-to-prison pipeline*** and law enforcement intervention (Heitzeg, 2009, p. 1; Teska, 2011), the theory that those who are suspended from school are more likely to ultimately run afoul of the legal system due to the increased potential of failing to graduate.
- In 2013, the American Academy of Pediatrics reiterated its 2007 statement about the undue harshness of zero tolerance discipline in favor of early intervention for those children whose behavior raises concerns.

The hindsight we have today is clear, based on the evidence accumulated at the great expense of the student guinea pigs used to come to the conclusion: Zero tolerance policies do not work and may have, in the long run, been more harmful than intended due to the collateral damage done by overreaction, flagrant abuse, and failure to take into account the exploratory and normal human development aspects of child and adolescent behavior, as well as the individual circumstances that should be analyzed before a decision is reached that denies a child access to education.

A CONFESSION

A confession is in order. During the origins of zero tolerance policies—and my own early educational career in the days of dinosaurs—I was a proponent of zero tolerance policies. They made life easier. I didn't have to think of the long-term consequences of penalties attached to kids who ran afoul of the system. If they did the crime, they did the time, even when the crime was not of their doing. In many cases, proximity was guilt enough to receive a punishment party favor. Best of all, they were out of my hair. That was probably the most important part.

My change of heart occurred when a high school student was penalized by her school for being in possession of alcohol found in her vehicle. It was in the trunk of her car and was seen by a teacher when the student went to get her gym clothes for an after-school athletic practice. Was the student in possession of alcohol? Yes. Was it hers? Depends on how one defined ownership. Her younger brother had stashed the bottle in his sister's car at home with the intent to get it later and share it with his peers after school. The sister knew nothing about it and was shocked to see the bottle under her gym bag when she pulled it from the trunk.

---

16. Data for most schools and school districts in the United States can be found in "Student Expulsion and Suspension Data, School Year 2009–2010," *Education Week*, at http://www.edweek.org/ew/qc/2013/ocrdata.html.

No amount of explanation in the days to come could rectify the situation, not even confession by the brother. She was suspended for five days for violating the zero tolerance policy of the school district on alcohol. No exception was made for the circumstances. The rules were the rules, and everyone paid the same price for their infraction. Except for the brother. Out of the same faulty logic that expelled the sister, the decision was made to not penalize the brother who had confessed to being the one responsible for the whole affair. After all, he technically was not in possession of the contraband. The fact that the brother was considered a valuable member of the current sport in season may have had a bearing on the decision, but we'll never know the conversations that went on behind closed doors.

The student did well academically prior to the suspension, but after her return, her grades and schoolwide performance declined. She transferred to another school the following year and finished below par for her prior performance.

How does this translate to bullying prevention? Zero tolerance policies designed to address fighting in school make no distinction between the instigator of a fight or the individual targeted by the harassment who is forced to defend oneself. This is not fair to those who are already being abused by the agents of mayhem. Untold numbers of kids who were the object of humiliation have been revictimized under this type of zero tolerance logic. It was wrong then, and it remains wrong today where such black-and-white, no room-for-thinking policies are enforced.

THE DEATH OF ZERO TOLERANCE?

Because of instances like the previous one and the disparate impact of zero tolerance policies on racial and ethnic nonmajorities, the US Department of Education and Justice strongly encouraged schools to back away from strict zero tolerance practices (Blad, 2014). Rather than continuing to enforce policies believed to feed the school-to-prison pipeline, the 2014 announcements hailed a reversal of the discipline paradigm set in the 1980s and 1990s. New guidelines were designed to pay attention to the individual student and the circumstances of the incident, as opposed to the application of a wholesale one-size-fits-all policy. The guidelines contained three overarching principles with action steps to better implement the recommendations (US DoE, 2014). A summary of the guiding principles follows.[17]

Guiding Principle 1: Climate and Prevention

Guiding Principle 1 is an acknowledgement that discipline is related to the level of in-school support that students feel from supervisory personnel.

17. For full details, see the *Directory of Federal School Climate and Discipline Resources*, US Department of Education (2014a), pp. 3–5.

While environmental climate has long been known to be a factor in behavior (Anderson, 1982; Gottfredson, Gottfredson, Payne, & Gottfredson, 2005), the recognition by the federal government that more attention should be paid to its influence, and the provision of resources to consider within the guideline document for potential implementation, was monumental.

The action steps recommended to improve school climate and build prevention initiatives include the "deliberate efforts" to use evidenced-based approaches to "promote positive student behavior." Included is the consideration of "tiered" intervention supports and strategies, the promotion of "social and emotional learning" as complimentary components to enhance academic potential, and the systematic and consistent training of all school staff to increase supportive behaviors interventions and strategies.

Two major components that might be considered nontraditional include a broad-based collaboration with "local mental health, child welfare, law enforcement, and juvenile justice agencies and other stakeholders." This recommendation alone is recognition that the success of students in educational endeavors is tied directly to community resources, inclusive of mental health options.

Guiding Principle 2: Clear, Appropriate, and Consistent Expectations and Consequences

Guiding Principle 2 recognizes that students learn best when they know what the rules are and that everyone expects and acts in accordance to making a positive school climate reality. The keys to the success of the principle lie in three descriptors: clear, appropriate, and consistent. School rules and accountability practices need to be clear and understandable; they need to be appropriate for the situation and the developmental level of the student involved; and they need to be enacted consistently so that all students know what is acceptable and what is not.

In order to increase the chances of Guiding Principle 2 being successful, supervisory personnel are encouraged to imbed behavioral expectations into the daily instructional domain. Stakeholders are considered to be an essential part of the "development and implementation" of policies. This includes "families, students, and school personnel." Particular emphasis was given to students with special learning needs and due process. When necessary, consequences should be "developmentally appropriate and proportional" to the infraction. Out-of-classroom suspensions or other forms of time-outs are to be considered a "last resort" tactic.

Guiding Principle 2 is particularly important in the two major areas. First, that stakeholders should be involved in the policy-making process and, second, that suspensions out of the educational setting are to be considered only as a last-chance option, rather than a first choice in the discipline arsenal.

Guiding Principle 3: Equity and Continuous Improvement

The third principle is directed solely at staff development to improve "policies and practices . . . [that] . . . ensure fairness and equity . . . for all students." The focus on staff improvement in the areas of equity increases the chances that disproportionate responses might negatively be employed against one who misbehaves. At the very least, it promises to heighten awareness of ***disproportionality*** in the application of disciplinary practices, allowing supervisory personnel the opportunity to think before they make a final decision about the necessity of an out-of-school discipline.

The use of "proactive, data-driven . . . [information and] . . . feedback" from stakeholders as elements to make better decisions about disciplinary decisions places a high premium on using empirical and tested methods, as opposed to approaches that have little or no basis as effective. "Proactive" likely equates and is synonymous with the use of preventive approaches prior to discipline, such as interventions using counseling and other diversions that might offset the eventual need for some type of disciplinary action.

The US DoE *Directory* document holds promise to provide policy guidance as new approaches to addressing the discipline needs among those who bully begin to emerge. It is hoped that the guidelines are given the time to take effect and are not subverted by the next swing of the education pendulum, which tends to reverse whatever trends and strategies are in practice at the time of a new election cycle, or the latest education fad to win the mindset of decision-makers.

TIERED INTERVENTION FRAMEWORKS

The use of "tiered interventions" as a framework of response to children with behavioral issues impairing their (and others') abilities to learn has emerged as one of the most promising developments in recent educational history. Though educational systems are just now recognizing the value afforded by such interventions employed throughout the entire school as a method of avoiding out-of-school removal of students, such methods are not actually as new as some would like to think. Tiered intervention and support methods hold the promise to be a critical factor in slowing the often knee-jerk disciplinary injustice that has been visited upon nonmajority groups within the educational system.

The tiered intervention concept has a history going back to the 1960s (Sugai & Simonsen, 2012). It was originally designed for use with students identified in need of special education services and based on a blending of behavioral analysis with determining less punitive methods of responding to student needs. Proponents of Positive Behavioral Interventions and Supports

(PBIS) were one of the first groups to consider the expanded use of interventions for behavioral problems outside the realm of special education. It gained traction in the 1990s after the reauthorization of the Individuals with Disabilities Act of 1997 and the creation of the University of Oregon's PBIS assistance center (Farmer, Lane, Lee, Hamm, & Lambert, 2012; Sugai & Simonsen, 2012). PBIS, in particular, is data driven and based on the foundation that responses to student behaviors should be based along a continuum of need as opposed to a one-size-fits-all approach as exemplified by zero tolerance policies. In effect, all students should know the expectations of the school community in an effort to improve overall school climate (Cohen, 2006; Klein, Cornell, & Konold, 2012) and student–staff connectedness (O'Brennan, Waasdorp, & Bradshaw, 2014) and how everyone will be held accountable when those expectations are violated or not met (Tier 1); some students may need additional assistance (Tier 2) and support in correcting misbehavior when they continue to be unable to follow Tier 1 expectations; and a small percentage of students may need more intensive attention and assistance with learning to gain self-control when they persistently run afoul of schoolwide expectations and Tier 2 efforts do not seem to be working (Tier 3). In 2013, over 20,000 schools reported using some variant of PBIS or related tiered intervention effort such as Response to Intervention (RTI; Samuels, 2013), Schoolwide Positive Behavior Support (SWPBS; Sugai & Horner, 2006) or Multitiered System of Support (MTSS; Hagans & Powers, n.d.).

Tiered intervention efforts have been well documented as a tool in addressing and reducing bullying behaviors within school settings (Bradshaw, 2015; Feuerborn & Chinn, 2012; Nese, Horner, Dickey, Stiller, & Tomlanovich, 2014; Ross & Horner, 2009; Stormont, Reinke, & Herman, 2011). Likewise, Goodman-Scott (2013) and Goodman-Scott, Doyle, & Brott (2013) address the positive role that school counselors in particular play in the implementation of PBIS at the elementary grade levels. It should be stressed, however, that schoolwide approaches using tiered interventions are not designed for exclusive usage by student service personnel—the very opposite. "Schoolwide" means just that, something that can be done by *all* supervisory staff within the school setting.

This is particularly important in designing and determining the best possible options for students who are identified as engaging in bullying behaviors with others. Tiered interventions provide differing levels of structure for those in need. The vast majority of students (assumed to be 80–90 percent of the student population; George, Kincaid, & Pollard-Sage, 2008) will be able to follow schoolwide expectations in most circumstances most of the time. Only minor redirection of behaviors will be necessary. Another 10 percent to 15 percent may be in need of more intensive assistance due to the inability to stay within the behavioral expectations of the school. Five percent to ten percent of the school population is assumed to be at high risk for the inability to consistently follow the overall rules and in need of intensive redirection of behaviors.

Let's take these tiered intervention population assumptions and apply them to the population of individuals who engage in bullying behaviors. If these percentages hold, most individuals who participate in some level of bullying will likely respond to minimal redirection of behavior (Tier 1), a smaller percentage will require more than one "dose" of intervention (Tier 2), and a very small number will require multiple attempts at learning new modes of behaviors which lesson their aggressiveness or other inappropriate behaviors toward peers (Tier 3). Those who persist in bullying others are the ones who require the most effort to encourage them to drop the behaviors that put them at risk of suspension from the classroom—hopefully only at the in-school level and not out-of-school.

Why should we not apply a tiered intervention framework to kids who bully? The answer is, there's no reason why we shouldn't. Children who bully do so for different reasons, under different circumstances, and at different levels of intensity. Our responses, our interventions, our positive behavioral supports, then, should be tailored to meet the needs of the individuals creating the problem. We should not treat those children who experiment with singular bullying behaviors the same way we treat those who chronically engage in them. There are different reasons in play for what drives the behaviors—we have to take the time and decipher those reasons in order to develop a better plan to help the child learn alternative ways of behaving. Some kids just need a mild redirection: "Whoa. You know that behavior doesn't fit with the way we treat each other at our school. Can I trust that you won't be doing that again and that we don't need to do anything else about it?" Others need a higher level of attention: "We've talked about that kind of behavior before, haven't we? Does what you just did fit in with the agreement you made to behave differently on the playground? I think we need to set up a time to figure out a better way of solving this problem. Let's go do that right now." Still others need intensive intervention: "Stop. Come here. That behavior is what we've been working on for a long time, haven't we? It seems as if you're still having problems following the plans we had in place and what you agreed to do to improve. I think we need to set up another meeting with your parents to figure out another plan and see if we can help you make better decisions before that happens again. Let's go right now and start."

There is no need, or rationale, to apply the same approach to every child in an attempt to solve problematic behaviors that evolve from different sources.

WANT TO LEARN MORE?

The law is a fascinating discipline, filled with both justice and contradiction. Those interested in pursuing how the justice system has shaped the development of bullying prevention and intervention legislation and policy can find more information in the following sources.

Parents are more likely to exercise their legal options more so than ever before when it comes to seeking protection for their children from perceived bullying in school settings. Examples include the following:

Culhane, J. G. (2013). Bullying, litigation, and populations: The limited effect of Title IX. *Western New England Law Review*, 322–351.

DiBlasio, N. (2011, September, 11). More bullying cases have parents turning to courts. *USA Today* Retrieved from http://usatoday30.usatoday.com/news/education/story/2011-09-11/bullying-lawsuits-parents-self-defense-courts/50363256/1.

Mueller, M. (2014, March 25). Bullies beware: Groundbreaking ruling allows schools to sue students who harass peers. *The Star-Ledger*. Retrieved from http://www.nj.com/news/index.ssf/2014/03/bullies_beware_groundbreaking_ruling_allows_schools_to_sue_students_who_harass_peers.html.

Flam, L. (2014, January 27). Parents fight cyberbullying with lawsuit. *Today.com*. Retrieved from http://www.today.com/moms/parents-fight-cyberbullying-lawsuit-2D11999975.

In addition, Michael J. Higdon's (2011) controversial article equating student suspensions within marginalized groups to metaphorical educational lynchings can be found at "To Lynch a Child: Bullying and Gender Nonconformity in Our Nation's Schools," *Indiana Law Journal*, pp. 826–878.

Opponents to enumerated groups pose specific challenges to efforts to provide comprehensive bullying prevention and intervention statutes. Some of those arguments are found at these sites:

Examiner.com. (2011, March 12). Conservatives oppose anti-bullying legislation that protects gay teens. Retrieved from http://www.examiner.com/article/conservatives-oppose-anti-bullying-legislation-that-protects-gay-teens.

People for the American Way. (n.d.). "Big bullies update. Retrieved from http://www.pfaw.org/rww-in-focus/updated-big-bullies-right-wings-anti-anti-bullying-strategies.

Rosenberg, L. (2011, March 16). Right wing gins up hysteria over Obama's initiative to curb bullying. Media Matters for America. Retrieved from http://mediamatters.org/research/2011/03/16/right-wing-gins-up-hysteria-over-obamas-initiat/177643.

PART II

Working With Those Who Engage in Bullying Behaviors

6

Will This Stuff Work?

©iStockphoto.com/Na

The following strategies and tactics *can* work for you and others because they *have worked* in *various settings* for *various situations.* Related professionals and I have used these approaches in dealing with difficult clients who brought us issues both simple and complicated. Additionally, I have consulted with and interviewed many others who have used aspects of the strategies and techniques contained in this section of the book.

Will they work for your specific circumstances, in your setting, and with the individuals whose lives you attempt to improve by stopping them from engaging in bullying behaviors? Maybe. Each child is different. Each set of circumstances and motivations is different. Each set of skills and abilities of those who attempt to implement these ideas is different. Some educators have better abilities to communicate with kids than others. The suggestions in this part may work for you. Or they may not. Which leads us to the last point.

Will every approach offered here work for you? No. In fact, none of them might work for you. As mentioned, each child, circumstances, and motivation to change is different. Likewise, each adult's ability to successfully engage kids is different. Some have more tolerance for chaos than others. Even the adults who are best at connecting with hard-to-reach kids sometimes cannot reach them all. So no claims or guarantees can be made as to how successful you will be in your particular environment when trying to use these approaches with any particular individual or set of individuals you are trying to reach.

But here's what we all know: If we do nothing, behavior that needs "assistance" rarely changes on its own. We call that ***behavioral inertia***—we do what we do because it works (whether good or bad, effective or ineffective in the long run, it gets the job done for us at the moment). Until we are given a compelling reason to behave in a different fashion, we just keep doing the same thing over and over. Children and adolescents who bully have little incentive to stop as long as what they do works for them. Oftentimes, not getting caught is one incentive, along with any actual tangible or status payoff they receive from the bullying behavior. Adult intervention is one method of interrupting that cycle of violence in the agent–target continuum. Whether you choose to use any of the tools in this toolbox and how successful you will be in doing so is a matter of skill set and personality match between you and the agent of bullying. Oh, yes, I almost forgot—add the willingness of the person you are working with to "work the program," whatever program it might be. It's not easy to work with those who choose to bully others, but if we have little other options available to us outside of penalty, then we miss the opportunity to engage a child who may well be on a path of destruction toward others and, perhaps, even themselves (Farrington & Ttofi, 2011; Hemphill et al., 2011; Huesmann et al., 1984; Huesmann, Eron, & Yarmel, 1987; Loeber & Hay, 1997; Renda, Vassallo, & Edwards, 2011; Ttofi, Farrington, & Losel, 2012; Ttofi, Farrington, Lösel, & Loeber, 2011).

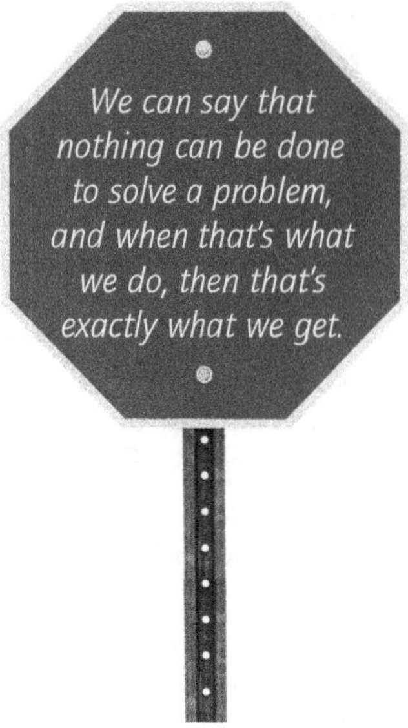

HOW TO USE THIS SECTION

The chapters in this section vary in length in order to highlight certain specific techniques, programs, and approaches that I have found promising in my career as a classroom teacher, school counselor, professional clinical counselor, violence prevention and mental health public policy advocate, and consultant. Some chapters are more descriptive than others due to the more complicated nature of the approach under review. When possible and relevant, I have tried to include potential scripts or verbal leads and prompts that the reader might find helpful in working with kids. Feedback through the years has indicated that the scripts and prompts contained in my earlier books were very useful in helping to start and keep kids engaged in whatever intervention is being undertaken. My role is to serve as a catalyst for your creative energies.

And speaking of creativity, here is one of the things you will find different about this section: In many instances, I have taken parts of strategies or approaches designed to work with the targets of bullying and have applied them to work with those who create the problem. This is a logical extension of the approach, based on the knowledge that many of the ***talk therapy*** approaches useful in helping us understand what life is like for the target of bullying are also useful for those who are causing the problem. Sometimes just a piece of a program or video is more useful and practical (***part-value***) than trying to force an entire program, curriculum, or movie into a situation or circumstance where it does not fit or will not work. However, it is essential to remember that the prime emphasis of this book is on the value of taking time to explore the thought processes of those who act with behaviors that are in need of redirection. If we don't talk, we don't learn, and when we don't learn, we cannot interact as successfully with those who need our help—and kids who bully others do need our help.

WANT TO LEARN MORE?

Readers may find it helpful to refer to my earlier works on bullying prevention and intervention in conjunction with this half of the book (Roberts, 2006, 2008) in order to further inspire your own creativity in what will work best in your particular setting and with your individual students. Likewise, there is a list of additional potential approaches found in the Resources for Consideration section at the conclusion of the book.

7

Essential Skills for Interveners

In order to be effective in interacting with children and adolescents who are difficult, one must first and foremost be able to exercise ***patience*** and ***tolerance***. Notice that I say "exercise patience and tolerance." One cannot just *be* patient or *have* tolerance. When working with difficult kids, one must actually turn those traits into *action*.

Patience is always a key in working with tough kids—not that all children who bully others necessarily fit the descriptor of being "tough." Some children are not so much tough as they are vexing. It takes tolerance to put up with many of the dodge-and-weave explanations that are offered by those under scrutiny from adults. Combined, patience and tolerance become powerful weapons in the cat-and-mouse game of getting to the root causes of what motivates those who intimidate others. They are characteristics that have often not been provided or offered to those who bully. When applied, they can throw a monkey wrench into the strategy of those who are used to not having to explain their behaviors since we have historically not taken the time—or had the patience or tolerance—to try and understand. It has always been easier to punish, suspend, or expel those who do wrong as opposed to doing the work necessary to get into the thought processes of those whom we need to understand the most. If we don't understand the logic of those who bully, how will we ever be able to intelligently craft an intervention for them?

THE INTERVENER

I refer to the individual who is involved in the intervention with those who bully others as the ***Intervener***, inclusive of the capital *I*. This is done with specific intent to highlight the role of that individual and should be emphasized that the designated Intervener can be any specific person either with the *training* and *skills* to work with kids who are challenging or who has a *special relationship* with that individual and who, due to that relationship, may be in the best position to increase the chances of positive changes among the child in need. Of course, skills to facilitate those changes always increase the odds that they will happen. Maybe that's why you're reading this book this very moment.

It is often best if the Intervener dealing with the agent of bullying is one with no or limited emotional attachment to the situation. The more neutral the adult doing the intervention, the less likely that false assumptions or misinterpretations will occur on the part of the interventionist. Perhaps the best ***neutral adult*** is someone who is not in or has not been in the direct disciplinary loop of the current situation and has nothing tangible to gain from what follows. This most likely makes members of a school (or agency) student services personnel team—the school counselor, school social worker, school psychologist, school nurse—the most logical people to consider, but that is not necessarily the requirement. *Any adult who can suspend temporary judgment for the sake of "getting to the bottom" of what creates the situation is acceptable from my perspective.* It may not be so, however, from the perspective of the child or adolescent who will most likely feel that what is about to occur is all about discipline and punishment, as opposed to accountability.

BEYOND PATIENCE AND TOLERANCE

Let's be clear about a very important element of working with difficult kids—*not everyone can or should work with them.* While patience and tolerance are the foundational traits essential for engaging those who bully others, they alone are not enough. There have to be actual skills employed to put those traits into action.

Professional counselors spend a great deal of their education acquiring the skills of communication, enabling them to assist their clients in self-exploration and the discovery of the motives behind behaviors that they themselves often do not understand. While it certainly helps to be in a counseling-related profession in order to work with kids who challenge our patience and levels of tolerance (isn't *that* a different way to phrase it?), it's absurd to think that every individual with problematic behaviors needs to be seen by a therapist of some sort. Certain people believe that, but not me. And while I'm on this thought, let's clear something else up—not every child who engages in some type of aggressive behavior needs "counseling," whatever that means to the general public. Most often what is needed is someone who can foster trust with kids, who has the basic skills of interpersonal communication to "hear" what is being said beyond the words on the surface (the ***metacommunication,*** or underlying message), and who is willing to help those who are amenable to changing their negative behaviors discover things about themselves that they likely did not know.

When we use the term ***interpersonal communications*** in this sense, we are talking about a level of interaction between two or more people in which one party has some knowledge of typical communication patterns and how communication between individuals commonly occurs. For our purposes, we will consider the basic skills that are necessary for successful communications during an ***intervention*** (an effort to stop negative behaviors of some sort) designed to prevent future instances of problematic behaviors on the part of the person causing harm to others. Let's examine some of the basic skills that an individual involved in an intervention with a child who has been exhibiting bullying behaviors can use with relative comfort, ease, and—with practice—success.

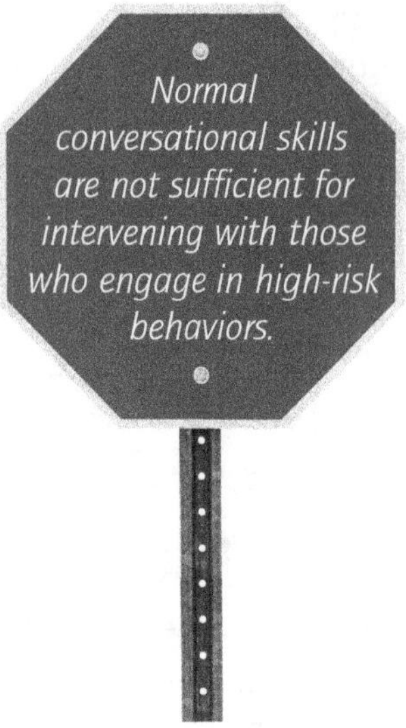

THE ABILITY TO TRULY LISTEN TO WHAT IS SAID

Without the ability to hear what the other person is truly saying, nothing helpful is likely to occur beyond what normally happens in friendly conversation. Covey's (2004) quote is never more true than in the field of skilled listening: "We typically seek first to be understood. Most people do not listen with the intent to understand; they listen with the intent to reply" (p. 239). The best example about how little listening goes on in our world is to pay attention to what you are actually doing while in a conversation with another person—usually getting ready to say something else. Most of us in normal discourse don't wait for the other person to finish the sentence before we are crafting the reply in our heads. How could we possibly be listening to what is being said when we are so busy listening to ourselves in preparation to respond to what we *think* we are hearing?

True listening is a skill. It takes practice. When we encounter others with truly effective listening skills, we know it. We value their friendship because we feel as if we are being heard at levels beyond casual conversation. Good listeners hear us in ways others do not. They get it because they have the ability to connect the dots of what we are saying—or not saying—and discard the detritus of our blather to understand us at that deeper level. They hear us at that metacommunicative level.

So how do we become more effective listeners? ***Focus***. Focus on the person whom we are supposed to be listening to and not on what's going on inside our heads. That includes focusing on what the individual is saying beneath and beyond mere words. What is his or her body revealing about what is going on inside the head that words can't convey? Focus takes practice. Focus takes skill. Focus takes—well, focus! When we listen to what is actually being said by another person, our responses will be different because we heard different things than if we had crafted our response in the middle of what the other person was saying. When we craft a response without truly listening, we respond on our *assumption* of what we think is *about* to be said, not what was *actually* said. In crafting our reply at the *conclusion* of a speaker's full statement, it also *slows down the verbal interaction* between both parties, increasing the chances that more thought will go into what is said between the two, rather than the rapid-fire pow-pow-pow of the typical conversation.

NONVERBAL COMMUNICATION AND BEHAVIOR

Listening also includes what is sometimes not said in words. What we commonly refer to as ***nonverbal communication*** is, as with virtually all we do to communicate with others, actually ***nonverbal behavior***. While we often do not think of quiet or nonverbal actions as behavior, they actually are. The lack of the use of words to express our feelings or thoughts is a behavior, just not a verbal one.

It has been estimated that upwards of 90 percent of how we express ourselves to others might be in a nonverbal fashion and that perhaps 65 percent of what is said when we do communicate verbally is expressed in a nonverbal fashion (Cormier, Nurius, & Osborne, 2009). Our choice of when we choose not to speak, the time we arrive for appointments, the posture we maintain in the presence of those we favor and those we do not, all communicate to others something about who we are and what we want to convey, even if and when we don't know it. Astute observers of people who understand the mechanics of nonverbals have the opportunity to understand the people with whom they are attempting to engage more so than those who depend merely on words alone.

The following are five different methods in which we choose to communicate with others in nonverbal fashion (see Cormier et al., 2009, and Egan, 2014, for greater details).

Body Posture and Movement: Kinesics

Kinesics pays attention to facial gestures, movements of the body, and posture. It is important to remember that all kinesthetic aspects of interaction must be viewed through a lens of culture (Ivey, Ivey, & Zalaquett, 2014). Perhaps the most important aspect of communicating the sense of connection or disconnection with others is through eye contact; however, eye contact is culturally sensitive. It may be considered a sign of disrespect in some cultures to look directly at a person in authority.[1] In stereotypical

1. In order to be most effective and reduce the chances of offensiveness or cultural insensitivity, individuals working with nonmajority, non-Western, or non-White cultural groups must avail themselves to the nuances of nonverbal communication. A good resource is Sue and Sue's (2013) *Counseling the Culturally Diverse: Theory and Practice.* In it, they note that nonmajority individuals have often learned through negative experiences that what people in power say cannot always be trusted and that a person's nonverbals often reveal more of the truth than the spoken word. It is important to remember, then, that interpreting nonverbals is a two-way street.

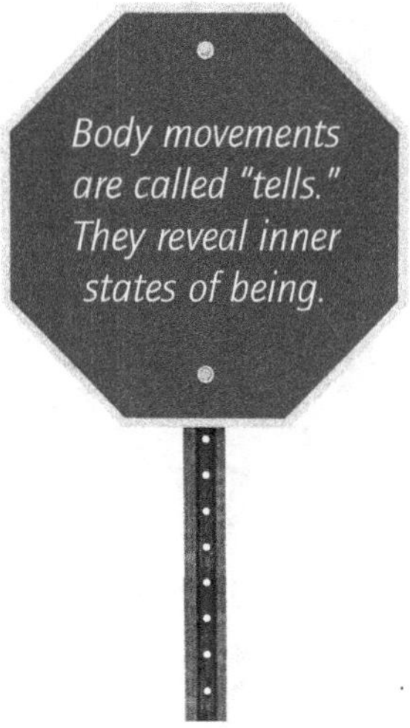

Western cultures, when an individual feels "closer" to or comfortable with another, the kinesthetics all indicate such via more open and relaxed posture, more direct eye contact, and less distance between the two during the interaction. It is just the opposite when an individual feels uncomfortable—there will be less eye contact, the body posture is likely to be more tense, and the individual in all likelihood will sit or position oneself as far away from the other as possible or in a position that makes it more difficult to read one's nonverbals. All of these are markers of how much connection is occurring between the two parties during the discussion of difficult topics.

How Something Is Said: Paralinguistics

Except in the rarest of instances—in which case it may well be an indication that something is awry—we typically do not share our stories in a monotone. We raise our voices (***volume***) and talk faster (***rate***) when excited and do the opposite when calmer. Our tone of voice (***intonation***) changes in direct relationship to stressors, and there are times when we are able to convey our thoughts in words better than others (***fluency***). Sometimes, we say little or nothing—silence is often the most powerful thing that can be said.

All of these factors of paralinguistics must be considered in listening to others. They provide a qualitative depth of richness to understanding exactly what the individual is trying to say—or avoid saying.

Physical Distance Between Speakers: Proxemics

As with kinesics, the level of safety one feels with another will impact the physical distance between the speakers. When we do not feel a closeness or sense of security with another, we prefer not to be around them, and if we must, we prefer to position ourselves as far away from the other as possible.

In all likelihood, when engaging individuals who are under scrutiny for violating a group rule, we are likely to experience individuals who are going to assume a ***defensive posture***—verbally, paralinguistically, and proximally. As we continue to interact with them, their level of comfort and sense of trust, hopefully, will increase so that we see changes in all three of these characteristics. Avoid encroaching in other individuals' ***personal space*** (commonly referred to as their "physical comfort zone"—different for each individual and culture according to the circumstances) to reduce the likelihood of automatically placing them on the defensive.

Where a Meeting Is Conducted: Environment

Usually, meetings between individuals who have run afoul of the rules and the authority enforcing them are conducted in the office of supervisory personnel. Expect, then, a defensive response from the individual since, in all likelihood, she or he will feel "captured." In the cat-and-mouse world of those who intimidate others and whose power derives from not being held accountable for their actions, being "called to the office" is the ultimate error.

The interpretive message the Intervener wants to send to the individual being interviewed sets the tone when he or she walks in the door. Is it the typical conference room for all sorts of meetings between individuals, or is it a special meeting room where only serious infractions are discussed? And who is in the room at the time of the initial intervention can also be considered an environmental factor. Is it just the Intervener and the individual who violated the rules; are there multiple adults in the room so as to send a ***"show of force" message*** to the individual; is law enforcement involved? Determine the type of message to send to those who bully by where the meetings are conducted and who and how many are present for the conference.

When People Show Up: Time

Time is a cultural concept. Business and education runs on Western culture time, which basically means that one should "be on time" to meetings. Adhering to dates and times for conferences is important for keeping order within the framework of those Western cultural expectations.

When we are serious about meetings, we show up "on time" in Western culture. If one is "late," it is considered a sign of rudeness or disrespect to authority. The world of business runs according to the calendar and clock—the world of people often does not.

As we know, not all individuals subscribe to the Western cultural concept of time—no matter the color of one's skin or nationality. Learning about adherence to time restrictions originates from one's family of origin, the ultimate cultural setting wherein we first learn what the outside world is supposed to be about.

In working with those who bully, here is the question that must be answered: Is it better to have the individual consistently show up six to seven minutes late for meetings and get *some* work done, or banish the individual from all future meetings for the sake of the fact that she or he couldn't make it to appointments "on time"?

INTENTIONAL INTERVIEWING

Those who intervene with children who bully are likely to find themselves involved in piecing together the stories and rationale behind the behavior. To best do so, a technique known as ***intentional interviewing*** (Ivey et al., 2014) is helpful.

Intentional interviewing is a method of gathering information. It is not a counseling technique, per se, but it does employ several basic counseling and listening skills that can be adapted to working with children who bully others to better understand what composes the logic of those who do it. As Ivey et al. (2014) explain, often the skills involved in interviewing, counseling, and psychotherapy intersect (p. 5). While it is not essential for an Intervener to be a licensed therapist—indeed, even if that were the case, there wouldn't be enough to go around—intentional interviewing is a critical tool that can be learned and used by most who have the desire to work with those who bully. It focuses on "providing information and advice to clients, and suggesting workable alternatives for resolving concerns" (Ivey et al., p. 5). It has utility across multiple professions and is extremely helpful in getting to the root causes of those who create problematic behaviors. Intentional interviewing is designed to be brief and help both parties in the intervention "cut to the chase" in exploring behaviors. Many of the prompts and dialogues used in this text use intentional interviewing techniques.

Interviewing Microskills

Ivey et al. (2014) mention multiple basic components of the helping process that are useful in the interview process. Called ***microskills***, once mastered, they compose the heart of one's ability "to listen effectively and help clients change and grow. . . . [They] enable you to anticipate or predict how clients will respond to . . . interventions [and enable] you . . . to shift . . . skills and strategies that match their needs" (p. 10).[2] Some of those basic microskills include the following:

Observation

Effective observation occurs at both the surface and metacommunicative levels. Elemental observation tells us what is happening through

2. What Ivey et al. call "microskills" are the foundational components of the counseling process as espoused by Carl Rogers' (1951) ***client-centered approach*** and elaborated on by Cormier et al. (2009) and Egan (2014). Sometimes, that which is most effective might be put in new bottles with flashy labels, but it is still the same basic wine—a common problem in educational circles.

surface and superficial behaviors and words. Metacommunicative observation takes into consideration the *totality of the story* from the individual—what is said, not said, how it is said, the underlying causes that lead up to the present interaction. Two kids may have a negative experience with each other that leads them to your office for intervention, but the odds are pretty good that the circumstances leading up to it didn't just start five minutes before it happened.

Advice: Do your homework before an interaction with those you need to talk to so that you know something of the background and history of an incident prior to an interview. It can shape the nature of your interaction and help you formulate questions and statements in a fashion that is more effective for the time you have with the individual.

Questioning

It's not about asking a lot of questions; it's about asking the *right* questions in the *right* way. Asking questions tends to put people off. It's often viewed as intrusive, makes them defensive, and often shuts them down, especially if they feel as if they are being interrogated. While gaining useful information is a critical part of intentional interviewing, knowing how to pose a question to an individual suspicious of the questioner's intent can make all the difference in the world in getting that relevant information. Remember, interviews between people of different power backgrounds can be considered an effort to gain information to be used against the less powerful.

Advice: People generally respond better to a request to help another individual who seems to understand their predicament rather than being directly asked an outright question. "I need your help in understanding what happened between you and Student B today" sends a different message than the commanding "Tell me what happened" or "What happened today?"

Encouragement

Kids prefer to feel as if they are being supported in their efforts, even when they're in the hot seat. Encouragement helps lower defenses by sending a message that the individual's efforts are worthwhile. Encouragement is important, even to those whose behaviors are the cause of problems—certainly not encouragement to keep doing the misdeeds, but support to participate in the process to make things better and encouragement when true behavioral changes start to occur.

Advice: Don't give encouragement when it is not warranted, but don't fail to provide it at the opportune moment. Carpe diem when you

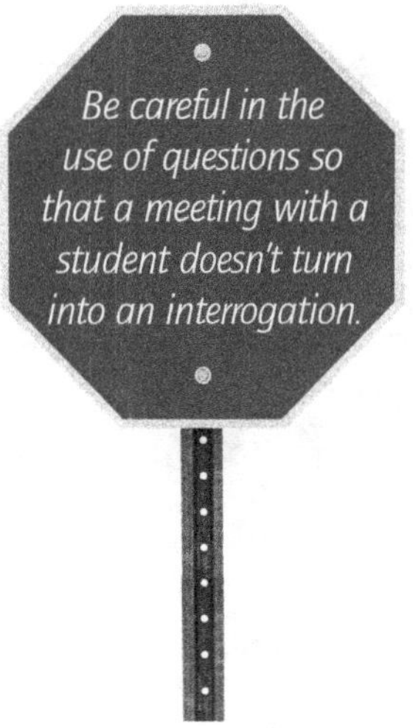

can! Acknowledge the reality of a situation: "I know you don't like being in here to discuss all this stuff, but I have to say you have been cooperative on several things that seem to be making the situation better. I appreciate that."

Paraphrase

A paraphrase is the use of one or two short phrases or sentences to, in the Intervener's own words, relay back to an individual what the Intervener understands that the individual has just said. It doesn't parrot back to the individual the exact words used, but it may incorporate some of them. The goal is to give the individual the opportunity to correct any misinterpretation on the part of the Intervener, as well as to let the person know that the story line is being followed.

Effective paraphrasing can help encourage the individual to continue to tell his or her story since the metacommunication is that the Intervener is following and "hearing" what is being said. In paraphrasing, one does not have to agree with what is being said—it is just a method of letting the individual know that you heard what was being expressed. There will be time to interpret, summarize, and challenge the story line later, if necessary. Paraphrasing just helps everyone move further down the story line and reduces the chances of an individual feeling as if the Intervener doesn't care what is being said or that his or her mind is already made up about whatever the outcome is going to be for the one in the hot seat.

Advice: Ask yourself this question as the individual is telling his or her story: "What is the main content/behavior/thought/feeling of what this individual is saying right now?" Identify those main points, then share that understanding with the individual. Example: "I get the impression you feel . . ." or "From what you've said and the way that you said it, you seem to be . . ." Try to keep paraphrasing in the moment by using the present tense. It makes what the individual just said active and in the here and now.

Reflection

Reflection of your understanding of another individual's experience (thought/feeling/behavior) is one of the most powerful tools likely to increase an interaction between two people. It sends both a direct verbal message and the metacommunication that "I hear you, I understand," even if it is not said in those exact words. Reflections of another's experience usually begin with ***sensate*** words: "It sounds as if . . ." or "It looks as if . . ." or "I get the sense that you feel . . ." are all effective prompts to help an Intervener get started expressing the understanding of what has been said by someone else from a metacommunicative level. A reflection is not a paraphrase, but the two often work hand in hand. Reflections go for deeper material. Look for ***themes*** or ***keywords*** used by the other person that give a better description of the experience.

Advice: Use reflections as summarizing points with individuals in conjunction with paraphrases. You likely will use more paraphrases than reflections in the early parts of an intervention because you don't have as much information or understanding about the individual as you do or will later in the interaction. An example of the use of paraphrase and reflection might go like this:

Student A has talked about how the actions of another student through the last few days led up to one final straw, which the aggressor considered the final insult.

Paraphrase: *"You were angry when he did that to you."*

> Student A continues telling his story about how a few days earlier, similar incidents had happened.

Reflection: *"And all those things seemed to just keep adding up as more and more frustration on your part because you tried several times to avoid the confrontation, and you thought you were being challenged to fight."*

> Student A continues to talk about how insulted he has felt with the behavior of the other student, although he isn't really sure if the insults were directed at him or not.

Paraphrase and Reflection combined: *"You wondered if those insults were meant for you and not anybody else, but you really couldn't be sure because every time you tried to ask Student B what he was doing, you felt as if he was encouraging everyone else around to laugh at you."*

A ***reflective synopsis*** might well be called a "minisummary" in which the Intervener offers a combination of content and reflection of what has been said in the previous few minutes:

> *"I get the sense from everything that you've told me that you don't like to be put on the spot in front of your friends and that you'd much rather go on the offense rather than have to play defense. It sounds as if from what you've said you sometimes try to put others down before they have the chance to do it to you."*

Summarizing

There are different types of summarizing statements. Some focus on content, some on thought, feelings, and behaviors, others on the entire metacommunication of what the Intervener heard the storyteller say. If paraphrasing and reflection go well, the Intervener will get the chance to summarize. If the relationship is going really well, the Intervener may get the chance to provide an ***interpretive summary***.

Summarizing the content of what has been said focuses on just that—the content *only*, nothing beyond. By summarizing content, once again the Intervener is letting the individual know that she or he has been heard and that this is what your understanding of the basic elements of that conversation was.

Advice: Summarizing content should play heavily off the previous paraphrases and reflections to the point of the summary—provided that they were correct (in which case the individual will have had the chance to give feedback to the Intervener to correct whatever paraphrase or reflection was considered incorrect). Focus on the main points of the content summarized since the last summary. Ideally, there should be several small summaries during the interaction. An example of a content summary might go like this:

> *"Let me make sure I understand what you've said in the last five minutes. You told me that you felt as if you were put on the spot in the cafeteria when Student B bumped you from behind and you spilled your milk. That made you angry, and you stood up and shoved him. You said you thought about hitting him but you didn't because you knew that would only make things worse. That sound like I heard you correctly?"*

Content, pure and simple. Everything that was said from the Interpreter was based on what Student A had shared of his experience to that point of the interaction. There was no effort to interpret from the Intervener's perspective what was going on "inside" the individual. Basically, summarizing content is a restatement of the "facts" as expressed from the storyteller.

Interpretation

Interpretations should be done minimally so as not to send the impression to the individual that everything that has been said is being considered in a way that gives little credence to the content and feelings of what has been said. Interpretation takes skill and a good ear to "connect the dots" of what has been said. It looks for the true metacommunication that has taken place and verbalizes it through the lens of the listener—in this case, the Intervener.

Advice: It is often better to interpret less and listen more to avoid giving the individual with whom we are working the impression that we are trying to "psychobabblize" everything that is said. Diagram 7.1 may be helpful in tying all of the components of intentional interviewing together into a visual conceptualization.

Using the sample information in Diagram 1, an effective interpretation might go like this:

"Let me see if I'm understanding you correctly. I'm going to give you my thoughts on what I heard you say, even though you might not have used these exact words: You get angry when you feel people don't respect you or your friends because you feel a lot of pride about who you are, and you intend to make sure people know that you're not going to be mistreated—which is

Diagram 7.1 Diagraming and Identifying Metacommunicative Themes

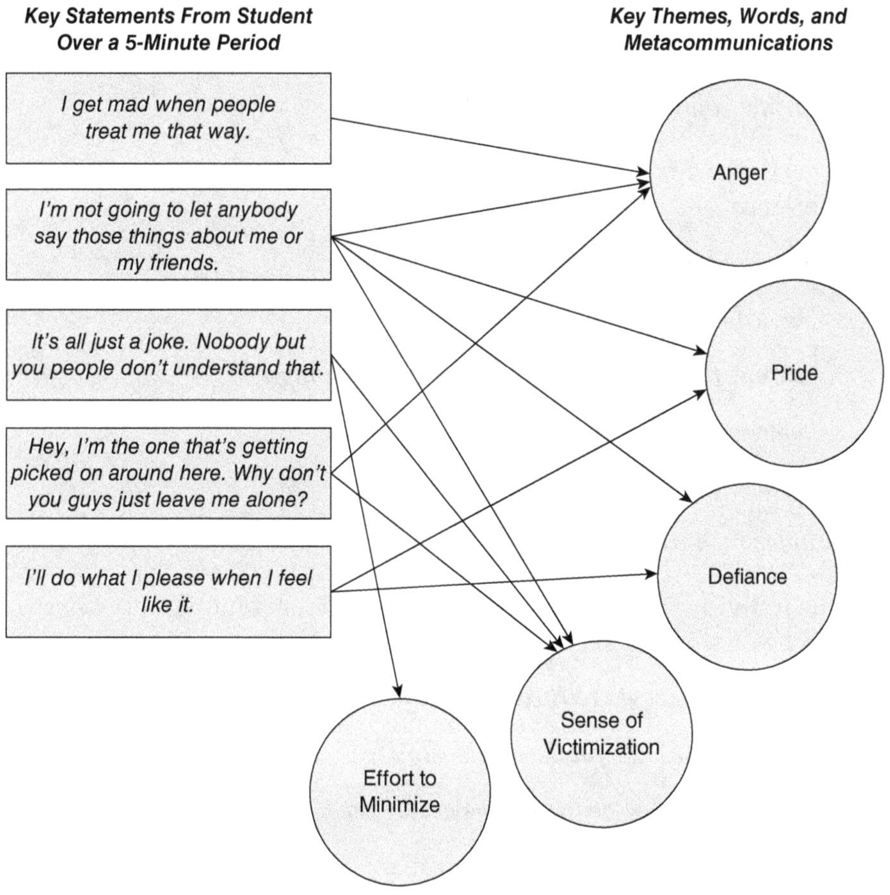

exactly the way you feel about this entire incident, that you're the one who's actually being bullied, not the other way around. I also get the sense that you don't think this whole thing is that big of a deal, that we adults are overreacting to the incident. Am I close on any of this?"

"Cheater" Words and Phrases

It's always helpful to have a few go-to words and phrases (*"**cheaters**"*) to use with people when trying to convey an empathic understanding of their experience. While each person's situation is different, there are usually certain emotions that are universal to everyone. Here are several cheaters that the Intervener may find useful in attempting to engage the difficult child. More detailed examples may be found in Cormier et al. (2009, p. 110) and in Hutchins and Vaught (1997, p. 72), the origins of these sample descriptors.

If the individual displays *minimal attachment* to an emotion or experience, he or she may feel . . .

annoyed bothered bugged irked ticked peeved

concerned caught pulled tense uneasy amused

pleased relieved sad disappointed mixed up

unsure confused bored relieved

If the individual displays *moderate attachment* to an emotion or experience, she or he may feel . . .

disgusted used hacked resentful locked in

blocked out pressured strained torn afraid

anxious frightened shook up worried discouraged

happy delighted joyful surprised up/upbeat

abandoned distressed drained empty lost

unhappy hurt lonely down distressed sad

If the individual displays *strong attachment* to an emotion or experience, he or she may feel . . .

angry boiling mad burned enraged fuming

furious pissed hateful desperate panicked

petrified terrified tortured crushed defeated

elated excited terrific thrilled helpless

hopeless overwhelmed humiliated

Of course, this list of potential descriptors must be modified for the age of the individual whom we are talking with, as well as the circumstances of the experience. This is particularly true in the case of children who may experience these emotions at levels of intensity equal to adults but who do not yet have the vocabulary to express it.

"IF I'D WANTED TO BE A COUNSELOR, I'D . . ."

I can hear all of you now: "If I'd wanted to be a counselor, I'd have gone to college to be one!" (Well, I can hear all of you who aren't already counselors.) My point is, you don't have to be a counselor or in the psychotherapeutic professions to work effectively with kids who are aggressive toward others. What is needed, however, is understanding and applying the skills of effective listening and responding in ways such as those presented earlier. Many of you doubtlessly already possess and have practiced these skills but didn't know that you did or what those skills were called. Some of you are just Kid Magnets. Others of you are natural helpers. You have the ability to connect with kids both in times of trouble and during the not-so-troubled times. That is a wonderful collection of traits to have and it serves as a beginning point to build toward increasing communication with kids. Speaking of which, in our next chapter we will look at the characteristics necessary for doing just that.

WANT TO LEARN MORE?

Eight great resources for *those interested in learning more about the art of higher order communication styles* often used in the helping professions and that were resourced for this chapter include *Becoming a Helper* by Corey and Corey (2016); *Interviewing and Change Strategies for Helpers* by Cormier, Nurius, and Osborn (2009); *The Skilled Helper* by Egan (2014); *Intentional Interviewing and Counseling* by Ivey, Ivey, and Zalaquett (2014); *Effective Helping* by Okun and Kantrowitz (2015); *Brief Counseling That Works* by Sklare (2014); *Interpersonal Conflict* by Wilmot and Hocker (2011); and *Learning the Art of Helping: Building Blocks and Techniques* by Young (2013). These texts contain hundreds of excellent strategies that can be adapted to the reader's particular situation in dealing with not only aggressive children, but children in general.

8

Making the Communication and Relational Connection

First and foremost in working with those who bully is making some kind of ***communication and relational connection*** with them. While not always easy to do, Interveners find that it is often a lot less difficult than they had originally imagined, especially when they drop their own defenses and beliefs about the individual going into the initial session. We must always remember to leave our own "baggage" outside the room where we hope to help others. Extra baggage just weighs us down and keeps us from seeing and hearing all we need to when engaged with other people.

THE FIRST CONTACT

The following scenario presumes an interaction with an agent of bullying who has, for the first time, been approached about the behavior.

The Setting

The contact between the Intervener and the individual responsible for bullying should be on a ***one-to-one basis***. This sends a strong message that the only focus in the room and topic to be discussed is that of the behavior of the individual. It gives little chance of others confusing the communication between the adult and the student, plus it increases the opportunity of avoiding misinformation being provided from multiple parties when the conversation is conducted in the absence of others. That means avoiding group interviews with multiple agents of the mayhem. It is a divide-and-conquer strategy that sends an elevated message to the individual that what is about to transpire will be listened to carefully. *The focus is solely on the individual and the problematic behavior.*

The first goal of increasing the likelihood of establishing a communication and relational communication is a ***calm and safe environment***. It is not recommended to attempt to make some type of relational connection with a child in the immediate aftermath of a heated event, particularly if the incident involved a physical confrontation. Whatever disciplinary action will occur, or has occurred, should be at some ***time-distant point*** away from the current effort to attempt the connection. Time tends to settle emotions and provide for greater clarity of thought. It also increases the likelihood of individuals who are in the hot seat being more willing to accept an offer to talk with a neutral adult about whatever it is that put them under the misbehavioral microscope in the first place.

When we talk about a calm and safe environment, we are talking not only about one in which an adequate time-distant point has occurred but one that is also a space with some level of privacy, with as little distraction as possible. That could be an office, or it could be an empty classroom. The key components are the relative ***sense of privacy***, the time-distance between when the agent of bullying came to the attention of the supervisory authority, and the current effort to talk calmly about the situation.

The First Contact

The first contact should always be one of both ***discovery*** and ***boundaries***. The Intervener should make it clear that the purpose of the meeting is to discover the agent's point of view along with the guidelines for how the two will proceed.

Intervener (I) 1: *Thanks for coming down, Student A. Do you know why we're here?*

Student A (SA) 1: *Don't have a clue.*

I 2: *I'll be straight up. It's about that conversation you had with Ms. Vice Principal* (VP) *earlier today.*

SA 2: *What conversation?*

I 3: *The one where she talked to you about what happened between you and Student B at lunch.*

SA 3: *I told her I didn't do nuthin' 'cept defend myself.*

I 4: *Well, that's what I want to hear about. I'm here to understand your side of the story and try to make things better for everybody.*

SA 4: [Says nothing. Just looks at the Intervener trying to figure out what the Intervener is really trying to do.]

I 5: *I have to tell you some ground rules right up front. I'm not the one that's going to put the hammer down on you. That's not my job. Whatever Ms. VP is going to do, that's between you and her. What we talk about in here stays in here, unless you tell me something that makes me think that you're going to hurt yourself or somebody else. In that case, you know we are required by law to make sure that everyone's safe and that*

	I have to contact whomever I have to contact in order to make sure that everyone stays that way. If you want me to share parts of what we talk about in here with Ms. VP, then you'll let me know. This is not an interrogation. You might find I can be useful in helping everyone understand your side of things.
SA 5:	[Still says nothing. Listens with a cautious look, sizing up the situation.]
I 6:	*Up front, I also have to be honest and tell you that you can't keep doing what you're accused of doing—if you're really doing it—because it violates school rules.*
SA 6:	*I said I didn't do nuthin'!*
I 7:	*OK, I'm listening. I just have to make sure you understand that, if you really are bullying Student B, that behavior is not allowed here, and if you do it, you will be held accountable. Do you know what accountability means?*
SA 7:	*It means I'll be punished.*
I 8:	*Not necessarily. It means that if you break the rules or treat others unfairly, the adults get to decide the best and fairest way for you to help right whatever wrong it is that you did.*
SA 8:	*That's punishment. Like I told you so.*
I 9:	*It might be. It also might not be. It might be trying to figure out what's a better way for you to make up for whatever you did—if you did anything—and still stay in school. You don't want to be kicked out of school, do you?*
SA 9:	*I don't care. You can kick me out for all I care.*
I 10:	*Well, we care that you stay in school for as long as you can because we know what's best for you at this age—it's about getting an education, as long as you can play by the rules and treat others with respect. Now, let's talk about what happened between you and Student B today. Why don't you tell me your version of exactly what happened?*

WHAT JUST HAPPENED HERE?

Here is what is happening, line by line, in that dialogue to help establish as neutral a connection as possible between the adult and the student.

It is clear from the student's reactions that he has no interest in what is about to occur. Everything that the student says is an effort to deny or confuse the Intervener (SA1–3, 6), if not an outright challenge to authority (SA6–9).

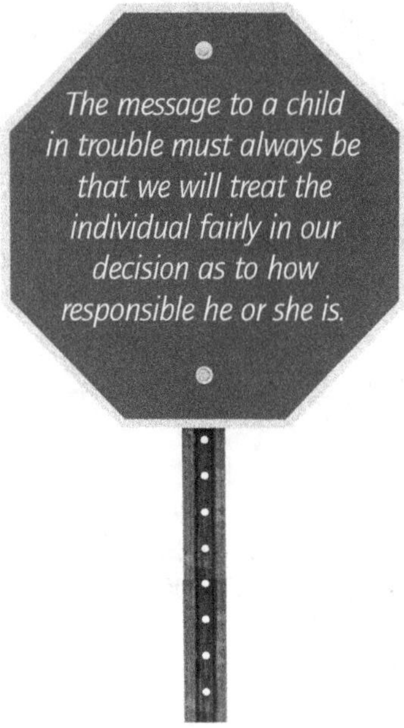

The adult's responses are *straightforward, firm, as friendly as feasible,* and *informational.* The purpose of why the student is in the meeting is set forth in I2 through I4. The ground rules for how things will progress are made clear in I5. I6 through I10 explain the limits of both what is expected of the student and the limits of behaviors that will be tolerated. At no time does the adult respond in kind to the student's efforts to challenge. There is no need to—the adult is in charge and in the power position. We have to remember that, when we find our personal buttons pushed by difficult students, not to relinquish our rational and logical position for the sake of an easy and cheap affective response. When we do that, we are losing control by stepping into the quicksand of emotion.

The Intervener is focused on delivering the goals and key messages of the session to Student A. The five prevailing messages to the student in this interaction are as follows:

1. We are here to discuss your side of what happened today.
2. These are the rules we will go by for this session.
3. Everybody has to follow the basic rules about behavior in school.
4. I'm not here to kick you out; in fact, I'm here to try figure out a way to keep you in school.
5. I want to hear your side of the story.

The less we respond to others from an emotional stance, the greater likelihood of establishing a communication and relational connection. It is often helpful to write down the main points of the messages and goals you want to stress with the student before beginning in order to increase the ability to focus and avoid becoming distracted by the instigator's efforts to create chaos and confusion (see Figure 8.1). Remember, our efforts to intervene and stop the behaviors of those who bully are a direct threat to the status quo of their behavioral inertia. They do not give up that inertia easily, especially when it is viewed as surrendering power among the peer group.

Continuing the Dialogue

What happens after the initial effort to establish some type of communication and relational connection depends on how successful the initial interaction was. The key to establishing the willingness of the individual to continue the most basic type of interaction will always be based on ***trust***—trust in the individual leading the intervention, trust in the process, and trust in the system.

Does the individual under the microscope trust you? Factors that will impact this decision on the part of the student include not only how successful the initial session went but also such things as the nature of past interactions and relationships between the two (positive, negative, or neutral); the circumstances of how the two of you came to be in the current situation; and the level of belief that the student holds that you can be of some benefit to him or her.

Does the individual under the microscope trust the process? As shown in the opening dialogue, the parameters for that opening session were clearly established by the Intervener in the five themes. However, it is the student who will make a judgment as to the worth of continuing the process based on the "what's-in-it-for-me" rule. If the student doesn't believe that there is anything to gain from continuing to play the game, then the game ends, or the student makes an effort to change the rules so that the game is now to his or her advantage. The message must be made clear that whatever is about to transpire (a) is not a game, (b) that the purpose of the meeting(s) is to discover all sides to the truth—whatever that is and wherever it leads, and (c) that while the individual is accused of engaging in bullying behaviors, this will be a fair process to all involved.

Does the individual under the microscope trust the system? This may be a factor over which the Intervener has no control. The level of success that the student has had in the past navigating whatever system she or he is navigating now may well doom efforts to create a bond between the Intervener and the student before the first interaction begins. If the student feels as if the system is biased to him or her personally or against whatever group he or she is a part of—racial, ethnic, socioeconomic, religious—the likelihood of wanting to cooperate with anyone who represents that system decreases dramatically. This is no different for any of us. If we feel the system is somehow rigged against us, we typically don't even try to engage in the process because we feel as if the outcome is predetermined against us. The more negative the interactions that individuals have had with a system, the less likely they are to believe or trust that the representative of that system—in this instance, the Intervener—will be any different from their perception of the way it has treated them in the past.

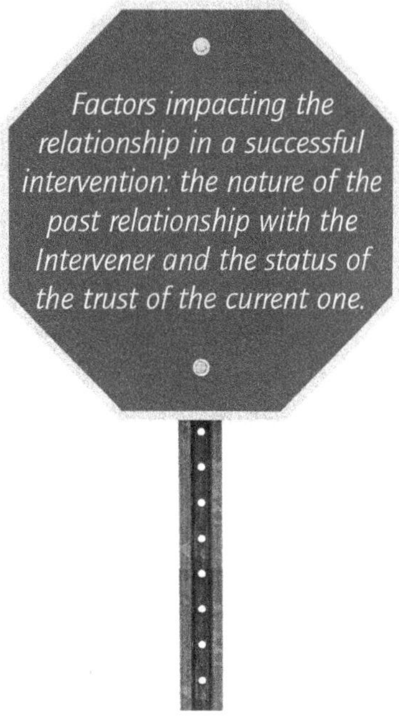

If the stars fall in our favor, if the individual accused of bullying behaviors has enough belief in you (even if just for the moment) to put aside any trepidations about what is about to occur and believes that the system just might treat him or her fairly, then the dialogue could continue. It is important to remember that this is a tenuous relationship and one that is always subject to the student backing out the moment she or he feels threatened or if there is nothing left to gain by continuing. This is a purely subjective decision on the part of the student. We can be as fair and just as Solon, but not necessarily in the eyes of the one who feels as if there is something to lose by continuing the conversation or that we are just going to perpetuate the injustices of the past.

HELPFUL LEADS TO INCREASE THE CHANCES OF COMMUNICATION AND RELATIONAL CONNECTIONS AND CONTINUING THE DIALOGUE

Always ***strive for neutrality*** when it comes to attempting to encourage those who may be suspicious of your motives or that the outcome is not one that will be in their favor. *What we say and how we say it can make all the difference in the world in overcoming hesitation on the part of these individuals.* Patience is more than a virtue here. It is the primary currency that will save both you and the student from jumping to responses from an emotional plane. Remember, your presence in the affairs of peer interactions in Kid World makes you suspect right off the bat. The wrong turn of a phrase, the misinterpretation of nuance on the part of the student and the entire effort can collapse—a house of cards if there ever was one.

Here are some leads that you might find helpful when making that effort to stay on neutral ground while discussing the viewpoints of individuals who have been accused of bullying:

Help me understand what happened today from your point of view.

It will help me to help you better if I hear it straight from you.

The only promise I can make is to be fair to everyone involved in this.

There won't be any decisions made until we get all the facts.

My role today is to get as much information as possible to make sure that all sides are heard.

I'm not going to respond to you the way you are responding to me. I'm treating you with respect, and I'm going to ask you to do the same.

Let's stay focused on the reason that we're here. We can discuss that other issue on another day.

I believe that, in your heart, you know what's right, and that's what I'd like us to focus on right now.

It's clear to me you don't want to be here. Guess what? I don't want to be here talking to you about this, either. I'd much rather be talking about more positive things in your life. So let's see how fast we can get this matter cleared up so that I can learn more about things that you like, rather than what you don't like.

All of these prompts are designed to ***avoid an escalation*** in a tense interaction between an individual who feels the heat of inquiry and who may well be responsible for the cause of the questioning at hand. When in doubt, remember this rule: Identify the ***neutral ground*** and move back to it when the interaction seems to be moving into emotional territory. Routing back to neutral ground may well be accomplished with some of the previous statements.

Figure 8.1 Intervention Rules

Rules to remember when opening an intervention with an individual who has engaged in abusive behaviors toward others.

Making Contact

Focus on the individual as if the problem had not occurred.

Focus on the behavior, not as if the individual is the problem.

Maintain a calm demeanor.

Avoid emotional enmeshment.

Ensure a safe time-distant point from the event.

As much as possible, allow for privacy.

Be patient.

Stay on neutral ground in terms of the conversation.

9

Forced Apologies and Mediations

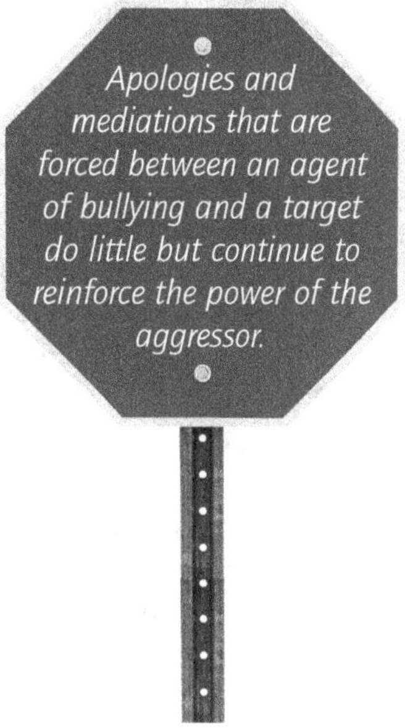

Two of the biggest mistakes ever made in all the efforts to address the relationship between those who bully and their targets were the one-to-one *forced apology* and being subjected to inappropriate mediation. These two techniques may have done more harm than good in the grand scheme of things. More likely, here's what that one-to-one forced apology did: It played right into the hands of the agents of bullying and increased their power over the target.

Forced apologies are fake. Besides the fact that neither party wants to be there—but for completely different reasons—there is no equity of power in the interaction. It is a *false situation* staged to force a resolution onto the two parties by the power of the authority making the interaction occur. It is doomed to failure from the beginning for that very reason—it doesn't originate as a genuine, mutually agreed upon method of resolving a wrong—as well as it's just plain unfair to the individual who has already been victimized by the abuser. In fact, forced apologies are likely *revictimizing* for targets because they feel as if they must accept the apology, no matter how insincere it happens to be.

Let's look at the motivations of the person who bullies and their targets when placed in that forced apology situation. Here's what the actor (and in this situation, the double entendre is intended) gains:

1. It gives the impression that she or he is cooperating.
2. It likely decreases the chances of punishment (if on the menu) or reduces the likelihood of receiving something believed to be onerous to the agent.
3. It forms an alliance of power between the authority forcing the apology and the agent of bullying by aligning the agent as a cooperative member of the agent–target interaction.
4. It maintains the agent's position of dominance by placing the target in a position of having to accept the apology. Additionally, it may well put the target in a position of seeming uncooperative in the eyes of the authority if he or she objects to the suggestion or demand of the adult.

Now, let's see what the target of bullying in the forced apology gets out of the interaction:

1. It forces the individual who has been bullied to cooperate with someone who has done nothing but cause him/her misery.

2. It places the individual in a position to feel obligated to accept the apology in order to show cooperation with the process.
3. It maintains inequity, if not further decreases, any power between the target of bullying and the agent.
4. It often forces the target to agree to "get along better with each other" in the future when the target has not done anything to deserve the mistreatment received from the agent of bullying in the first place.

Forced mediation is sometimes little better for many of the same reasons. The purpose of ***mediation*** is to bring together two parties who disagree for the purpose of finding a solution to the problem. But here's the forgotten element when bullying is involved—there is no "problem" to be "solved" when one of the parties has wronged the other. There is nothing to "mediate," no "common ground" to be found between the two. Making amends is certainly in order on the part of the agent of bullying, as is likely restoration for the wrong that has occurred—but these aspects are more appropriately addressed in a restorative justice process, rather than mediation. The individual who has been bullied has no reason to be placed in a forced apology or forced mediation situation. The target of bullying has no reason to be further inconvenienced or intimidated by the misbehavior of the one who created the situation in the first place.

It *is* appropriate to consider the merits of a genuine apology on the part of the aggressor *if* the origin of that apology is (1) a sincere effort on the part of the person who bullied; (2) a workable solution to the actions of bullying that occurred (i.e., what is offered by the agent of bullying moves toward true restoration of the self-worth of the target); (3) a sincere apology and restorative action can be crafted along with a responsible adult or peer; or (4) if the one who was abused is amenable to accepting the apology.

Likewise, the one victimized by the aggressor should not be forced into face-to-face meetings with the agent that can create additional stress for the one who has been attacked. If the target indicates that she or he finds a suggested meeting acceptable, the supervisory authority should still determine if the target has the cognitive and affective strength to do so. Those who are victimized, especially chronically, are often highly suggestible to what is offered from those in power positions because they either want to please the adult making the suggestion, avoid additional conflict, or have "accepted" their social status as one with little or no power to voice their own opinions—sometimes all three. Above all, give adequate time to the individuals who have been targeted for abuse to offer their own ideas as to what should occur. It may be the first time they have been given voice—and power—to do so.

FORCED APOLOGIES ARE NOT RESTORATIVE JUSTICE

What is far more appropriate for determining the best course of action between an agent of bullying and the target is likely to evolve from the restorative justice process, which is discussed in Chapter 10. While there are similarities in the physical structure of forced apologies, mediation, and restorative justice techniques—primarily in that both the agent and target are in the same room at the same time—the ***power dynamic*** of who is controlling the interaction is very different.

In a forced apology or mediation setting, the pressure is on the target to accept the terms of remediation whether that is in the best interest of the target or not. Restorative justice places more power in the hands of the target through the control of the group process by the leader, especially if a talking-circle format is used. Restorative efforts also focus on the experiential perceptions of the target.

Let us now go to Chapter 10 to see how restorative justice differs from mediation and forced apologies, as well as why it is one preferred method of intervention between the two parties.

10

Applying Elements of Restorative Justice Techniques With Those Who Engage in Bullying Behaviors

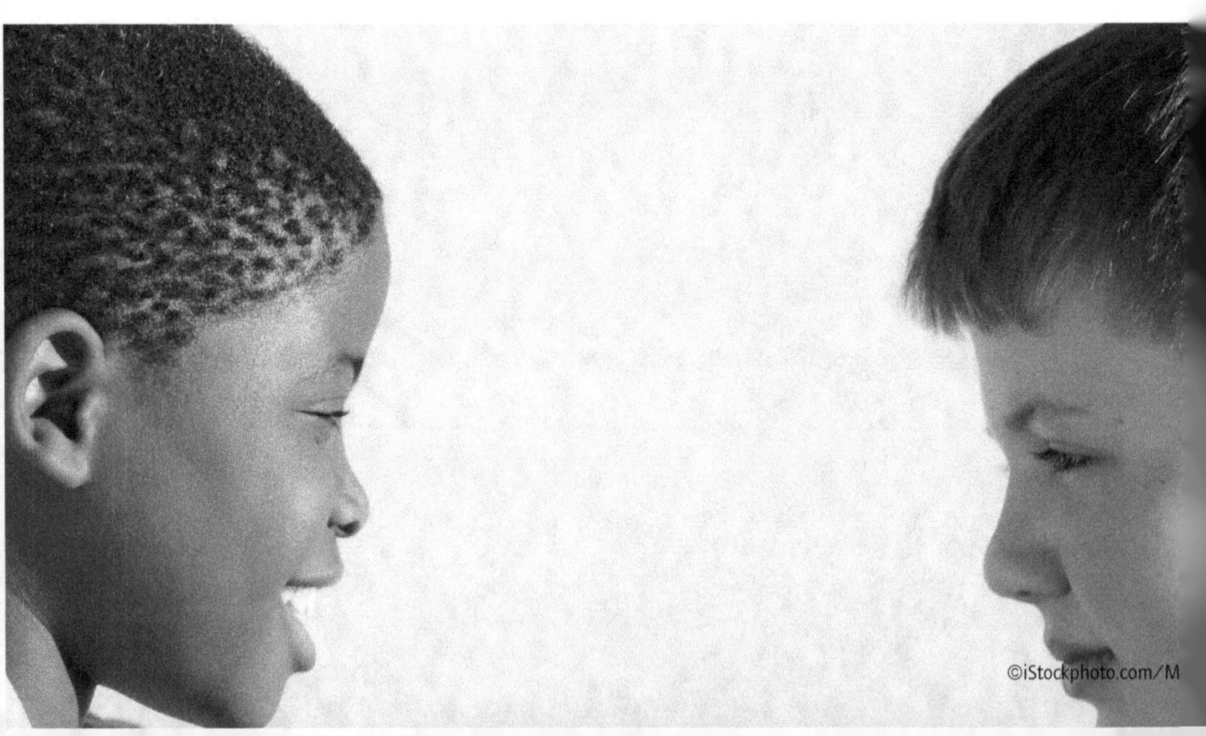

Restorative justice is not new. However, it has been introduced to the vast majority of educators over the past decade due to its expanded use within schools as an alternative to mediation.

Riestenberg (2012) provides one of the most practical explanations of the need for restorative justice:

> *Restorative justice offers a paradigm shift in the way we think of crime or breaking rules. Its principles teach us to think not only about the offender but also about the victim; not only about the court but also about the community; not only about the law that was broken but also about the impact of its breaking on people. The shift is from rules to relationships.* (p. 12)

Restorative justice has had a long history of use worldwide within the criminal justice system and is based on efforts to help those who have committed crimes hear and learn what their actions have done to victims beyond the tangible ("History of Restorative Justice," n.d.). While its use in the criminal justice system escalated in the 1970s, its roots lie deep within many Native American, First Nation, and Aboriginal nations across the world (Daly & Immarigeon, 1998; Gavrielides, 2011). More may know of or have heard of the use of ***talking circles*** (also called ***healing circles***), a primary technique used in restorative justice wherein those who were wronged have a chance to tell their stories to those who wronged them (Riestenberg, 2012). Let's review the basics of restorative justice as a foundation for what we will be discussing as we move forward in this chapter.

THE CONCEPT BEHIND RESTORATIVE JUSTICE

Western culture has been predominantly and historically punitive when it comes to dealing with those who make mistakes. Its basic method of dealing with those who commit some type of moral, social, or legal infraction involves giving short shrift to the reasons and causes which may have contributed to the error as long as we punish the guilty. Punitive measures are simple to administer and do not involve a lot of critical thinking skills. Zero tolerance policies are the poster child for that type of approach: You do a wrong, you get punished. Bazelon (2013) noted, "Bullying is supposed to be clear-cut. There's a bad kid and a victim, and once you know who's who, you know whose side to be on" (p. 14). People who do wrong are "bad," and we punish bad people. What's not to like?

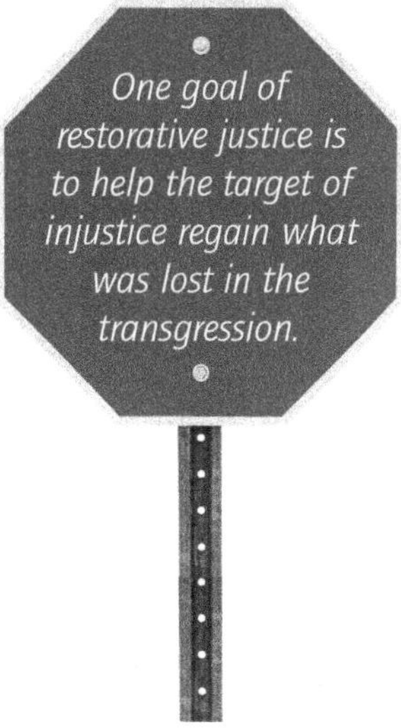

Well, quite a bit, actually. While punishment is simplistic to enact, it does little to investigate the cause of the circumstances surrounding what helped create the opportunity for the misdeed or mistake. Even though the explanation offered by the apprehended party in an act of bullying—"But wait, I can explain!"—may well be just as lame as the way the line has been used in so many bad crime movies through the ages, when we go straight to punishment we actually forego the chance to understand the logic and rationale behind the individual who holds the key to bullying. We also deny the perpetrators one of the most valuable opportunities that they may be afforded prior to holding them accountable—that being the chance to learn the true meaning and depth of what one's actions did to another.

Restorative justice is designed to address just this very thing, and it has proven successful when used properly in both the juvenile court and educational systems. There is a key phrase in that last sentence that must not be overlooked—*when used properly*. As with many activities used, too often people attempt to put in play techniques or strategies of which they are not as well trained as they should be, if trained at all: "We need a solution to this problem, quick. I read an article online that said this restorative justice thing worked with kids in Blovovia. Let's throw it against the wall and see if it sticks!" So much for the merits of research and thoughtful consideration.

THE TALKING CIRCLE

One of the major concepts behind a restorative approach is to show support from the relevant community[1] to those who have been victimized in some fashion. All who participate in a restorative action are considered equals, although the group leader navigates the basic traffic flow of the process. In restoration, the target is provided the opportunity to tell his or her story in a safe, controlled environment, usually through the use of the talking or healing circle.[2] The key to this intensive interpersonal exchange is that the interaction is highly structured and under the supervision and guidance of an adult who knows basic group dynamics and how a restorative intervention is supposed to work. Training and additional education in using restorative justice practices is recommended before using it as an intervention tool in any setting.

---

1. In this sense, think of the "community" in terms of the community in which the problem behavior takes place—a school, a grade level, a classroom, a team, a cohort group. A personal recommendation is to employ the geography of problem solving (see Chapter 18) in composing a talking circle. Think small and only involve those necessary to keep the process as manageable and relevant as possible.

2. One of the most powerful aspects of the talking circle is the use of the symbolic ***talking piece***, a token object of some sort that gives the holder permission to speak, according to group rules, during the session. Only the person who holds the talking piece can speak. The group leader controls access to the talking piece and reminds the group of the rules should someone speak in the absence of possessing the talking piece for the moment. All will have equal access to the talking piece at some point as long as they follow the rules for the group.

There are two main groups of participants in a restorative intervention—those who have been harmed by an action and are stakeholders (or representatives of the stakeholder group) within the community, and those who are responsible for creating the harmful situation. The composition of the group is up to the group leader but must take into consideration the ultimate well-being of all involved. Should the group be composed only of a target and other members of the community with the purpose of helping to support the target's effort to feel welcomed? While the target did no wrong, those who are victimized often feel ostracized from the larger community. Riestenberg (2012) notes that "being a victim of harm or crime sets a person apart. Receiving messages of care and concern helps pull the victim back into the community. . . . Having a chance to articulate what one needs to be safe . . . helps to increase the . . . sense of personal power" (p. 43).

Should the restorative action have the target and agent in the same group? Isn't that a contradiction to what we said earlier about forced apologies and not having the agent and the target in the room together forcing the target to be subjected to possible revictimization? It could be, but not if the talking circle is handled correctly.

The heart of a restorative justice intervention assumes that this will be the place where the agent of the wrong doing has the opportunity to hear from those whom have been harmed. Care must be taken so that (1) those victimized are not forced to participate if they do not want to; (2) those who were targeted have complete control of the decision to participate or not; and (3) the other members of the circle include those targeted plus other members of the community who have a vested interest in the overall health and well-being of that community. While it is important that the agent of bullying not be allowed a position of power within the group, it is also just as important that the agent feels safe and that the group not be used as a method to attack or settle old scores between the two parties. It is a healing and talking circle, not a revenge circle.

Participants are not required to speak when their time comes. They can "pass" on their opportunity to speak by handing the talking piece to the next person. Once the group leader sets the rules for the group, the talking piece is passed around the circle for introductions by name and why they are participating in the group. The group facilitator then begins the circle by asking a question relevant to all in attendance, something that everyone is likely to be able to answer in some form or fashion (e.g., "What brings us together today?" "What is the reason that you are participating in this group?" "What do you hope is the outcome of today's talking circle?"). The talking piece is passed around the circle, each person given equal time to respond. The group leader will ask a second and third question for group response and reflection, depending on the amount of time allotted for the circle. There should be time for closing statements by all in the circle, followed by a final closing statement by the group leader that sums up the sentiment of the total group experience as it relates to the goal(s) of the restorative effort.

The idea of bringing victim(s), stakeholders of the healthy community, and perpetrator together so that the individual who did the wrong can hear firsthand from the person targeted what that action did to her or him is conceptually designed to increase empathy on the part of the aggressor. This is where restorative measures differ primarily from the one-to-one forced apology and mediation. Those that were victimized are given power and are supported by the strength of the community in the talking circle. The focus of the group is on healing, not punishment; on giving voice to all who have a stake in the overall health of the community; on creating an ***equity of power*** among everyone who agrees to participate in and honor the goals of the circle outside the group.

Restorative justice brings the two parties together in a controlled environment so that they can "learn" from each other (primarily, so that the aggressor can learn what his or her actions do to others). Learning *can* be a two-way street in a restorative justice effort between those who bully and their targets, especially when children have social skills deficits and they act in ways with their peers that tend to provoke negative responses in kind, the so-called ***provocative victim*** (Olweus, 1978, 1996). In essence, an understanding of "When you do that, this is what it does to me" can be of benefit to both parties in cases where neither one truly understands the reasons or motives of the other, and all behaviors and interactions between the two are interpreted from an attack-defend mindset.

IS IT REALLY RESTORATIVE JUSTICE OR RESTORATIVE AND REMEDIATIVE EFFORTS?

While I highly endorse restorative justice[3] and talking circles as a healing and educational technique when used in the appropriate setting with leaders who are appropriately educated and skilled in the process, I don't believe that it can or should be used in its pure form with those along the bullying continuum in the same fashion as the method is applied with those who are being adjudicated in the juvenile justice system. My primary concern is the protection of the target. *If the restorative effort or talking circle is not efficiently monitored and regulated, it could become another forced apology or mediation fiasco.*

3. Additionally, the National Education Association "supports restorative practices that use empathy over authority," according to Steven Grant (2015, p. 7). See "Moving Beyond Zero Tolerance," *NEA Today*, Winter 2015.

Perhaps we should call the use of restorative justice concepts with those who bully ***restorative*** or ***remediative efforts***. Applying the formulaic restorative justice template may not always be appropriate or workable in instances of bullying. Here are several components and concepts of restorative justice that can be applied in an effort to *restore* the dignity and self-worth of the individual harmed and *remediate* the harm that was done:

- First and foremost, those who act in ways to physically or psychologically injure others must know that they will be held accountable for their actions. This accountability will be fair and consistent with the established rules of the school, institution, or organization.
- Everyone is responsible for her or his actions.
- It is important that aggressors understand that, in addition to the specifics of whatever was done in the instance(s) under consideration, that bullying others extends beyond just the mere act(s) alone.
- Those who harm others must learn that their behaviors disrupt the ability of everyone in the environment to feel safe about forming relationships within their respective peer groups.
- Those who injure one member of the relevant peer group are perceived to be acting against the welfare, safety, and security of the entire group.
- Only through making efforts to restore and repair whatever was taken from another or remediate and repair the harm done to another can those who do wrong begin to do what is right at both the individual and group level.
- Not everything that is done to others can be restored or remediated.
- Remediation and restoration must conceptually take into account everyone (the group or community within the specific school, organization, or institution) who may have been impacted or harmed by the action(s) directed toward a specific target.
- Offering an insincere apology is not an honest act of either remediation or restoration.
- It is acceptable to not like another or have disagreements with them. It is not acceptable to act toward those individuals in ways that are demeaning, degrading, take away their self-worth, or deprive them of their friends. That means the individual who bullies will not interfere with others' abilities to be a full member of the community.
- If an aggressor does not like another, he or she should choose to not associate or have interactions with the individual.
- Whether we like or dislike others, we will treat them with respect.

Guidelines 10.1 Basic Guidelines for Restorative and Remediative Discussions With an Aggressor.
It helps to have basic rules or guidelines to shape conversations and educational opportunities with those who bully. These 10 suggestions are based on some of the foundations of restorative practices. Naturally, the reader should adopt the most developmentally appropriate language for the clientele and setting.

Things We Believe and Do

1. We are all responsible for our actions.
2. All of us are accountable for those actions.
3. An act of harm goes beyond the simple act itself.
4. Unsafe behaviors make everyone feel unsafe.
5. If an individual harms another, she or he is responsible for making amends for that harm. However . . .
6. Not everything that is done to harm another can be undone or repaired.
7. An apology that is not real is not being truthful.
8. It is OK to disagree with others and even dislike them, but it is not OK to act in ways to harm them.
9. If an individual does not like another person, he or she can make the choice to avoid them when possible.
10. Whether we like another person or not, we will still treat them with respect.

A SAMPLE DIALOGUE ABOUT RESTORATION AND REMEDIATION

Let's continue our conversation with Student A (SA) that we started earlier and incorporate some of the components already outlined into that discussion to see if we can help educate our student who has run afoul of the rules as to what is expected of everyone in the future.[4]

Intervener [I] 1: *Thanks, again, for coming down to see me.*

Student A [SA] 1: *Like I gotta lotta choice.*

I 2: *Well, actually, SA, you do. You have a lot of choices, and that's a part of what I'd like us to talk about today.*

---

4. This is still a one-to-one conversation with Student A, not a sample dialogue within a talking circle.

SA 2: [Says nothing. Waits for the Intervener to drive the conversation.]

I 3: *What I'd like us to do today is make sure that we're on the same page as to what you and Ms. VP worked out last week and how that fits into us being able to make sure that everyone gets along here at school. Can you remind me of what she said about what you have to do from here on out?*

SA 3: *You know what she said.*

I 4: *In all honesty, I know some of it, but not all. I'm not involved in that discipline stuff. I'm here to try work things out between students when they have disagreements to see if everyone can make things work better. So help me out, will you? What did the two of you end up working out?*

SA 4: *She said she won't kick me out if I don't pick on Student B* [SB] *anymore.*

I 5: *Well, that sounds workable.*

SA 5: *Easy for you to say. I hate SB's guts.*

I 6: *We can talk about that, too, as we move forward. Anything else Ms. VP and you talked about?*

SA 6: *She said I have to do what you say, too, or she'll kick me out.*

I 7: *Now is that what she really said, or was it something slightly different?*

SA 7: *Close enough.* [Doesn't offer any additional information.]

I 8: *OK, SA, you're really going to make me work, aren't you? Let me tell you what I remember of the conversation I had with her. Ms. VP told me that if you and I could work something out so that there's no more trouble between you and SB and that your overall behavior improves, she will hold off on applying any additional school rules.*

SA 8: *You mean punishment.*

I 9: *That may be a matter of opinion. You might see it as a punishment because you don't like it or because you want to do whatever it is you have to do. We see it more as just holding you accountable for your actions. Do you know what that word means?*

SA 9: *I'm not stupid.*

I 10: *Oh, we know that, SA. In fact, you're one of the smartest kids around this place. That's why we figure you also understand why holding people responsible for their actions when they mess up is the right thing to do.*

SA 10: *If it's fair.*

I 11: *It'll be fair. That's the way things should be. When we make a mistake, we still should be treated fairly and given a chance to make up for the wrong we did. I gave you my word that I'll do everything I can to see that everybody is treated fairly as we move forward. Have I respected you enough to do that to this point?*

SA 11: *I guess.*

I 12: *I think I have. I think I've worked really hard to make sure that everybody in here is treated both fairly and with respect because that's what we all want. We all want to be treated fairly and with respect.* [Pauses a moment for that to sink in.] *Even SB.*

SA 12: *SB don't deserve respect.*

I 13: *We disagree on that. Everybody deserves the respect they earn. But we earn that respect through the way we behave, and the way you've been treating SB lately doesn't show that you either respect him or that you are doing a lot to earn the respect that you want other people to give you.*

SA 13: *I said SB don't deserve respect so that's why I don't give him any.*

I 14: *We can talk about your relationship with SB in the days to come. But for now, I want to make certain that you remember the way we try to operate around here. Here's what's important to remember: This is supposed to be a safe place for everyone. When someone acts in a way that makes it seem like it's not, that behavior and the person who does it is going to be held accountable. If someone does something wrong to someone else, we're going to give him or her the chance to correct the mistake, but that person has to be willing to do right by both the rules and their relationship with everybody around here because, in its own strange way, a school is like one big stinky family.*

SA 14: [Laughs.] *Especially the stinky part!*

I 15: [Chuckles.] *Yes, and sometimes more than others. But in order to help make this school family work, we have to (1) follow the rules, (2) treat everyone with the respect they earn, (3) own up to when we make a mistake, and (4) do what we can to make that mistake right by the person we wronged. Is that too much to ask of everybody?*

SA 15: *Sounds like a whole lotta rules to me.*

I 16: *Not as many as are in the student handbook.*

SA 16: [Smiles and stifles a laugh.] *Got that right.*

I 17: *Let's do this. Let's talk about some of what we've discussed to this point today and see if we can make more sense out of it, OK? Give it your best shot, and I'll be able to tell Ms. VP that you're making progress on keeping your nose clean. Deal?*

SA 17: *I guess. Don't have much of a choice.*

WHAT JUST HAPPENED HERE?

What happened in this exchange? The Intervener structured the conversation in an effort to introduce Student A to some of the concepts of remediative and restorative practices. Student A was informed that everyone is responsible for the behaviors directed toward others (I 14); when individuals violate the rules, they are accountable for their actions (I 9–11,14); that accountability will be applied fairly to all (I 11–12); and that the safety of the group and school trumps the individual's behavior that disrupts it (I 14). The Intervener even exemplifies with Student A that disagreements can be handled respectfully (I 11–13) and that even if two people do not get along, it is important that they treat each other with respect (I 13, 15).

This interaction between the Intervener and Student A is an effective example of an Intervener-led structured interview as discussed in Chapter 8. This session is not so much an effort to explore with the student the reasons for the actions that got him into trouble as it is a ***structured educational session*** informing him of certain ideas and concepts that, hopefully, will bear fruit in the future. Some interventions with those who bully have to be educational in nature, and there is no reason not to presume that both education and relationship building cannot be done simultaneously. Effective interventions combine education, relationship building, and opportunities for insight for both the agent and Intervener.

WANT TO LEARN MORE?

For those wanting to learn more about how restorative justice and talking circles work, readers are highly encouraged to read Nancy Riestenberg's (2012) *Circle in the Square: Building Community and Repairing Harm in School* and Mark Umbreit's (2003) "Talking Circles" from the Center for Restorative Justice and Peacemaking at http://www.cehd.umn.edu/ssw/rjp/resources/rj_dialogue_resources/Peacemaking_Healing_Circles/Talking_Circles.pdf for a clear and concise methodology of creating restorative practices in appropriate settings. Additional information on the major components of restorative justice can be found in Bilchik's (1998) *Guide for Implementing the Balanced and Restorative Justice Model*, from the US Department of Justice Office of Juvenile Justice and Delinquency Prevention at http://www.ojjdp.gov/pubs/implementing/balanced.html#principles; Burke's (2013) *An Inventory and Examination of Restorative Justice Practices for Youth in Illinois* at http://www.icjia.state.il.us/public/pdf/researchreports/inventoryandexaminationofrestorativejusticepracticesforyouthillinois_042013.pdf; and the Conflict Resolution Center's (2009) "What Is Restorative Justice?" at http://www.cscsb.org/restorative_justice/what_is_restorative_justice.html.

11

Building Empathy Within Those Who Bully

Perhaps the best tool against bullying is building a sense of empathy within those who are considering doing wrong to others. That is often much easier said than done.

Having a concept of and applying ***empathy*** has been identified repeatedly as a silver bullet of bullying prevention. Szalavitz (2010) notes the following:

> The capacity for empathy is believed to be innate in most humans, as well as some other species—chimps, for instance, will protest the unfair treatment of others, refusing to accept a treat they have rightfully earned if another chimp doing the same work fails to get the same reward. (para. 5)

Empathy may well appear in the earliest days of childhood, as observed when infants cry when exposed to other crying newborns and when infants as young as fourteen months make efforts to assist adults who seem to be in need of help in reaching an object (Coloroso, 2003; Szalavitz, 2010, para. 6). Espelage, Mebane, and Adams (2004) write that "there is a general consensus that attending, fostering, and promoting empathy in children and adolescents . . . relate to the development of prosocial behavior and to the prevention of aggressive behavior" (p. 38). Empathy is closely attached to one's moral compass, and from a societal viewpoint, chaos and anarchy evolve when one's ability to think, feel, and act only on behalf of self-interest is the driving force behind decisions. At its worst, lack of empathy is one of the characteristics of psychopathology, marked by the ability to harm others without remorse (Bazelon, 2013, pp. 55–56; Dolan, 2013).

Having empathy allows children and adolescents to regulate impulsive behaviors and think before they act. It increases the likelihood of self-intervention to stop acts of bullying due to one's own sense of extension of the self into the situation observed in others. This is particularly important in motivating bystanders to get involved on behalf of those targeted for abuse.

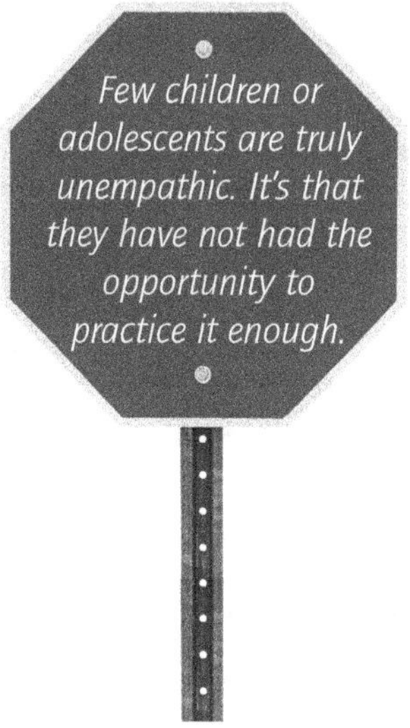

Funke and Hymel (as cited in Macklem, 2003, p. 99) defined empathy as the "ability to appreciate another person's feelings." Espelage, Mebane, and Adams (2004) added that empathy involves "both cognitive and emotional facets" (p. 38). Some adolescents are rated higher than their peers in the ability to understand others' experiences as rated on emotional intelligence scales (Lomas, Stough, Hansen, & Downey, 2012). It is the proverbial capacity to walk in another person's shoes or, as Riestenberg (2012) noted, "take the perspective of another and recognize how it feels to be that person" (p. 34). Curtner-Smith, Smith, and

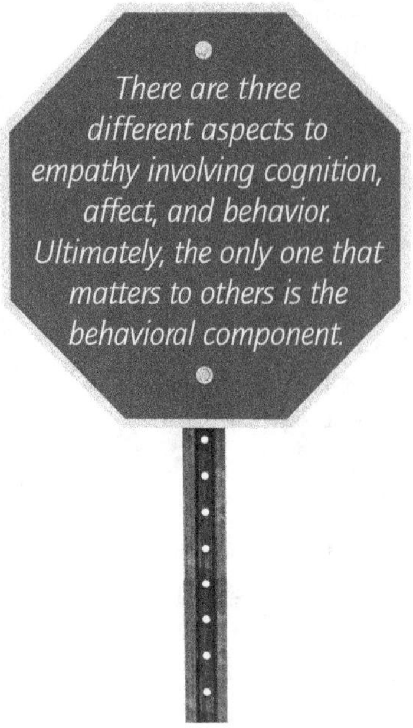

Porter (2010) add that empathy is the "vicarious sharing of another's emotions" (p. 86). Curtner-Smith et al. (p. 86) consider it two dimensional: ***cognitive empathy*** refers to one's ability to identify the emotions occurring in another person; ***affective empathy*** refers to one's ability to have a conception of another's emotions. Affective empathy is likely the type most people understand when the term *empathy* is used.

There is a complex interaction between having the characteristic and practicing it. Indeed, children and adolescents may well be empathic toward others but not have the skills to put the affect and cognition into behavioral gear. It is important to note that empathy involves all three domains of the human experience. In order to have a ***feeling of commonality*** toward the experiences of another, there is also a ***thought process of recognition*** to trigger that link of similarity. At some level, cognition takes place in order to feel the pain of another. Whether the individuals experiencing empathy understand that they are engaged at both levels or not is another important aspect of making a determination as to what to do next—the behavior—if the they choose to do anything at all.

EMPATHY VERSUS SYMPATHY

Empathy and ***sympathy*** are not the same. Sympathy involves reacting to a situation occurring with others because we have actually had the experience ourselves. When we respond to another who has lost a cherished pet because we, too, have lost one, that is a sympathetic response. The closer we are in similarity to the details of an experience gives us a heightened sense of awareness and understanding. For instance, the experiences of losing a pet versus losing a parent are very different, yet both involve having had the experience of dealing with death, grief, and loss.

It is important to remember, however, that everyone experiences phenomena differently, so it is never acceptable to say to another "I know how you feel" because you do not, you cannot—you are not that person. When we have a sympathetic response to another, we are offering tacit approval of that person's reaction to an experience (Egan, 2014). In reality, one's reaction to a situation may not be appropriate; it could well be an overreaction or a minimization of what has occurred. In the instant we offer support, sympathy becomes an endorsement of the behavior. It is likely more effective (and true) to say to another "I've had a similar experience, and while I would never try to say what it's like for you, I know that when it happened to me I felt . . ." In all likelihood (and intentionally), the words you use to describe your experience will be similar to the experience of the one you are attempting to comfort. Empathy is an effort to share an understanding of similar experiences in order to increase the likelihood of ***bonding*** with another person.

That being said, most individuals experience empathy through a sympathetic lens because we experience varying degrees of the basic emotions through the normal human development process. Age and exposure to life's challenges provide us with our personal road map of response patterns to happiness, sadness, surprise, fear, disgust, and anger (Sauter, Eisner, Edman, & Scott, 2010). While basic emotions seem universal, how one expresses them are nuanced based on family of origin and cultural norms. All the more reason that we are well advised to remind ourselves as potential helpers that our reaction to an incident of bullying and someone else's reaction may be quite different.

CAN WE TEACH EMPATHY TO OTHERS?

Is it possible to teach empathy to others? The answer is yes, but as with all other things in life, it's not that simplistic, and there are strings attached.

It is far easier to build on one's capacity to engage in empathic actions if empathy already exists to some degree within an individual. The less inclined one is to understand what empathy is or to have had caring, empathic actions extended toward the individual, the more difficult it is to both teach the concept and encourage turning thought and emotion into action.

Increasing an individual's knowledge of what empathy is and its value is not just "kid stuff" anymore. Increasing empathy among educators is not new, and its practice now extends into the nursing (Hojat, 2009) and medical fields (Shapiro, Morrison, & Bokor, 2004; Shapiro, 2008) out of the need to respond to criticisms of the "poor bedside manner" often displayed by members of the professions. Exactly how best to do so, however, seems to be rooted more in providing those who need an increase in the attribute the opportunity to both learn what it is and to be given chances to practice and apply it in daily life. Practice may not make perfect, but it certainly increases the likelihood that those who do so may perform a particular task or skill better than those who do not.

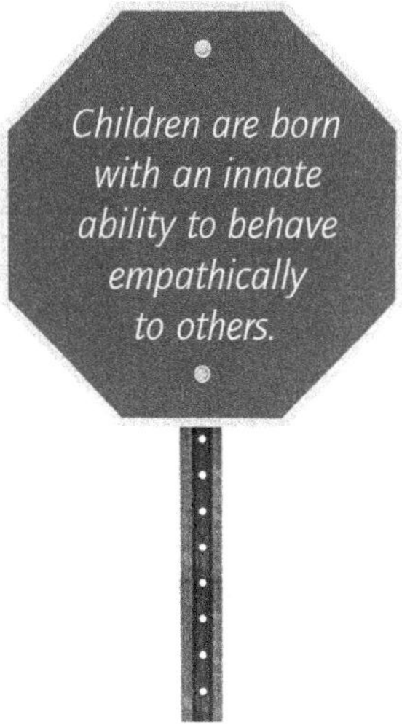

TEACHING EMPATHY BY CONCEPT

While I agree with Coloroso (2003) and Szalavitz (2010) that most children are born with some type of innate sense of empathy, I also subscribe to the belief and

experience that some may lose their capacity to engage in it as a result of lack of encouragement and nurturing to do so. As with any skill, one must use it or lose it—perhaps not lose it entirely, but at least the likelihood increases that one becomes a little rusty without practice. Though they may not know the word, most children understand and can describe the concept of empathy, as well as practice it in some form, without any type of formal training or education in the art. Whatever "inborn quality" (Coloroso, 2003, p. 114) they bring with them into this world[1] is enhanced through vicarious learning within the family along with what limited peer group experiences they have prior to the much larger socialization that occurs once the child enters kindergarten and travels through the elementary years.

Children who do not receive the chance to talk about empathy and practice it, or who do not receive its blessings via peer or adult interactions, begin a journey of withdrawal from its influence. This is particularly true for those who are exposed to hurtful and abusive peer relationships. If not provided the opportunity to experience empathy in real life, they lose additional chances to reinforce the behavior either vicariously or through practice. When Coloroso (2003) notes that, as children get older, "by the time they are six or seven, [they] are more intellectually capable of responding constructively and more emotionally capable of responding with compassion," so too are they equally intellectually capable to begin withholding such behaviors based on support from their immediate peer groups and adult influences.

Adolescents are at a developmental stage to consciously and willfully choose whether or not to actively participate in an act of empathy. Increasing peer pressure has much to do with this. If peers support the activity, it greatly increases the chances that the adolescent will follow through with the act since peer opinion and support are so critical during this period. If the behavior is not supported or actively scorned by peers, few adolescents have the courage to resist and act in the face of opposition from friends.

This was the basic premise behind Coloroso's (2003) seminal work on the influence of ***bystanders*** in breaking the cycle of harm between agents

1. This is not to say that empathic understanding or behaviors exhibited during infancy are instinctual. To the contrary, humans as a species do not have the same kind of true instincts as do other animals (e.g., children have to be taught to swim). They do, however, maintain certain instinctual-like behaviors activated and enhanced by learning opportunities or triggers in the environment for which there is some type of reinforcement. For example, Szalavitz's (2010) example of infants crying in the nursery when exposed to other crying infants is based on the reinforcement the child receives when subsequently attended to by its caregiver.

of bullying and their targets, further amplified by Peck's (2012) *STAND TALL* video training program. Both concepts maintain that there are many individuals involved in the bully–victim dyad besides just the two opposing parties. Those who are aware of the bullying taking place play roles in tacitly endorsing it when they observe it and either vicariously or directly do nothing to attempt to stop it. The assumption behind all bystander intervention work is that there are far more individuals who do not engage in bullying than there are who do. The missing link, then, is to somehow convince those who do bully to either get involved in stopping those who do or protect those who are targeted. We will discuss more of the importance of bystanders in Chapter 16.

REINFORCING COGNITIVE EMPATHY AND KINDNESS

We are more likely to engage in behaviors we may feel uncertain about if we understand the rationale behind it. Children are naturally more altruistic than adolescents, primarily because they have not yet been exposed to the travails of life, which tend to teach them about the fickleness and questionable integrity of peers and adults. As we grow older, we discover that people do not always honor their words or do what they say they will. We learn about betrayal, one of the biggest factors to damage relationships. As these experiences happen, we begin to pull back from offering the kindness to others that we naturally extended as children. We grow more cautious in trusting others because we have learned to be skeptical, maybe even cynical, and that not everyone is honest or operates from the same level of altruistic motives.

Even though children are generally more charitable and kind, some children lose that innate ability to engage in empathic behaviors due to lack of opportunity or practice. They are not exposed to strong enough role models in their immediate environments to nurture that natural kindness, which is, as Hoffman (2000) reminds us, the way that we learn to "gain understanding and respond affectively to the circumstances, feelings, and wishes of . . . [others]" (p. 7). It is important to remember that few children or adolescents truly have not been exposed to empathy; instead, they have lacked the encouragement to practice it, which decreases the likelihood of them doing so. Use it or lose it.

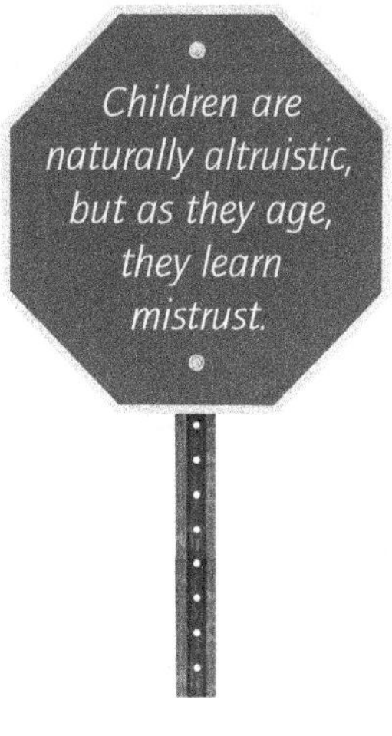

So when we encounter a child or adolescent who exhibits a ***softened sense of empathic abilities*** (please note how that is phrased to emphasize that the commonly termed *lack of empathy* is more a manifestation of the lack of receiving it and of having the nurturance to practice it), it is incumbent upon us to help determine their understanding of what it is, as well as to begin the process of practice. Some leads might include the following:

> *Do you remember a time in your life when someone acted in a kind way and helped you when you needed it? Can you tell me about what that was like for you?*
>
> *When we were younger, we often helped each other more than we do now. What do you think has changed to make it so that we don't do that as much today?*
>
> *We all have role models from whom we learn kindness. Are there people in your life that helped you learn kindness when you were younger? Will you share with me who those were and what it was that made them good role models for kindness?*
>
> *Who are the kind people in your life today?*
>
> *Everyone needs a helping hand now and then. When was the last time you helped someone? Tell me about how all of that came about.*
>
> *Let's talk a little bit about what you were thinking about when you wrote that stuff on your Facebook page about . . .*

The purpose of all of these leads is to start strengthening the cognitive empathic "muscles" in order to encourage individuals to think about how receiving and giving kindness relates to their past and current experiences. It is always easier to get an individual to *think* and *talk* about an action in a safe environment before she or he goes out and does it. Developing cognitive empathy, then, is the first step in helping individuals reengage their empathetic behavior capabilities.

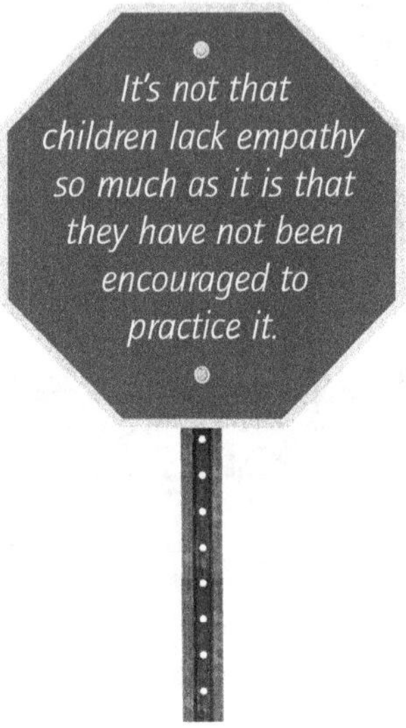

None of those leads address the aspect of affective empathy. That is purposeful in that what we often *act* on *feelings* without first *thinking* about the *consequences* of those actions. This is the basis behind rational-emotive behavioral therapy (REBT; Albert Ellis Institute, 2014; Ellis, 2011; Sharf, 2016), something that we explore in another chapter. When we act on affect, we often do not make the best decisions. An all-too-common exchange between supervisory personnel and a student goes like this: "*What* were you *thinking*?!?" "I didn't *think* about it, I just *did* it." Further evidence of how individuals often need to be reminded to slow down their *choosing*—and it is a choice—before acting on impulse.

The reason we avoided asking any leads related to affect is for that very reason. We want to steer clear of reinforcing actions based on emotion. That is not to say that we will not eventually return to addressing the connection between affect and its relevance to the actor, but not just yet. The best decisions are usually made through some sort of logic that can be explained so that a reasonable person (that same reasonable person back in Chapter 5) understands how the dots are connected to the behavior and avoid the "I didn't *think* about it, I just *did* it!" school of mistaken behavior.

REINFORCING AFFECTIVE EMPATHY

As we have discussed, children and adolescents tend to pull back from their natural altruism as they age. ***Amorality*** is a symptom of certain behavioral and mental health disorders. Although we may be challenged to think otherwise by their behaviors, few children are absolutely amoral. Likewise, few children or adolescents are truly nonempathic. They are more likely ***empathic-hesitant*** for many of the reasons we identified earlier. We still declare, however, that some children and adolescents "lack empathy." While some may well be ***emotionally hardened*** so as to not extend themselves to being helpful to others, the capacity to do so remains inherent in all but the most abused of souls.

Assuming, then, that we likely will not run across many children or adolescents who are truly either amoral or nonempathic, how do we help remind individuals how to get in touch with their ***natural affective empathy***? Actually, this may be one of the easier things to do because of the location of where emotions lie within our memory banks and everyday living—near the surface.

Kids talk about their emotional lives regularly. In many respects, their entire existence is one big seething mass of basic emotions, and those emotions can be accessed and acted upon intensely. If in doubt, talk to teenagers in the throes of their first true love—doesn't get much more intense than that. Those early experiences and understanding of happiness, sadness, surprise, fear, disgust, and anger[2] emerge from the family of origin, and those impressions, as with all early learning that develops from the home, create a basic template for whatever modifications will follow during the normal human development cycle. Of course, not all home experiences are pleasant ones, and not every child has the chance to experience basic emotions in ways that benefit healthy emotional interactions with others. However, because virtually all children have experienced the basic

---

2. There is new debate over exactly how many basic emotions there may be—six or seven. A study in 2014 postulated that two of the emotions may be combinations of others. See Jack, Garrod, and Schyns's (2014) "Dynamic Facial Expressions of Emotion Transmit an Evolving Hierarchy of Signals Over Time," *Current Biology, 24*, 1–6. However many there may be, the point remains the same—we learn to read other people via a template of basic emotions that we commonly share as a species.

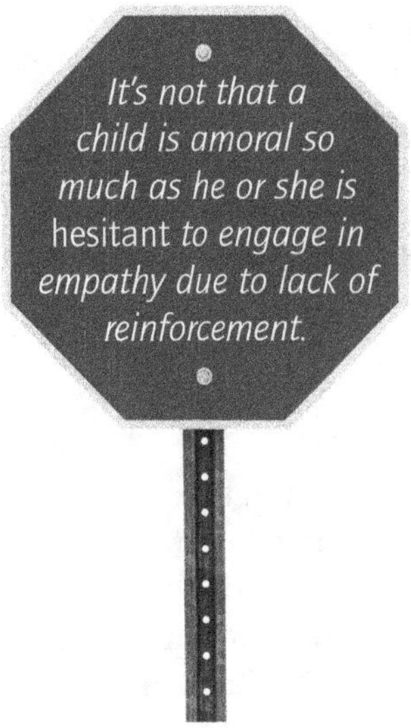

emotions to varying degrees, that becomes the foundation for our work in helping them remember their altruistic and empathic abilities with others.

When we encounter kids who seem reluctant to share empathy with others, it is helpful to use leads similar to the ones we used in helping them connect with cognitive empathy. The leads should, of course, be age appropriate in their phrasing. The templates offered here are designed to help get that part of the conversation going:

> *I need your help. The other day when you and Student B were involved in that incident in the hallway and he fell and hit his head, I got the impression that you didn't seem to care that he was hurt. Is that accurate on my part?*

> Choose whichever basic emotion is relevant for the situation: *When was the last time you felt happy/sad/surprised/afraid/mad/disgusted? What was going on when that happened?*

> Focusing on one particular basic emotion so as not to overwhelm the individual: *What makes you happy/sad/surprised/afraid/mad/disgusted?*

> Again, focusing on one particular basic emotion: *When you feel happy/sad/surprised/afraid/mad/disgusted, what do you do with that?*

> Continuing to focus on one particular basic emotion: *How often do you feel happy/sad/surprised/afraid/mad/disgusted?*

Each of these leads is searching for different aspects to the makeup of the individual's ***persona,*** or that part of our character that we allow others to see. We reveal our persona through our behaviors, but the persona that we show to others, of course, is only a small part of our true selves. When we share our viewpoints with others, such as through dialogue and conversation—if we are honest—we can reveal those hidden aspects that we normally keep to ourselves. But again, no matter what we *say* we think or feel, it is ultimately only through our *actions* that we give truth to our words.

So what do we have in these leads? First, one of the most important leads is the request for assistance: "I need your help." Those four words open more doors to understanding others than any directive or command with which we might hope to garner the same information. Asking for help ***equalizes power*** between two people and is an ***invitation of trust*** to whom it is offered. The metacommunication is "I am asking you to help me understand you better because it will help us as we move forward in what we are trying to accomplish." Without trust, the interaction will stall or stop, particularly when it involves needing the other party to be a part of helping to solve a problem.

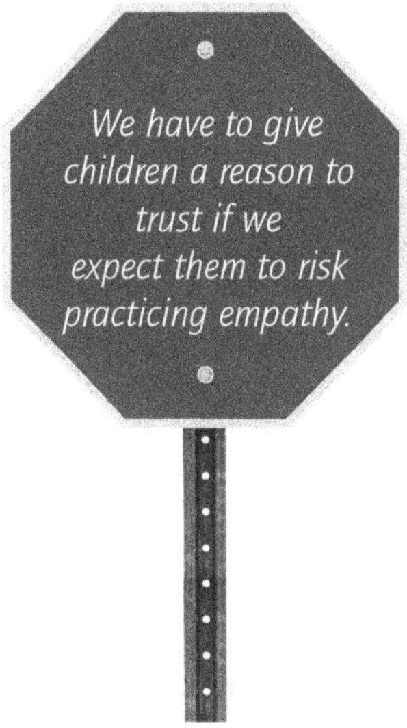

The rest of that first lead identifies what is confusing to the person making the inquiry. It is not an accusation when couched with the phrase "I got the impression . . ." It is not the same as the statement "You didn't care that he was hurt." The invitation is made to the student to help clarify the assumption that the Intervener has about what the behavior *seemed* to indicate. If the student reacts defensively to the inquiry, the Intervener can further clarify the nature of the impression: "No, I'm not saying that you didn't care, I'm saying that *I* couldn't tell exactly what you were thinking or feeling when it happened. That's what I'm trying to understand. That's what I need your help with."

Identifying when and what makes the individual feel a basic emotion is critical in creating a map of the individual's emotional world. Those with limited experiences with happiness and positive surprises are less likely to take the risks necessary to extend themselves to others when compared to those who experience happiness and positive surprises on a more regular basis. We need to discover what the basis for an emotion is for the individual. If the goodness that one finds in life comes from the misery of others, that is certainly a critical piece of information that we need as we move forward.

Interestingly, four basic emotions are related to negative life experiences (sadness, fear, anger, disgust). An argument might be made that five basic emotions could be negative if the surprises one experiences are not happy or joyful. Being surprised with the threat of harm would certainly not be considered either happy or joyful. Along with the fact that sadness, fear, disgust, and anger can be considered a negative experience, especially if they occur in large doses or are chronic in the life of the individual, they also tend to weigh more heavily on our emotional well-being than can be offset by happiness.[3] Children and adolescents whose lives are filled with these four negative emotions and do not have much opportunity to have happiness to offset the accumulative stressors associated with fear, sadness, disgust, and anger are more likely to view the world and act through those lenses.

The last lead in the previous examples has to do with helping to broaden the behavioral lens of what one *does* when he or she experiences a basic emotion. This becomes critical in determining how to structure

---

3. That is not to say that negative emotions should be always be viewed as negatives. There are times when fear, sadness, disgust, and anger are certainly appropriate, and their presence would be a marker of atypical behavior in a child or adolescent who did not show such emotions under the proper conditions. Specifically, it is healthy to show sadness during loss, and even anger is appropriate when wronged. How we manifest the behavioral component of those emotions, of course, is the key.

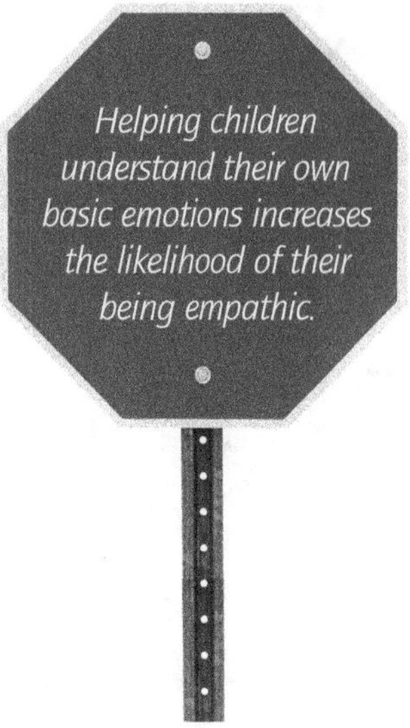

alternatives to negative behavioral reactions. If the responses to negative emotions show a negative pattern (e.g., they all involve some kind of physical outburst to level the emotional playing field), then that requires a different intervention than one in which only certain emotions elicit negative behaviors. We will see how this works in our sample dialogue at the end of this chapter.

FINDING THE LINK TO APPLYING EMPATHY TOWARD OTHERS

Now we come to the most important piece of the empathy puzzle: How do we get the individual who seems not to be empathic toward others to begin to be so?

If the student who chooses to bully understands the concept of how painful the experience can be, the big leap is to now connect and extend that conceptualization outward toward peers. That comes in stages, and like discovering whether or not the individual comprehends the concept of empathy, the first step toward that expansion will be to talk about what it might be to act in an empathic fashion to others.

We are hesitant to engage in actions and behaviors of which we are uncomfortable or have uncertainty when we don't know what the general outcome might be. If it's risky, we hesitate. As unexpected as it may seem, those who engage in bullying need a level of comfort and certainty that they will win in the risky behavior of which they engage, since what is likely at stake for them is a perceived (or real) loss of power. ***Role play*** is a powerful tool to encourage behaviors on the part of individuals, but role play is most effective when the actions and motives behind engaging in future behaviors in real life are first thoroughly discussed and practiced in a safe environment. This helps alleviate some of the uncertainties and decreases anxieties on the part of the people who are about to do something different or outside of their comfort zones. An individual who does not engage in empathy and who is about to do so for the first time will likely be anxious about doing so.

Here are some prompts that might prove helpful in starting that conversation toward encouraging the shift toward cognitive and behavioral empathy:

> *Have you ever thought of what it must be like to be on the receiving end of* [insert whatever bullying action was directed toward another]? *What do you think that might be like?*

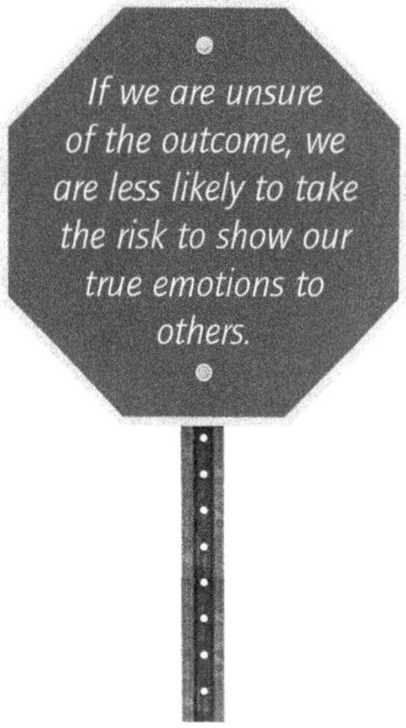

If someone were to do that [referencing the offending action] *to a friend of yours, what do you think she or he might feel?*

If someone were to do that [referencing the offending action] *to you, what might you feel?*

These three prompts go from the abstract directly to the personal. The first lead inquires about the individual's *thoughts* about an infraction happening to an unspecified other person. Notice that the emphasis is on thoughts, and the person to whom the injustice happened is unnamed. How the individual responds to this question can be quite revealing. First, an answer will reveal to some degree whether or not the individual has actually thought about what his or her actions might be like for another person. Second, who does the person choose to be the recipient of the improper behavior? Is it a generic boy or girl, or someone more readily identifiable and realistic? These answers are markers as to the depth of thought that the individual has expended at the point in time when the question is asked.

The second prompt brings bullying behavior closer to home, yet is still not specific to the agent of bullying. It continues to keep the behavior "out there" in the abstract. The question focuses on how a "friend" might respond to the behavior. Again, whom the student chooses to pick as that friend can be revealing. Is the person chosen a close friend or an imaginary one? Does the student indicate that he or she is friendless? Likewise, what is the reaction that is offered by the student on the friend's behalf? Is it similar to the agent of bullying's behavior? More intense? Less intense? All of these answers are indicative and revealing as to the mindset of the actor.

The last lead is intensely personal and may well be the most intimidating to the individual. The question focuses on the "you"—definitely not in the abstract—and about what the individual feels during an act of aggression against another. The agent of bullying may balk at answering this one because it holds the promise to be extremely revealing. If the individual does not feel safe or trust the Intervener, she or he may well choose to not answer the question or shut down the intervention. We can often talk about how others may feel to hypothetical situations in an abstract sense—which may well be the exact way we would respond to the real life scenario. But when you ask me in such a way that I have to acknowledge ***ownership to the action,*** I may clam up, shut down, or try to divert attention to another issue or person. I can talk about *you*, but maybe I can't talk about *me*. Or maybe I don't want to talk about me with you. Or maybe I don't actually know about me enough to be able to give an answer. All of these are possibilities.

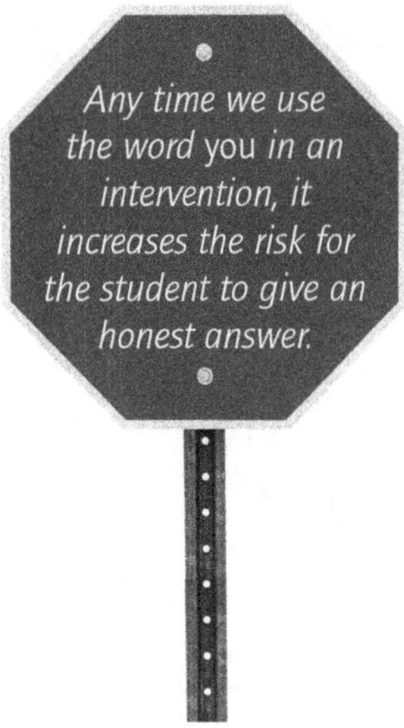

The object at this stage is to see if the individual who mistreats others is open to the possibility that one's actions may negatively impact or damage those to whom the action is directed. The amount of honesty toward that possibility is an important road map as to what direction the Intervener may need to go next.

A SAMPLE DIALOGUE ATTEMPTING TO LINK THE ACTIONS OF THOSE WHO BULLY WITH THE EXPERIENCES OF THEIR TARGETS

Intervener [I] 1: *Student A, good to see you again. We've had a good few weeks working together. I really appreciate all the effort you've put into making things better for both this thing with Student B* [SB] *and for yourself.*

Student A [SA] 1: *It's all good. We're making it work.*

I 2: *Yes, we are. I'm glad you feel that way. More importantly, you're the one making things work. You've shared a lot of yourself with me over the past few meetings that have helped me understand you much better than before. I appreciate that and your honesty. It's clear there's more to you than meets the eye, which, you know, is sometimes the only thing we judge about other people. I think that's been an issue for you, hasn't it, that the adults think they know you only by what they've seen of your behavior?*

SA 2: *Yeah, I guess that's right. I understand that better now.*

I 3: *Great. What I'd like us to do today is to have you help me understand even more about the way you see the world by asking a few questions. Like always, you can answer them if you want to, or not. Whatever. It's up to you, but because of what you've shared with me to this point, I think it's helped both of us understand each other's points of view better and get to where we are today.*

SA 3: *I'm OK with it. Whatever you want to ask.*

I 4: *Well, not all of it is about questions. Some of it will be sharing with you what we believe and practice here about treating each other fairly and with respect. You don't think I'd let you get out of here without trying to teach you something, do you?*

SA 4: [Laughs and smiles.] *No way. You do that to me all the time. You can't help yourself.*

I 5: [Laughs.] *I'm glad you feel that way about me. Seems as if we're understanding each other better each day we meet. When we started meeting four weeks ago, things were pretty tense between you and SB, you and me, and you and Ms. Vice Principal* [VP]. *It was kind of a mess. We started out making sure that you understood that everyone has to follow the rules and that we are going to do everything possible to keep this a safe place for everyone. Including you. And we talked about what would be best to try make things right with SB. What did we decide together on that?*

SA 5: *That I wouldn't apologize to him if I didn't really mean it because that would be a false apology, that not everything that's done to a person can be made right, and that when we do something wrong to one person we also send a message to everybody else that it's OK to do that stuff everywhere even though it's really not OK.*

I 6: *Excellent. And you remember that word for trying to make things right again for the people we wronged?*

SA 6: *Restoration.*

I 7: *Correct. Sounds like you remember things really well. More importantly, sounds like you've been practicing some of it. So here's what I'd like us to talk about today . . .*

I 7 A: *I'd really be interested in knowing more about how you get along with the world when things don't go your way, say, like when you're . . .* [Choose one of the basic emotions to explore. But choose only one so that the focus is on that emotion.]

or I 7 B: *I'm really interested in the things that happen to you or around you that make you . . .* [Again, choose one of the basic emotions to explore, but focus only on that emotion for the session.]

or I 7 C: *What do you do when you feel* [choose a basic emotion]? *What I mean by that is what goes through your head and your body when you feel* [the basic emotion under discussion]?

or	I 7 D: *We all feel certain things from time to time—anger, sadness, happiness, disgust. Sometimes we even are surprised by things. So how often do you feel* [pick one of the basic emotions] *in a* [day/week/month]*?*
SA 7:	[Responds to whichever question and emotion is chosen for focus in this particular session.]
I 8:	*Thank you for being so honest with me. It shows how hard you're working to try help me understand the way you see the world. Let me make sure that I'm hearing and understanding you accurately. You believe . . .* [Intervener summarizes the main points of what SA just said]. *Does that sound right?*
SA 8:	*That's pretty close. Except for this one part where you said . . .* [SA makes a slight correction in the Intervener's interpretation.]
I 9:	*Thanks for making that clearer for me. I want to be certain that I understand exactly what you're trying to say. Now I want to take a big risk with you and ask you a question that's really personal. Same rules apply—you don't have to answer if you don't want to, but—well, you know the rest.*
SA 9:	*It'll help you understand me better if I do.*
I 10:	[Chuckles.] *Right. You know how we adults are. Always trying extra hard to be understood.*
SA 10:	[Big laugh.] *Well, some of you do and some of you don't.*
I 11:	*I'll take it that you think I'm one of the ones that does.* [Grins, showing that he knows it's a joke.]
SA 11:	*You're all right for an old man.*
I 12:	*A compliment! I'll take it! So here's my risky question . . .* [Choose the one question most likely to make the most gains for the interaction at the moment.]
I 12 A:	*Have you ever thought about what it might be like to be treated like you treated SB in the cafeteria?*
or	I 12 B: *If someone did to a friend of yours what you did to SB in the cafeteria, how do you think that person would feel?*
or	I 12 C: *If someone had done to you what you did to SB the other day, what do you think you might have felt?*

WHAT JUST HAPPENED HERE?

There is a wealth of information to be gleaned from choosing any particular direction to take this sample dialogue.

First, the early part of the conversation serves as a method of ***checking for comprehension*** as to what the individual remembers and understands about previous topics covered between the two (SA 2, 5–6, 8). It also gives ***feedback*** in that it allows the Intervener to let the actor know how well his or her behaviors have been perceived by others since the intervention started. Both of these elements are extremely important. In the check for comprehension, we learn what main elements of the educational piece of the intervention the individual has retained. By giving feedback, we let the individuals know the type of benefits of both perception and reality they are receiving from their current change in behaviors (if any are, indeed, occurring). Feedback can provide reinforcement to people, encourage them to continue to move in a desired direction, or provide a message that the current behavior is not receiving the type of positive gains everyone hoped it would.

Another important element of checking for comprehension is that it allows the Intervener to understand exactly what and how the creator of the misbehavior interprets the intervention (SA 5–6). In this instance, Student A is showing not only that he understands the *content* of the conversation (e.g., SA 6), but also the *intent* of the larger lesson (SA 5). Often during interventions, fear, suspicion, and mistrust may prevent an individual from truly hearing the metacommunication of the conversation. In this scenario, there seems to be a higher level of trust between the two parties, as evidenced by exchanges of good-natured humor (SA 4, 10–11, I 10–12). Neither the Intervener nor the student is acting in a defensive manner. A level of trust has been created.

A major aspect of checking for comprehension and providing feedback is that the feedback goes both ways. Not only can we let the agents of misbehavior understand how we view their efforts (or nonefforts) to change, but we can also alter our direction with an intervention if we discover that something needs to be tweaked. The classic example of a ***redirection of intervention*** occurs when Student A lets the Intervener know that the Intervener's interpretation of what Student A said in one instance was only partially correct (I 8–9, SA 8). Armed with that new information, the Intervener can *more effectively respond to the needs of the child* by addressing misinformation or misinterpretation on either party's behalf.

UNDERSTANDING THE LOGIC OF THE AGENTS OF BULLYING

If we don't take the time or make the effort to understand the thought processes of those who act aggressively toward others, we are missing the point of this entire book. And the starting point for doing that is continual efforts to engage the agent of bullying in discussions about what motivates them to do so.

What follows is a continuation of the conversation between the Intervener and Student A. This meeting follows an interaction between Student A and his peers in which questions were raised about the appropriateness of the behavior, a setback in the forward progress that had been made until this incident. Student A is not as agreeable as he was in the last interaction. However, for the sake of trying to move forward and not get stuck on the most recent incident, the Intervener has chosen to try steer the conversation back to the positive decisions that Student A has been making.

I 1: *Student A, thanks for coming down again to see me. What is this, the third or fourth time we've met now?*

SA 1: *Yeah. I guess. If you say so.*

I 2: *I talked to Ms.* VP *right before we met just to see how things have been going for you and* SB *the last few days. She says things have been better. There haven't been any incidents that have come across her desk, and the rest of your teachers seem to think that things have quieted down between the two of you. But there was something that came up yesterday between you and some of your classmates. You want to talk about that?*

SA 2: *Yeah, well, I don't have much choice in the matter now, do I?*

I 3: *We've talked about that before. We always have choices in our actions. We just have to make the decision to act on the right ones.*

SA 3: *Whatever you say.*

I 4: *It's clear you've made decisions over the last week to avoid having problems with SB. That's a choice that you made. We didn't make it for you. You could have decided to do whatever you felt like and go back to pestering him, but for some reason, you decided not to. I, for one, appreciate that, and I'm pretty sure SB does, too. And whatever it was that happened yesterday apparently died down pretty quickly. What is it that's different now?*

SA 4: *I don't want to get booted out of school.*

I 5: [Waits to see if SA offers any additional reasons. He doesn't.] *That certainly sounds reasonable to me. But again, you've made the decision to follow the rules set up to keep you from being suspended. You. Made. That.*

Decision. You had and have a choice, and you've chosen to avoid something that you don't want to happen to you—getting booted out of school.

SA 5: *Like I said, I don't have much choice.*

I 6: *SA, we've spent the last few meetings talking about what we need to do to keep you in school. I would really like to know a little more about what you think about all of this stuff and how we can make it better for everyone so that you don't get into trouble again, and everyone in school feels safe about being here. You game to give that a try?*

SA 6: *Depends.*

I 7: *Let's give it a shot. And you don't have to answer anything if you don't want to, but if we talk a bit about how you see the world, it might help me understand you better.*

SA 7: *Whatever.*

At this point, the Intervener can choose whichever prompt seems most relevant from this chapter to continue the conversation.

I 8: *You know, when I was a kid, I know that there were times when people helped me out when I needed a helping hand. That ever happen for you?*

SA 8: [Looks at the Intervener, but doesn't say anything. Unclear if he's thinking of an example or trying to figure out if he can trust the direction that the exchange is about to go.]

I 9: *Not everyone was kind to me, but enough were to make a difference in my life. I can't help but think that there must be somebody in your life who helped you out a time a two when you needed it.*

SA 9: [Still silent. The Intervener gives SA the silence he needs to decide whether or not he wants to answer.] *Yeah, maybe.*

I 10: [Gives SA a chance to continue and waits patiently to let him take the lead.]

SA 10: *Yeah, when I was in elementary school, there were lots of people down there who seemed like they cared.*

I 11: *When we're younger, we often help each other more than we do when we get older. Why do you think that is?*

SA 11: *I think the older we get, the more we forget about what it's like to be a kid.*

I 12: *What do you mean by that?*

SA 12: *When we get older, we get meaner because we have to. Not everybody's as kind as they used to be. We're not little kids anymore, and we have to be tougher to survive.*

I 13: *I hear that a lot from people. But you mean nobody's kind to you at all today?*

SA 13: *Not many. Well, yeah, I mean, I've got friends, but they're not all kind.*

I 14: *Help me understand that.*

SA 14: [SA provides some examples to the Intervener that are helpful in describing what his experience is like among his peers. It includes information on the most recent incident.]

I 15: *Wow. That explains a lot. And I guess that's a part of the reason why you responded the way you did to SB that day in the cafeteria. You thought he was going to do something to embarrass you in front of your friends like some of them have done to you in the past. And some of them tried to do yesterday before you walked away.*

SA 15: *You got it. He's no real friend of mine, and I wasn't about to give him a chance to do that. I have to put up with it from my friends but I don't have to put up with it from him.*

I 16: *SA, I think I understand much better what you were thinking that day. And I presume you also understand what we've been talking about over the past couple of weeks as to why you can't treat SB or anybody else the way you two have been getting along—or rather, not getting along—here at school.*

SA 16: *I get it. I don't like it, but I get it.*

I 17: *We don't have to like everything that we have to do; we just sometimes have to learn how to get along for the sake of getting along for the good of everybody. You know, if you and SB or anybody else can't get along, then you can just agree to disagree over whatever it is that you disagree on and not have anything to do with one another. Do you understand that "agree-to-disagree" thing I just said?*

SA 17: *You mean that we can just disagree with each other, but leave one another alone and let it be.*

I 18: *Exactly. Just let each of you be who you are, and go on about your business without messing with one another. Can you do that?*

SA 18: *I can try.*

I 19: *Well, that's a better place than where we were a few weeks ago.*

WHAT JUST HAPPENED HERE?

Here is what has transpired in that last session.

The opening of the dialogue was designed to ***keep the conversation as relaxed as possible*** (I 1), especially in light of the recent setback. Student A was welcomed and approached in a manner that was ***nonconfrontational.***

Much of the tension from the immediate aftermath of the initial incident has been reduced at this point—at least, that is the optimum objective—even though it is apparent that Student A seems to have something bothering him and is not as cooperative as in the last meeting (SA 1–8). Some type of relationship, even if it is a cautious one, should have developed between the Intervener and Student A if this approach is working. ***Patience*** is key during these types of interventions with kids who tend to be suspicious of adult motives and who may, in fact, view the world from an aggressive and defensive stance (SA 2–8, 12–13, 15). As long as the actor is following the rules, improving behavior, and not creating mayhem, we have to be willing to give one the time necessary and required to make a major ***cognitive shift*** (Beck & Weishaar, 2011, p. 277) within. A cognitive shift is a change in the way an individual views and thinks about the world (the ***worldview***; see reference to Glasser's works at end of chapter) in which she or he lives (Sharf, 2016), which is, along with the all-important behavioral change piece, one of the ultimate goals of making the effort to intervene with the actor. This is a delicate balancing act in which both parties are learning how to dance with the other, yet one in which the Intervener, ultimately, has the lead in the direction the dance will go (I 4–7). The partner in this metaphorical dance, remember, may not be so willing to follow that lead, which is the main reason why patience is in order when working with those who are used to being in charge and not having to surrender their power.

Feedback is presented on how Student A's behaviors have been viewed since the last session (I 2, 4). Student A was also reminded that it is *his* decision and choice as to whether or not to follow the rules in order to stay in school (I 4–5). ***Encouragement*** is key here. He is supported in his efforts to both follow the rules and in *his* choosing to make the decisions necessary to do so. It may seem counterintuitive to talk of encouraging an agent of bullying, but the focus of the encouragement is on the behaviors we want to support and increase, not the negative ones. ***Positive reinforcement of target behaviors*** is one of the primary foundations of the Positive Behavioral Intervention Strategies (PBIS) approach (PBIS World.com, 2012; US Department of Education Office of Special Education Programs Technical Assistance Center on Positive Behavioral Interventions and Supports, n.d.), particularly as it relates to interventions in the bullying continuum (Stiller, Nese, Tomlanovich, Horner, & Ross, 2013).

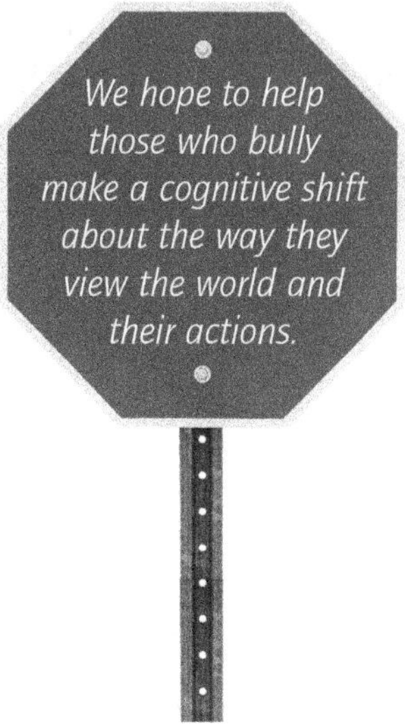

The session begins to turn more personal after the review and feedback of recent behavioral changes. The Intervener steers the conversation to Student A's personal world and perceptions with his entreaty to him to get to know "a little more about what you think about all this stuff" (I 6–7). There is no guarantee that the actor will accept the invitation to delve into those inner thoughts and feelings. Student A could have shut down at that point, but he chose not to due to the strength of the growing relationship between him and the Intervener. If the individual backs away from going in a particular direction, it is an indication that she or he is not ready to go there, that the trust level is not yet high enough. The individual may choose to never allow the Intervener to "go personal" out of the desire to prevent exposure of vulnerabilities, out of the rejection of the process, or as an act of rebellion against the intervention or Intervener. When this happens, more patience is in order if time and current behaviors allow for it. If not, then the intervention may come to a grinding halt. It's up to the choices that the individual makes in tandem with the skill of the Intervener to convince the agent of bullying why it is in one's best interest to continue working the process.

The Intervener uses ***self-disclosure*** to begin moving into the more risky private world of the individual (I 8–9). Self-disclosure is an extraordinarily powerful tool in intentional interviewing when used properly, but cautions are in order. While we want the individuals with whom we are dealing to disclose what is going on in *their* heads, what is going on in *ours* is (1) not necessarily important and (2) not the focus of the intervention. Because it is so powerful in shaping the direction of an interview or conversation, self-disclosure should be used sparingly and only if relevant to helping assist the actor in moving forward toward self-discovery. When the Intervener uses self-disclosure, suddenly the focus of the conversation turns to the discloser, and those who are master manipulators are more than willing to escape through the door of someone else's disclosure if it takes the pressure off discussing their issues. The phrase *when I was a kid* can also send a message that *our* experiences are more important *theirs*. Our experiences should not overwhelm and cloud the current experience of the person we are trying to help. Sharing should be a near-equal experience. When we use the ***language of equity***, we are trying to convey to another that we may have experienced something in common—not that our and their experience is the same, only that we have both "been in the neighborhood" of an experience, and because of that, we may be able to find common ground on which to navigate our current and future conversations.

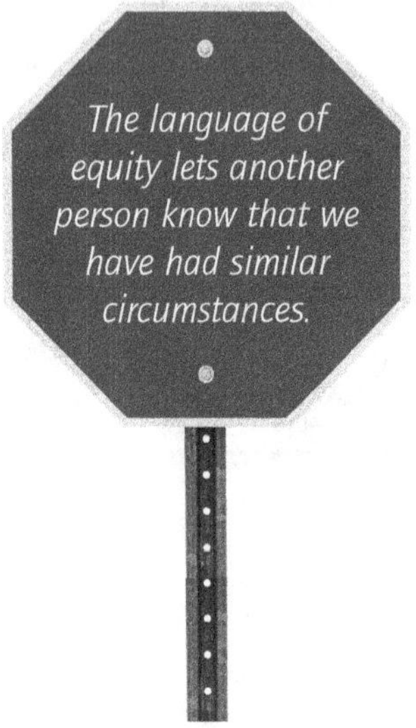

Silence was also used in this conversation as a method of encouraging additional disclosure on the part of Student A (I 10). Silence in conversation and problem solving can be interpreted in different ways, based on how it has been used with an individual in the past. Unfortunately, silence is all too often used as a weapon of passive-aggressiveness to show disapproval or as a tool of intimidation. It is often taught to us that way in our families of origin. When a parent disapproved of our behavior, we got the silent treatment, something we didn't forget (and then make the mistake of passing it along to our children).

Silence has another powerful use in conversations about difficult or awkward subjects, that being to give people the opportunity and option to think and formulate a response to the topic being discussed. The Intervener in this dialogue (SA 9 and I 10) is "backing off" of peppering the student with too much information or too many questions. It sends an unspoken metacommunication to Student A from the Intervener that "I want to hear what you have to say" and "I'm willing to give you the time to figure out what and how you want to say it." This is important in helping build a bond with kids who may be distrustful of our motives since they are used to being bombarded with the "blahblahblahblah" of supervisory personnel all throughout their school lives. Even when we ask for their opinion, we seldom give them the chance to actually give it to us.

Because the Intervener was patient and used silence effectively, the student eventually offered a response about who he viewed as helpful from the past (SA 10). That allowed the Intervener to then press forward with a follow-up statement and questions (I 11–12), which the student felt secure enough in answering (SA 11–12).

Student A's answers to the questions related to why he believed that kids are less kind as they get older reveal the all-important worldview. His metacommunication is that, as his peers get older, they have had to engage in behaviors that are designed to survive in his world (SA 12–15). This is a common perception held among individuals who bully others: It's a dog-eat-dog world out there; therefore, I have to do unto others before they do it to me. This mindset creates ***perceptual flaws*** that see other people's actions as being designed to be harmful whether they really are or not—remember the faulty logic of the reactionary target–agent? Student A's reasoning, however, is not to be assumed to apply to every individual who bullies others. Some just do it from an abuse of power position and the thrill of it.

The Intervener's response to Student A's rationale is not one of ***challenge*** or ***confrontation*** (I 13–16), but one of trying to convince him that he has heard what the student had to say. What good would it do for trust building if you ask people a question about a personal experience or opinion, they give it to you, and then you criticize it? That won't do much to build trust. ("Here, kitty, kitty, kitty . . ." WHACK!?! Nope, I won't be trusting you ever again.) If trust is going to be created between the Intervener and someone who is mistrustful of authority figures, the Intervener must

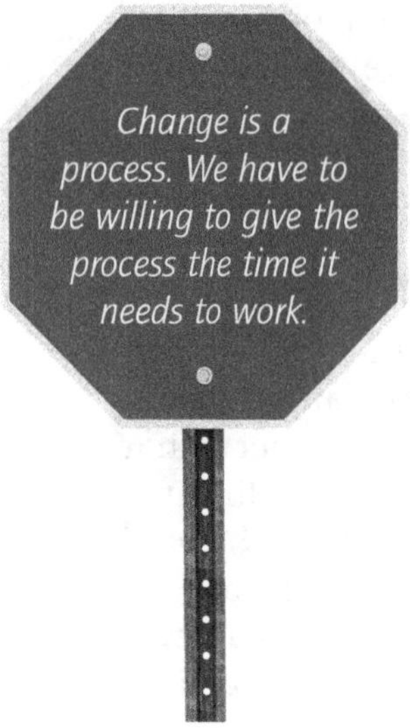

be honest and genuine in honoring the questions asked. If the formula works and trust continues to build, there will be plenty of time for conversations about changing misguided behaviors in the days and weeks to come. *This is a* ***process***. Change of long-ingrained behaviors does not occur overnight. The best tools we have at our disposal are ***patience*** and ***time***.

We have to be willing to be patient and put in the time with those that we might prefer not to while the change occurs. *They* have to also be willing to put in the time and effort in making the changes that are necessary to break or modify the behavior patterns causing the problem in the first place.

This section of the ongoing dialogue with Student A closes with points that are emphasized for him to remember. The Intervener assures him that he has a better understanding of the basis for his prior actions (I 16); the student is reminded that it is acceptable to disagree with others as long as it is done in a socially acceptable manner (I 17–18); and he is encouraged, again, as in the session's beginning (I 2), that what he has done in the past few weeks is the direction that the Intervener believes will be most helpful to Student A (I 19).

In summary, the session opened with a positive and closed with a positive. There was information exchanged between both the Intervener and the individual, which was reacted upon by both parties without raising the tension or mistrust levels. No challenge or confrontation was used or needed to stress a particular viewpoint by either individual. They both seem as if they are hearing each other at a level that will allow a continuing dialogue in the future, which is exactly what we want in order to increase the chances of successful change in the student.

WANT TO LEARN MORE?

Choice therapy (formerly called control or reality therapy) is an approach designed by William Glasser in the late 1960s and 1970s to assist clients to "resolve the discrepancy [between what is wanted and what is actually needed], to put the scale back in balance [and help the individual understand that] individual choices . . . generate behavior(s)" (Wubbolding et al., 2004). It has a long history of application in K–12 educational settings and is highly relevant for use with those who bully by assisting them to understand that because their behavior is a choice and decision they make, they can also make the conscious decision to *not* behave in that fashion.

12

Thought Before Action

Slowing Down Impulsive Behaviors

One of the central characteristics of those who choose to bully others is the lack of forethought about the consequences. Most times it is a matter of ***impulse*** or ***reactivity***—the desire to strike back at someone who has, in the aggressor's view, committed an infraction. The behavior is reactionary and knee-jerk, often driven by an intensity of emotion that drives the response. This is a characteristic of logic peculiar to the agent.

When affect drives a behavior, cognition is generally on the losing end. It's two against one, and even when cognition is brought into the equation to temper a behavior, affect often outweighs it. Adolescents, in particular, are filled with emotions that find an outlet in impulsive behaviors. However, before we adults forget, all of us are prone to acting in impulsive ways if we do not have the skills to stop and think before we act. And thinking is exactly what has to be done in order to help curb the all-too-expedient urge to get immediate satisfaction or retribution for a perceived wrong in the heat of the moment.

UNDERSTANDING RATIONAL AND IRRATIONAL THOUGHT

Humankind has long recognized that we tend to not see things as they really are, particularly when emotions are involved. The Greek philosopher Epictetus is said to have observed that "men are disturbed, not by things, but by the principles and notions which they form concerning things. . . . An uninstructed person will lay the fault of his own bad condition upon others" (from the *Enchiridion*, circa 135 CE). The desire to blame others for our own misfortunes or be blind to our own creation of our miseries is ancient. One would think and hope that by today we would be intelligent enough to know and act better, but such is clearly not the case, as evidenced by the many ineffective behaviors we continue to engage in as a species.

There is a relatively easy solution—at least on paper—to responding impulsively from an affective state, and that is to insert cognition into the equation before the behavior. This is the basis behind the work of Albert Ellis's (1962, 2011) ***rational emotive behavior therapy*** (REBT).[1] Here is a simplified explanation of an REBT-like approach to addressing impulsive behaviors, along with some like-minded viewpoints to help us understand how our thoughts influence our behaviors.

1. Originally called rational therapy (RT) and later rational emotive therapy (RET).

A QUICK REBT PRIMER

We all have a basic view of the world that emerges from our family of origins and our interactions with the environment—remember Glasser's worldview that we introduced in the last chapter? Within that worldview, we develop a system of beliefs about what things mean and the basis behind the way our worldview evolves. These ***schemas*** (Beck & Weishaar, 2011), originally identified by Aaron Beck, shape the way we interpret whatever happens to us, regardless of whether or not it is reality. Schemas can be both positive or negative. ***Negative schemas*** are the ones that create problems for us and everyone else in our presence. Metaphorically, if we go about life with "dirt" on our "glasses," then we see the world with muddy lenses every time it rains. Our "cup" of happiness is always half empty, never half full. We are the personification of Winnie the Pooh's Eeyore: "End of the road . . . nothing to do . . . and no hope of things getting better. Sounds like Saturday night at my house" (Geurs & Shay, 1997).

REBT holds that, like Epictetus, we act and react based on the views we hold of the world around us. The beliefs under which we operate serve as the primary interpretative filter for our decisions. No matter what the actual event is that occurs, if our belief system views it as negative or a threat, we will respond to it in that manner.

A few simple illustrations of Ellis's REBT are included to show how we can end up acting out of proportion to an actual event. REBT's use of simple A-B-C analogies make it very useful in explaining the process to children and adolescents, and its simple explanation increases its applicability by both therapeutic and nontherapeutic personnel. In this instance, the letter *A* refers to an ***activating event***; letter *B* refers to the ***belief system*** in which an individual operates (similar to Glasser's worldview and Beck's schema); and the letter *C* refers to the ultimate behavior, or ***consequence***, as a result of responding to the activating event through an impulsive and skewed affective belief system.

It makes no difference what the actual activating event was. If we react purely through a faulty affective belief system, then the resultant behavior,

Figure 12.1 The A-B-C Model of Ellis's Rational Emotive Behavior Therapy

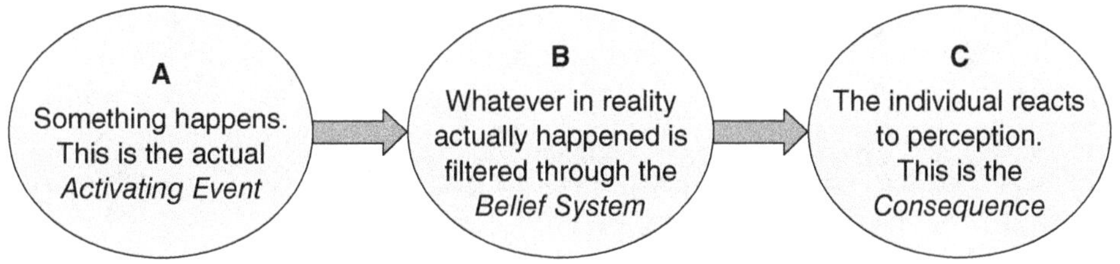

the consequence, will be based on affect and not logic. Let's go back to Student A's reaction to Student B in the event that came to light in the cafeteria and see how REBT might be applied to the intervention.

USING AN REBT APPROACH WITH STUDENT A

For some reason, Student A (SA) began to dislike Student B (SB) several months earlier. Perhaps it was based on a misinterpreted exchange of words or peer misinformation. Whatever the case, at some point, the relationship between SA and SB soured, and SA made the *choice* to view any and all of SB's comments and behaviors from that point forward through a negative filter. SA held a negative belief system about SB. Again, this was a *choice* that SA made, although he may well have had reinforcement of his ideas from peers who wanted to generate hostility between the two. A belief system can hold both ***rational*** and ***irrational*** thoughts. If an individual's belief system is based on reality—in this instance, if SB's negative beliefs about SA were based on some type of actual mistreatment that SB had inflicted upon him—then perhaps SA would have been justified in holding a negative belief system about SB. Unfortunately, we tend to hold on to negative interpretations of others as a form of safeguarding ourselves from future hurt. We have to learn to let go of our suspicions (irrational thinking) and make decisions based on fact (rational thinking). REBT helps us to learn how to do that.

But it is not the belief system alone that created the problem between SA and SB. Our beliefs and opinions may make us grumpy and miserable inside, but remember, it is only when we *act* on the basis of those beliefs that a problem may occur. I may dislike you, you may dislike me, and that is entirely acceptable in the grand scheme of things as long as our behaviors toward each other are civil and tolerable. Perhaps the most civil and tolerable thing we can do in that instance is just avoid having anything to do with one another. Not only do we agree to disagree, but we can also agree to stay away from each other if that is what is best for the good of the order and to keep the peace. The problem in Kid World is that there is hardly any way for one individual to get away from another anymore, not at school and, today, not even at home with the encroachment of cyberspace through the fiber-optic keyhole.

However, SA acted on his negative belief system about SB while in the cafeteria. SA was seated at a table with his friends when SB walked by and accidently bumped into him from behind, causing SA to spill his drink on himself. SB tried to apologize, but before he could, SA was up off his seat, yelling and pushing SB back, which caused him to drop his tray, spilling food everywhere. There were no punches exchanged, but it might well have escalated to that point if supervisory personnel in the immediate area had not broken up the fracas by prompt action.

So what was going on in the cognition, affect, and behavior of SA during that incident? The only way we will know is if we spend the time to engage him in an REBT-type analysis and exploration of just that. And when we do, here is what we find using the A-B-C model of an REBT approach.

The activating event is what actually happened. It is *reality*. What happens from this point on, however, will be based on how SA *perceives* what occurred.

Figure 12.2 The Activating Event

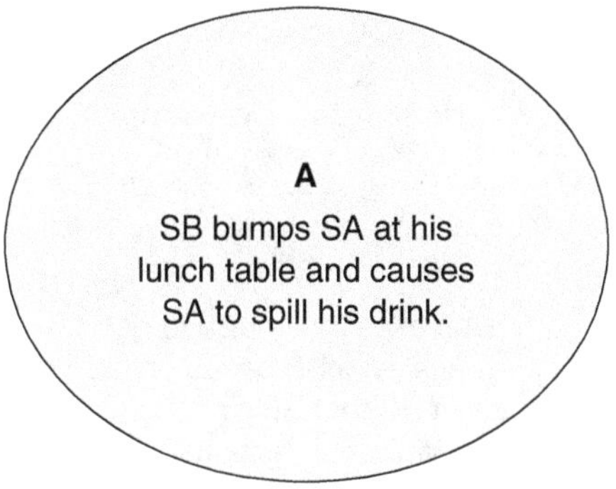

SA interprets SB's bumping him as intentional, based on his *belief* that SB dislikes him as much as he dislikes SB. There is no basis in fact for this *assumption,* as SB has tried to avoid SA since their dispute started weeks ago. SA's belief system at this time does not allow him to assume any other motive for the bump. His thought pattern is geared toward the negative, based on his dislike for SB and his desire to view any of SB's behaviors as negative. These are irrational thoughts in reality but not in SA's mind at the time of the incident. For SA, the incident is viewed with malicious intent. For SA, SB's bump is a *confirmation* of his reality because of the belief system that SA holds.

Figure 12.3 Student A's (Faulty) Belief System

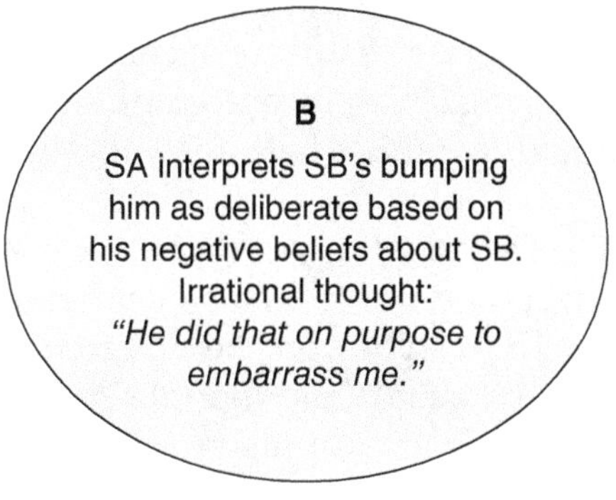

SA's behavior, his pushing SB, was the consequence of a faulty belief system that viewed SB's bumping him as verification of what SA wanted to believe about SB. If SA was looking for a reason to fight or otherwise engage in some type of intimidating behavior toward SB, the accident in the cafeteria certainly provided that opportunity and excuse due to SA's negative filter. No matter what SB might say in the form of an apology, at that moment, SA was going to hear none of it or view it as sincere. In SA's mind, because of his negative belief system, SB had just proven all the nasty assumptions SA had been carrying around in his head about him.

Figure 12.4 Student A's Consequential Decision

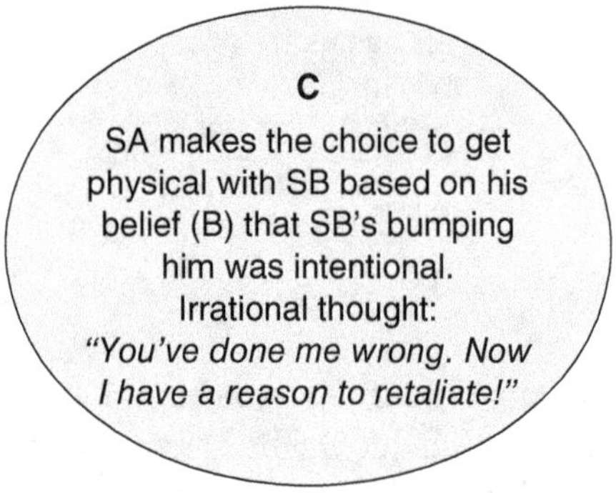

LEARNING NEW WAYS OF BEHAVING—STTA: STOP. THINK. THEN ACT.

What Student A must be helped to learn is to not act on the first impulse that comes to him when faced with a situation that might have negative consequences. He has to learn to think before he acts, rather than act on the emotion that is most convenient. In essence, he has to change his current emotive-behavioral pattern. To do so, we must help him understand what he is currently doing to both himself and others when he allows himself to act (behavior) on impulse (emotion/affect) and not from a cooler head (logic/cognition).

This can be done best by first talking with SA about exactly what his thought processes are when he engages in an impulsive act. One of the most helpful of leads is one of the most obvious:

When you and [Name] *were involved in that incident the other day, what were you thinking when you* [insert the action of the individual]?

The answer given provides insight into how impulse driven the behavior may have been. The standard variation (so often heard)—"I didn't think about it. I just did it"—indicates a highly impulse-driven motive for a behavior. An answer in the neighborhood of "I thought about not doing it, but then went ahead and did it anyway, because . . ." is indicative of an individual who is closer to the direction that we want our impulsive people to move.

In SA's case, it will be helpful to explain to him in language that is developmentally appropriate about the basic concepts of the REBT A-B-C model of behavior. Draw it out on paper, on a whiteboard, or a SMART board, but do draw it out. It helps to visualize what is occurring when the explanation is being provided so that it more fully can be remembered with the student.

The critical element now becomes helping SA understand a method of moving toward a more cognitive and rational approach to problem solving, one that does not ignore the affective component of his experience, but puts a stopgap in place to slow the expediency of responding on impulse. It is time now to introduce the "Stop. Think. Then Act." approach (STTA). STTA can be pronounced as "stay" to further help the individual remember the acronym when needed the most, as well as providing an internal prompt to stop and think before acting.

The purpose of STTA is to *slow down the impulsivity of reacting immediately* to an activating event. It is designed to increase the chances of cognition coming into play before a behavior is undertaken. Explaining STTA comes into play after there is evidence that the individual understands the A-B-C model of behavior. A sample dialogue introducing STTA might go like this:

A SAMPLE DIALOGUE INTRODUCING STTA

Intervener [I] 1: *SA, you've done really well explaining to me how you understand this A-B-C stuff we've been doodling with here over the last few minutes. It's clear to me that you get the ideas of the problems that can happen when we do things because we are simply reacting to too much feeling rather than thinking about things before we do them.*

Student A [SA] 1: *It's not that hard to understand.*

I 2: *Whether it is or not, you've done well in convincing me that you understand it. Now I think you're ready to move forward to learn the ways to start doing it.*

SA 2: [Says nothing for awhile.] *What's the catch?*

I 3: *No catch. It's just something simple to help you figure out a way to maybe not act on your gut before you have a chance to think about the consequences of your actions.*

SA 3: *So what do I have to do?*

I 4: *For now, just talk through it with me and see if it makes sense to you. Game?*

SA 4: *Might as well. You're just full of all sorts of things for me to remember, aren't you?*

I 5: *As long as you're working the program and continuing to show improvement, I don't see any reason to stop now. Here's how this next part works. It's called "Stop. Think. Then Act." Some people call it STTA or "stay" for short, just to help them remember it.*

SA 5: *Well, it's not spelled that way.*

I 6: *Nope, but sometimes we try to remember things with little memory tricks to make it easier for us to use when we need it. Here's how it works. It's really simple. The next time you find yourself in a situation with someone you don't like, don't do anything. Just stop—stay. There's the "Stop" part of STTA, get it? Just stop and figure out what exactly is going on. Listen to what is really being said by the other person—remember that A-B-C stuff we talked about earlier? This is where you're going to actually see and hear what is happening instead of just reacting to it. Are you with me so far?* [Stopping along the way during descriptions of new activities or explanations of new concepts to check for comprehension is critical before moving forward. If things need to be explained again or clarified, this is an opportunity where that can be done.]

SA 6: *I'm not stopping if somebody's about to hit me. That's crazy talk.* [Laughs.] *That's some of that irrational stuff we were talking about a while ago.*

I 7: [Smiles with SA at his use of the concept of the A-B-C model to justify his current thinking.] *Well, that's not exactly the point I was trying to make. I'm not talking about if you're being attacked by someone else. Let's use what happened with you and Student B [SB] in the cafeteria. That's probably a better example. When SB bumped into you at your table that day, what did you think?*

SA 8: *That he did it on purpose to make me spill my milk.*

I 9: *I can see where you might assume that based on the way you've told me you used to think about your relationship with SB. But in reality, what was all that you could truly know in that moment when you felt that bump and the milk went all over the place?*

SA 9: [Looks skeptical, but is thinking.] *Well, all I could really tell was that somebody had bumped me—I didn't even know who it was until I turned around—and that my milk went flying out of my hand and down my shirt.*

I 10: *Right. Exactly. All you knew for certain was that someone had bumped you and the milk went all over you and that it was a mess.*

SA 10: *And that SB did it on purpose.*

I 11: *You didn't know that for certain at the time, did you? And we've discovered that that wasn't the case, was it? Let's think about that a minute. Now that we're applying the Stop in STTA, let's move into the "Think" part. You assumed at the time that SB bumped you on purpose to make you spill your milk, but you didn't know that for a fact, right?*

SA 11: *Well, yeah, but it doesn't take a genius to figure out what was happening. Or could have been happening—or what I thought was happening.* [It's clear that SA is still trying to validate his response to SB that day, but the STTA formula has begun to make him begin to doubt his irrational thinking and assumptions.]

I 12: *But let's stay focused on what was really happening and what you could have figured out if you had allowed yourself the time to use that Stop phase of STTA to Think about things. If you would have stopped to take the time to understand everything that had happened, what exactly would you have learned when you turned around and saw that it was SB that had bumped you? Talk it out step by step, as if it was a series of photographs.*

SA 12: [Is quiet as he recalls the incident.] *I saw SB behind me out of the corner of my eye.* [Pauses as he thinks more.] *I felt the milk all over me. I heard SB saying, "I'm so sorry, I'm so sorry, it was an accident!" I heard people laughing. And then I stood up and pushed him.*

I 13: *Let's take out the pushing part because that's where the train ran off the tracks for you. If you hadn't pushed SB because you assumed he bumped you on purpose, all you really knew was just exactly what you described before that moment: Somebody bumped into you, which caused you to spill your milk all over the place, you turned around and SB was right behind you apologizing. That's it. That's all you really knew for certain. You didn't know if SB had done it on purpose or not. You can't read somebody's mind. That was your assumption.*

SA 13: *I had my reasons for thinking that way.*

I 14: *That's that irrational thinking stuff. Was your assumption that he had done it on purpose really the truth this time?*

SA 14: *Not according to him.*

I 15: *You don't believe SB after everything he's told us about his view of things?*

SA 15: [Doesn't want to say what he is about to say.] *Sort of. Maybe yeah. I guess. I don't know.*

I 16: *I think that you believe now that he really didn't mean to bump into you that day and that it really was an accident. So now let's take just the facts of what we know and do some of that Think in that STTA stuff to see how things might have gone another way. If you had stopped and thought about exactly what had just happened in the cafeteria, how might that have changed what you ultimately did to SB?*

SA 16: [Still doesn't want to admit that he might have been able to respond differently to SB.] *I might not have done it.*

I 17: *You "might not have done it." I believe that. And you might not have done it because . . . ?*

SA 17: *Because maybe I would have just thought about what was really happening instead of what I thought SB meant to do.*

I 18: *Right. Because you would have thought before you acted. And when we think before we act, we are more likely to make a positive decision based on facts and not assumptions. Those assumptions can get us into trouble because they're not always based on reality; they're often based on the things we want to believe about people because we don't take the time to get to know them better or because we decide we just don't like them. Does any of this make sense to you?*

SA 18: *I guess it does.*

I 19: *Can you tell me in your own words what all of this stuff we've talked about today means to you?*

SA 19: [Pauses to collect his thoughts. The Intervener gives him the time and space to do so.] *It means that sometimes we do things that we shouldn't because we think that something is happening when it's not and that maybe what we need to do is stop and think about what we're about to do before we do it.*

I 20: *Because . . . ?*

SA 20: *Because when we do things without thinking we sometimes don't make the best decisions.*

I 21: *Excellent! You nailed it! Right on target. I think you've done a lot of good work today, SA. You've cooperated with me in an honest way to try learn about what happens when we act before we know all the facts and before thinking about what those actions might mean to others. This has been a really good day for you—and us. Let's set up a time to meet again to see how things are going, OK?*

WHAT JUST HAPPENED HERE?

This was a pivotal day for Student A (and my wish for all of us is that we have this kind of breakthrough success during interventions with those who choose to bully others on multiple occasions). What has happened to make this meeting with him so successful?

Student A has made the conscious decision to work the program. While he has shown signs of skepticism and resistance at points along the way (SA 2, 6, 11), he has basically not made too many efforts to avoid the process designed to prevent him from being removed from his educational setting and has even, at times, shown a sense of playfulness (SA 5, 6). Humor generally increases the chances of success when an individual is at least willing to try follow the rules. It gives an Intervener more time to employ a variety of approaches and options to try figure out a ***best fit strategy***, one that will work best with a particular child. What is working with SA may not work with the next student or the next or the one after that. A large part of successful intervention with those who bully is figuring out exactly what will work with whom and under what conditions. It also

matters who the Intervener is and what skills and relationships he or she brings to the equation.[2]

In this session, SA was given the opportunity to share his understanding and comprehension of not only the A-B-C model of reacting to misperceptions and the first two stages of STTA—the Stop and the Think—but, more importantly, he was able to share his thought and action (or reaction) in terms of what happened on the day of the incident in the cafeteria (SA 8–13). This is essential in designing any future interventions with SA because it reveals the basis of his logic and his level of rationality in making the decision. He reacted to Student B's bumping him primarily from his long-standing and chosen beliefs about SB—that he didn't like him—which, therefore, led to the perception that SB could not have just accidently bumped into him that day in the cafeteria. If it happened, SB must have done it on purpose with malicious intent to embarrass SA (SA 8, 10). But SA also revealed in his conversation during the intervention that he was open to other possibilities, based on his walk-through of the STTA model. SA was not so closed-minded and full of dislike for SB that he could not entertain the possibility that what happened *could* have been a simple accident and nothing more (SA 9, 12). Because SA was open to that possibility, it set the stage for future conversations and learning options with him about backing away from a reactionary state of mind the next time he finds himself in a similar situation.

HELPING KIDS SLOW DOWN TO THINK BEFORE THEY ACT

Getting an individual to stop and think before acting is critical in slowing down responses based upon affect alone, the basis of reactionary and impulsive acts. There are many "tricks of the trade" floating around in the universe of impulse intervention. Many of those ideas work extremely well within the STTA framework to help children and adolescents move from ***affect-impulsive reaction*** to ***affect-thought-conscious action***.

So what are some of the techniques to help those who bully move from an impulsive or reactionary mindset to one of think first? Let's start here . . .

---

2. This is what Raymond Corsini (2008) called the *whohowwhom factor:* "I have come to believe that what counts . . . is who does it and how and to whom it is done. . . . Sometimes the *how* variable will be of less importance than the match between the *who* and *whom*, because differences in actual technique may be relatively small for some systems. . . . At times an apparently circumscribed method . . . may achieve superior results for some people when other, more complex methods will fail" (pp. 10–11).

Counting Techniques

One of the oldest and most time-tested methods in education, counting becomes a ***spacer*** or ***bumper*** between acting on affect and thinking before acting. It's simple to teach and almost everyone can do it:

> *Here's what I want you to try the next time you find yourself angry/mad/wanting to hit someone* [insert the proper emotion or reactionary behavior here]. *Remember STTA? As soon as you feel as if you're going to lose it, use the Stop, and immediately start to count quietly to yourself until you feel that you have calmed down. This will give you time to Think about what is going on before you do something that's not based on what's really happening. How far do you count? As far as you need to so that you can to calm down. Ten? Twenty? Fifty? One hundred? Whatever it takes. And count slowly, too. In fact, let's put a "one thousand" in between each number—one thousand one, one thousand two, one thousand three. Don't get in a hurry. That's how we could get right back into acting without thinking—because we counted too fast. Take your time. Slow. Things. Down.*

Learning "When You Feel It, Start to Stop It"

It's vital that kids know what is happening to them physiologically and that they can learn to read their bodies as an indicator of what is going on inside them. Children and adolescents often report that they can feel their bodies changing (***triggers***) when they have certain emotions, particularly anger, which they verbalize as "feeling hot" or "like a knot in my stomach" (which, by the way, are physiological reactions many adults experience to intense emotional stimuli). Whatever the description is, if they are lucky enough to have that indicator, it can be a marker that they need to start their own intervention as soon as it starts:

> *You say you can feel your body tense and your face start to get hot when you get angry. You know, you're lucky that you feel those things because that's your body's way of telling you that you're overwhelmed with a particular emotion.*
>
> *Here's what might help when you feel your body starting to make those changes. As soon as you feel yourself getting hot, start the STTA process to make sure you don't act on your feelings and do something you'll regret later. So that means Stop whatever it is that's going on at that moment—do that counting stuff we talked about last week or some of the other things we've talked about—and do whatever it takes for as long as it takes until you feel your body start to relax. You know then that you're getting control back over your emotions when your body tells you it's calming down; plus, when you realize you're getting calmer, it will increase the*

chances of your being able to start to Think more clearly about how to solve whatever problem it is you're having to deal with at that moment.

Leaving the Scene of the Accident Before Something Happens

In Psychology 101, we learned a concept called ***leaving the field*** (Lewin, 1939; Wheeler, 2008), a method of ***conflict avoidance***—basically, when we are faced with some type of overwhelming challenge or no-win situation, one solution to deal with it is to walk away from the stressful environment. Metaphorically, it's the equivalent of walking off the football field, taking one's football and going home, except in this instance the "football" is likely the irrational response to affect. In essence, it is a preemptive move to avoid something getting worse or, even better, leaving the scene of an accident before it occurs:

The next time you feel your body telling you that you'd like to do something that you know in your heart or head would get you into trouble, do the STTA thing, Stop and start counting. If you feel as if that's not going to work, then here's another option. Leave the area where the problem is happening. Stop, count, and walk away to Think. Go somewhere where you can cool down, and if the problem follows you, go to an adult to talk about it. It's not going to do you any good to stay where the problem is and just get more upset.

Walk Away

Similar to leaving the field, walking away, avoiding the conflict and the residual fallout that usually goes when one does not walk away, may not be a long-term remedy to every problem, but it can provide a short-term avoidance to a temporary annoyance before it becomes a major calamity. Another problem with this technique is that a student in the classroom typically just can't "walk away" when the pressure begins to build without it likely being viewed as a disciplinary matter. However, it's often better for a student to walk away and out of a classroom to defuse a situation than to have an interaction build to a point wherein something more drastic occurs. One way to avoid this is by prior arrangement with those with whom the student has daily interactions:

OK, here's the deal. You can walk away from your anger only as a last resort if some of the other coping skills we've talked about aren't working. I've arranged with your teachers that if you find yourself losing control, you can simply get up and quietly walk to the back of the room and stand.

That will be a signal for the teacher that you're having a difficult time. If that doesn't work, then you can quietly leave the room and come to me—but only if standing at the back of the room doesn't work first. You and I will work stuff out when you get down here, and leaving a classroom is only to be used as a last resort. But if that's what it takes to prevent you from getting into trouble, then I've arranged for it as an option.

Burn It Off

Physical activity is another stopgap method used in education to help individuals deal with frustration. When we corral that energy and channel it in somewhat of a purposeful and productive manner, we call it extracurricular activities. When we don't, we call it a problem.

Encouraging individuals to channel affect into societally-acceptable physical endeavors has proven to be the saving grace for many students in school settings that would likely have not been successful if all they had at their disposal was sitting in a desk the entire school day. It has also had a tempering effect of tamping down some individuals' tendencies to be impulsive, as they have had to learn a modicum of self-discipline in order to participate in those activities in which they feel as if they get more immediate satisfaction. The expectations of the peer group (e.g., a team) to which one has affinity, allegiance, desire, and values the rewards of following the team rules in order to be allowed to play on game nights may well outweigh the benefits of immediate gratification by reacting emotionally to conflict.

Am I advocating encouraging those who are disrespectful or hurtful to others to get involved in athletics or other extracurricular activities? Maybe, as long as they can conduct themselves appropriately within the entire system that sponsors the activity: "You want to play drums in the band, then you have to follow the rules all over school for the privilege of getting to do so." I would argue that any program that can channel a current negative behavior and turn it into a positive one, while at the same time helping the individual to learn self-control and self-discipline, can't be all bad. If we reframe misbehavior to view it in terms of ***misdirected passionate energy***, then helping children to find what they are passionate about in order to give them the chance to channel negative energies into positive, productive outcomes is certainly worth the chance. This by no means excuses misbehaviors that are abusive or disruptive to others: "It's really simple. If you can't follow the rules in Mr. Math's class, then you're disrespecting your teammates who do follow all the rules all the time in all their classes—even Mr. Math's.

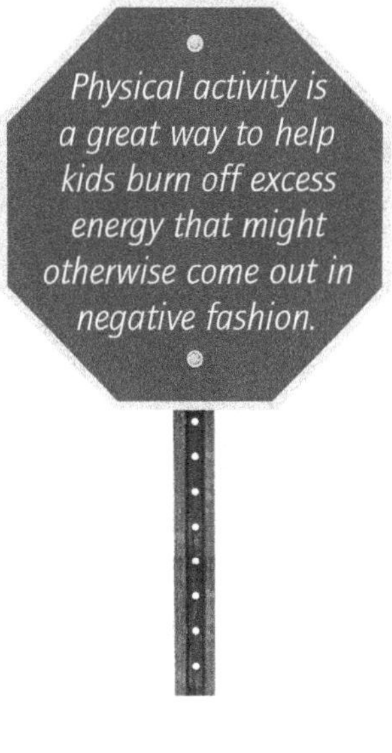

So you get right with Mr. Math, and you'll be playing Friday night." It does, however, challenge us to dig deeper into the passions of "bad kids" to see what they are "good at."

What about those who choose not to participate formally in organized extracurricular activities? The main point of this suggested alternative is using an individual's passion or physical exertion as an offset to physical and psychological frustration. Arranging for some type of physical energy burn, whether organized or not, is a coping skill to pent-up frustrations. Do they like to dance? Then get a version of their favorite tunes and have them dance themselves into exhaustion in their spare time. Do they like to run? Let them run laps around the parking lot, schoolyard, or track during recess. Basketball? Take them to the gym and have them shoot hoops until their arms fall off. Shoot some hoops with them. Let them win. There's nothing better than when kids best their supervisors in simple, fun games. Just don't be thin-skinned about it because they *will* tell everybody about how lousy you are at whatever it is that they just beat you in.

WANT TO LEARN MORE?

For those interested in REBT as a possible approach to helping kids slow down on their impulsive behaviors, readers are encouraged to explore the REBT approach and modify its basic principles and language for use with children and adolescents. REBT in its purest form as advocated by its originator, Albert Ellis, can be very confrontational. Ellis was often considered quite acerbic by those who preferred more sweetness with their morning tea and therapy. Two good starting references can be found in DiGiuseppe and Bernard's chapter "REBT Assessment and Treatment With Children" in Ellis and Bernard's (2006) *Rational Emotive Behavioral Approaches to Childhood: Theory, Practice and Research* and *A Primer on Rational Emotive Behavior Therapy* by Dryden, DiGuiseppe, and Neenan (2010). Gonzalez et al. (2004) found that, in many instances, children responded to REBT activities and approaches better than adolescents and that nonmental health professionals outperformed their mental health professional counterparts when applying REBT toward changing behaviors. All the more reason for all those in supervisory positions with adolescents to learn more about REBT and its potential for use with their specific clientele.

Aaron Beck's cognitive approach, sometimes referred to as ***cognitive behavioral therapy***, and Ellis's belief system are similar and are often useful in helping explain impulsive behaviors. An excellent source on cognitive theory can be found in Creed, Reisweber, and Beck's (2011) *Cognitive Therapy for Adolescents in School Settings.*

13

Morality as a Component of Bullying Prevention

What is our role in addressing the issue of morality when we interact with others? It's one thing when we do so with adults who, theoretically, have the free will to discuss the pros and cons of their opinions and behavior. But what about doing so with children and adolescents? Can we do so in educational settings and not violate or contradict the religious or philosophical beliefs accompanying children and adolescents from the home or the legal sanctions designed to protect and keep church and state doctrines separate?

I believe we can, and furthermore, I believe we do it on a daily basis whether we know we do so or not.

Acting in what is defined as a moral fashion is a learned behavior. We are born biologically amoral (Tomasello & Vaish, 2012). We learn what is "moral" or "immoral" behavior from our immediate caregivers. Those first caregivers are, usually, the family of origin. We learn of different values as we age and increase our interaction with greater society. In the most basic respects, acting in a moral fashion is a cooperation necessary among civilizations. Without a sense of right and wrong, there can be no order, no sense of safety, no foundation on which to base decisions. A culture's morality provides the springboard for the ***moral emotions*** of empathy, shame, guilt, and pride (Malti & Latzko, 2010).

When we act in an ethical fashion, we teach moral behavior. Ethics and morality have a lot in common, but they are not always the same. The primary nexus between the two is that they focus on the application of "right behavior" toward others. We act in a moral fashion toward others because of the social rules taught to us in our basic institutions—family, faith, education, the legal system—all which teach components of empathic behaviors toward others. While often thought of in religious terms, one does not have to adhere to a religious philosophy in order to be a moral person. Morality is based on a sense of fairness for the good of all and to protect the weak from those who would take advantage of them. True morality is applied equally without concern to superficiality—color of skin, sexual orientation, religious affiliation. When people are wronged, we apply the concept of justice to right that wrong, and that justice must be fair and moral in itself. Moral behavior occurs every day in our homes, schools, courts, and greater society, though we may not think about it as such as we go about our day.

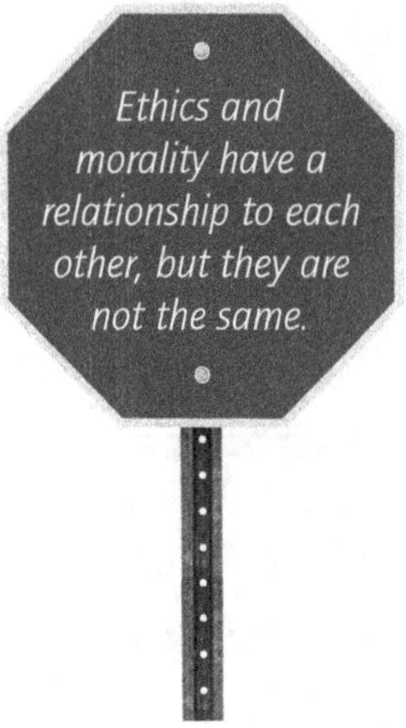

Unfortunately, people also interact with others in ways that do not take a moral perspective of right behavior into account. When people bully others, they may or may not be violating the law, the interpretation of the tenets of their faith, what they have been taught at home or in school, but they are acting in an immoral fashion from the standpoint that they are engaging in behaviors that violate the social order, take dignity and self-esteem away from others, and abuse those who are weaker in whatever circumstance the behavior occurs.

COGNITION AND MORAL INTELLIGENCE

Borba (2001) defined ***moral intelligence*** as the "capacity to understand right from wrong; it means to have strong ethical convictions and to act on them so that one behaves in a right and honorable way" (p. 4). Borba identified many of the causes of the lack of moral intelligence among children, including the lack of "acquired moral intelligence . . . poor impulse control, underdeveloped moral sensitivity," the belief that "the moral atmosphere in which today's kids are being raised is toxic," and that "our kids are being steadily bombarded with outside messages that go against the very values we are trying to instill" (p. 4). One can generalize this statement for children and adolescents in the broadest of senses and include individuals from all races, ethnicities, faiths, and family background. We are often frustrated and make the observation—true or not—that what moral or ethical behavior one learns in the home is undone at school and vice versa.

Moral cognition follows a "distinct developmental trajectory" (Malti & Latzko, 2010, p. 2). We "generate understandings of the social world by making inferences and forming theories about experienced social events" (Turiel, p. 1, as cited in Packer, 1985). Regardless of one's opinions of the origins and maintenance of a child's morality, hopefully we can all agree that a child without a moral compass is a child at risk and one more likely to have fewer internal resources to think twice before acting in a fashion that, later, might be deemed a mistake. Bandura (1991) and Bandura, Barbaranelli, Caprara, and Pastorelli (1996) spoke of ***moral disengagement***, a phenomenon in which individuals set aside their moral scruples under circumstances for the benefit of personal gain. Pozzoli, Gini, and Vieno (2012) found moral disengagement to be a factor in elementary children's bullying behaviors. Apparently, just as quickly as children can learn moral foundations, they can be convinced by their peers and even themselves that circumstances supercede application of moral convictions in specific instances—again, the peer group reigns supreme.[1] Gini, Pozzoli, and Hymel (2013), in a meta-analysis of prior studies, also found a link between moral disengagement and aggressive behaviors. In essence, the less one ascribes

1. Such behaviors, conforming to the norms of the group or to those in authority, are an extension of the classic obedience experiments of Stanley Milgram (1963) in which participants were encouraged to deliver what they thought were painful electric shocks to others by the assurance that it was safe to do so, no matter how badly those receiving the shocks begged them to stop. While the shocks weren't real, the rationalizations for forsaking the values and empathic preferences of the unknowing participants were. Group power becomes authority if an individual wants to be accepted by a group badly enough.

to some semblance of moral standards, the greater the likelihood of some type of aggressive behavior.

In teaching children to act empathically toward others, we automatically provide and strengthen some of those internal resources to better enable them to put the brakes on impulsive behaviors. It is more difficult to harm others when one considers what that harm might be like if directed toward him or her.

Borba (2001) identifies seven "essential virtues" (p. 8) for building moral intelligence and character. These include the following:

Empathy—the ability to understand others' concerns

Conscience—knowing the right way to act and then doing so

Self-Control—the ability to act rationally without giving in to peer pressure or internal beliefs

Respect—valuing others

Kindness—acting in a fashion that takes into account the welfare of others

Tolerance—respecting others and their beliefs, even when they are different from the individual's

Fairness—being open minded and acting in a just way toward others

All of Borba's (2001) essential virtues can be incorporated into interventions with individuals who have been involved in bullying others. They are embedded in the strategies and techniques advanced in this book in one fashion or another. Perhaps some concrete examples of conversational leads would be helpful in highlighting ways to incorporate those seven virtues of moral intelligence into an intervention.

CONVERSATIONAL LEADS EMBEDDING BORBA'S MORAL INTELLIGENCE VIRTUES

The following leads are offered as starting points for engaging individuals who have in some way wronged others, based on Borba's (2001) seven essential virtues.

Empathy

"I can't help but wonder what it might be like to be put in a situation like the one you had with Student B. What if the roles were reversed? What might you have thought in the same situation."

"Sometimes we forget what it's like to receive that kind of treatment. Do you think it would have made a difference if you had been the one who had been treated that way instead of the other way around?"

"Have you ever heard of the term empathy? *It's when you understand how others feel in similar situations. If you were applying empathy toward Student B in this instance, how might that look/sound/feel?"*

Conscience

"When you and Student B got into the shoving match today, did it occur to you that behavior might not fit in with the school rules?"

"Since the incident today in the cafeteria, what have you thought about how it all fits in with our school rules?"

"How did today's behavior match what we teach here in school about doing what we know is the right thing?"

Self-Control

"One of the things that makes us good citizens is the ability to not automatically react to things that make us mad. Did you do what you did today because you thought about it first, or did you just do it without thinking about it?"

"What would have been different about today if you had thought before you acted?"

"There are lots of times we want to do things in the heat of the moment, but if we give ourselves a little more time, we often cool down and then don't feel so strongly about them."

Respect

"Was what happened today between you and Student B based on respect? If not, how did it happen?"

"What was respectful about what happened today between you and Student B?"

"Respect is when we value everyone enough to treat them as if we would like to be treated ourselves. Did that happen today?"

Kindness

"What was kind about what happened today?"

"Help me understand how raising your voice and shoving Student B was kind."

"Would you want what happened between you and Student B today to be done to another member of your family? Would that be very kind?"

Tolerance

"You know that tolerance is one of our basic school values. We've spent a lot of time on it this year in student advisory groups. Can you tell me how you were practicing tolerance yesterday when you said those words to Student B?"

"Is what you have been saying about Student B on your Facebook page a good example of tolerance?"

"It's OK to disagree with someone else. We don't have to believe the same way everyone else does, but as long as no one is hurting anyone else, people have the right to be who they are, whether we approve of it or not. We have to learn to tolerate other people because there are a lot of people on this planet who are different from us."

Fairness

"Is what happened to Student B today fair when it comes to the way we want people to be treated in our school?"

"Is it fair if one person is not capable of defending himself or herself to try get that person to fight another?"

"Fairness means we try to give everyone an equal chance to achieve and be successful. When you don't treat others fairly, it prevents them from being the best they can be because they worry about not getting that equal chance. Have you treated everyone fairly today? If not, what could you do to change that?"

A MAGIC QUESTION

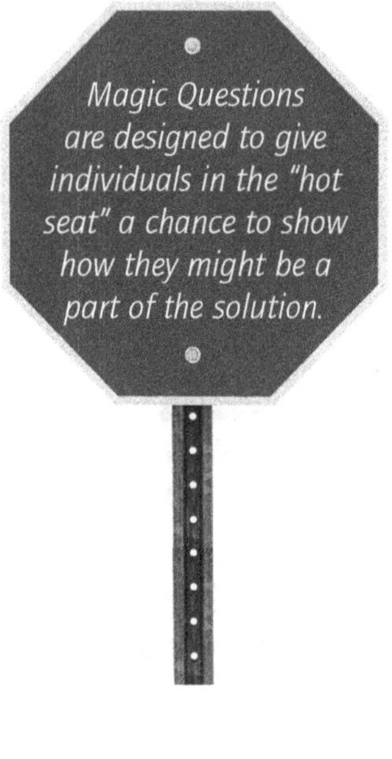

That last question in some applicable format in the previous section is an important one: "What could you do to change that?" It's a ***Magic Question***. It could well be applied in virtually any conversation with an individual with whom behavior is a concern. The purpose of having an intervention conversation with another individual is not to pepper him or her with a million questions—it's not a test or an effort to trick one into giving the "wrong" answer. The ultimate goal is to help the individual explore the thoughts, feelings, and behaviors that lead to specific problematic behaviors. The only way to do that is to give the individual the opportunity to think, verbalize, and, perhaps if possible, role-play new methods of correcting current misbehaviors.

SHAMING IS NOT AN OPTION!

The phrase *You ought to be ashamed of yourself!* is a weapon. ***Shaming*** as a tool of intervention and restoration does damage to both the individual to whom it is directed and the credibility of the one using it as the self-esteem exterminator that it is. One does not intelligently shame another into proper behavior. Shame has no therapeutic utility, and truth be told, countless adults have spent years in therapy trying to rid themselves of the damage done when shaming was inflicted upon them in childhood and adolescence. Stuewig, Tangney, Helgel, Harty, and McCloskey (2010) addressed the issue of shame and guilt as "moral emotions that regulate social behavior" (p. 92) and that shame has been shown to be "positively linked to hostility and aggression" (p. 92). They go on to note a litany of additional studies wherein shaming creates situations in which individuals feel "***shame-rage*** or ***humiliated fury*** [emphasis added] . . . [and] . . . aggressively lash out in an attempt to regain a sense of agency and control" (p. 92). Such rage and fury is often reported by those who have been the targets of bullying behaviors as the basis of acts of vengeance to rectify the sense of past wrongs (Newman, Fox, Harding, Mehta, & Roth, 2004). Additionally, shaming encourages individuals to hide the behavior deemed shameful (Stuewig et al.), which makes it even harder to encourage the agent of bullying to talk about the logic behind the actions.

We must not, then, inadvertently (or on purpose) do to others what they choose to do to their targets. In place of shame, we must use intelligent conversation to move those who misbehave toward making more ethical and rational decisions based on an empathic foundation. No matter how much those who intimidate others get under our own skin—either because they make us angry or because they intimidate *us*—we cannot be guilty of using the same tactic on them under the guise of an educational intervention.

Can we express that we are "disappointed" in their behavior? Yes—as long as it is tempered with ". . . because I know that you are capable of acting in a more positive manner." But we must avoid the parentlike, stand-alone admonition of "You ought to be ashamed of yourself!" because the truth may well be that the individual is not ashamed, nor feels guilt for what has occurred. That is why it is so important to spend the time to get underneath the thought processes of those who bully others so that we can craft more effective interventions to counter the logic that is creating so much misery toward their targets.

14

Dealing With the Demon That Is Anger

Anger is a demon. It is invasive, pernicious, toxic, and all-consuming. It eats at the soul of decency and blinds logic. We see it every day in larger society, among children in our schools, in homes, and—if we are honest—even within ourselves. In that sense, anger is something we can all understand on a first-hand basis.

Anger is also contagious. Like a virus, it can spread from one person to another, especially when those in power use it as a tool to get what they want. Kids are exposed to more than enough poor role models in real life, media, and in cyberspace to learn how people obtain their goals through the use of anger. That anger can range from the controlled silence of shunning to the rage of physical violence.

Embedded under most acts of bullying is anger: anger at self, anger at others, anger with one's station in life, sometimes anger at things one cannot identify. Bullying others can be a way to settle the score of the injustices felt by those who lash out in their efforts to level the playing field. Yelling, hitting, or demeaning others are sometimes efforts to exorcise the demon of anger from oneself. At other times, they are intentional inflictions of pain and misery designed to spread the disease to others so that everyone can be as miserable as the person who is the carrier.

If we fail to recognize the role that anger plays in acts of bullying, we are missing an important opportunity to craft more effective interventions. That is why it is important to understand both the logic of the agent of bullying along with helping educate him or her in ways to avoid using it as the key of entry to everything desired.

DON'T UNDERESTIMATE THE DEMON

One of the most frequent mistakes we make in intervening with children who are bullied or who bully others is to tell them that they will "grow out of it," "it will go away," or "just don't do it." When we say these things to kids, we send the metacommunication that (1) their problems are not that important to us, and (2) we adults either have forgotten, want to forget, or don't have a clue what the thoughts and feelings are like to be a child of that age. To pass off the intensity of childhood experiences as just a passing phase is dismissive at best, demeaning at worst.

Learning how to handle anger is a critical life skill. It begins in infancy and receives some of its most memorable lessons in early childhood and the elementary years. Adolescence is another critical period of time when we learn how to understand and control anger since it is during this period that our emotions are also impacted by raging surges of hormones, further fogging the cognitive processes.

Anger is one of the most intense emotions we feel. It is primordial. We were hardwired to use it as a survival mechanism (Bilodeau, 1994). While the days of fighting saber-toothed tigers might be over and the direct anger-survival mode of response might not be as necessary as it once was, the underlying hardwiring remains to help us respond to perceptual threats. Bilodeau's description of this response is relevant for helping us work with children and adolescents who use their anger as a basis for behavior to overcome their frustrations:

> Anger is the emotion that provided the incentive against the elements and to accomplish what would have been physically impossible without the additional strength that seems to accompany anger. Adrenaline, the chemical involved in anger arousal, produces a numbing effect on the body which allows a persona to continue fighting when hurt. The individual doesn't experience pain until after the struggle, when the adrenaline level drops. . . . Anger also creates a tunnel-vision effect that concentrates attention onto the opposing force. . . . Self-doubt and fear of failure do not impinge on the combatant's ability to struggle. (p. 18)

Let's use just these few passages to create an intervention with an individual brought to our attention for his intimidation of others. Here are some possible key prompts that might work well in this situation:

"You know, anger is something that we all feel from time to time. That's a natural part of who we are. It can become a problem, though, if we feel it all the time. Is that something that happens to you? Do you mind telling me what that's like for you?" or "Help me understand what that's like for you."

"Anger can make us feel physically strong when we use it against others. Have you ever noticed that? Do you mind telling me what that's like . . .?" or "Help me understand . . ."

"When we get angry, our body changes to turn us into fighting machines like we used to have to be when we lived in caves and fought wild creatures. Even though we don't have to do that anymore, our bodies still act as if we're about to be attacked by a dinosaur. Do you ever feel as if you're about to be attacked by some monster when you get mad? Do you mind telling me what that's like . . .?" or "Help me understand what that's like . . ."

"Sometimes when we get mad, we strike out at others and don't feel anything. It's as if getting mad makes us numb to the way we really feel, and when we're mad, we don't feel things like hurt or sad. Do you ever feel hurt

or sad before you get angry? Do you mind telling me what that's like . . .?" or "Help me understand what that's like for you . . ."

"Some people say that when they get angry, they can only focus on what it is they're angry at. It's almost as if everything else goes away, like they're in a tunnel and the only thing they can see is the face of the person they're angry with. Does that ever happen to you? Do you mind telling me what that's like . . .?" or "Help me understand what that's like . . ."

"When I get angry it's because sometimes I'm really feeling something else inside and getting mad is the easier thing to do—like sometimes I feel as if I'm not sure of myself or that I can't be a failure in front of everyone, and if I act tough and yell or fight back, then nobody will know how I really feel. Does any of that ever go on inside of you? Do you mind telling me what that's like . . .?" or "Help me understand what that's like . . ."

The prompt "Help me understand what that's like for you" prevents a simple yes-or-no response to the closed-ended question right before them. There are two kinds of questions: closed- and open-ended (Egan, 2014). ***Closed-ended questions*** do not allow for expansion of an answer. They are typically answered one of two ways—yes or no. Closed-ended questions give us minimal information and do not encourage the individual to provide more in-depth responses. They make the Intervener do more work since the individual we are working with sits back and waits for us to ask the next question that they can answer with a yes or a no. Closed-ended questions often give the impression of interrogation. ***Open-ended questions*** and in-depth questions, on the other hand, provide the individual with the opportunity to tell us more about their experiences, their impressions, thoughts, feelings, and behaviors. Yes or no are not sufficient answers for open-ended questions. Individuals have to verbalize more in order to fully explain an open-ended question. Of course, the best interventions use both closed- and open-ended questions to help both the Intervener and the person being interviewed to fully explain the experience.

The answers we get in response to these statements and questions tell us a great deal about what's going on inside the head of those who bully others. Possible responses might well be categorized into these three groups:

Open to Change

Respondents admit or indicate that they act in anger as a cover-up for underlying emotions, even if they cannot identify them at that moment. This opens the door for exploration of what those emotions feel like in an effort to specifically identify what lies underneath the angry behavior.

Possibility of Change

Respondents are hesitant to admit or indicate that their actions may be a cover for another emotion, but do not shut the door on the possibility. They may vacillate between agreeing to change and not agreeing. As with the Open to Change group, further exploration is necessary to help individuals put specific words to what they feel in addition to anger.

Resistant to Change

Respondents actively dispute that they feel anything beneath the anger on which they act. They openly express their disdain for any type of intervention and do not see a reason to change. This group likely requires a focus on the specifics of what their behaviors do to others before they can begin to work on their own thoughts, feeling, and behaviors.

Working to help individuals identify the emotions behind the anger they feel in tandem with the STTA (Stop. Think. Then Act.) process (see Chapter 12) can be effective tools in further discovering what makes those who intimidate others tick.

IN THE END, IT'S MORE ABOUT ANGER MANAGEMENT

If anger is an all-consuming issue with a student, it likely always will be unless new patterns of behavior are learned to replace the automatic-anger response. The challenge, then, becomes not one of anger elimination, but anger management.

Anger management requires self-awareness of three important factors on the part of the individual. First, we have to know as much as we can about who we think we are and who others think we are. Next, there is the knowledge of the ***triggers*** that encourage an individual to act in a negative fashion. Last, the individual must learn the behaviors to respond to anger in prosocial ways, most likely contrary to the ways they are used to behaving.

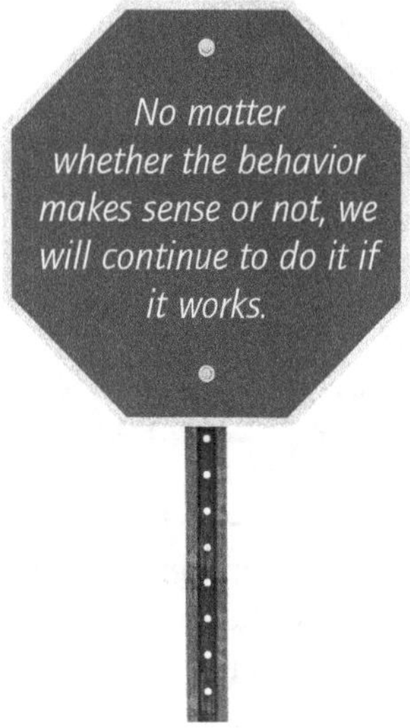

A little reminder—remember that ***behavioral inertia*** that keeps cropping up time and time again in our discussion? We do what we do because it works. That's the reinforcement of the behavior, and we continue to behave in that specific way until acted upon by a greater force, or reason, to change. Sometimes that decision to change comes from within before an intervention. More often, however, especially in the case of those who bully others, the reason to change is an imposition from the outside letting the individuals know that they will be held accountable or penalized for behaviors deemed unacceptable.

We don't "unlearn" behaviors. We either learn new ones to take the place of the old ones, or we stop old behaviors when we discover that they are not as useful anymore to accomplish our goals. Such is the basis of learning anger management skills.

Learning Who We Think We Are

One of the simplest ways to learn about who we think we are and how others see us is through the use of a simple diagram called the ***Johari Window***[1] ("Johari Window Workbook," n.d.; Luft & Ingham, circa 1955, 1961). The Johari Window can be modified and used with any age group and can be a fun exercise of self-exploration. It can also be risky when individuals learn about the areas of themselves that they did not know existed in the eyes of others.

Figure 14.1 The (Basic) Johari Window

Pane 1 "The Public Person" Known to Self Known to Others	Pane 3 "The Blind Spot" Not Known to Self Known to Others
"The Secret Self" Known to Self Not Known to Others Pane 2	"The Great Unknown" Not Known to Self Not Known to Others Pane 4

1. The Johari Window (sometimes also called *Johari's Window*) has a humorous origin, named after a combination of part of the first names of its originators, Joseph Luft and Harry Ingham in the mid-1950s. It has appeared in various forms over the years in counseling and human relations programs, but surprisingly, not so much in the general education field. Perhaps all educators would benefit from working on their own Johari Window to help discover those blind spots that need assistance to make them better teachers, administrators, student services personnel, and family members.

Figure 14.2 An Active Johari Window With Student A

Awareness efforts of nonthreatening and beneficial characteristics increase the likelihood of sharing more of the Public Person with others. Pane 1 expands.	As nonawareness decreases, areas of awareness increase. Blind Spots shrink. Pane 3 decreases.
The Secret Self may remain the same if the individual chooses, or could decrease if the decision is made to share more with others via the Public Person. Pane 2 could decrease or remain the same.	As self-awareness and the Public Person increases, areas of nonawareness decrease. Pane 4 decreases.

The beauty of using the Johari Window is the simplicity in its explanation and application with those participating. The Johari Window has four "knowledge panes." Each pane contains different regions of self-awareness, ranging from fully aware to didn't-have-a-clue.

The goal is to try to move what may not be known by the individual (Panes 3 and 4), either because that knowledge is a true ***"blind spot" of self-awareness*** or a subconscious defensive denial, into an area of greater self-awareness (Panes 1 and 2). All individuals have a right to their own secrets and privacy (Pane 2), and there are always aspects that we have yet to discover (Panes 3 and 4), which can be both excitingly positive or frightfully negative.

In practice, one's Johari Window is dynamic and not in equivalent proportions of self-awareness. The panes are always changing as we move through life. They should be. It's mentally healthy for us to want to learn about ourselves and how we interact with others in the world. An active Johari Window during diagramming with a student, then, may actually change to look like Figure 14.2.

One of the great aspects of the Johari Window is that it is simple to use, simple to understand, and simple to apply in an intervention. (It also doesn't take much artistic skill, which is really nice if your abilities, like mine, only extend to whatever you can do with circles, squares, and arrows.)

Using some of the suggestions that follow in conjunction with the Johari Window can produce a road map of an individual's triggers, the second major component of increasing the self-awareness of those who choose to maliciously dominate others.

Understanding the Idiosyncrasy of Anger

Anger comes in many forms from different sources. It's unique for each of us, or ***idiosyncratic***. Sometimes biology and genetics may make us more prone to react from a hardwired, visceral level. In other instances, we learned to respond through a lens of anger, and we have had no reason to change. What makes you angry might not bother me in the least and vice versa. However, we can learn ways to avoid responding to anger if willing to do so. We can learn methods of shifting responses from the affective to the cognitive and increase the chances of logic slowing down a hasty response.

One of the foundational components of helping this cognitive shift occur is understanding what pushes our buttons. Sometimes this knowledge is out front and center (Johari Window Panes 1 or 3), though we may not be aware of what others know about us. We can make a conscious choice as to how we use that which we know and share about ourselves (Panes 1 and 2). Things that we don't know about ourselves may get under our skin and make us wiggle because they are buried (or we deny and repress them) from our consciousness so deeply that we can't readily access them (or choose not to) for identification or recognition (Johari Window Panes 3 and 4). The goal of the Intervener is to help the individual understand how she or he thinks and responds to triggers by mapping them on the Johari Window.

The simplest method of identifying those triggers is to ask the agent of bullying outright, "What are some of the things that make you angry/tick you off/get under your skin?" If the relationship is working, the individual will likely be able to name people, places, and situations that do just that.

If the student seems hesitant, doesn't know, or doesn't want to answer, the information may be gleaned from additional conversations that occur during the course of an intervention. Or they may need some prompts. Drew (2010), in an activity book designed to assist children in addressing the necessary components of anger management, conflict resolution, and empathy building, provides a list of potential triggers applicable for students in Grades 3 through 6. The sample dialogue that follows uses one list from Drew's Activity Session 33, "What Real Kids Have to Say About Anger Triggers" (p. 85). This activity book is highly recommended and filled with creative ideas that can be modified for use in virtually any bullying exploratory intervention. This interaction is with a different student, Student C, who was involved in another incident and falls into the Possibility of Change group as described earlier in the chapter, but who either is hesitant to identify her triggers or has difficulty doing so:

SAMPLE DIALOGUE FILLING IN THE JOHARI WINDOW

Intervener [I] 1: *You have been very helpful with me as we've spent time together these last few days in telling me the reasons that you and Student D got into that shouting match the other day. But I noticed today that when we were talking about things that helped to make you upset and angry, it was difficult for you to give some examples. So here's what I'd like to try to do. I'm going to read a list of imaginary situations or things that happen to kids, and I'd like you to tell me if any of these things make you angry, mad, or feel like you would like to yell or hit at the person who did them. When we finish, we'll have a list of things you don't like, and then we can talk about ways to avoid going straight from mad to doing something that gets you into trouble. Do you think we might be able to do that?*

Student C [SC] 1: *I guess.*

I 2: *Remember, this is just an imaginary list of things that happen. You can add anything to the list that you want to after we get started or when we finish.*

SC 2: *OK.*

I 3: *All right. Here we go. I get mad when people . . .*

talk behind my back

say I did something I really didn't do

hit and pick on me because of my [insert a reason here: size/color of skin/ religion/gender identification]

make fun of me because [insert a reason here: where I live/the clothes I wear/my family]

hurt me for no reason

pick on somebody younger than they are

make me feel like I'm invisible

talk down to me/talk to me but don't listen

make threats

judge me because of who I am

[The remainder of Drew's (2010) list is read to Student C, who has responded with a *yes, no, maybe* or *depends* to each situation that has been offered. At this stage of the intervention, the focus is on information gathering using closed-ended questions. The Intervener may choose to add additional potential items or situations directly dependent upon knowledge of and relationship with the individual. Once the basic triggers are identified, more open-ended questions can come into play to enrich the experience of the student.]

I 4: *Great. You've been really honest. I appreciate that. Now, are there any other situations that you can think of that we could add to this list?*

SC 4: [Student adds three additional scenarios to the list of things that make her angry.]

I 5: *Very good. Now, let's look at the things you said are likely to make you angry and see what they tell us. I'm going to list the things that you knew made you mad and upset on this page, and the ones that you listed as "maybes" or "depends" or that you "hadn't thought of that, but it probably would" make you angry on this page. What I'd like you to do is look at these lists and tell me if you think that other people also know that you are likely to get angry in these situations or if you are the only one who knows. While you're doing that with your lists, I'm going to look at the list, too, and write down the things that I think that other people and I know or think would make you mad. We'll have three lists. It's sort of like a puzzle. And when we finish, I'll tell you what all of this means and how it fits together. OK, now look at these lists, and tell me who knows what about you.* [The Intervener begins to transfer the list of situations on the two lists onto large, poster-sized sheets representing each pane of the Johari Window. When completed, Student C's sheets look like Figure 14.3.]

Now the fun begins. Using the list of characteristics and situations listed, the Intervener gives an age-appropriate explanation to Student C of the Johari Window, how it works, and what each of the panes might mean for her. It also explains that nothing can be written in Pane 4 for the moment because no one knows, yet, what is to be discovered in the future. However, at the end of the exercise, Student C can be given the opportunity to speculate what might end up being there to keep her intrigued by the whole Johari Window experience.

Figure 14.3 Sample List of Johari Window in Intervention With Student C

I know and other people know that I would get mad if people . . . talk behind my back say I said something I really didn't call me weak call me names because of my race judge me exclude me from the group steal stuff from me	I might not think so but other people know/think that I would get mad if people . . . say I said something I really didn't call me weak call me names because of my race judge me steal stuff from me make fun of my parents or family say I am ugly or use other names make fun of me because of my good grades
I know but other people don't know that I would get mad if people . . . make fun of my parents or family say things about my religion hurt someone else for no reason	Things I don't know and other people don't know, either . . .

SAMPLE DIALOGUE REVIEWING INFORMATION GAINED FROM JOHARI WINDOW EXERCISE

[Following the brief explanation of the Johari Window.]

I 1: *So here's what I see when I look at what we have written here.*

First, Pane 1 is what everybody knows because it's pretty much out in the open. You don't like people to talk behind your back, or for people to

put words in your mouth. You consider it an insult if people consider you weak, which probably is one reason that you feel like you have to act tough all the time. You also find it insulting when people make comments about your race—I have to tell you, I don't like it when people do that, either.[2] *I find it disrespectful, but I also don't resort to hitting them when they do it. I usually call them on it and let them know I think they're being rude and inappropriate. We can talk about other ways to respond to that as we go along. Let's see, you also don't like people to assume things about you that aren't true, and you also don't want to be left out of activities that your friends are involved in. And stealing—nope, you don't want people to steal things from you. Another little secret? Me, either,*[2] *and I'm not sure many people do.*

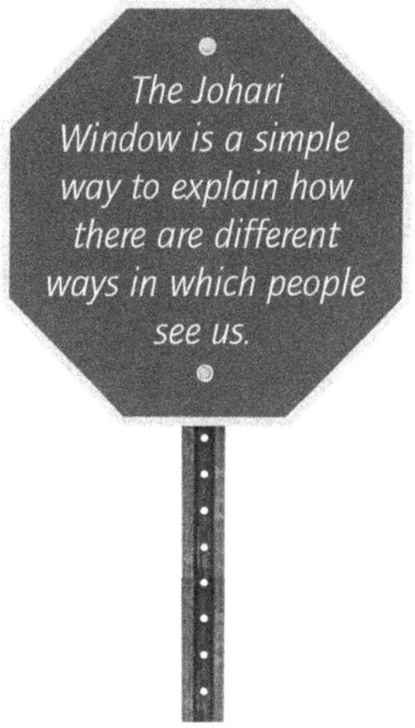

[At this point, a decision can be made to ask if a student agrees or disagrees with the list in Pane 1 and if there are any other items that might need to be added. Depending upon the nature of the interaction and feedback from it, an Intervener can move on to the Pane 2 list at the most appropriate time. Note: It may be beneficial to just focus on one pane per meeting so as not to overwhelm the individual with too much information. That is a decision that must be made from a developmental and relational standpoint.]

I 2: *Remember what this second pane in the Window represents?*

SC 1: *Things that I know but others don't.*

I 3: *Right. Very good. So let's see what you were willing to share with me about yourself that other people don't know. And I need to tell you here that I appreciate your trusting me enough to do that. Let's see. You don't like it if people make fun of your family or your religion. And you also don't like it when people hurt someone for no reason. Anything else we need to add?* [The Intervener gives Student C several seconds of silence. She indicates that there is not.]

This is really interesting to me. We have something in common[2] *here on all three of these behaviors. But I'm wondering about the third item on your list, that you don't like it when you feel or see people hurt someone else for no reason. I'm curious about two parts of that. Are there times when you've seen that happen? And what about the times you think*

---

2. Remember, self-disclosure is very powerful, and it sometimes can be distracting to the flow of a conversation. On the other hand, and in this instance, it can also be an opportunity to increase the trust level and find common ground between the Intervener and Student C.

that it's OK to hurt someone for a reason? Help me understand what you're thinking about those two examples.

[Items in Pane 2 ("Secret Self") can be somewhat risky and threatening to the individual, particularly if there is a trust issue involving a fear of the revelation of secrets by the Intervener. Choosing how to proceed, as with Pane 1, should be based on the response of the individual. Does he or she feel safe? What is the trust level between the two? Would it be better to discuss any of the items at a later time if they are considered to be too threatening for the individual at this time?]

I 4: *You've done really well on these. You've shared a lot of information that helps me understand the way you see the world and the way you think other people see you—which brings us to that third list* [Pane 3]. *What's that one about?*

SC 2: *The stuff that other people think they know about me—but they probably don't!*

I 5: *Well, you might be right, or you might be wrong. We need to see if any of these items fit you or not and talk about how they might have gotten on the list. I noticed that you picked some and I picked some others—and we both picked some of the same ones!* [Laughs.] *So let's see what you think about the items on this list.*

[It is important to discuss with a student the impressions of how specific items got listed in Pane 3 and what might have contributed to those impressions. Additional questions or leads related to this line of inquiry might include:

What do you think might have happened to give others the impression that item belongs on the list?

If you disagree that you should be judged that way, what might be occurring to give people the impression that it is?

So what might you do to stop people from thinking that item is a part of who you are?

[The focus on Pane 3 should be on current behaviors that are causing others to have the impressions they do about the student and the changes that might occur to alter them in the future. As the intervention moves forward, speculation about what might occur in Pane 4 could prove helpful, especially if Student C has displayed a willingness to change.]

I 6: *Well, we don't have much on this list. Wonder why?*

SC 3: *Because that's the one that talks about what I don't know about myself and nobody else does, either.*

I 7: *Right. Hmmmm. So if we were to list some things down there that we would want to discover about you—let's focus on the positive things—what might they be? What are some of the things that we're going to find out about you that are going to change the way everybody views you now—maybe some things that you can do to surprise people?*

Discussions in Panes 1, 2, and 3 are "now oriented," in that they refer to behaviors, thoughts, or emotions that are currently occurring. Pane 4 is "future oriented." It provides an opportunity for Student C and the Intervener to brainstorm about positive changes that Student C can engage in to change future impressions.

WHAT JUST HAPPENED HERE?

One of the major advantages to the Johari Window exercise is that it provides a higher level of interaction between those who participate in it. The exercise is not merely conversational. It also provides a visual "product" at the end of the day and something that can be referred to in future interactions.

Here, the Intervener provided a highly personal review of the student based on exactly what Student C had revealed about herself. While the focus was solely on the student and her world, it was not a total vanity project. There's work going on here. Each pane of the Johari Window was carefully examined, and feedback from the student was solicited to add or subtract from Student C's viewpoints.

In the end, time spent on a Johari Window can be both fun and enlightening, and it can provide a road map to gauge progress in the future.

WANT TO LEARN MORE?

Intrigued by the Johari Window? There are lots of samples of ways to use the Johari Window floating around on the web. A Google search in September 2015 resulted in over 16,000 possible options. Most of the links are for use with adults. It is always important to remember that any recommended example or resource should be modified for what is best developmentally and individually appropriate for the kids with whom we work.

A great resource for teaching anger management in the elementary years is *How to Take the Grrrr Out of Anger* by Verdick and Lisovskis (2003).

15

When Bullies Live in Space

Of course, this chapter is about cyberspace, that ethereal and nebulous "out there" that no one can really get a handle on when it comes to bullying and intimidation. Cyberspace can be a paradise for those who choose to hide behind the cyberbushes and throw the rocks of hate and cynicism. It can be the origins of great misery when groups of cybergremlins band together to launch an attack against a single target. While social media has become the new currency of interpersonal relationships, it has also opened the opportunity to intimidate others on a 24/7/365 basis, leaving no respite from abuse.

Cyberbullying occurs when an individual uses an electronic communication medium to harass and intimidate others. Sample methods of electronic social media communications bullying are found in Figure 15.1. The U.S. Center for Disease Control and Prevention considered cyberbullying to be a form of ***electronic aggression*** (David-Ferdon & Hertz, 2009). Cyberbullying is an effort to disrupt the normal psychological functioning of a target through attacks aimed at lowering the self-esteem. As a result of the intimidation, taunts, and threats that occur via the electronic medium, it can lead to physical confrontations between those who are directly or peripherally engaged in the cyberbullying activity. As with physical bullying, harassment, and intimidation, cyberbullying may or may not be defined as a criminal act. Such determinations are defined by state and federal statutes. Usually, however, the use of electronic means to harass others makes the agent of the action subject to both federal and state laws that regulate the use of the Internet and wireless communication devices.

SCOPE OF THE PROBLEM

As with physical forms of bullying, we really don't know the true scope of cyberbullying. Early reported trends in the mid-to-late 2000s indicated that a vast majority of students did *not* intimidate or harass their peers via electronic media (Hertz & David-Ferdon, 2008; Kowalski & Limber, 2007; Williams & Guerra, 2007), but that old-fashioned, face-to-face verbal and physical aggression was still in vogue. Perhaps contributing to these early results were the facts that large majorities of those who were cyberbullied often did not report the abuse to school personnel (Ybarra, Diener-West, & Leaf, 2007), usually because they did not know or could not prove the exact identity of the individuals creating the mayhem (Kowalski & Limber, 2007). Likewise, even Kowalski and Limber (2007) noted that "if anything, the statistics underestimate the true frequency" (p. 26) of cyberbullying. Parents, too, are virtually clueless when it comes to understanding social media, particularly its latest incarnation.

Recent data suggest that the incidences of electronic aggression increase with age and the evolution of technological usage among children and adolescents ("Cyberbullying: Statistics and Tips," 2004 [iSafe]; David-Ferdon & Hertz, 2009). Unlike the trends that show that, as adolescents physically mature, the incidences of physical bullying decrease—most likely a phenomenon in direct proportion to one's physical, cognitive, and emotional maturity—data today show that electronic abuse is more likely to occur in inverse proportion to the decrease in physical bullying (Hinduja & Patchin, 2009). Intuitively, the more time one spends in online and wireless activities, the greater the chances of being exposed to cyberbullying (Hinduja & Patchin, 2008).

Those who are targets of abuse usually suspect they know who is responsible for it. Hinduja and Patchin (2009, p. 58) found in their studies that the most frequent abuser in cyberspace was known to the other person in the school setting, followed by a friend of the target—in fact, a friend was *more likely* to *be* the origin of cyberbullying than an ex-friend. With friends like that—well, you know the rest of that old adage.

GONE IN SIXTY NANOSECONDS

Authority will never be one step ahead of technology, particularly when it comes to attempting to provide oversight with social communication among children and adolescents. In less than two decades, social communication has gone from what today is considered the stone age of dial-up to the crystal-clear, digital era of Telepresence. By the time we all see this book in print, who knows how long it will be until we have live holographic communication?[1]

Though the first e-mail was delivered in 1971, it was not until the 1990s that mass use of web communication came into the general public domain. With the advent of public access to the World Wide Web, new and creative methods of communication evolved. In mid-1993, there were no more than 150 websites—in total. By July 2015, it was estimated that there were over 849 million websites, with a September 2015 estimate of 4.79 billion indexed pages ("July 2015 Web Server Survey"; WorldWideWeb.com).

Along with the expansion of websites came new opportunities for communication. ***Connectivity*** (van Dijck, 2013) became the synonym for communication. No longer were we communicating with others on a unidimensional level. Web communication allowed us to communicate at increased sensory levels. Never before had so many people had the capacity to "connect" with each other in so many different electronic methods. One could restrain the connection to a single person via a single e-mail,

1. Apparently sooner than we think. See "Definition: Holographic Telepresence," complete with a live demonstration of how it works, at http://whatis.techtarget.com/definition/holographic-telepresence.

Figure 15.1 Methods of Electronic Aggression

Common Methods Used to Intimidate Via Electronic Aggression

Adapted and Modified From Willard (2007, p. 1)

Cyberstalking

Repeated attempts to harass a target via electronic means. Meets the common definition of harassment in most instances and employs any or all of the techniques cited here.

Denigration

Put-downs and derogatory comments. Includes gossip and rumors. Includes posting photos intended to do the same.

Exclusion or *Shunning*

Refusing to let an individual into an electronic group. May include blocking or deleting that individual from prior access.

Flaming

Efforts to increase the tension or heighten denigration by making inflammatory statements or posting photos intended to do the same.

Harassment

Repeated efforts to harm another's reputation via any of the methods cited here. The key to harassment is in the repetition of the abuse.

Impersonation or *Identity Theft*

Posts made under some sort of anonymity or false electronic name/identity to make others believe that another individual is making the comments. May occur when the target's cyber account has been hacked or passwords stolen.

Malicious Website

A website created to demean a target. Usually contains embarrassing photos along with anonymous statements about the individual.

Outing

Posting secrets of another individual in a public cyberspace or venue so that some (via restricted or members'-only access) or all (no restricted access) can view.

Polling

Posting surveys asking respondents to reply to derogatory questions about a target—for example, "Who is the ugliest girl in ninth grade?" or "Who all has had sex with [named person]?"

Figure 15.2 Top International Networking Sites as of May 2015[3]

- Facebook
- Twitter
- LinkedIn
- Pinterest
- Google Plus
- Tumblr
- Instagram
- VK
- Flickr
- Vine
- Meetup
- Tagged
- Ask.fm
- MeetMe
- Classmates

share with multiple e-mail users via a *cc* of the same, or jump into the pool of mass communication via chat rooms and bulletin boards. The access of MySpace in 2003 and Facebook in 2005 to adolescent audiences cemented social networking as the hottest communication tool ever available to those groups (boyd & Ellison, 2008).

Though the first webcam was available in limited circles in 1991, its use in social media was not widely expanded to the general public until the advent of YouTube in 2005. So widespread was its use, along with its use in conjunction with related social communication sites, that *Time* magazine declared "You" and the "Information Age" as its person of the year in 2006.[2] The addition of video-posting capabilities as a means of social communication greatly upped the ante in terms of the ability to heighten sensory response to the written word. Now, not only could we be informed, delighted, confused, or infuriated by what was in print, but we could also add intensity to those messages with video postings.

Classmates.com was created in the mid-1990s, one of the first social networks. Since then, many social networks have come and gone. Figure 15.2 highlights the networking sites that were recognized in 2015 as the top sites used and trafficked by the general public for social networking purposes.

IT'S ALL FUN AND GAMES UNTIL . . .

Of course, all sites have the potential for misuse. Some, however, have gained reputations for being used primarily as a tool for abusive behaviors

2. Grossman, L. (2006, December 25). "You—yes, you—are *Time* magazine's person of the year." *Time*. Retrieved from http://content.time.com/time/magazine/article/0,9171,1570810,00.html

3. See US traffic ranks links from eBizMBA at http://www.ebizmba.com/articles/social-networking-websites, Compete Analytics at https://www.compete.com/, and global traffic ranks link from Quantcast at https://www.quantcast.com/.

among children and adolescents. One even shut itself down before it got much of a start.

Snapchat is a photo-sharing platform launched in 2011 that allows users to upload photos on a limited-time basis before vanishing from user access. The time limitations for a photo to be uploaded range from one to ten seconds. At the end of the time limit, the photo is supposed to be dropped from the Snapchat server for public viewing so that the viewer only has the chance to see the posting during the time duration of the initial post.

For whatever legitimate purpose the poster of a photo might have intended, there have been plenty of abuses of Snapchat by those whose major goal was to embarrass, bully, or intimidate others. Additionally, it has been used to send sexually explicit images. Contrary to the early perceptions by its users that a photo would be posted and only available for viewing before vanishing forever, it was entirely possible to capture a photo posted on Snapchat via a screenshot command on the device on which the picture appeared if it was taken during the duration of the photo's original posting. Once the screenshot was saved, it could then be uploaded on any other social media platform that accepted the format of the saved image. A five-second time-limited post of the bare buttocks of a student taken in the locker room after a gym class sent to 20 classmates via Snapchat as a prank could suddenly go viral if just one of those classmates captured a screenshot of the photo, then reposted or e-mailed it on another social media platform. To add insult to injury, it was later revealed that photos going into the Snapchat universe that might not have been screengrabbed during their time-limited posting in cyberspace did not actually vaporize into nothingness as promised. The "media file remains . . . [making it] . . . simple for users to retrieve it" ("Exposed," 2014).

By 2014, Snapchat had proven financially successful enough that four up-and-coming social media startups intended to challenge it: Whisper, Secret, Rumr, and Confide.[4] All applications worked under a premise of sharing information within a network of designated friends, though identities may or may not be anonymous depending upon the app chosen.

Of course, all that glitters in the gossip world is not gold. American-based Yik Yak went live for college-aged audiences in the fall of 2013 as an anonymous "feed of what people are saying and doing around you without having to know them" (Yik Yak, 2014).[5] By the spring of 2014, the app had—to its credit—dialed back its access (via a process known as ***geofencing***, designed to block Yik Yak usage on school grounds) due to unintended use and abuse among middle school- and high school-aged kids. Schools in Decatur (Alabama), Chicago (Illinois), Fulton County (Georgia), Marblehead (Massachusetts), and San Clemente (California) were particularly negatively

---

4. See Yarm, M. (2014, March 13). Hot apps: The race to be the next snapchat. *Rolling Stone*, p. 24.

5. Yik Yak. *CrunchBase*. Retrieved March 17, 2014, from http://www.crunchbase.com/company/yik-yak.

impacted. Bomb threats and personal attacks were common. In one instance, posters to the site verbally attacked the victim of a sexual assault. Yik Yak was compared to a virtual "bathroom wall where users [could] post vitriol and hate" (Valencia, 2014, para. 8).[6]

Similar concerns have been raised with the use of Latvian-based Ask.fm, which has been blamed for contributing to suicidal behavior among those who have been targeted in posts such as "drink bleach," "go get cancer," "go die," "fat," "a loser," "slut," and "ugly" that were attributed in part to the self-harm decisions made by adolescents in multiple countries.[7] The CEO of Ask.fm, in an interview, did not offer much in the way of empathy for the negative impact that the company may have had on the lives of those targeted for negative online abuse. In terms of Ask.fm being used for cyberbullying purposes, the CEO responded with the following:

> Well, the truth is that parents do not know where kids socialize. They think that when kids go to school . . . all they do is solve math problems. If parents knew what kids actually talk about, they would be a lot more scared. This is what happens with Ask.fm as they can see it right in the open. However, the truth is that it happens everywhere, both online and offline.[8] (quoted in Sarle, 2013, para. 5)

The problems of Ask.fm were similar to those of Formspring, which, launched in 2009, went offline in 2013. Formspring, too, had been accused of allowing anonymous posters to cyberbully targets, some of whom engaged in self-harm behaviors resulting in suicide.[9]

WHO'S THE SHERIFF IN CYBERSPACE?

The major challenge that schools and related entities have in dealing with cyberbullying is determining whether or not they have the jurisdiction to

---

6. Valencia, N. (2014, March 10). Yik Yak chat app stirring up trouble in high schools. *CNN Tech*. Retrieved from http://www.cnn.com/2014/03/07/tech/yik-yak-app-high-school-problems/.

7. As mentioned earlier in Chapter 2, there is not a direct causal link between bullying behaviors in and of themselves and the decisions made by the targets of such behaviors to harm themselves or others. However, there should be no doubt that being on the receiving end of bullying behaviors weakens the resiliency and positive decision-making skills of those who are targeted.

8. Sarle, D. (2013, May 13). Ask.fm responds to cyberbullying allegations. ArcticStartup.com. Retrieved from http://www.arcticstartup.com/2013/05/13/ask-fm-responds-to-cyberbullying-allegations.

9. Seifert, D. (2013, March 15). Social question and answer site Formspring to shut down on March 31. *The Verge*. Retrieved from http://www.theverge.com/2013/3/15/4110196/social-question-answer-site-formspring-shut-down-march-31st.

do so. Courts have sent mixed messages when it comes to determining if restrictions can be applied to those who are—or are not—engaging in what might well be deemed free speech (Clark, Orman, & Schulz, 2011; Trainor, 2012). The "falsely shouting fire in a theater and causing a panic" principle (Holmes' opinion from *Schenck v. United States,* 1919) still applies in cyberspace—for the most part. A person cannot threaten others, defame, or libel another in a public online forum. However, with the exception of threats, legal defamation or libeling others is often a matter that the courts must determine. That rarely happens in the raucous world of cyberspace among kids, and as with adult defamation or libel, by the time something can be done to hold the offending parties accountable, the humiliation and the damage to one's reputation has already been done.[10]

One of the determinants for liability issues is whether or not a responsible or supervisory party engaged in deliberate indifference. The ***deliberate indifference standard*** basically implies that a professional in charge of an activity or responsibility willfully ignored a condition of inordinate risk to one for whom the professional had an obligation (Julka & Lewis, 2008). Knowledge of the risk is important. A supervisory entity cannot be held accountable if a risk is unknown. While one could make the argument—and it is made—that it is impossible to know whether or not a communication of some sort in cyberspace outside the realm of a direct threat will result in *actual* harm, it cannot be said that supervisory personnel in particular settings are not more aware of the *possibility* than in other populations. Such is certainly the case when dealing with school-aged youth, particularly in light of the number of instances where such cybercommunications have played some role in harm to others (e.g, the 2013 Sedwick bullycide case in Florida [Creston, 2013]).

An entity may or may not be held to the deliberate indifference standard depending upon the role of the supervisory personnel. The average person who chooses not to get involved in some type of dispute between two people—even in cyberspace—with whom she or he has no responsibility does not meet the deliberate indifference standard. An educator, however, does not have the luxury of "looking the other way,"[11] particularly if it

10. It is important to note that "while it appears that bullying lawsuits against school districts are on the rise, plaintiff's success rates are not" (Trainor, 2012, p. 15). However, parents are far more likely to bring lawsuits today than ever before against school personnel over the issue of perceived neglect or indifference related to bullying behaviors. Associated Press, 2014.

11. This is particularly the case when the individual in the supervisory role is a designated mandated reporter by law.

involves a student with whom the educator has some kind of supervisory responsibility—either directly (e.g., a student in a teacher's classroom) or indirectly (e.g., a student in the school, but not one under a teacher's direct supervision or control)—and the dispute has potential to disrupt the educational process. Does this also include accidental discoveries of cyber disputes among students which the educator stumbles across? The answer is yes, if the communications portend a high degree of probability that to ignore the communication would result in some type of inordinate risk to a target or to the health and safety of nontargets who might be harmed in some way by the subsequent disruption of the agent of the threat.

So who *is* the sheriff in cyberspace? It depends. If the origin of the problematic message comes from property owned by the school, then clearly the owner of the property has the authority and responsibility to address the issue.[12] If the problematic message originates on school property or during a school-sponsored activity, either on or off school grounds, school personnel have the authority and responsibility to address the issue. If the problematic message originates off campus and has no real or potential likelihood of disrupting the educational process, then it is likely that school personnel have no authority to interfere or address the communication. However, if there is ***reasonable cause*** to believe that the cybercommunication will or does disrupt the educational environment or learning process, school authorities likely have grounds for addressing the issue.

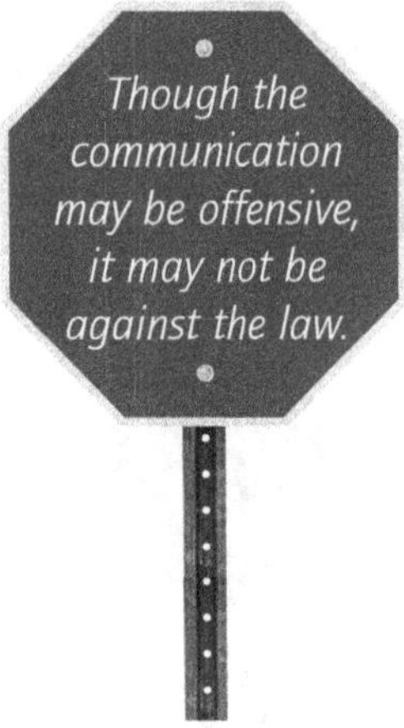

What exactly does "addressing the issue" mean? Again, it depends on the nature of the communication. Answering that question may well be based on the answers to two more. First, is it in the best interest of the student to intervene? Second, if the answer to that question is yes, then is there existing jurisdiction to allow school personnel to do so? Even when the answer to the first question is yes, if the answer to the second question is no, then to act in the absence of authority by virtue of legal standing places the person who intervenes at risk.

Here is the dilemma: What is "right" morally and "right" in the eyes of human compassion may not have legal standing for action on the part of an Intervener. I may want to stop offensive behavior among students that I stumble across in cyberspace, but I may not legally be able to do so with the authority of state statute, my employer, or as a part of the scope of practice of my profession. When I act in the absence of that foundation, then I act as an individual and am individually responsible and liable for the outcome of what happens as a result of my individual action.

---

12. Caveat: If allowed by state laws. At the time of publication, there were no federal laws requiring school districts to specifically address cyberbullying or potentially related problematic communications unless the offensive message violated another existing federal statute (e.g., civil rights).

WHO'S NOT THE SHERIFF

Here's what cannot be done. No authority outside the courts or parents has the right to force a minor to surrender access to a personal online account. Notice, that says *personal* online account. If the account or equipment is owned by a school district, then the district has the ability to restrict or block access to the use of the technology or account.

Case in point: A twelve-year-old female student posted a statement on her Facebook account from her home that she "'hated' an adult school monitor who had been 'mean' to her" (Forliti, 2012; Post, 2012; Protalinski, 2012). The school principal, in an effort to address what was interpreted as cyberbullying, placed the student in detention and instructed her to apologize. The student responded by posting another comment, which included profanity, on the account. The principal meted out another punishment, and in what can only be deemed (at best) an error in judgment or (at worst) outright intimidation, a school counselor forced the student to surrender her passwords to personal online accounts in the presence of a sheriff's deputy after another student's mother complained that the girl and her son were engaging in sexting activity. The girl's mother sued specific school personnel, the district, and the sheriff's department on behalf of her daughter for violation of First (freedom of speech) and Fourth (unreasonable search and seizure) Amendment rights and damages. A federal judge ruled that there was enough evidence to pursue a case.

In 2014, the case was settled and "as part of the agreement the School District [sic] agreed to strengthen privacy protections for its students and pay damages" (American Civil Liberties Union [ACLU] of Minnesota, 2014). The district and all individually named plaintiffs were allowed to make no admission of liability but did agree to changes in school and student handbook policy as related to handling matters of electronic communications and the right of a student to withhold consent in voluntary searches of personal items, along with training to be provided to all staff regarding such changes (*R.S. v. Minnewaska School District*, 2014). A total of $70,000 was split between the family of the student and the ACLU of Minnesota, which represented the plaintiffs.

What went wrong here? Perhaps the better question is, was anything done correctly? Regardless of the ultimate outcome of the case, school personnel in this situation clearly overreacted to the student's original Facebook post. While students may make the decision to rant against the adults in their lives—and a good question might well be, is that any different from the adults who rant from the cyberbushes in the comments sections following news stories they don't like?—they still maintain a certain level of First Amendment rights to free speech as long as their comments or rants are not threatening or disruptive to the school environment (*R.S. v. Minnewaska Area School District*, 2014):

> The law on out-of-school statements by students can thus be summarized as follows: Such statements are protected under the First Amendment and not punishable by school authorities unless they are ***true threats*** [emphasis added] or are reasonably calculated to reach the school environment and are so egregious as to pose a serious safety risk or other substantial disruption in that environment. R.S.'s Facebook wall postings were not true threats or threats of any kind. While her statements may have been reasonability calculated to reach a school audience, that possible fact is not sufficient to justify her punishment. (p. 21)

Were the student's Facebook comments disrespectful? Apparently so. Were they potentially abusive to their targets? Probably. Might they rile the adults to whom they were directed? Apparently they did. Was it the wisest thing to do on the part of the student? Certainly not. The public utterances of students in a public space—in this case, cyberspace, where those comments might be viewed by the adults to whom they are directed or who have supervisory responsibility—are no different than a student verbally railing against a punishment received being overheard by a teacher while walking down a crowded hallway. The principle is the same—the student made statements that, while not reaching the bar of true threat, might need to be addressed by supervisory personnel because they are inappropriate, demeaning, or abusive. To address a student under those circumstances is acceptable and, I would argue, should be done from a "teachable moment" paradigm.

What is additionally problematic in this instance is the forcing of a minor to surrender passwords to private accounts that have information, comments, and other personal observations unrelated to the issue relevant to school personnel; the presence of law enforcement in the absence of the girl's parent during the student–school personnel conference to obtain the online passwords, which ultimately was one basis of the challenge in court as a de facto warrantless search; and the use of a supposed neutral party (the school counselor) in the role of interrogator.[13] Perhaps in the broadest of interpretations, an argument might be made that there was a need to access those private accounts to see if true threats existed toward school personnel or students. However, there was no evidence that any of the comments rose to that level of concern. Indeed, what was posted on the Facebook account seemed nothing

13. Student services personnel, such as school counselors, school social workers, and school psychologists, are trained to be neutral observers and assist their clients to make effective decisions. They are *not* trained to serve as interrogators to extract and divulge confidential information to third parties unless there is a ***duty to warn*** issue (e.g., potential for harm to self or others) involved. Placing student service professionals in disciplinary roles that are the responsibility of administrative personnel is unethical and is a disservice to their profession.

more threatening than the normal developmental expression of frustration and anger, however inappropriate, on the part of a twelve-year-old with access to a very powerful method of transmission of that opinion.

Ironically, it should also be noted that the student at the center of the controversy should not have had a Facebook account in the first place. According to Protalinski (2012), at twelve years of age, she was one year too early for registration of an account with Facebook. Of course, we all know that that never stops underage children from accessing online accounts: "Millions of preteens and children use [online accounts] by simply lying to get past sign-up restrictions" (Protalinski, p. 4). Imagine that! A preteen bending the truth a bit. Who would have ever thought that?

INTERVENTIONS FOR THOSE WHO BULLY VIA ELECTRONIC MEANS

Intervention strategies for those who choose to bully others using cyberspace as a launching pad are similar to strategies for those who engage in more traditional forms. The message is simple: The behavior is not acceptable, no matter if it occurs physically, face-to-face, or in cyberspace. However, there is an added twist of leverage that can be applied in the discussions—what is posted in cyberspace is most likely traceable to its source, and what was posted may be illegal. This changes several components of how the intervention might have to be handled.

Let's examine a possible dialogue with a middle school-aged student who has been accused of making harassing statements on his social media page and who denies being the source of the material.

SAMPLE DIALOGUE DEALING WITH A CYBERBULLYING INCIDENT

Student E (SE) 1:	*I didn't do it. I. Did. Not. Do it!*
Intervener (I) 1:	*Well, let's you and I go over everything and see if we can figure out who did. Sound fair?*
SE 2:	*You can go over anything you want, but I'm telling you I'm not responsible for what's been going around.*
I 2:	*So you've seen the comments and the photos?*
SE 3:	[Laughs.] *Everybody has. It's out there.*
I 3:	[Chooses to stay focused on the problem of the postings, not on the distraction or the laughter.] *That's exactly part of the problem. It's out there and everybody can see it.*
SE 4:	*That's not my problem.*

I 4:	*Maybe not, but let's make sure that we all understand what the rules are.*
SE 5:	*I know the rules about cyberspace—there are no rules! That's what makes it so cool! Nobody can tell anybody what to do or not to do—even you. It's freedom of speech, you know? You can't stop me from saying what I want to say.*
I 5:	*Well . . . that's not exactly true. I know a lot of people think that's the case, so I want to make sure you are aware of exactly what the rules really are when it comes to online postings so that you don't get into trouble.*
SE 6:	[Looks, but says nothing. Seems either interested or stumped.]
I 6:	*I'm not going to lie to you. There are a lot of things that people can get away with on the Internet, and you do have freedom of speech for the most part—but not total freedom of speech. No one does. If you say something about other people that isn't true and it hurts their reputation, that's not allowed. That's called* libel *if it's in writing or* slander *if it's spoken—ever heard of those words?*
SE 7:	*Yes. No. Well, maybe.*
I 7:	*Do you know what it means?*
SE 8:	*What you just said. You can't tell lies about people. Yeah, I guess I've heard of that before. But that doesn't count online. Not on the Internet. People write goofy stuff all the time that everybody knows isn't true.*
I 8:	*Sorry to say, yes, it does. Libel and slander applies in all settings. Everywhere. You can't just go around and say nasty things about people that are hurtful and untrue, especially if it's done intentionally.*
SE 9:	[Stays quiet for a moment.] *So what if it wasn't done on purpose or a person says it wasn't done on purpose? What if they didn't mean it?*
I 9:	*That might need to be sorted out by other people—which brings me to who those other people might be. If an individual is accused of slander or libel—even when it occurs in cyberspace—he or she might have broken school rules or even the law and might be charged with a crime. Either way, it gets to be a big mess, especially if an individual is charged with a crime.*
SE 10:	*Well, I'm a kid, and they don't charge somebody my age with a crime. I'd just say I didn't mean it. If I'd done it, I mean. But I didn't.*

I 10:	*That might work. But it also might not work. Kids your age can be charged with crimes if what they do is serious enough to break the rules too badly. But let's not worry about that right now—I just wanted you to know that that's a possibility if somebody who was targeted for cyberbullying decides to turn the information over to the police or something like that.*
SE 11:	[Sits and thinks.] *So what if a person just forwarded something that somebody else already said or posted a picture that somebody sent them?*
I 11:	*It depends. It might not amount to much. Or it might. Remember what I said a minute ago about if something is posted intentionally? Intent to harm someone is a big factor in figuring out if someone's responsible for libeling or slandering someone else.* [Intervener can see Student E thinking about that last piece of information. Gives him the silence to see if he wants to say anything. Student E does not, so Intervener proceeds.]
I 12:	*The other thing everyone needs to know is that if you post someone's—*
SE 12:	*I told you I didn't do it!*
I 13:	*Yes, you did tell me that. Let me rephrase that. The other thing that young people need to know is that if someone posts something in cyberspace that interferes with the right of all students to get the education they deserve here at school, then that person can be held responsible for what was said.*
SE 13:	*Well, that's stupid! It's not like whatever was said happened on school property. You can't punish a person for something that happened off campus.*
I 14:	*Maybe. Maybe not. Let me give you an example. If someone posts something on his* [name of social media] *page that makes somebody else mad and then they post insults back and forth all night long on it, and one person says to the other that he's going to hurt that person the next time he sees him at school, do you think the school is going to let that happen?*
SE 14:	*If nothing happens, you can't punish people for something that they didn't do.*
I 15:	*Good point. But the school is responsible for everyone's safety, and if we get wind that there's going to be a fight on school grounds, and we know who said what to who, we're not going to stand back and let someone run the risk of getting hurt.*

We have the right to step in and prevent something like that from happening. Make sense?

SE 15: *No. Because cyberspace isn't here on campus. You can only punish us if we post something like that from a school computer.*

I 16: *The problem is that cyberspace is kinda everywhere and kinda all the time—at home, at school, before school, after school. The more I think about it, it's really everywhere and all the time. So, yes, school rules—and the law, too—say that people can be held responsible for something they post on the Internet if it's going to disrupt the school day. Let me give you another example. If someone were to make a threat to shoot up the school on* [name of social media] *and a hundred of her friends saw it, and they all reported that to us here at school, do you think we couldn't do something to stop it from happening just because it was said in cyberspace?*

SE 16: *Shooting up the school and pulling a joke on somebody aren't the same thing.*

I 17: *You're right, but the same basic idea applies to both in terms of what is said out in cyberspace has the potential to do something to harm people at school or interfere with their right to learn. Look, we don't know yet who's responsible for what got posted last night and has the school all in an uproar today. But we do know that it's causing a lot of disruption, and a lot of your classmates are upset. You know we already had two fights today over it. And you know and I know that your name is in the middle of this mess—*

SE 17: *But I didn't do it!*

I 18: *You keep saying that, and I'm going to give you the benefit of the doubt. But I wanted you to know the facts on what can happen when things get out of hand with stuff like this. I also want you to remember that everything's that's posted can be traced back to where it came from and that that's exactly what's being done right now—*

SE 18: *By who?*

I 19: *By the police.*

SE 19: *Well, I don't have anything to worry about.*

I 20: *I hope not. I also hope that you'll help us sort all this out if you know something.*

SE 20: *Oh, you want me to be a snitch, huh?*

I 21: *I prefer to see it as helping to solve a problem that's creating a lot of chaos here at school. It's not a safe place if people are fighting, and we can't allow that to happen. If you didn't have anything to do with the posts, then you're in the clear. And if you did or if you know who started it all, then a little cooperation from you could help me help you when the dust settles, and we start having to figure out who's going to be held responsible and what kind of accountability is fair.*

SE 21: *You mean punished.*

I 22: *You keep talking about punishment, and it may end up being that. I'm not the one that makes those decisions. I hope that whatever happens to the ones responsible will hold them accountable for their actions and be designed to help them make up for the wrong they did to the people that have been harmed. That may be distasteful to those who have to do it, and they may view it as a punishment in their minds, but I hope that whatever is designed will help them learn that what they did was not acceptable and help them think before they do it again—and maybe even help them to never want to do it again.*

Now, you have to go back to class and I have to talk to some other people. Let me write you a pass and get us both on our way. And don't forget, my door is always open if you need to come talk to me about this or anything else that's important. There's nothing we can't talk about if it's going to help make life better for all of us around here. But we are all responsible for our behaviors—you, me, everybody—and sometimes when we make a mistake, the best thing we can do is do what we can to make it right. Never forget that.

WHAT JUST HAPPENED HERE?

Let's look at the major components of this intervention to see how the Intervener used an educational approach with the student to address the issue under consideration.

First, throughout the entire intervention, the *Intervener stayed calm* and *refused to let the discussion escalate*. Notice the Intervener *avoided getting drawn into the wild goose chase of the distractors* that the student kept throwing out. The focus was on *providing the information* to the student (I 4–6, 8–11, 13, 15–18, 22), not on the student's demeanor, challenges, or protests (SE 1–2, 4–5, 12–13, 20–21). It's so tempting to respond to the challenges and zingers thrown at the Intervener. Usually designed to provide a defensive shield by the person being interviewed, some may choose to attempt to escalate the verbal exchanges to the point of insult. Such challenges, of course, must be dealt with according to the policies in place within the institution.

Next, notice that the *Intervener weaved educational information into the conversation* without specifically making it pedantic (I 6, 8–11, 13, 15–18). There was information about how interpretation of the school rules on cyberbullying might be perceived as a violation of both them or the legal system (I 6, 9, 13–15); about how what is posted in cyberspace might, indeed, fall into the legal system (I 6, 9, 8–11, 16); about what might happen to an individual who crossed the line (I 5, 6, 8–9, 10, 13, 15–16). It wasn't a here-read-this-list-of-rules approach or a reading of the riot act, but more a subtle, oh-by-the-way-in-case-you-didn't-know approach to making sure that important information was distributed during the course of the intentional interview. It also *avoided the* ***question-answer interrogation effect***—"Did you know that . . .?" or "Don't you know that . . .?" When we throw nothing but questions out to people, especially closed-ended questions, they just sit and wait for the next one and don't expand on any of their thoughts because—well, you know—they know we're going to ask another question, sometimes even before we let them finish the answer to the one we just got through asking them. Be patient. Use silence. The *Intervener gave the student room to think* about the barrage of information that was coming his way (SE 6, 9, 11), and the *Intervener did not expect a period of silence to be followed by a comment* from the student. Sometimes, they need the silence to organize their thoughts or think about what it is we want them to consider. It helps if we don't always fill their heads with additional noise. That's one thing that kids have plenty of already.

The *Intervener never did accuse the student of being the one directly responsible* for having created the problem (I 1, 13, 18, 20). The fact is, at that point of the intervention, no one actually knew yet, so it would have eroded whatever trust might be in the making between the two parties if the Intervener went on the attack. But *what was known as general information and was not confidential was presented to the student as fact* (I 2–3, 17–18)—the student was involved somehow in that day's chaos. In doing so, the Intervener put the student on notice that he may end up being held accountable for his actions at some point in the future (I 18, 21, 22).

The student viewed any action to be taken by school personnel to be punitive. The *Intervener kept the focus on accountability and education.* There was the acknowledgement that, in the end, whatever accountability that may be meted out to the responsible parties may be viewed by them as a punishment but that the Intervener hoped it would have a more educational and beneficial focus than one of pure discipline.

Finally, *the student was encouraged to provide information he might have about the incident from the perspective of being a solution* to the problem, not a part of it (I 1, 20–22). While the student tried to spin the offer as "snitching,"

Figure 15.3 Key Points to Keep in Mind During Intervention With Agents of Bullying

Intervention Tips to Remember

Stay calm.

Identify the issue (usually the behavior).

Do not let the person with whom you are working "punch your buttons."

Always move to de-escalate the tension.

Keep the focus on the "issue" and not the "person."

Avoid distractors—things and people that are not the issue.

Weave education and information into the intervention. Make it a teachable experience.

Avoid closed-ended questions as much as possible. Encourage open-ended answers.

Give people "room" to think about what it is they want to say.

Let silence speak for itself.

Avoid accusations. Stick to the facts.

Focus on accountability, not punishment.

Allow individuals the opportunity to provide input to the solution.

the Intervener preferred to view the offer as a way to assist the student if it was later discovered that his role in the incident was more direct than indirect. Was the offer some kind of partial immunity? Not really. It was more of an offer to remind whoever ultimately decides the accountability piece that the student did, indeed, contribute to the effort to resolve the matter.

WANT TO LEARN MORE?

For an interesting read on exactly how clueless kids think their parents are when it comes to social media, see Kelly Wallace's (October 16, 2013) "Parents, Beware of Bullying on Sites You've Never Seen" at http://www.cnn.com/2013/10/10/living/parents-new-apps-bullying/.

Just how many websites are floating around in cyberspace today? See "July 2015 Web Server Survey" at http://news.netcraft.com/archives/2015/07/22/july-2015-web-server-survey.html and WorldWideWeb.com at http://www.worldwidewebsize.com/ for fascinating and updated information on the growth and size and of the web since its creation.

For more information about cyberbullying, see http://www.cyberbullying.info/ (particularly useful for young children), "What Is Cyberbullying?" at http://www.stopbullying.gov/cyberbullying/what-is-it/index.html and "What Is Cyberbullying, Exactly?" at http://stopcyberbullying.org/index2.html.

Examples of how badly students can be injured when social media goes awry can be found in Jordan Valinsky's (May 29, 2013) "The Real Story Behind Snapchat Leaked, the Site Publishing Screenshots of Your Embarrassing Snaps" at http://betabeat.com/2013/05/snapchat-leaked-creator/; Sarah Perez's (March 13, 2014) "Amid Bullying and Threats of Violence, Anonymous Social App Yik Yak Shuts Off Access to US Middle and High School Students" (from *TechCrunch* at http://techcrunch.com/2014/03/13/amid-vicious-bullying-threats-of-violence-anonymous-social-app-yik-yak-shuts-off-access-to-u-s-middle-high-school-students/); Taylor Amerding's (March 24, 2014) "Teen Cyberbullying Grows With 'Anonymous' Social Chat Apps" (from *CSOonline* at http://www.csoonline.com/article/750184/teen-cyberbullying-grows-with-anonymous-social-chat-apps; and Kim Bellware's (March 10, 2014) "Anonymous Message App Yik Yak Faces Backlash From an Entire City" (from *Huffington Post* at http://www.huffingtonpost.com/2014/03/10/yik-yak-app_n_4921365.html); Sarah Perez's (August 12, 2013) "In Wake of Teen Suicides, Ask.fm Faces a 'Myspace' Problem" (from *TechCrunch* at http://techcrunch.com/2013/08/12/in-wake-of-teen-suicides-ask-fm-faces-a-myspace-problem/ on March 18, 2014.

16

Bystanders or Upstanders?

©iStockphoto.com/kali9

Bullying prevention is a total community effort. While it "takes a village to raise a child," when it comes to bullying prevention and intervention, the peer group is also a major part of the solution. Adults have historically been asleep at the wheel in their responsibilities to address the issue. Let's be blunt: Adults have been dragged into the solution equation because the courts have ruled that they have liabilities if they ignore the problem when in a supervisory capacity. But adults alone cannot, and should not, be the only ones solely responsible to respond to the problem. *We cannot solve the problem of bullying without the contribution of the people most frequently impacted by it—the kids themselves!*

Coloroso (2003) coined the term ***bystander*** to identify a critical group of individuals involved in the bully–target relationship—and make no mistake about it, those who bully others and those they target *are* involved in a relationship, whether those that are targeted choose to be so or not. Bystanders are those who "aid and abet the bully through acts of omission or commission. They can stand idly by or look away, or they can actively encourage the bullying or join in and become one of a bunch of bullies" (Coloroso, 2003, p. 62). The challenge is to educate the bystanders to not stand by and give tacit approval to the bullying behaviors of others, but to learn the skills to actively intervene in whatever way they can to either disrupt or stop the negative behaviors and assist those that are targeted. Coloroso calls those who attempt to help the target of bullying behaviors as ***"defenders of the target"*** (p. 66). Yet another group, the ***"possible defenders"*** (p. 66) are those who do not endorse bullying behaviors, but do not come to the aid of their peers either because they are passive or do not have the skills to be able to do so.

Coloroso (2003) noted four main reasons for the failure of bystanders and possible defenders to get involved in the bullying of their peers. They include the following:

1. Fear that they will be injured themselves
2. Fear that they will become the next target of the aggressor
3. Fear that intervening will make the situation worse
4. Lack of knowledge on the part of the bystander so as to know what to do (p. 67)

It's not difficult to pick up two main themes here—***fear*** and ***lack of skills to intervene***. If bystanders believe that they operate in an environment that is unsafe, they report that they fear for their own safety. When we feel unsafe, we are less likely to be willing to risk to help others because, after all, the first rule of survival is to ensure that we are safe ourselves. If bystanders believe that their interventions will place them in the crosshairs for the aggressor's next bullying behaviors because they do not believe that the supervisors will effectively support or protect them when they do, then they are less likely—if at all—to place themselves in a position of risk. And if bystanders feel as if they do not have the skills to either effectively intercede on behalf of their peers or that their intervention will aggravate the already abusive situation, they are less likely to take the risk to do so. Are adults any different in these respects?

A lot has changed since the publication of Coloroso's (2003) *The Bully, the Bullied, and the Bystander*, much because of it. Recognizing that enlisting passive bystanders was a missing link in increasing the chances of intervening on behalf of the targets of bullying, programs emerged to educate children and youth on ways to do just that. So powerful is the effort to increase bystander intervention in the bully–target cycle that even the US government began active educational efforts in 2011 through its StopBullying.gov website to funnel prevention and intervention information from the US government agencies and departments of Education, Health and Human Services, Justice, Centers for Disease Control and Prevention (CDC), Health Resources and Services Administration (HRSA), and Substance Abuse and Medical Health Services Administration (SAMSHA). In 2013, the AdCouncil created four informational commercials dealing with the issue of bullying, a part of which focused on the issue of encouraging peers to be more than bystanders. Amazingly, the concept of bystanders as a part of the solution to bullying intervention rose to national prominence and national government advocacy in less than a decade.

MOVING FROM BYSTANDER TO UPSTANDER VIA THE STAND TALL APPROACH

The challenge, however, remains. How do we turn passive bystanders into active peer interveners, or ***"upstanders"*** (Peck, 2012)?

First, we must address the first two fear factors identified by Coloroso (2003): the fear that bystanders who intervene will be injured themselves or the fear that they will become targets. These two fears are systemic problems and require an honest assessment of the institution's social climate. How safe are potential peer interveners if they become actively engaged in trying to stop bullying behaviors in the setting? Such answers can come informally through reported anecdotes from students, daily observations, or more formal instruments such as comprehensive school climate assessments. Specific instrumentation recommendations for the measurement of bullying climate within the school setting can be found in a compendium from the CDC.

There are two sources of anxiety which create fear—internal and external. They are closely intertwined. One's internal sense of security is enhanced by the sense of safety within the environment in which she or he operates. If we don't feel safe, we will be less willing to take risks because we know that no one "has our back." On the other hand, if we know that we are supported in our risk taking, we will be far more likely to take the chance to extend that helping hand to another during a tense confrontation.

One of the most recent efforts to provide an educational program to help turn passive bystanders into peer interveners is called the STAND TALL program (Peck, 2012). STAND TALL is based on three core competencies of respect, discussion, and action (p. 21) and is geared for Grades 4 through 6, the prime age when negative stereotypes about race and religion begin to form (Leadership Conference on Civil and Human Rights, 1995).

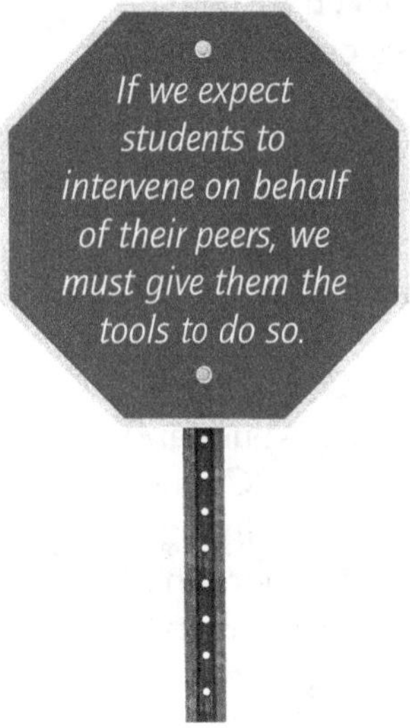

There are three parts to the STAND TALL program. The first part involves watching a video segment running approximately ten minutes in which students talk about their experiences dealing with difficult interpersonal interactions played out in realistic scenario format with a professional actor. The second step involves an in-class discussion among students about the video examples they have just seen so that they can personalize the just-observed scenarios and make them most relevant for their situation. The last step involves practicing the skills learned from watching the video and interacting with their peers in class.

It is unfair to expect individuals—especially children—to engage in instances of conflict de-escalation without the education and skill building to do so. To expect otherwise is both foolish and unsafe for those whom we hold to the expectation. Only when we give individuals the skills to intervene in bully–target interactions do we begin to address the last two of Coloroso's (2003) four identified factors that prevent individuals from being willing to intervene in bullying situations.

Using the STAND TALL program as a stand-alone program in and of itself is one method of increasing the chances of moving passive and hesitant bystanders into the active column. Using it in conjunction with other programs (as is age appropriate) can provide a powerful enhancement to an existing bullying prevention and intervention initiative within an educational setting. A few of the more well-known, currently cited as effective, and internationally recognized bullying prevention and behavioral management programs include the following:

Character Counts

Steps to Respect and Second Step

Olweus Bullying Prevention Program

Roots of Empathy

Promoting Alternative Thinking Strategies (PATHS)

Tribes Learning Communities (TLC)

Positive Behavioral Interventions and Supports (PBIS)

Response to Intervention (RTI)

A NEW TWIST: AN ARGUMENT FOR PENALTIES AGAINST "BAD SAMARITANS"

Samaritan laws have an antiquated history in civilization. The principle is based on the expectation that those in a position to assist others who are imperiled have a moral obligation to do so. ***"Good Samaritan" laws*** provide a ***hold-harmless shield*** to those who act in ***good faith*** toward those who are endangered in the event that the endangered are further injured in some way by the person rendering assistance.

Samaritan laws have not always been so benign. In ancient Egypt and Greece, stiff penalties were often inflicted upon those who failed to act in helping the needy (Benzmiller, 2013). Such individuals were considered ***"Bad Samaritans"*** (p. 945). Within Western jurisprudence and legislatures, there has been the general expectation that those in a supervisory position or with a special helping relationship (e.g., medical, mental health, or public protection function) are obligated to act affirmatively to assist the endangered as a function of the relationship with a client or the public trust—the ***fiduciary responsibility***. Failure to do so is a violation of that fiduciary duty and might have legal strings attached.

Benzmiller (2013) proffered that bystanders who fail to act to intervene when acts of bullying occur are de facto Bad Samaritans and are responsible for encouraging or approving an act of bullying by their intentional or neglectful inaction. Such justification is based on the "growing trend in American law toward acceptance of affirmative duties to aid" (p. 947) those in distress.

The application of an ***affirmative duty to act*** in instances of bullying among minors creates an entirely new set of considerations in who should be held accountable for passive observation and inaction by bystanders. Use of an affirmative duty principle with adults in supervisory positions, however, might well be justified. Let us look at the possible ramifications of Bad Samaritan rules or laws for both children and adults.

APPLICATION OF BAD SAMARITAN RULES TO MINORS

Education and juvenile justice have long been based on the assumption that children and adolescents are going to make mistakes during their normal cognitive and affective development (Rosado, 2000). Adults in supervisory capacities then, particularly those in education, must be willing to seize on instances of error and turn them into "teachable moments." Even when discipline is administered, it is wisest to do so with education in mind. The word *discipline* originates from the Latin *disciplina* for "instruction given, teaching, learning, knowledge" (*Online Etymology Dictionary*, para. 1, n.d.). Discipline need not be punishment, although, as we have shown in several instances in this book, an individual may perceive it as such. The loss of a privilege may be interpreted as a punishment by the individual who must comply, but it may be an appropriate lesson for an infraction when the reason and learning goal of the loss of the privilege is explained in detail. Too often, unfortunately, education or seizing a positive teachable moment is not the true goal of most discipline administered today—the goal is, indeed, designed to punish individuals, to "teach them a lesson."

Punishment for the sake of punishment does teach a "lesson" to children, but it's not the one that turns it into a building block of wisdom. Instead, it teaches that those in power get to inflict punishment on others who do "wrong" simply because they have the power to do so. In those instances, the abuse of power becomes just one more example to others of bullying. Using this as background, let us examine the educational benefits of asserting a Bad Samaritan framework on child and adolescent bystanders to bullying behaviors.

First, the theoretical pros: If individuals know that they will be held accountable for a failure to act when a peer is on the receiving end of mistreatment, it will encourage bystanders to actively intervene. It will increase the number of individuals who feel empowered to act against bullying behaviors if they know that their efforts are supported by the supervisory authority. And if the majority of students actively challenge bullying behaviors, it will decrease the overall number of such behaviors within the student community.

Now the more realistic cons: Individuals might not have the tools to know what to do in situations when they observe their peers being bullied. They may feel that they have to act to intervene regardless of their skills to be able to do so. Action on the part of possible defenders could well be based on efforts to avoid their own punishment for failure to do so. Last, all individuals who intervene in conflict risk the possibility of becoming a part of the conflict itself. One wonders the benefit of a physically smaller child feeling compelled to confront a larger aggressor based on the fear of being disciplined as a Bad Samaritan under school rules.

We should not compel children to intervene in confrontational situations without having given them the tools and support to do so. Such tools might well include the knowledge that physical intervention may not be the best course of action, but knowing who to contact (e.g., a responsible adult supervisor) in times of such conflict is a better option. Indeed, we do want to provide children and adolescents with the conflict resolution skills so that they are capable of de-escalating tense interpersonal interactions, but we need to recognize that children also need to know how to find the nearest adult when their skills of intervention will not resolve the conflict in which they find themselves.

APPLICATION OF BAD SAMARITAN RULES TO ADULTS

Adults, on the other hand, are more responsible for coming to the aid of those with whom they have supervisory responsibilities. One of the major reasons that bullying behaviors have existed for so long is the reality that adults have been complicit in allowing it to happen. In some instances, they have condoned it intentionally (e.g., "The only way a bully stops being a bully is when they get a dose of their own medicine") or acted negligently as actual de facto Bad Samaritans. When we make no effort to change the status quo of bullying behaviors, then such behaviors likely do not improve, and they may very well get worse.

What are the theoretical pros of applying Bad Samaritan expectations upon adults in supervisory capacities? They are perhaps much the same as the pros for children and adolescents as outlined earlier. Because supervisory personnel know that they will be held accountable if they fail to act when they observe or are made aware of bullying behaviors, they will likely feel more of an obligation to be proactive in stopping it. Adults who know the institution in which they work will back up and support their interventions are more likely to feel empowered to do so. And when the supervisory personnel act as a unit with the same level of expectations and behaviors designed to stop bullying, everyone in the environment knows that the mistreatment of others will be addressed—not *maybe* addressed or addressed by *some* but not by others—but addressed and dealt with by *everyone* in the institutional setting because that is the expectation of those who attend that particular environment.

Adults are not children, and they are not deserving of the excuses and oversights that we provide for kids when adults fail in their fiduciary responsibilities to act in an affirmative manner to stop misbehavior among the population that they supervise. While the application of Bad Samaritan rules or statutes to children would be a mistake, it is less so with adults. In reality, most adults who supervise children are already held to a Bad Samaritan standard, though it may not be called such. Adults in supervisory capacities are expected, if not required by law, to prevent harm to children. The extent of how far their authority reaches for such prevention will vary. In some settings, professionals may be expected only to act in a preventive capacity during the exact hours of their workday and only within the walls of the buildings in which they operate. In others, their responsibilities may extend 24/7/365 both in and outside the brick and mortar (or cyberspace, in the case of online supervisors) in which they operate. Failure to act when one's charges are imperiled is ***negligence***, and the penalties for negligence may well be both criminal and civil. All adults who work with children are well-advised to be knowledgeable about the reach of expectations and limitations regarding their responsibilities when it comes to responding to bullying behaviors of which they have knowledge.

WANT TO LEARN MORE?

To see the AdCouncil's "Be More Than a Bystander" public service campaign, go to http://www.multivu.com/mnr/63684-ad-council-ddb-new-york-new-psas-for-national-bullying-prevention-month.

For an expansive list of assessment possibilities related to the measurement of school climate, see the Directory of Federal Climate and Discipline Resources (2014) at http://www2.ed.gov/policy/gen/guid/school-discipline/appendix-1-directory.pdf and Hamburger, Basile, and Vivolos's (2011) *Measuring Bullying Victimization, Perpetration, and Bystander Experiences: A Compendium of Assessment Tools*, available at http://www.cdc.gov/violenceprevention/pdf/BullyCompendiumBk-a.pdf.

Which bullying prevention or intervention program works best? At the time of the final edits of publication, no one specific bullying prevention or behavioral intervention program could prove its effectiveness at a level of statistical consistency so as to be declared the "most successful" of any such programs. One study even found that those participating in bullying prevention programs "were more likely to have experienced peer victimization, compared to those attending schools without bullying prevention programs" (Joeng & Lee, 2013, p. 1). Certain programs seem to offer some improvement in reducing bullying behaviors in certain settings, but the myriad of noncontrolled and nonexperimental applications of the various programs do not lend themselves well to definitive conclusions. "Whole-school interventions" that "address bullying as a systemic problem meriting a systemic solution" (Vreeman & Carroll, 2007, p. 86), however, seemed to have the best promise. In spite of all the flurry of concern over bullying behaviors and its prevention, the United States remains nascent in its efforts to prove statistically what works and what doesn't. See Casebeer (2012), Farrington and

Ttofi (2009), Polanin, Espelage, and Pigott (2012), and Ross and Horner (2009) for further insight into the difficulties of declaring a "winner" or "best in show" of current bullying prevention programs.

Those interested in learning more about the concept of applying Bad Samaritan regulations are encouraged to read Benzmiller's (2013) full article. It provides a fascinating introduction to a potential approach to compel individuals to move from passive to active bystander status in dealing with bullying behaviors, as well as raises provocative questions of the practicality of its use for educational purposes.

State laws vary on sometimes minor nuances regarding what might be considered negligence under mandatory reporting statutes. An excellent source of generic information on state laws regarding a whole host of child welfare related laws can be found at the Child Welfare Information Gateway website, https://www.childwelfare.gov/systemwide/laws_policies/state/. A caveat: Clearinghouse-type sites are often not updated as necessary to report the most frequent laws or policies impacting practice. Always consult with state and local resources to cross-validate accuracy of generic clearinghouse-type information.

17

Engaging the Parent

©iStockphoto.com/Christoph

We cannot work with children who bully others without also working with their parents and guardians.[1] Regardless of parents' receptivity to working with supervisory personnel during an intervention, we have to take the position that no matter how difficult they may present in the early stages of that intervention, in the end, we will be able to convince them the wisdom of acting in the best interest of their child. That must be the starting position of the intervention—if *we* don't believe that the parent will be a willing partner in the intervention, we've lost half the battle before it has begun. We have to assume that parents do not know or understand the seriousness of what the child's behavior poses for the future. It is our job to educate the parents and present them with the information, regardless of whether or not they seem receptive to it in the early stages. We must hold the position that, if our evidence is strong enough, it will overcome even the strongest of disbelief on the part of the parent. The unbiased facts should speak for themselves. Whether or not the parents choose to believe the information or desire to be an active participant in solving the problem is a decision they have to make for themselves.

Parents of children who bully come in all flavors. They typically, however, fall into two major groups—those who want to play an active role in the solution of their child's behavior, and those who are, either through neglect, incapability, or willfulness, less inclined to do so. That "less inclined" group runs a continuum from the skeptical "I'm not so sure I agree with your assessment that my child is a bully, but I'll listen and maybe try to do something if I can" end of the spectrum, to its polar opposite: "You're crazy. My child is not a bully! How dare you call her one! She's just doing what I told her to do, standing up for herself. I have a good mind to sue you for slander!"

Let's consider how we might work best with both groups.

THE PARENT WHO IS RECEPTIVE TO INTERVENTION

The parents who are receptive to intervention on behalf of a child involved in questionable behaviors make our jobs much easier. They are generally receptive to suggestions we may have to offer and are willing to try do their parts in improving the situation. They may have the personal resources to tackle the job head on, or they may need suggestions and assistance in helping to address the issue in the home.

---

1. We will refer to both parents and guardians as *parents* in this chapter for the sake of convenience.

We must nurture and support parents who are an eager part in the solution to the problem behavior of their children. They likely will welcome the initial conference with the Intervener. They may not like what they hear, but they trust the source of information as valid. It is important to engage the receptive parent as an ***equal partner*** in addressing the behavior of the child.

DIALOGUE WITH THE PARENT WILLING TO HELP

In the following scenario, a parent and an Intervener are having their first informational conference:

Intervener [I] 1:	*Thanks for coming in today, Mr. Parent.*
Parent [P] 1:	*She's my child, and I'm responsible for her. Now, can you help me understand what all this is about?*
I 2:	*Absolutely. We've been getting some reports lately of Student G being involved in some behaviors that are causing problems for other students in her grade.*
P 2:	*What kind of behaviors?*
I 3:	*I'll just lay it all out here and we'll see if we can figure it out.* *When we first heard Student G's name mentioned in these instances, we were as surprised as you were. So all of her teachers met first to see if we were all hearing the same information. It seems as if we were, and it was coming from enough different students who don't know one another to hear the same story that we decided we needed to follow up to see if we could notice it, too. We paid closer attention to Student G for a full week, and here is what we observed—we met again yesterday and compiled a list of behaviors that are either clearly problematic or close to the line.* [At this point, a paper is handed to the parent with a list of seven instances where Student G was disrespectful to her peers or borderline physically aggressive in settings when she thought she was not being observed. The Intervener gives the parent plenty of time to read the list and ask any questions she may have about the specifics of the behaviors.]
P 3:	*I'm embarrassed. We don't raise Student G to do these things, and if we had known she was, we would have done something before now. All of these things look like she's bullying the kids in her grade.*

I 4: *Let's set your mind at ease about a couple of things. First, let's not put a label on the behavior. We prefer to say that Student G's been doing some things that are causing problems to her peers and are impacting their abilities to learn in school. There is no need to give something a label because it might not be what we think it is. And no one believes you encouraged these kinds of behaviors. We know you well enough here at school to realize that if you'd known before now about these behaviors, you would have already started working with us on stopping them. That's the purpose of this conversation, to take that first step of informing you of what we've observed and to let you know that we would like to work together to find a solution to stop it.*

P 4: *Well, I'm certainly on board with that. What do you suggest that we can do at home to help?*

I 5: *First, I want to ask you if you have any questions about anything on this list. Any doubts about what we've seen, or any questions about any of the behaviors?*

P 5: *That one incident three days ago when Student G took another girl's books when she thought the teacher wasn't looking and then gave them right back when she found out she had been seen and said she was only joking—we've seen some of that at home with her younger brother recently.*

I 6: *That's helpful to know. Let's look at some of the material I have to share with you about what parents need to know about bullying behaviors with their children. You can take all of this home with you. And right after we discuss some of these handouts, I'd like for us to leave here with another short list of three immediate things that you can do at home to help us start addressing these behaviors together.*

WHAT JUST HAPPENED HERE?

Wouldn't the world be a wonderful place if all parents were as receptive to information about their children as this particular one was? Actually, many of them are when they are approached in a *nonadversarial manner* (I 1). One key is to arrange the initial conference as soon as there is enough *factual information available to structure a coherent picture* of what is occurring (I 2–3). The parent is provided a list of what has been observed by several teachers in multiple circumstances (I 3). Another key is to *approach the parent as an equal partner* (I 3–4) in the problem-solving equation. While the truth may well be that supervisory personnel can apply enough reason, pressure, structure, or discipline to Student G to cause her to correct misbehavior

Intervention Tips With Parents

Facts connect the dots to complete the total picture.

Assume the parent is an equal partner, and move forward from that perspective.

during the periods of time when she is under supervision, when parents are brought into the picture and are cooperative (P 3, 4), it expands the potential for adult supervision exponentially. Parents should always be viewed as willing partners and given the benefit of the doubt until there is a reason to consider otherwise.

DIALOGUE WITH THE PARENT WHO IS SKEPTICAL ABOUT INTERVENTION

Maintaining the high ground in our intervention, we assume that all parents want what is best for their children, even when they are skeptical after being presented with the facts. Sometimes, this skepticism is directly related to the concern of parents that they don't have the skills to be of assistance in helping solve the problem—sound familiar? It should. That is one of the same reasons that Coloroso (2003) reported that kids refused to move from passive bystander to active intervener status. Think about that.

The challenge for the Intervener, then, is to convince the parents about the positive outcome likely to occur if they choose to make themselves available as partners at home in solving the problem. Skeptical parents need lots of encouragement and convincing to overcome their skepticism. We have to work with them to find their strengths and address their concerns about whatever is at the root of their doubts.

In this scenario, we join the Intervener right after awkward pleasantries have been exchanged. The anxiety of the parent comes out early when she jumps ahead of the planned information exchange:

Parent (P) 1: *I have to tell you, I'm really nervous about all of this. Student H has told me he's been accused of bullying his classmates, and I'm not really sure I believe it's true. He says they're the ones picking on him. And I don't want Student H to be labeled a bully.*

Intervener (I) 1: *Well, let me assure you that I'm not here to put a label on Student H or call his behavior bullying. But I am here to share information with you about what we've observed and discuss with you what you think we might be able to do together in order to make the situation better.* [Here the Intervener reviews the observation techniques used to gather the facts about Student H's behavior in a similar way to the scenario with the receptive parent earlier. The parent listens but is uncomfortable about what she hears and remains skeptical.]

P 2: *I still have a hard time believing that Student H is responsible for causing all of those problems.*

I 2: *All I'm doing is giving you the facts of what we've observed. There were six of us involved in making these observations, and all six of us saw the same kinds of behaviors from Student H all week long.*

P 3: *Well, you probably all compared notes.*

I 3: *Actually, we didn't. We purposely agreed that we would not talk to each other about Student H until the end of the week so that we would avoid influencing each other in any way. What you see on that list was gathered independently from any conversation any of us had until yesterday when we met to discuss how the week with Student H had gone.*

P 4: [Is getting the message that her child may have, indeed, engaged in the behaviors that are being reported.] *So what's the point?*

I 4: *We want to help Student H stop engaging in these behaviors, and we need your help.*

P 5: *Look, I don't know anything about how to do any of that stuff. That's all your job, anyway.*

I 5: *Parts of it. But not all of it. We know that the best chance of success we have with helping Student H stop what's been going on is if we address the behaviors both here and at home. That's where we need your help.*

P 6: *But I already said I don't know how to do any of this stuff.*

I 6: *I understand that you feel that way. But what if I said that you and I could today, right now, this afternoon before you leave, come up with three things you can do over this next week to help us all work together to try stop Student H from maybe getting into more trouble?*

P 7: *I'm not sure I could do them.*

I 7: *What if I told you I believe you are more capable that you think you are?*

P 8: [Doesn't quite know how to respond. The encouragement flies opposite to the way she anticipated the conversation to go.]

I 8: *Look, let's review these materials that I'm going to give to you, and when we finish, let's see if you feel the same way you did before we started, OK?*

WHAT JUST HAPPENED HERE?

Skeptical parents may need help understanding that their child has been disruptive and how that conclusion was reached (I 2–3). Again, we need to have the facts on our side to demonstrate that the meeting we are having is both to discuss the problematic behavior and improve the outcome for all involved (I 4–6).

The main message to skeptical parents is that we *believe that they have more skills than they believe they do* (P 6–7, I 7) and that *we are willing to invest the time with them* (I 6, 8) to help them discover how supportive they can really be. It is important to remember that *skeptical parents are at a* ***tipping point*** in terms of their beliefs and decisions as to whether or not they have the capabilities or even the desire to help. The Intervener's role is to tip them into the "can-do" side. Reviewing plans with parents (I 6, 8) is an excellent way to encourage them to, if nothing else, help them understand what is about to occur.

THE PARENT WHO IS RESISTANT TO INTERVENTION

Then, there are those parents who, no matter how well the information is presented or how clear the evidence, refuse to want to be a part of the

Intervention Tips With Parents

Parents often question their abilities to help solve their child's problem in the school setting.

Believe in and convince the parents of their existing skill set in helping solve errant child behavior.

Have resources available to provide the parents to build on their skillset.

solution equation. These parents are not skeptical. They are firm in their resolve to stay out of the intervention process, usually because they are antagonistic to either the intervention itself or they do not believe that their children have created the problem.

In this scenario, we have a parent who falls on the outer fringe of the less-inclined spectrum—one might even find this parent a part of the problem. We join after the first few minutes of introductions and background information in which the situation has been shared. The parent is clearly on the offensive.

Parent [P] 1: *I really don't believe that Student I is the problem here.*

Intervener [I] 1: *I understand that it seems from your perspective that Student I isn't responsible for what has been occurring, but—*

P 2: *There's no doubt in my mind that it's not Student I's fault. He's just responding to what those other kids have been doing to provoke him.*

I 2: *Six different teachers reported that Student I was the one who started the negative interactions with all of his classmates.*

P 3: *That's just you people seeing what you want to see. You did the same thing to his older brother two years ago. Come to think of it, I got treated the same way when I was a kid in school.*

I 3: *I'm sorry that you feel as if you were not treated fairly in school, but we'll have to disagree on how your children have been treated here. We work hard to make certain that we treat everyone as fairly as possible. One way we do that is to make independent judgments on student behavior when there's a question about exactly what the behavior means. As I explained, we had six teachers observing Student I throughout the week—*

P 4: *See! You were spying on my kid, trying to make it look like he was acting up!*

I 4: *Please let me finish and fully explain. All six teachers observed Student I independently for a week and didn't report back on what they saw until the week was over. We did that specifically to avoid any accidental influence we might have had on one another in terms of what we were observing. At the end of the week, the instances on that list that I gave you were the conclusions that six different teachers came to about what was going on between Student I and his classmates. It's really not a matter of the school trying to gang up on your child and making up things that didn't happen. This is actually what six different people saw happen over the last week between Student I and other students, and in every instance, he was the first to start some kind of negative interaction.*

P 5: *I just don't believe it. And besides, if he did do anything on that list, he was just doing what we told him to do to defend himself. We don't let our kids be punching bags to anybody!*

I 5: *And we don't want anyone's child to be a punching bag to anyone, either. However, we also don't allow any child to behave in a fashion that is disrespectful or abusive to others. We don't want anyone to mistreat Student I, and we don't want Student I to mistreat anyone else. We want this to be a safe place for everyone. So let's see if we can move forward to figure out a way to make this situation better for everyone. We can agree to disagree on whether or not what was reported about Student I's behavior was 100% accurate, but I am going to be honest and tell you point blank that even if 10% of these behaviors continue, Student I will be held accountable for his actions.*

P 6: *So you're going to pick on him, too.*

I 6: *No. Quite the opposite. We are going to be very fair to Student I, but we are going to hold him accountable when he behaves outside the rules. Here is a list of what we do to try help students learn from their mistakes. We believe that when students misbehave, we want them to learn ways to not make that same mistake again.*

P 7: *You really mean punish them, don't you?*

I 7: *Not necessarily. Our first goal is to try help the child who has made a mistake to make amends for that mistake to those that may have been wronged. That's called* restoration. *If that doesn't or won't work, then we move toward discipline. Discipline is not always punishment—it's not about hurting. It's about trying to figure out what the student who did the wrong can learn from the behavior so that he or she can make better decisions the next time. We want to keep all our students in school for as long as we can. We don't want to have to send any student home because of misbehavior. But that is an option we sometimes have to consider if a student's behavior is so out of line that others are endangered or the behavior disrupts or prevents other students from learning.*

P 8: *Well, I don't like any of those ideas.*

I 8: *Then we'll have to agree to disagree because that's the way we're going to proceed with Student I if these types of behaviors continue.*

P 9: *So it doesn't make any difference what my opinion is?*

I 9: *Yes, it does. That's why we're meeting right now, and that's why we need you to help us at home to prevent these things from occurring again in the future. In fact, we'd like to include some of your ideas into whatever plan it is we think will be best for everyone.*

P 10: *So what can I do? I don't even trust you people that you're treating Student I right.*

I 10: *Then maybe the first thing we need to do is talk about what we need to do to raise the trust level between your family and the school. You have to believe me when I say, I want to help you and Student I to have a better future here at school than the one you believe he's had in the past. So might we go over some of these handouts I have about how we might start to do that and start today, right now, in trying to make that happen?*

WHAT JUST HAPPENED HERE?

As with the skeptical parent, ***trust*** *is the main hurdle that must be overcome with parents who are resistant to change* (P 1–5). Parents often are hesitant about partnering with supervisory personnel because of *past negative experiences* with their other children in the school setting (P 3). Sometimes, it is their own past experience with authority that manifests itself during parent–teacher conferences (P 3). Whatever the reason, the *major challenge is to prove to these parents that the supervisory personnel is not out to "get" their child,* but is trying to assist everyone in making the situation better for everyone involved (I 5–6). It is a difficult task and one not always achieved. As with working with students who bully, applying patience and tolerance are always the two major ***temperaments*** that help.

The main challenge for all concerned is to persuade the skeptical or resistant parent that everyone who is attempting to intervene and the child will be better served if all three legs of the corrective action stool are the same length (I 9–10). That may well take some major convincing on the part of the Interveners (I 6–7,10), especially if the mistrust is based on perceived past wrongs directed toward the child or the parents (P 3). The skeptical *parent needs to know exactly what will happen* in the intervention,

Intervention Tips With Parents

Distrust is the major stumbling block that causes interventions to fail.

Parents may have had bad experiences themselves as children. They do not forget.

Mistrustful parents view interventions as reasons to "get" their child for misbehavior.

We have to be patient and tolerant with parents, too.

both if the child cooperates (I 6–7), or if the child does not (I 6). *Make sure the parent understands that his or her opinion matters* (P 9, I 9) and that, as much as is possible, it will be taken into consideration as a part of whatever plan is finalized (I 9).

WHAT PARENTS NEED TO KNOW

Parents of children who antagonize others need to know specifically what the rules are that will be applied to future instances of bullying behaviors exhibited by their children. Whether we get the indications that the parents are more or less agreeable to being parties in the ***solution equation,*** we keep to that high road of assumption that we still have the responsibility to do everything within our power to provide the information to those parents to help them make the best decision on behalf of their children. Failure to do so is a failure show by deeds that we truly do have the best interest of all children in mind, even the ones with parents who challenge every fiber of our patience and tolerance.

With that in mind, here is a list of important things that parents of children who bully others need to know:

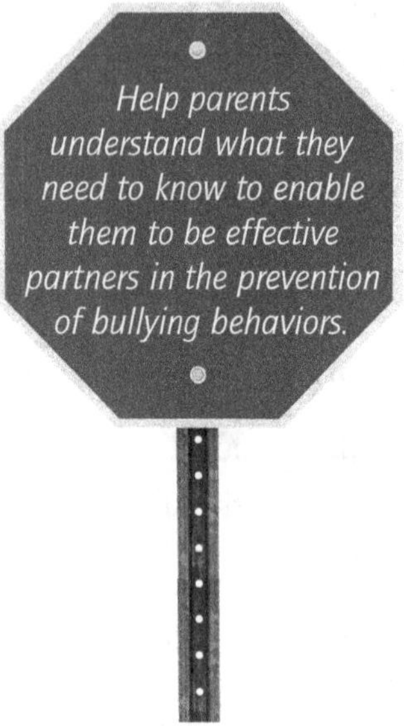

Provide a copy of the institution's rules on bullying-related behaviors. This is nonnegotiable because it serves as the foundation of everything else that can legally result from violations of the rules. Supervisory personnel cannot enforce rules for which they have no authority. More importantly, however, is that parents need to understand what is at stake if their child's behaviors do not change for the better.

Stick to the facts of observed behaviors. Parents need to know the *specifics* of what their child has been observed doing that qualifies as inappropriate behavior. This is best presented in a matter-of-fact format that can be discussed with the parent without additional room for editorial comments from supervisory personnel. It's not what we *think* is happening, it's what we *know* is happening because the behavior has been *observed* and *documented*.

Assure parents that the goal of intervention is to make the institution a safe place for everyone so that they can learn and achieve the goals of the institution. A *safe* and *distraction-free learning environment* increases the likelihood of improved learning. Parents need to know that this benefits everyone, including their children. They also need to know that supervisory personnel will do whatever is necessary to make sure that happens.

Inform parents that, if necessary, their child may face an intervention designed to improve the learning environment for everyone. Every child in the institution who displays inappropriate behaviors is subject to an intervention conference, first between supervisory personnel and the student. The purpose of that conference is to try to stop future similar behaviors from occurring. If the original conference works, no further action may be needed. If not, then the parents will be increasingly drawn into the solution equation.

Explain the incremental disciplinary process. Based on the institution's rules, parents need to know that intervention and discipline will be administered from a least- to a more-restrictive or intrusive manner based directly on how well the student responds to the initial intervention. The goal is to reduce bullying behaviors as soon as possible without further intervention. However, if lower levels of intervention do not work, additional applications of strategies may well be necessary.

What Parents Need to Know About Becoming Partners in the Solution Equation to Correct Negative Behaviors With Their Child

A copy of the school rules and which rules the child's behavior violates

Specific behaviors of the child that are problematic

An explanation that the child's behavior impacts the total learning environment for all children

The accountability measures that will be attempted to correct the misbehavior

The incremental disciplinary measures that may have to be enforced if early intervention does not work

Parents play a critical role in the solution to the problem by reinforcing at home what is expected to occur in the school setting.

Above all, assure parents that the ultimate goal is to keep the student in the learning environment. The purpose of intervention with a student who bullies is not to punish or deprive the right to an education. The goal is to help the student learn more positive ways of interacting with peers during the educational day. This information is best presented to parents both in writing and during a review of the information during a parent conference. It is important to keep the conference as low threat and nonconfrontational as possible. Always remember, the mere act of requesting a parent conference is often perceived as a "summons" by parents, an indication that their child has done something "wrong" even before they arrive at the institution.

HELPFUL TIPS FOR THE PARENTS OF CHILDREN WHO BULLY

Parents are often at a loss to know what to do if their children are identified as engaging in bullying behaviors. Perhaps that is because educators are often at a loss themselves. Search any database for information on intervention strategies for parents of children who bully and you don't find much. What is out there, too, has often been pilfered from the same source and reposted by others in cyberspace as original.

What follows is a list of suggestions for working with parents of children who bully gleaned from what is a consensus among various legitimate sources at the time of publication. Sources for these suggestions and where to go to discover more about helping parents work with the child who exhibits bullying behaviors are found at the end of the chapter.

First and foremost, the parent and the child need to have a conversation about the information related to the reason why the child's behavior is being considered bullying. Clarify if there is there some kind of misunderstanding or misinterpretation of the behavior. Does the child know that the behavior is being viewed by others as intimidating? Are others involved with the child in the behavior? The parent needs to be as objective as possible and avoid angry reactions so as to avoid increasing the odds of shutting down communication.

Determine if there is a developmental foundation for the cause of the behavior with the child. Some parents do not understand that there may be legitimate reasons why a child acts out against peers. Sometimes it has a basis in a formerly diagnosed learning or behavioral disability. At other times, children act out in response to some type of traumatic event ongoing in their lives (e.g., grief and loss). If the behavior is recent in its origin, consider what is different in the life of the child that might create the acting-out behavior.

Do not downplay the seriousness of the reports. Too often parents pooh-pooh the idea that their child is the cause of disruptive or aggressive behaviors. All parents need to realize that under the right circumstances any child—yes, even their own—can engage in behaviors that might be considered intimidating to others. Take reports at face value first until they can be clarified by additional information from both the child and supervisory personnel.

Make parental expectations clear. Parents must make it clear to their children that they are expected to follow the rules of the institution. If there is a disagreement between the home and the institution as to exactly what those rules are or if the rules contradict those of the family, then a parent should immediately request a conference to avoid placing the child in a double bind.[2]

Hold children accountable for misbehavior related to bullying. In instances when children do, indeed, engage in bullying, hold them accountable for their actions. Since most instances of bullying occur outside the home, children need to know that they run the risk of double jeopardy at home if they are responsible for bullying behaviors someplace else. Such accountability, however, needs to be fair. Parents should not become bullies themselves in the dispensing of heavy-handed discipline to their children.

Be a role model for responding to bullying behaviors. This may seem difficult to do on the surface, but it can be done through the responses adults give to intimidating situations during the times when their children are present. Someone cuts off the parent in traffic? Don't respond in anger! Someone rude in the checkout line? Don't say it! How the adult responds sends a strong message to the child about how to properly handle boorish people.

Encourage empathy and compassion. Be kind. Children are exposed to much anger in their daily lives. Children can understand the applicability of the Golden Rule[3] with or without any religious affiliation. Help them see

---

2. A ***double bind*** is when an individual is faced with two requirements that are seemingly opposite in expectation. To do one is to fail to do the other. Double binds are particularly difficult to solve when punishments are attached for failing to follow both sets of expectations. For example, if following family rules flies in the face of school rules, then which does the child choose?

3. It is amazing that all the world's major religions—and many of the not-so-major ones—ascribe to some sort of empathic and compassionate application of interaction with others. Also called the ***ethic of reciprocity***, all applications basically describe the same behavior of "Do to others as you would like done to you" or "Don't do to others what you would

themselves in the lives of others. Ask them, "What would you feel like if that had happened to you?" Then ask, "What prevented you from acting in that manner in this instance?"

Help your child understand the difference between taking responsibility and blame. Taking responsibility for one's actions is a way of acknowledging that when mistakes are made, we are willing to do what is necessary to move toward accountability. Responsibility is the first step toward accountability. Taking responsibility also reduces the chances of being blamed for misbehavior since blame typically is an accusation directed toward individuals when no one will accept responsibility.

Work with supervisory personnel to help your child learn the necessary skills to avoid, reduce, and eliminate behaviors that are interpreted as intimidating others. Parents and personnel who work in schools, community centers, and other child-centered gathering places must combine their resources in order to discover the best-fit approach to solving behavioral problems with children who intimidate others. There should be strong communication between the home and supervisory personnel in order to help monitor the child's behaviors as much as possible.

When the child behaves properly, be sure to note it. Only criticizing what goes wrong in a child's life without providing positive reinforcement when things go well sends a message that we are only interested in the negative behavior. If we don't water the seeds we want to grow, then they die before ever seeing the light of day.

At the end of the day, be realistic. Sometimes children do engage in bullying behaviors. Those kids belong to somebody, and they just might end up belonging to the parents who are sitting in front of us today. Help parents understand that if their child is involved in bullying, there are ways to address it. Acknowledging that fact can be the first step toward finding a solution that best suits the child, the institution, and the parents.

THE BOTTOM LINE

Here's the bottom line: A child is less likely to be successful in slowing or stopping bullying behaviors without the support of parents. No matter

not like done to you." See "Shared Beliefs in the 'Golden Rule' (aka Ethics of Reciprocity): Passages From Various Religious Texts" at http://www.religioustolerance.org/reciproc2.htm for a delightful review of the various ways in which the same concept is expressed.

Helpful Tips for Parents of a Child Who Engages in Bullying Behaviors

Talk to your child about the behaviors that must be corrected.

Don't downplay the importance of the need to change the behavior.

Set expectations for your child. The child is expected to follow the school rules at a minimum.

Hold your child accountable for both school and home misbehaviors.

Be a role model when it comes to avoiding bullying behaviors.

Encourage the child to be kind to others and think about how he or she might feel if the misbehavior was directed toward him or her.

Give your child permission to make mistakes and ask forgiveness without fear of punishment.

Work closely with supervisory personnel. Communicate. Collaborate.

When your child behaves properly or makes a good decision, support it.

Be realistic about bullying behaviors. All kids may do it at one point in their lives, but kids who do so all the time are in need of help to stop it.

how difficult a parent may be to deal with in terms of requesting their assistance in the process, *the invitation must always be extended,* if for no other reason than to let them know that if the behavior does not improve, additional restrictions and discipline are likely to occur to ensure the safety and well-being of all. Even "difficult parents" often surprise us in their willingness to cooperate when asked to be a part of the solution to a problem behavior with their child. Sometimes, it's all in the way they are approached and maybe even given the respect that they are not used to receiving.

WANT TO LEARN MORE?

Additional sources for helping parents work with their child who engages in bullying behaviors can be found at the following:

Anti-Defamation League. (2012). *What to do if your child exhibits bullying behavior.* http://www.adl.org/assets/pdf/education-outreach/What-to-Do-if-Your-Child-Exhibits-Bullying-Behavior.pdf

Lee, K. (n.d.). What to do when your child is a bully: How to handle this tough situation and help your child correct his behavior. *About.com.* http://childparenting.about.com/od/socialdevelopment/a/What-To-Do-When-Your-Child-Is-A-Bully.htm

PACER Center. (n.d.). *What if your child is the bully?* http://www.pacer.org/parent/php/PHP-c109.pdf

Sizer, B. (n.d.). What to do when your child is a bully. *PBS Parents: Education.* http://www.pbs.org/parents/education/going-to-school/social/what-to-do-when-your-child-is-a-bully/

Steiner-Adair, C. (2013, November 18). What to do if your child is a bully. *Wall Street Journal.* http://blogs.wsj.com/speakeasy/2013/11/18/what-to-do-if-your-child-is-a-bully/

18

Documentation

©iStockphoto.com/michaeljung

The major premise of this book is based on what we are calling an ***intervention***. An intervention has two main purposes. First, it is an intentional act to alert the individual creating the problem (and, when necessary, the parents as well) that the current behavior is deemed inappropriate and that it must improve. Second, it places the individual on notice that if the behavior does not improve, increasing levels of behavioral education, restoration, remediation, restriction, or discipline will be considered.

THE GEOGRAPHY OF PROBLEM SOLVING (GPS) APPROACH

An intervention with an individual who bullies should always start as soon as the problem is noted with the ***Geography of Problem Solving (GPS) approach***.[1] GPS is a very simple concept for addressing problems of most types and can be amazingly effective in stopping issues from becoming larger at the time of initial engagement. GPS operates from the belief that problems are solved best at the "lowest level" at which they occur. What does that lowest level mean? In an interpersonal disagreement, it could mean two people calmly talking among themselves over some misunderstanding before the two of them take rumor, innuendo, and paranoia to the next level. (GPS, of course, would put an end to most reality shows currently dominating the media since conflict is the gasoline on the fire that makes them work.) Remember, the more people brought into a conversation to address a problem, the more potential solutions—or disagreements—emerge.

Clearly, for interventions with children who bully others, the earlier an intervention can occur, the better. However, an intervention should not be an overreaction to a misunderstanding between two parties—sometimes a disagreement is just a disagreement without anything else attached to it. Our job is to discern which is which and what is what, and the only way that happens is through thorough investigation.

---

1. The exact origin of this approach to problem solving is a mystery to me and one that I have not been able to unravel, though not because of lack of trying. I first learned of it during my undergraduate years from a wise gentleman, Dr. Francis Christie, who taught classes at Hendrix College during the mid-1970s. Try as I may, I have never been able to find an official citation for the concept and, after consultation, have come to the conclusion that it may well have been a concept of his own creation. Regardless of its origins, I teach the approach in all of my counselor education coursework and use it in my consultations as a method of de-escalating tensions in the early stages of interpersonal disputes.

INVESTIGATION BEFORE INTERVENTION

An "investigation" sounds rather ominous. It might turn out to be that way, but using a GPS approach in the early stages of some type of bullying behavior likely decreases the chances of that occurring.

When we talk about an ***investigation*** in this instance, we are talking about a low-level intervention that *simply gathers the facts* of what is or has been occurring which is considered to be inappropriate behavior. The facts should answer the following four questions:

The Four Critical Questions of Investigating Incidents of Bullying

Who is involved?

What specific problematic behavior occurred (or is occurring)?

When did (or does) it occur?

Where did (or does) it happen?

Notice that there is no "Why . . . ?" question. There's a very good reason for that. "Why?" is often too large a question to answer. The answer to "Why?" is found in the "Who? What? When? and Where?" that precedes it. The "Who? What? When? and Where?" are based on facts. "Why?" is most often a summation of those four contributing factors and is the conclusion we draw from them. However, "Why?" is often a subjective conclusion on the part of both those attempting to analyze behavior and those who engage in it. Individuals who engage in problematic behavior can often provide a reason, in their minds, as to "Why?" they did something, but the accompanying facts may show little connection. For the sake of our investigations, let's stick to as much of the hard-core factual information that we can discover and leave the "Why?" to speak for itself.

In the best of worlds, as much information as possible is gathered *before* an intervention. Additional information will come out during the intervention, but to begin one without the background behind what is known to that point is a mistake. Factual information helps keep an intervention focused and on track. The purpose of an investigation is to add additional information to what is already known or not known so that the intervention can proceed as smoothly as possible. *An investigation is not an interrogation.* An investigation uses many of the techniques of intentional interviewing discussed in Chapter 7. Another way to view the Intervener's role in the investigation process is that of a ***facilitator of information gathering***.

Let's look at a scenario (Documentation 18.1) in which the four critical questions listed earlier have been applied prior to further intervention

Figure 18.1 Documentation of Incident Report 18.1

First Documentation Filed on Initial Incident Between Two Students

Incident of Concern # 34 / 2016–17 School Year

Name of Individuals Involved: Student J and Student K. Both are in the same classroom, Grade 5.

Date of Incident: Behavior seems to be ongoing. Date of onset unclear. Last incident was on the playground 3/2/17. Incident observed by Mr. Teacher A from the window in his room during the lunch break.

Describe the Incident: Student J pushed Student K off the slide during lunch break. Student J was observed taunting Student K right before he shoved Student K at the top of the ladder of the slide. Duty teachers were not in the area where the incident occurred, but responded immediately when other students brought it to their attention. Mr. Teacher B and Ms. Teacher C were on the playground at the time of the incident.

Student J was interviewed immediately after the incident by Ms. Principal and claimed that Student K fell on her own. Student J did not waver from his claim.

Student K was interviewed immediately after the incident and claimed that Student J had been calling her names in a whisper all during the morning in class, including the use of profanity ("bitch," "whore," and "slut" were specifically mentioned). Student K also said that there had been other incidents over the last few weeks, but she wasn't sure how long ago they had started.

Other students on the playground at the time of the incident verified that Student J had been calling Student K derogatory names that day, including the ones mentioned by Student K, and had been doing so for at least three weeks prior.

When Student K was asked what prevented her from reporting the behavior to school staff, she indicated that she was "scared of what Student J might do to her" if she did.

Location of Incident: The 3/2/17 incident was not directly observed by school staff (mentioned above) on the south playground. Student K, however, claimed that Student J had engaged in use of profanity directed toward her and other students, had stolen pencils and paper from her, and had shoved her multiple times in her main classroom when Ms. Teacher D was not looking.

Follow-up/Recommendations: Ms. Principal referred the matter to Ms. School Counselor for further investigation and recommendation on further steps. Ms. School Counselor will meet individually with Student J and Student K. Formal behavioral intervention and conference with both Student J and Student K's parents (separately) may be in order if warranted. Ms. Principal and Ms. School Counselor will consult on next steps within 72 hours.

with a student in an upper elementary grade who has created repeated problems by his behavior.

This documentation provides the basic information necessary to start an effective intervention. It describes the incident; identifies the main players involved, including school personnel; and, perhaps most importantly, notes *what* will happen after the incident, *who* will be responsible for the follow-up, and sets an expectation for *when* that follow-up will occur.

COMPONENTS OF THE INTERVENTION

In this scenario, further investigation revealed that Student K had, indeed, been subjected to abusive behavior from Student J for an extended period of time. Ms. Teacher D, the teacher in the classroom, had been oblivious to the cues of the bullying and had observed nothing out of the ordinary between Students J and K. This is not uncommon. Students often report that bullying goes on "right under the teacher's nose." Whether an exaggeration or not, kids have learned many surreptitious and devious ways to punish their peers when supervisory personnel's backs are turned.

Chapter 15 provides a scenario and sample dialogue involving an incident of cyberbullying. Interventions for incidents of electronic, physical, or verbal bullying are basically the same. Interventions come in ***levels***, depending upon the number and seriousness of an incident(s). The potential levels of intervention with those who bully are listed below.

Notice the use of the term *minor* in Level 1. The definition of what constitutes a minor incident needs to be clarified. While bullying behaviors should not be tolerated, supervisory personnel must have the ***professional discretion*** to determine all aspects of the circumstances of the behavior under consideration. As previously discussed, zero tolerance policies do not work and are not in the best educational interest of the student. What might be considered a minor

Levels of Intervention With Individuals Who Bully

Level 1: First incident or incident determined to be minor

Level 2: Second incident or incident determined to be more problematic, serious, or severe

Level 3: Repeated incidents

Level 4: Repeated incidents with little or no improvement in student behavior incident between two students of equal power differential might be a major incident when age and cognitive and developmental abilities are thrown into the mix.

Each level of intervention should have different ***behavioral outcome goals***. These goals should be discussed with the student—collaboratively in Levels 1 and 2, perhaps less collaboratively in Levels 3 and 4—and documented in a format that makes it clear what the behavioral expectations are for all who are responsible for implementing it.

What follows is a sample dialogue between an Intervener—in this case, the school counselor—and Student J in the scenario outlined in this chapter. The decision was made to move directly into a Level 2 intervention since the fact gathering verified that Student J had, indeed, been harassing Student K for several weeks prior to the first observed incident on the playground.

Intervener [I 1]: *OK, we've spent the first few minutes going over what happened on the playground—what the teachers saw and what you said was going on. For the most part, you seem to disagree that you pushed Student K off the slide ladder, but you don't seem to disagree too much with what everybody else says they saw. Can you help me put those two pieces of the puzzle together?*

Student J [SJ 1]: *I don't believe I intentionally pushed Student K off the slide. It was an accident, but I can't fight everybody else if they said I did it. It's their word against mine.*

I 2: *Well, that's what we're here for, to make sure that you can explain everything so that we can get to the bottom of what happened.*

SJ 2: *Whatever.*

I 3: [The Intervener gives Student J the silence to add anything else, but it becomes clear that he is not going to do so.] *So for the moment, let's leave the incident about the slide. There are a few more things I need help understanding from your viewpoint. I understand that what happened on the slide was not the first time that you and Student K had some kind of not-so-nice behavior between the two of you.*

SJ 3: *What do you mean?*

I 4: *It's my understanding that you had been making some inappropriate comments to Student K—calling her names—for several weeks before the push on the slide. I have several reports that you had taken some of Student K's pencils and paper and that there had been some times when you had*

	even pushed and bumped her in the classroom when Ms. Teacher D wasn't looking.
SJ 4:	*Who says that?*
I 5:	*It's floating around.*
SJ 5:	*Well, if nobody saw me do it, then I guess I didn't do it.*
I 6:	*What if I told you that people had seen you do it?*
SJ 6:	*Like who?*
I 7:	*Enough people to make Ms. Principal and me concerned that there might be truth to what we've been told.*
SJ 7:	*I didn't do anything.*
I 8:	*Fine. Let's say you didn't. And let's say for the sake of our meeting today that you really didn't shove Student K off the slide ladder the other day. Let's just focus on the school rules for the rest of our visit today so that you have a clear understanding of exactly what they are when it comes to the way we are expected to treat each another during the school day.*
SJ 8:	*I read the rules already. I was made to when Ms. Principal talked to me the day Student K said I pushed her off the slide.*
I 9:	*Then let me ask you what your understanding of the code of conduct is for everyone here.*
SJ 9:	*"Students are expected to treat each other with respect." Ms. Principal made me read that out loud in her office.*
I 10:	*I'm impressed that you can quote the rules. Can you quote any more about student behavior?*
SJ 10:	*There's so many stupid ones.*
I 11:	*How about the ones that deal with bullying?*
SJ 11:	*"Bullying is not allowed at Alfred Adler Elementary School. Students who do so will be held accountable for their behaviors."*
I 12:	*Wow. You really know the rules, don't you?*
SJ 12:	*"If a student believes he or she has been bullied, that student should report what happened as soon as possible to the nearest teacher or other adult in the building." Want me to go on?*
I 13:	*I think what you've just said will be enough for us to talk about the rest of today. Here's the deal. We've got a problem. There's plenty of evidence that you have broken the rules when it comes to the rules of behavior we expect of everyone here at Adler Elementary School. And if that's the case, then*

we've got to figure out a way to stop that from happening again. You and I have discussed some behavior problems before, and you know that I want to help you stay out of trouble. But I can't do that without your help. I need you to work with me on helping you be able to stay in school because there are strings attached if you don't follow the rules.

SJ 13: *Even when those rules are stupid?*

I 14: *We can't change the rules, at least not today. They are what they are. But we do have to live by them—even me. So if that's what we have to do, let's first make sure that we know what might happen to us—or in this case, you—if the rules aren't followed. I'm going to be very clear: You have to follow the rules. That's the basics. Next, if you don't follow the rules, there are consequences. What those consequences are depends on what's best for you and everyone in our school. But I am officially telling you and putting you on notice that you have now broken enough of our school rules enough times that you have entered the "consequence zone," and things are going to start to change, with or without your help. You are an important part of this school, and we want you here, but you have to follow the rules—and it's clear to me you know what those rules are because you quoted a bunch of them to me just two minutes ago.*

SJ 14: [Sits and listens. Doesn't quite know what to say because he can't figure out if he should agree or disagree with the way the information is presented to him.]

I 15: *I can see you're thinking. So let's put our heads together and think about ways we can improve your behavior. But before we do that, let me make sure I understand that you understand what's going on right now. What is the one thing that's got to happen in order for me to be able to help you avoid additional problems here at school?*

SJ 15: *I have to follow the rules.*

I 16: *Yes. And what might be the next thing that has to happen at the same time?*

SJ 16: *I have to change some of the things I've been doing.*

I 17: *Yes. You've got it. Now, let's start figuring out exactly how we're going to work together to start making things better for everyone here at Adler Elementary.*

WHAT JUST HAPPENED HERE?

This is a sample dialogue of what a Level 2 intervention might sound like. Six things happened in this conversation between the Intervener and the student.

Student J was placed firmly on notice that (*if* he had, indeed, shoved Student K off the slide) the following had happened:

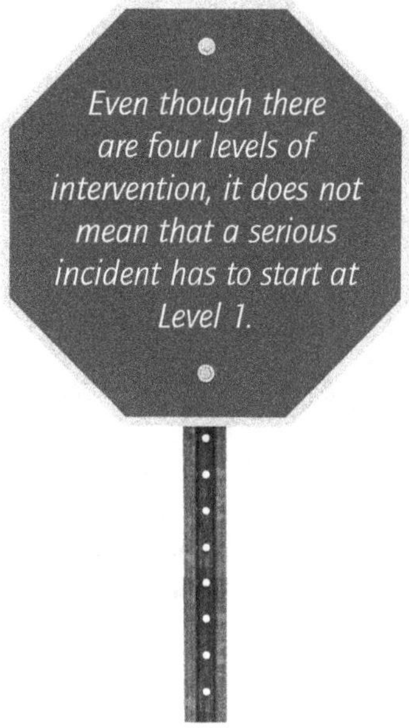

1. His behavior had broken the school rules.
2. He had crossed the line into unacceptable behavior.
3. Such behaviors placed him at risk for some type of accountability or disciplinary action.

At the same time, he was given the following:

1. An indication that the Intervener was impressed with his ability to learn the information he needed (i.e., Student J's verbatim recitation of some of the school rules on bullying)
2. Encouragement to change his behavior so that he could move back into the regular school day without running the risk of disciplinary measures
3. The chance to collaborate with the Intervener in whatever next step might be about to occur

This ***"sweet and sour approach"*** provides both the *hard information that the student needs to know about what is expected* of the misbehavior, as well as *highlights those attributes that the student brings that will be an asset* to the intervention and whatever future steps are necessary. When possible, try to *avoid providing only the "hammer" without the "cushion"* to soften the blow. This is especially important in working with individuals who are used to the hammer of discipline and authority and grow suspicious of *any* type of adult intervention during a behavioral problem, even when that intervention provides a possible solution for the one creating it.

DOCUMENTING THE INTERVENTION

All interventions should be documented in some fashion. It need not be lengthy, but it does need to cover the scope of the following details:

Documentation Essentials of Intervention With Those Who Bully

1. Dates of intervention relative to the initial report of incident
2. Who was involved in the intervention
3. Generic details of what was covered in the intervention
4. Plans for corrective/collaborative action

Documentation provides written proof that supervisory personnel are actively involved in trying to work out some type of solution to the problem that has been brought to their attention. Documentation is important as a safeguard against accusations that "nothing is being done" to address the issue. Some may argue that documentation leads to a "paper trail" for lawsuits. This may well be true if the documentation does not indicate that the supervisory authority has taken an incident of bullying seriously with proper intervention strategies. The reality is that more supervisory personnel and their employers are likely to lose a court challenge if there is no documentation of efforts to address an incident of bullying. Documentation of even the weakest of intervention efforts can indicate an effort at providing ***due diligence***, the effort to avoid further harm to others after a potentially dangerous situation is brought to supervisory personnel's attention. And as we have previously noted, failure to provide evidence of due diligence with incidents of bullying can become the basis for a claim of negligence against the supervisory agency.

Intervention Plan 18.1 provides documentation of the intervention dialogue we have just completed between the Intervener and Student J.

Intervention Plan 18.1 Initial Written Plan to Address Behavior Problems of Student Involved in Bullying Behaviors

Intervention Report #1

Incident of Concern # 34 / 2016–17 School Year

Name of Individuals Involved: Student J and Ms. School Counselor (designated by Ms. Principal as Intervener at this stage)

Date of Intervention: March 3, 2017

Date of Original Incident: March 2, 2017

Level of Intervention: 2 (Note: No Level 1 intervention was conducted due to late discovery of prior bullying behaviors.)

Prior Interventions: No formal interventions to this point. Original incident involved discussion between Student J and Ms. Principal and a disciplinary warning that other actions would likely follow after investigation of original incident was concluded.

Details of Intervention: Intervener met with Student J for 20 minutes the morning of March 3. Purpose of the meeting was to initiate formal intervention due to observed incident of bullying on March 2 and to ensure that Student J was familiar with school rules related to bullying and related inappropriate behaviors.

Student J was not completely cooperative during the meeting. Verbal responses indicated he did not want to be in the meeting and did not always believe that all the school rules were necessary. Additionally, he still maintains that he did not purposefully push another student from the slide in the initial incident. Student J was able to recite several of the basic rules related to bullying during the intervention. Though he indicated by his body posture and comments that he was not a willing participant in the intervention, Student J did not make an effort to negatively impact the meeting's purpose.

Intervener verbally formally notified Student J that (1) he had been observed engaging in behaviors that violated school rules; (2) that such behaviors were not appropriate at Adler Elementary; and (3) that additional misbehaviors would likely result in accountability actions or discipline. Student J was also informed that he would be given the opportunity to participate in collaborative efforts to make better choices in the future.

Follow-up/Recommendations: The following recommendations are made: (1) Intervener will provide Intervention Report #1 to Ms. Principal; (2) Intervener recommends additional meeting with Student J to gauge changes in current behavioral issues; (3) Constructive Behavioral Change (CBC) plan will be initiated in consultation with Student J's teachers and parent(s).

THE CONSTRUCTIVE BEHAVIORAL CHANGE (CBC) PLAN

Following intervention meetings, a Constructive Behavioral Change (CBC) plan is in order. The CBC plan becomes the written guideline for all future planning purposes to deal with the original or subsequent incidents of bullying. It establishes guidelines for expected behavioral outcome goals and begins a process for monitoring the success of reaching them. With a CBC plan, progress or nonprogress can be noted. Without a CBC plan, there is no documented evidence that an effective intervention has taken place.

A CBC plan should have the following components:

Essential Components of an Intervention Constructive Behavioral Change (CBC) Plan

1. Basic background information relative to initial report of incident(s)
2. Who was involved in implementing the CBC plan
3. Major goals of the CBC plan, with modifications as necessary
4. Progress notes on how the CBC plan was implanted
5. Recommendations for future action

The following is the CBC plan on Student J several weeks after the initial observed incident with Student K. Student J was not a willing participant in the plan to repair the damage done to Student K, but school

Constructive Behavioral Change Plan 18.1 Proposed Interventions for Student Involved in Bullying Incidents

Intervention #1

Constructive Behavioral Change Plan

Incident of Concern # 34 / 2016–17 School Year

Name of Individuals Involved: Student J, Ms. School Counselor, Ms.

Principal. Teacher D (primary classroom teacher for Student J),Teachers E, F, and G (specific subject teachers with Student J for math, music, and P.E.).

Date of Intervention: March 3, 2017

Date of Original Incident: March 2, 2017

Date of Original CBC: March 10, 2017, after consultation and meeting with parents.

Goal of March 10, 2017, CBC: A CBC plan was developed for Student J following the initial incident documented in Incident of Concern #34 of March 2, 2017. This CBC plan was developed after meeting with Student J's parents on March 7. In addition to Student J and his parents, Ms. School Counselor and Ms. Teacher D attended the meeting. Teachers E, F, and G were consulted prior to the meeting in order to gather their input on ways they could also assist in the CBC plan due to the fact that they also taught Student J during the day.

Mr. and Mrs. Student J were supportive of intervention efforts on behalf of Student J. Student J, however, did not indicate his support of any effort on his behalf, but agreed to the plan in an effort to "get it over with."

The following CBC plan was agreed to on March 10:

1. Student J will be given the opportunity to provide Student K restoration for the pencils and paper he had previously taken or destroyed.
2. Student J will be given the opportunity to apologize to Student K, but only if the apology is sincere and only if Student K feels comfortable.
3. Student J is instructed to limit his direct interaction with Student K unless she initiates the contact. Student J was instructed that if Student K does interact with him that he is to behave properly and respectfully.
4. Student J will continue to meet with Ms. School Counselor (the designated Intervener for Student J) during the next several weeks to discuss behavioral changes and learn new ways to interact with other students in more positive ways.
5. Ms. School Counselor will discuss and report on Student J's progress with his parents, teachers, and Ms. Principal.

All of the parties at the meeting on the CBC plan were in agreement with the exception of Student J. He refused to agree to the plan, but he did not say that he would actively refuse to participate in it. He was, again, put on notice that his behavior had to change in order to ensure that everyone felt safe in school, and if it did not change, he would face possible additional accountability or disciplinary measures as stated in the student handbook.

Progress Report 1: Date of report—March 17

Student J has met with Ms. School Counselor twice during the past week. The following behavioral outcome goals were addressed.

1. Student J gave his impression of how he had changed his behavior during the past week during both sessions. He indicated that he thought he was doing better, even though he was "not doing anything different" than he had in the past.
2. Ms. School Counselor worked with Student J on two handouts from the *Owning Up* curriculum. Student J was assigned worksheets, and then they discussed his answers in both sessions.
3. There have been no negative behavioral incidents reported with Student J in any of his classes during the past week.

Update on 3.10.17 CBC: Date of update—March 20

A meeting of Student J's teachers and Ms. Counselor was held on March 19 to discuss a recent incident between Student J and Student K. Student J had been following the CBC filed on March 10, but on March 18' he and Student K had a loud argument in Ms. Teacher D's room before lunch. Ms. Teacher D described the argument as the result of Student J "flipping" Student K's hair as students were lining up to leave for the lunchroom. Ms. Teacher D observed Student K tell Student J to stop, but Student J repeated the behavior, at which point Student K raised her voice at Student J, telling him, again, to stop. Student J yelled in Student K's face, "Stop being such a baby!" Ms. Teacher D intervened and stopped the negative interaction after that point. She reported the

(Continued)

Constructive Behavioral Change Plan 18.1 (Continued)

incident to Ms. School Counselor since she is the primary Intervener for Student J's CBC plan. It was not felt that a new Incident of Concern report should be filed on this incident. This is considered to be related to and an extension of Incident of Concern #34.

Ms. School Counselor called Student J's parents to inform them of the most recent incident. At that time, the parents were told that an adjustment would be recommended to his CBC plan (see below). The parents gave verbal approval to the recommendation.

Revision of 3.10.17 CBC: At the March 19 meeting, Ms. School Counselor met with Student J to notify him that the following changes were being made to his CBC:

1. Student J was to avoid having any interaction with Student K until his behavior was deemed positive enough to do so.
2. The rest of the 3.10.17 CBC was still in effect.

Progress Report 2: Date of report—April 15

There have been no additional negative behaviors on Student J's part during the past two weeks.

1. Ms. School Counselor and Student J have met twice a week since the start of the CBC plan. Each week, they continue to discuss Student J's behavioral progress.
2. Student J continues to complete worksheets from the *Owning Up* curriculum for discussion. The focus on these worksheets and discussion have been on Student J "owning" the behaviors that have been problematic for him and others in the past.
3. Student J and Ms. School Counselor will start the teen reader *Vicious* in the next two weeks as a focus of future discussions.

Progress Report 3: Date of report—April 30

There have been no additional negative behaviors toward other students on Student J's part during the past two weeks. However, there was an incident in which he and Ms. Teacher D had a verbal dispute over whether or not he could or could not partner with Student K during a group activity. The matter was resolved between Student J and Ms. Teacher D.

1. A total of 11 meetings have been held with Student J since the start of the CBC plan. Student J has not missed any of the biweekly sessions.
2. Student J has fully completed his worksheet assignment for each session and participates in conversations freely with Ms. School Counselor.
3. Student J has been particularly insightful on his thoughts related to the book *Vicious*.
4. There have been no negative reports from any of his other teachers in the past two weeks.
5. It is recommended that the meetings fall back to once a week with Student J, as long as his behavior continues to remain appropriate.
6. It is recommended that a parent conference be held shortly to report on the progress Student J has made since the beginning of the CBC plan.

personnel continued to apply *persistent, pervasive,* and *patient* remediative pressures to ensure the best for the school environment.

A CBC plan can be as extensive or simple as necessary. Something similar to a CBC plan may already exist in some agencies or as mandated by state law, and if such is the case, that likely meets the intent behind the basic concepts of such documentation. Individuals must follow whatever the policy or laws are within their jurisdiction. As prevention and intervention efforts increase, so too will the requirements of documented efforts to stop bullying. Woe be unto the individual or institution that cannot provide solid evidence of its efforts to stop legally prohibited behaviors.

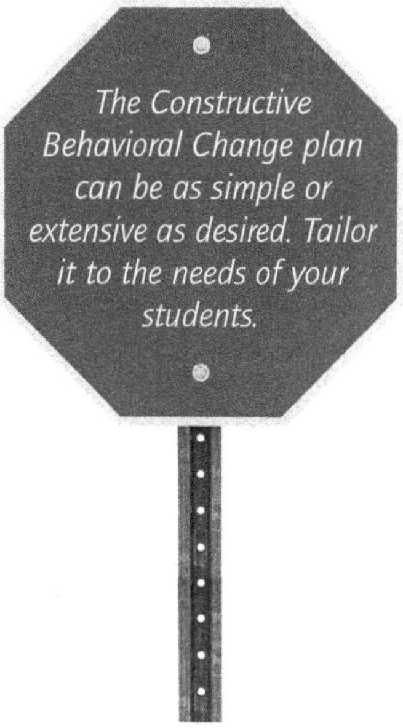

19

Bibliomedia Therapy

©iStockphoto.com/Wavebr

One of the defenses of aggressive individuals is that they disengage the emotional strings attached to their actions by ***dehumanizing*** the target. If the target is "less than human," if it is not a "person," not like "us," and all the better if it is a designated "enemy" of some type, then the likelihood of one's ability to strike out against that not-like-me "thing" is increased. Grossman and DeGaetano (1999, p. 49, 60–64) addressed this learned ability to ***desensitize*** young children through their exposure to environmental violence:

> Conditioning our children and teens to want and need to act out violently starts with environmental saturation of visual violence. . . . [W]hat surrounds the child . . . teaches the child. . . . [C]hildren learn from what's around them. . . . When it comes to the question of what our children are learning, the answer is simple: violence, mayhem, and murder. (p. 49)

Case in point: Here is an excerpt from the review of the 2014 movie *300: Rise of an Empire* (Colvert, 2014):

> [The film] plays like a collaboration between the Marquis de Sade and Michael Bay. Or maybe the History Channel and the "Saw" [horror movie] franchise. Catering to audiences that savor chest-thumping machismo, in-your-face eruptions of blood and hyper-pumped male musculature fetishized in slo-mo, it's unlike anything else in theatres today. . . .
>
> Disturbingly, the film gives [the writer and producer] another forum to explore his fascination with hate-sex. For all the violence onscreen, nothing tops the punishing scene of rage and intercourse between [two of the main characters]. . . . He's the rape-iest major movie maker working today. . . . [The writer and producer] would be better served sharing those fantasies with a professional than with the *impressionable young male audiences his films attract* [emphasis added]. (pp. E1, E6)

At least the film was given an R rating, not that that will prevent younger audiences from viewing it once it is available via streaming or disk format.

THE MECHANICS OF BIBLIOMEDIA THERAPY ON THE BRAIN

One of the most powerful methods of reaching those who bully others is through the written word and film. Creative endeavors activate those receptors in the brain that are less prone to shielding from intellectual defenses. When we know that we are likely to be engaged in some type of affectively stressful event—for example, aggressive behavior directed toward others, especially those aggressive behaviors that we know may be injurious—we can cognitively tamp down our natural tendency to be more affectively impacted by the action. Creative endeavors often "outsmart" these defenses and go straight to the affective areas of the brain.

We learn to override the innate tendency for empathy by a variety of methods. Two are particularly important and easily accessible—*observation* and *practice*. We have already noted Grossman and DeGaetano's (1999) environmental saturation of visual violence theory and have seen an example of it in practice in modern media. The social setting of schools and related youth-oriented institutions and venues become the Petri dishes where kids practice what they see on their peers. Ironically, the very same mediums that can encourage individuals to act negatively toward others can also be used to shape more positive behaviors and help them remain in touch with their natural-born affective affinity to behave more empathically.

Bibliotherapy has been defined in several ways. Riordan and Wilson (1989) noted that it "refers to the guided reading of written material in gaining understanding or solving problems relevant to a person's therapeutic needs" (p. 506). It has been used in the treatment of a wide variety of mental health issues inclusive of addictive chemical use (Apodaca & Miller, 2003; Fanner & Urquhart, 2008), harmful behaviors directed toward the self, panic disorders, sexual dysfunction, and the improvement of social skills (Fanner & Urquhart, 2008). It has also been reported useful in working with those dealing with grief and loss (Briggs & Pehrsson, 2008), as well as increasing multicultural awareness and sensitivity among elementary-aged children (Kim, Green, & Klein, 2006). Its effectiveness is well documented, although most of the research has been directed toward the use of nonfiction works. Detrixhe (2010) indicated that most of the reviews of the efficacy of bibliotherapy have been on children and adolescents, perhaps because "adult problems are thought to be too complex to be captured by a mere story" (p. 63)—as if the lives of youth are not as complicated! Bibliotherapy is considered an avenue to self-improvement through "self-help reading" (Bruneau, Bubenzer, & McGlothlin, 2010, p. 217). It is an activity toward self-improvement and self-awareness that can be done outside the confines of the office or classroom.

Bibliomedia therapy is a logical extension of bibliotherapy—the inclusion of both print and electronic media as resources for increasing self-awareness and insight with those in need or want of such. Bibliomedia therapy is more expansive than what has been referred to as ***cinematherapy***, or the use of movies as a learning and therapeutic tool. In this day of ever-expanding media technology, *all* electronic resources must be considered as potential learning mechanisms at our disposal. This is particularly true in the case of the omnipresence and ubiquity of YouTube, which—though there is often much to create dismay—also has powerful positive lessons of particular interest to children and adolescents readily available to the masses.

The brain responds differently to the affective stimuli afforded to us via bibliomedia resources. Paul (2012) reported that while the brain tends to gloss over words or hackneyed phrases we commonly hear, evocative words and phrases tend to activate areas of the brain related to that particular sensory mode. Fiction, in particular, often held the most stimulative potential, lighting up the brain as did "computer simulations run on computers."[1] Paul goes on to specifically note the relevance of the potential use of bibliomedia therapeutic devices to increase empathy:

> Fiction—with its redolent details, imaginative metaphors and attentive descriptions of people and their actions—offers an especially rich replica [of real live situations and experiences]. Indeed, in one respect novels go beyond simulating reality to give readers . . . *the opportunity to enter fully into other people's thoughts and feelings* [emphasis added]. (2012, para. 6)

This observation gives support to Detrixhe's (2010) advocacy for the increased use of fiction in bibliotherapy.

Likewise, the brain responds differently to different types of cinematic genres. Braff (2011), in an article for the *Chicago Tribune*, notes psychologist Birgit Wolz's opinion that "by eliciting emotions, watching movies can open doors that otherwise might stay closed" (para. 3). Comedies and laughter tend to put distance between one's problems and stressors, if only for a brief period of time. Laughter also lowers blood pressure. Horror films often do the opposite—increase those physiological functions preparing the body for fight or flight. Movies filmed in 3-D can even heighten

---

1. Keith Oakley, emeritus professor of cognitive psychology at the University of Toronto, as cited in the Paul (2012) article.

these responses due to the increased realism of visual perception—not only is the monster chasing you, it is leaping out of the screen and into your lap!

USING BIBLIOMEDIA THERAPY WITH THOSE WHO BULLY

Bibliomedia therapy is designed to increase self-awareness and empathy within those who bully others. It will not, however, work by itself and as a stand-alone effort to change the behavior of individuals. Bibliomedia therapy does not require a "therapist" be employed with those who bully, but it does require an Intervener who is willing to spend the time exploring the interpretations of the reading or viewing materials with those for whom it was assigned.

Bibliomedia approaches to self-awareness need to follow specific guidelines in order to be most effective. Those guidelines follow.

Use developmentally and age-appropriate materials. First and foremost, all materials must be developmentally and age appropriate. Do not use materials that are inappropriate for the designated audience, as it will likely confuse and befuddle the learning opportunity. Mature and stress-invoking materials are likely not suitable candidates for younger users. This is particularly true with the use of visual media, as it engages more senses during its use. Likewise, do not insult the intelligence of those who would benefit from materials within their behavioral continuum.

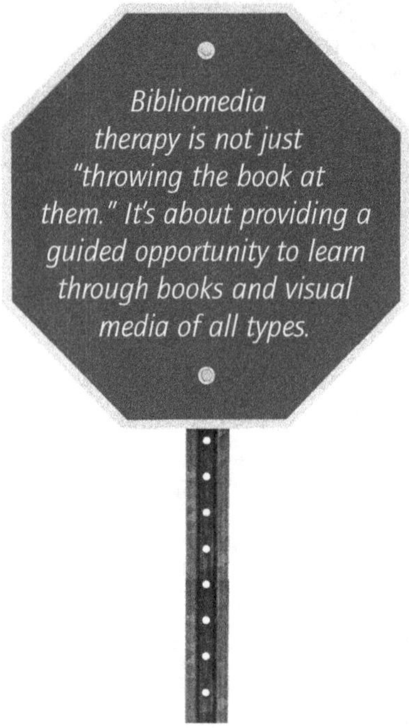

The challenge is to determine what materials are appropriate for the behavior of the individual. A sixth grader who engages in behaviors more akin to those of a student in high school will likely benefit from exposure to materials related to that high school behavior rather than something supposed to be more suitable for his age and grade. The appropriateness of the material, then, may well be more aligned with the behavior rather than age.

Be familiar with the material assigned. Always preview or read materials before use. Never use materials with which the Intervener is unfamiliar. That is a disaster waiting to happen.

This means that the Intervener must have read the articles or books and watched the films or videos that will be discussed. There must be a point to the assigned materials—watching the 2011 movie *Bully* just because "it's about bullying" does not mean that it will be relevant or appropriate for specific students. (Hint: It's likely too intense for younger or sensitive viewers.)

An important question to be answered before material is chosen: "What is the most important lesson(s) or objective(s) for improving the student's behavior that we can get from reading this story/watching this movie/video clip?" Having answers to that question will go a long way in meeting the next guideline.

Structured questions can help guide the individual toward greater self-exploration within the discussion. Any discussion of bibliomedia materials should be structured toward the goals of the interaction between the Intervener and the individual. This helps the Intervener to stay focused and prevents the likelihood of being led astray by any nonrelevant distractions that the student may bring up during the discussion.

Some sample questions or leads may include the following:

"What do you think [the main character] was thinking when he [did what he did] to [the target of the behavior]?"

"If that had been you who had received that kind of treatment, how would you have [felt/reacted]?"

"Sometimes, we do things without thinking about the consequences. Do you think that any of that was going on here in [this book/this movie]?"

"What do you think [the main character/the target of the behavior] was feeling when [the incident] occurred?"

Have the ability to entertain and encourage a discussion of the material. Sometimes we have to keep the momentum going in a discussion, especially with reluctant individuals. Many (if not most) individuals under supervision for bullying behaviors likely do not want to be under such scrutiny. As a result, they may not be overly eager to participate.

The Intervener must be able to encourage, if not coax, the individual to explore the cognitive and affective energies behind the behavior causing the problem. Individuals who do not want to participate in a "forced activity," such as being held accountable for their behaviors, are more than willing to let the intervention die on the vine without their input—remember those open- versus closed-ended questions? We have to be wise to the individual's potential desire to keep motives and explanations for his or her behavior under the cloak of secrecy, even to themselves.

Do not be shocked or surprised by the opinions offered. Expect the unexpected. As much as possible, avoid showing a reaction to a student's response that is specifically designed to get a reaction. For those whose early objective seems to be to derail the bibliomedia intervention, the Intervener should try as hard as possible to steer the conversation back toward something meaningful.

Individuals who bully do sometimes admire those characteristics when they see it in others. That is one of the drawbacks to bibliomedia, particularly film—it can promulgate myths and stereotypes (Wedding & Niemiec, 2003). Likewise, it could well serve as inspiration for negative behaviors among those prone to doing so. This is all the more reason for a structured and guided conversation about what is actually portrayed in a book or film and how that portrayal is interpreted.[2]

The focus of the discussion should be on assisting individuals to compare their actions with the topic of the assigned materials. It is important to help those who intimidate others compare their behaviors to both the standards of expectations within the institutional setting, as well as their reactions to any bibliomedia assignment. A key lead question is this: "Is there any difference between the behavior of [the main character] in this [book/film] and you? If so, what and how?"

Engaging aggressors in a discussion and exploration of ***comparison behaviors*** can give tremendous insight into how they view their actions through the lens of the actions of others. Individuals who see no wrong in their behavior, yet see the same actions as wrong when done by a character in a book or movie are telling us that they are either in denial about their own behavior or unaware of how their actions are viewed by others. Both of these viewpoints on the part of students are worthy of further exploration in an intervention.

Exploring and increasing the individual's sense of empathy is critical. The main purpose of a bibliomedia assignment is to explore the current level of empathy within an individual in hopes of increasing it as necessary. Individuals may not be able to tell us to our faces about their sense of empathy because they don't have the words, they may be obstinate, or they just may not know how to be empathic—all of these can

2. Case in point: In 2014, VH1 ran an antibullying public service announcement called "Revenge of the Nerds." Set to the music of Gloria Gaynor's "I Will Survive," the video showed the prototypical not-too-cool kids being bullied by their peers as the targets sang their own lyrics about how they would one day rule their tormentors in the business world as adults. While at face value the video is humorous, one can't help but wonder if the overly dramatic inflictions did not end up inspiring a new wave of incidents as a direct result from the graphic role modeling displayed in the film. See "Del Campo Saatchi and Saatchi Present First Campaign for VH1" at http://saatchi.com/en-us/news/del-campo-saatchi-saatchi-presents-first-campaign-for-vh1/.

be gleaned from a discussion of material that takes the focus off the individuals and into the abstract third-party actions of a main character in print or film. In other words, "I may not be able to feel it in me, but I can feel/see/understand it through that character." As Interveners, we will gladly take the assist of whatever helps the self-exploration process on the part of the individuals with whom we are working to achieve positive behavioral change.

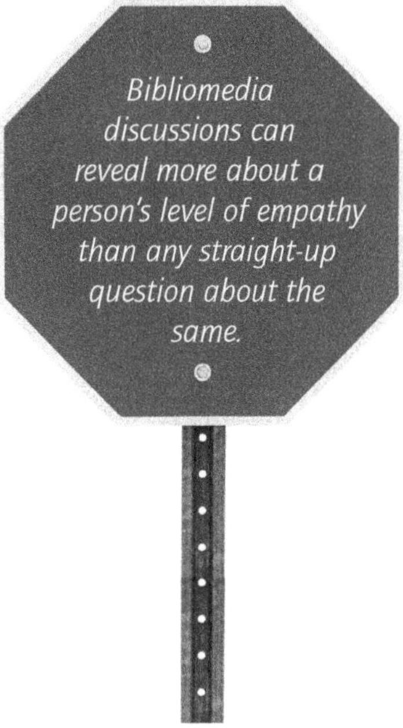

Listen to the metacommunication of what is said and the themes individuals continue to return. Do they seem to feel any connection to the misfortunes of others? Most do, in varying degrees. Very few are so detached from the influence of their peers and the world around them that they feel "nothing" (something which we especially need to know since kids who cannot sense the discomfort or pain of others are more likely to engage in intimidation and aggression). Exploring and helping individuals identify exactly how much they feel about the pain of others is a significant process goal in the discussion following a bibliomedia assignment.

The Resources for Consideration section contains a list of several relevant resources potentially useful for bibliomedia interventions with children and adolescents who bully.

A DISCUSSION USING BIBLIOMEDIA THERAPY WITH AN INDIVIDUAL WHO BULLIES

The student in this dialogue, a ninth-grade male, has been working and meeting with an Intervener for several weeks. Much progress has been made. The Intervener determined that the student was mature enough to be assigned the 2011 movie *Bully* for a discussion the next week. This is the discussion of that bibliomedia assignment:

Intervener [I 1]: *So how was it?*

Student L [SL 1]: *Not bad.*

I 2: *What did you think?*

SL 2: *It was pretty realistic.*

I 3: *Yep, that it was. Sometimes, it was hard to watch. Did you ever feel that way while you were watching it?*

SL 3: *Sometimes.*

I 4: *Want to share an example?*

SL 4: *Yeah, like that time they were picking on that kid on the bus. That was whack.*

I 5: *"Whack" in that it was . . . ?*

SL 5: *Sick. I mean, you don't say those things to a kid who's like him. It ain't right.*

I 6: *"Like him?"*

SL 6: *You know. Retarded.*

I 7: *And you know how it makes me cringe when people use the R-word.*

SL 7: *I'm sorry. I should have said something else.*

I 8: *Like maybe . . . ?* [The Intervener is trying to let Student L talk as much as possible, even when he has said something inappropriate or insensitive. The key is to make corrections as necessary without shutting down the conversation because Student L feels as if he is being reprimanded for what was, perhaps, a slip of the tongue.]

SL 8: *That special ed kid. I should've said something else.*

I 9: *That's better and probably nicer. We might even go so far as to use the term student with special needs. But let's don't use that R-word. We've been working really hard in the entire school to be respectful of everyone, remember?*

SL 9: *Yeah, yeah, I know.*

I 10: *You said that that scene on the bus bothered you.* [Intervener makes a statement and then lets it hang there to see what type of response it drives from Student L.]

SL 10: *It really made me mad. It's not right to pick on a kid like that—a student with special needs. Did I get it right this time?*

I 11: *Better. Thanks for thinking about what you were going to say before you actually said it. What is it about the way they were treating him—let's call him by his real name. It was Alex, wasn't it? What is it about the way they were treating Alex that you found wrong?*

SL 11: *It's just not right to pick on somebody who can't fight back.*

I 12: *That's important to you—that whoever's getting picked on can defend himself.*

SL 12: *It's not a fair fight unless they can.*

I 13: *So you're sharing with me that the times there have been conflicts between you and other students, when they've claimed you've been bullying and harassing them, that you've always considered that they could defend themselves and fight back if they needed to.*

SL 13: *Pretty much.*

I 14: *That's a real eye-opener for me. I'm not sure I ever considered that as something you might be thinking about when those incidents arose.*

SL 14: [Student sits quietly. Doesn't say anything. Seems to be thinking.]

I 15: [Gives Student L more time to think.] *Let me ask you a question related to the movie. What do you think Alex was thinking and feeling when he was getting hammered on that bus by all those other kids?*

SL 15: *I'm pretty sure he felt alone. And probably scared. And maybe even mad. How'd you be able to put up with that and not get mad?*

I 16: *I think those are wise insights into what anyone might feel in that situation. Maybe even you.* [Intervener lets that last observation sink in to generate some thoughts, but Student L does not respond to it.] *So if you had been on that bus with Alex and those other kids had started abusing him like you saw they did in the film, what would you have done?*

SL 16: *I would've told them to knock it off, to stop messing with Alex, that he wasn't doing anything to bother them. I would've stood up for him and made them stop. I might have even gone up and sat next to him.*

I 17: *That would have been a brave thing to do.*

SL 17: *I don't know about it being brave, but it would have been the right thing to do.*

I 18: *Yes, it would have. And it would have been brave. So let me ask you this: If you would have stood up for Alex in the movie because it was the right thing to do, because you don't believe it's fair to pick on someone who can't defend himself, what stops you from doing the same thing among your own classmates here at school? What is it that makes you pick on them instead of take up for them?*

SL 18: *The people I mess with are jerks. They deserve what they get. And half the time, I'm just giving them what they'd like to do to me if they could.*

I 19:	*Well, that's interesting. It's the first time you've shared that with me. I appreciate it. But I have to ask, do you think it might be possible that some of the people you've been accused of bullying might feel the same way you think that Alex must feel on that bus?*
SL 19:	[Student L is quiet for a few seconds.] *I don't know. I never thought about it.*
I 20:	*Why don't we explore that for a little bit with the rest of the time we have in here today?*

WHAT JUST HAPPENED HERE?

Here's what has happened in this dialogue. First, the Intervener gave the student every *opportunity to be an active part* of that day's meeting. The *Intervener was patient* with Student L (even when he used inappropriate language to refer to an adolescent with special needs in SL 6–8, I 7–9) and "waited him out" for answers to the structured questions or observations offered (I 8, 15–16). The *discussion stayed focused on the student's cognitive and affective reactions* to one particular scene in the movie (I 10–16). In this session, the *student was even given the option of revealing what he might have done* behaviorally in the scenario (I 16–18, SL 15–17). Because the student's answer was positive, *he was encouraged* (I 17–18). Then *the discussion began to turn from the abstract to the personal* (I 15–16, 19, SL 15–19). The last part of the conversation was headed toward a very ego-threatening *exploration of a comparison* between what the difference was between how the students in the film made Alex feel and how Student L might make his targets feel by his own behaviors.

In essence, the session moved from the "out there" (the abstract of the character in the movie) to the "in me" (the actual student in the room). This is usually a safe tactic to use to move the focus of a discussion from the safety of the external (the "not me") to the insecurity of the internal (the "very me"). It's also a method to explore and discover the "Secret Self" and the "Great Unknown" panes of the Johari Window discussed in Chapter 14. If the relationship is strong, this movement will proceed more easily. If the individual with whom the Intervener is working is uncomfortable or defiant about discussing what is going on inside, more resistance is likely to be present. Resistance can manifest itself in a variety of ways—along a continuum of outright defiance and obstinance all the way to shy compliance. It is not uncommon for individuals in the "hot seat" of scrutiny to be cautious about inquiry.

20

When All Else Fails

©iStockphoto.com/omgimages

In the end, when all avenues of restorative and remediative efforts have not worked in attempting to resolve and correct the misbehavior of those who bully, the only option left may be some sort of punitive discipline, including the removal of the individual engaging in the offending behavior from the setting in which it occurs.

Suspension from organizational activities and privileges should be a last resort for any child. The removal of a student from an educational endeavor places that individual at risk for any host of additional dangers. Unsupervised time is a calling card for mischief.

THE PROBLEM WITH SUSPENSIONS—DISPROPORTIONALITY

Out-of-school suspensions have been proven to exhibit ***disproportionality*** in who is impacted most. The facts are clear: Nonmajority demographic groups are more disproportionately subjected to suspensions and expulsions for running afoul of institutional rules than are those of the majority (Flannery, 2015). The average secondary school student in America has an 11 percent chance of being suspended for a rule infraction during the course of an average year (Kelman, 2013). Nationally, according to Losen and Gillespie (2012, pp. 6–7) at the Center for Civil Rights Remedies at the Civil Rights Project:

- More than three million K–12 students lost some type of direct instruction in the 2009–2010 academic year due to suspensions, "the number . . . it would take to fill every seat in every major league baseball park and every NFL stadium in America, *combined* [sic]."
- The "risk of getting suspended is not borne equally by all students."
- One out of six (17 percent) African American children in a K–12 school was suspended at least once. This compares to one in thirteen (8 percent) among Native American children; one in fourteen (7 percent) for Latino children; one in twenty (5 percent) for Whites; and one in fifty (2 percent) for Asian Americans.
- Students receiving special education services or with related mental or physical disabilities (13 percent of the total, all ethnic and racial groups combined) were twice as many times to have been suspended than those not receiving such services. Within this group, 25 percent of the suspensions were directed toward African Americans. In one state, Illinois, 42 percent of the total suspensions were among African American students receiving special education services.
- African American students and students receiving special education services were more likely to be suspended repeatedly. This was inverse in proportionality to students of other racial or ethnic groups

or students not receiving special education services. Male nonmajority students receiving special education services in the largest districts included in the sample were most likely to be suspended, as high as 33 percent in some instances.
- States did not suspend students equally: some states rarely used suspension as a method of discipline (South Dakota at 2.2 percent), while others did more so (South Carolina at 12.7 percent).
- In virtually all instances, African Americans were suspended more often than other racial or ethnic groups. However, certain states stood out: African Americans made up 25 percent of all suspensions in Illinois; and in North Carolina, Native Americans made up 18 percent of all suspensions. Illinois had the largest proportional disparity among racial and ethnic groups in the entire country.
- In the school districts included in the survey, 12 percent of the sample (839) had 10 percent of their student bodies suspended at least once. Nearly 200 districts (2 percent) suspended more than 20 percent of their entire enrollment at one time or another.

Lest one think that out-of-school suspensions were reserved for repeat offenders, consider this: In 2010 in North Carolina, 32 percent of African American students were given out-of-school suspensions for *first-time* violation of cell phone–use policies as compared to 15 percent of their White peers, and 43 percent of the African American student population was suspended out of school for a *first-time* public display of affection compared to 15 percent of their White compatriots (Ferriss, 2011b).

THE PROBLEM WITH SUSPENSIONS—THE SCHOOL-TO-PRISON PIPELINE

Many suspensions are a direct result of the enforcement of inflexible zero tolerance policies. Hoffman (2014) found that the expansion of zero tolerance practices resulted in a net increase of suspensions among the African American students in an urban school district. Out-of-school suspensions have repeatedly been considered to be a major contributing factor in the student dropout rate for those receiving the suspensions (Knefel, 2013b), as well as contributing to the school-to-prison pipeline. In one instance, 31 percent of all Texas students were found to have received an out-of-school suspension at least once in their middle or high school years, and when in- and out-of-school suspensions were totaled, the rate almost doubled to 60 percent (Schwarz, 2011). Of the Texas disciplinary actions, 97 percent were "discretionary [and] not based on mandatory laws for suspension or expulsion" (Ferriss, 2011a, para. 8) The actual in- and out-of-school suspension rates nationally may never be known with accuracy; "while the federal government collects suspension statistics, it doesn't record suspension causes, and discipline codes vary widely between each state, district, and even some schools" (Kelman, 2013, para. 11).

The increased emphasis on school security following the late 1990s high-profile incidences of school shootings saw an increase in police presence in American schools.[1] As a result, rather than viewing misbehavior as a normal developmental issue to be dealt with from an educational perspective, school personnel often referred behavioral problems to available in-school law enforcement liaison officers or considered such behaviors through a legal lens:

> In recent years, an influx of law enforcement officers in schools has done even more to direct youth of color toward prison. With law enforcement actively patrolling school hallways, student infractions that once merited a trip to the principal's office now have a greater chance of leading to a police ticket or arrest. . . . Schools with a designated school law enforcement officer on duty had disorderly conduct arrest rates close to five times those of comparable schools without such an officer. (Wilf, 2012, para. 4)

Law enforcement was more than willing to provide encouragement and assistance for such referrals. Indeed, it often validated the existence of law officer employment within community schools. Both necessity and invention, it seems, has contributed to unintended consequences for those who support orderly educational attainment and those who can least afford to lose them.

THE PROBLEM WITH SUSPENSIONS AND SERVING THE NEEDS OF CHILDREN WITH SPECIAL NEEDS

American school personnel have long known that one disciplinary size does not fit all. This has been especially true in dealing with students who have special learning needs, handicaps, or disabilities.

We have rightly determined, though not without a history of legal wrangling, that it is unfair to deny students with special learning needs the opportunity for an education. The history of meeting the needs of children with specific learning challenges was one first of total exclusion from education (if not seclusion and institutionalization) prior to the 1960s, to one of limited access in the 1960s and 1970s, to more equal access and accommodation with the passage in 1975 of the *Education for All Handicapped Children Act* (Public Law 94-142), today's Individuals With Disabilities Education Act (20 USC §1400 et seq., renamed in 1990 with periodic revisions).

---

1. To compound insult to injury, violence in American schools was not a new phenomenon prior to that time. What was new was the visible encroachment of violence in White, suburban, middle- and upper-middle-class schools. For many, "school violence" only became a reality when it reached that demographic.

A central key to meeting the needs of those with special learning abilities is *accommodation*. That includes the recognition that behavioral issues among students may not always be within their abilities to control or regulate in comparison to their peers. The accommodation of such behavioral needs is often a flashpoint when it comes to school personnel and their willingness to see such behaviors from a special needs viewpoint. In 2014, the US Department of Justice (DoJ) reported that during the 2011 to 2012 school year this occurred:

> Although students who receive special education services represent 12 percent of students in the country, they make up 19 percent of students suspended in school, 20 percent of students receiving out-of-school suspensions once, 25 percent of students receiving multiple out-of-school suspensions, 19 percent of student expelled, 23 percent of student referred to law enforcement, and 23 percent of students receiving a school-related arrest. (as cited in US Department of Education, 2014b, p. i)

The argument, as with the disproportionate suspension of other nonmajority group students, is always one of the chicken and the egg: Are students within nonmajority groups unfairly targeted, or are they actually subject to more discipline due to unruly, intentional, and unmanageable misbehaviors?

Students with special and differing learning abilities are not to be "legally . . . subjected to long suspensions for behaviors that are manifestations of their disabilities" (Hook, 2014, p. 1). The laws of the Individuals With Disabilities Act and of the Americans With Disabilities Act are clear in these respects. This does not mean that students receiving special education services cannot be held accountable for their actions. Students who are legitimately deemed a danger to themselves or others, or who engage in activities or behaviors that are deemed dangerous, unmanageable, or so disruptive so as to meet one or more of the earlier mentioned criteria, may be removed from existing services for up to forty-five days until school personnel and other relevant professionals can determine the best placement setting (Hook, 2014).

We have no data available on the number of special education students who are involved as agents of bullying behaviors. The numbers are likely few. We know that students receiving special education services and who may be involved in the bullying dyad are far more likely to be the targets of such behaviors (Carter & Spencer, 2006). If, however, students with special needs are determined to be the aggressors within bullying behaviors, they should be held as fairly accountable for their actions, as should all others within the confines of their developmental and intellectual needs.

It is highly recommended that, as relevant, a student's individual educational plan (IEP) be revised to include educational opportunities to change behaviors of aggressors or teach the appropriate skills of de-escalation or assistance seeking of students who are targeted. By including such into the

IEP, the learning opportunity is shifted from optional to required and increases the likelihood that effective intervention and learning will take place.

FEDERAL INTERVENTION TO DISRUPT DISPROPORTIONATE SUSPENSIONS

In 2014, the US Departments of Education and Justice joined forces in an effort to stop the disproportionate rate of suspensions among the racial, ethnic, and special education populations by issuing guidelines addressing not only school discipline but also the overarching school climate, which often contributes to student alienation (US DoE, 2014a). The document was a milestone in that it recognized that it is not enough to deal with the individual student in isolation of the environment in which the student acts. In essence, the student who runs afoul of the system impacts the system for all within it and vice versa. The document also focused on prevention as a way to reduce school discipline issues.

SO WHAT SHOULD WE DO WHEN ALL ELSE FAILS?

If anyone *legitimately* endangers or disrupts the educational mission of an institution, and the individual either refuses to alter those behaviors or accommodations cannot be made so that everyone can continue to learn in a safe environment, then it makes it difficult to argue on behalf of keeping that particular individual in the setting. Notice I emphasize "legitimately" because too often suspensions and punitive discipline have been used as the first choice of "correcting" misbehavior. As we have discussed throughout this book, the focus for correcting those who bully others should be on education and remediation of the misbehavior and restoration of the wrong committed. Most of those who intimidate others can be moved in that direction if we commit ourselves to the time and resources necessary—primarily adult supervisory personnel with the skills to actively engage children and adolescents who are challenging—to do what needs to be done.

However, there may come a time when all options are exhausted for those who bully others—alternative and creative solutions have seemed to not had the desired effect of making the positive behavioral changes necessary for the success of all concerned. When that moment comes—when all possibilities, consultations, parental conferences, accommodations, and student interventions have been exhausted—there may be no other option but to remove the individual from the setting. This is just the hard-core reality of working with individuals who are aggressive toward others and who act in ways that are so disruptive to the educational mission and focus of the institution that they impair the learning or safety of others.

Removal of an individual, however, should not be considered the "end of the problem." Whatever the removal is—in-school, out-of-school, short-term, or long-term—it should be done with the *goal of getting the individual back into the educational setting as soon as possible*. We know the damage that bullying behaviors do to those who are targeted by it, but we also know the damage that can be done to those who are removed from the educational setting. And because we know, we cannot ignore its negative potential, no matter how much easier it would seem to make everyone's life in the short run.

The goal of getting the individual back into the education setting as soon as possible is only accomplished when the individual who has created the behavioral problem begins appropriate efforts to change those prior negative behaviors or the appropriate accommodations are made to begin that process. The likelihood of immediate 180° change in one's demeanor, modus operandus, or long-term behavioral pattern after a removal or suspension is slim. People do not change overnight, but we should and must allow them the opportunity to begin that process of change, as long as their efforts show the progress toward the positive behavioral change that is charted and as long as their progress along with those efforts does not provide additional disruption in the mission of the institution.

WANT TO LEARN MORE?

The full federal report on the impact of disproportionality in school discipline can be found in *Opportunities Suspended: The Disparate Impact of Disciplinary Exclusion from School* at http://civilrightsproject.ucla.edu/resources/projects/center-for-civil-rights-remedies/school-to-prison-folder/federal-reports/upcoming-ccrr-research.

For additional insight into the impact of a police presence in American schools, see Knefel's (September 13, 2013) "When High School Students Are Treated Like Prisoners" in *Rolling Stone*, online at http://www.rollingstone.com/politics/news/when-high-school-students-are-treated-like-prisoners-20130912, as well as the November 7, 2013, *Rolling Stone* article "The School-to-Prison Pipeline: A Nationwide Problem for Equal Rights," online at http://www.rollingstone.com/music/news/the-school-to-prison-pipeline-a-nationwide-problem-for-equal-rights-20131107.

A state-by-state statistical breakdown of disciplinary actions directed at students receiving special education services can be found in the US Department of Justice Civil Rights Data Collection at http://ocrdata.ed.gov/.

21

Potholes, Gravel, and Road Tar

Knowledge is power. The power to make sound, informed decisions. The power to choose. The power to choose to do good—or not.

We make choices every day about how we intervene with children and youth who engage in bullying behaviors. While we are ultimately not responsible for the choices made by those who engage in bullying behaviors, we *are* responsible for how we contribute to that mindset. Are we a part of the solution equation or a part of the problem? Oh, maybe we don't *actively* encourage others to bully their peers, but we also don't *actively* engage ourselves to challenge the behaviors in others when we see it. If we turn our heads to the problem, if we assume that somebody else will take care of it, if we assume that it's somebody else's responsibility to do something about it, then we *are* a part of the chain of events that encourage others to make the decisions to intimidate. If we choose to benignly neglect a problem for any of these reasons, then we have also benignly allowed ourselves to become a part of it.

I don't believe you got to this point in the book because you're a part of the problem. Consider yourself now one of the many who wants to do something to help stop those who create bullying problems for others and who is willing to take the time to educate yourself about ways to do what, to this point, few have done—go upstream to address the causes by engaging those who create the problem in the first place.

It won't be an easy task. Not everyone believes that those who engage in bullying behaviors deserve a second chance. It's always easier when we just cast our troubles by the wayside and keep moving along the happy road of life that we choose to create in our happy little heads. But we all know that life isn't like that. Life is messy. That happy little road of life is full of potholes. Every once in a while, a piece of gravel will crack the windshield. Oh, we can always replace that windshield, but soon, we may find that we get whacked by another piece of gravel further down the road, and then another and another, until one day we ask ourselves, "Shouldn't somebody fix the road we're on so that this doesn't keep happening to me and everybody else?"

While this analogy may be a poor one when it comes to working with those who bully, I would argue that it's perfect. When it comes to the way we have been dealing with solving bullying behaviors, our current path has not been very effective because we have chosen to ignore the reasons why those potholes and loose gravel are on the road in the first place. We haven't done a very good job of preparing a path for long-term success because we've ignored one of the basics on which it is founded. We've chosen to ignore addressing the problem at its base. *We've failed to address the needs of the person who causes the problem in the first place.* Oh, yeah, we've patched the potholes here and there and swept off the loose gravel by applying the quickest method and largest dose of Carnation Instant Justice we could get our hands on—usually by using the same disciplinary hammer to all situations, regardless of what the cause of the problem actually was. But we've never dug underneath the pavement to investigate where the fault lies in the composition to determine which part of the different layers of the base are the weakest, which ones don't hold up well under pressure, and which ones are just plain faulty.

We have that chance when we take the time to work with those who bully others. They will tell us what parts of our strategies are weak, where the cracks are in the techniques that we use, and which approaches are doomed to failure quite simply because they don't work.

Welcome to the road crew. Get out your reflective vest and shovel. There's lot of pavement to replace.

I'll be out there sweating under the hot sun with you.

Resources for Consideration

As I noted in my first book, *Bullying From Both Sides* (2006), there is no shortage of resources in the Solution Universe when it comes to purporting to solve education woes of all types. So it is with efforts to address bullying behaviors. Most of the solutions, however, have been directed toward dealing with problems *after* they have occurred, not before.

These resources are offered for your consideration from a different angle—as potential resources to working with those who seem to create bullying behaviors. Not all of these resources may be relevant for your setting. You have to make a determination as to *what works* best, for *whom,* and under *what circumstance.* We just can't pick up a book, video, or curriculum and throw it at problems to make them go away. We have to be selective and strategic in our approach to complicated problems.

Readers are encouraged to cruise resources beyond the few offered here by searching for additional materials by topic or subject matter on Corwin (http://www.corwin.com/), Sunburst Visual Media (http://www.sdteach.com/bullying.html), Free Spirit Publishing (http://www.freespirit.com/), Research Press (https://www.researchpress.com/), or Amazon.com (http://www.amazon.com/). But be forewarned—you *will* be overwhelmed by what you find! Perhaps the few resources noted here will serve as a starting point from which you can branch out and find the best resources for your particular setting. Good luck!

CLASSROOM CURRICULUM, ACTIVITIES, AND STRATEGIES

Alvord, M., Zucker, B., & Grados, J. (2011). *Resilience Builder Program for children and adolescents: Enhancing social competence and self-regulation.* Champaign, IL: Research Press.

A comprehensive cognitive-behavioral collection of sessions with CD printouts. Can be modified for K–12 grade levels.

Beane, A. (2011). *The new bully free classroom: Proven prevention and intervention strategies for teachers K–8*. Minneapolis, MN: Free Spirit.

Allan Beane was one of the first to develop classroom materials to address school bullying. This revised edition brings the classic into a new century and is still as relevant as the original.

Breakstone, S., Dreiblatt, M., & Dreiblatt, K. (2009). *How to stop bullying and social aggression: Elementary grade lessons and activities that teach empathy, friendship, and respect.* Thousand Oaks, CA: Corwin.

For those who want activities in the K–6 grade levels, the grades that are perhaps the most important in helping kids to learn the skills of self-control.

Coombs-Richardson, R., & Meisgeier, C. (2001). *Connecting with others: Lessons for teaching social and emotional competence.* Champaign, IL: Research Press.

While written for Grades 9–12, this activities book may be better suited for reluctant readers in those grades or Grades 9–10.

Davis, S., & Davis, J. (2007a). *Schools where everyone belongs: Practical strategies for reducing bullying* (2nd ed.). Champaign, IL: Research Press.

Davis, S., & Davis, J. (2007b). *Empowering bystanders in bullying prevention: Grades K–8*. Champaign, IL: Research Press.

Davis, S., & Nixon, C. (2014). *Youth Voice Project: Student insights into bullying and peer mistreatment*. Champaign, IL: Research Press.

The "Davis Trilogy" contains two resources (Davis & Davis, 2007a, 2007b) and one extensive research effort (2014) on the causes of bullying and suggestions for addressing it. The 2014 report details the opinions of 13,000 students in the United States on their views of the nature of bullying and how to combat it. Maybe we *should* listen to the kids, eh?

Dillon, J. (2012). *No place for bullying: Leadership for schools that care for every student.* Thousand Oaks, CA: Corwin.

Looks at the perspective of solving bullying from a leadership position within the schools. A great resource for principals and others faced with turning policy into practice.

Drew, N. (2010). *No kidding about bullying: 125 ready-to-use activities to help kids manage anger, resolve conflicts, build empathy, and get along.* Minneapolis, MN: Free Spirit.

What more could I possible add? The title says it all! For Grades 3–6. Great for resistant readers. A true Kid Friendly classroom resource.

Horne, A., Nitza, A., Dobias, B., Jolliff, D., Raczynski, K., & Voors, K. (2012). *Empowering teen peers to prevent bullying: The Bully Busters Program for high school.* Champaign, IL: Research Press.

An effort to build on peer leadership, this book includes activities and strategies to train students in the upper grades to work with elementary students on ways to prevent and intervene in bullying behaviors.

Peterson, K. (2012). *Activities for building character and social-emotional learning: Grades 3–5.* Minneapolis, MN: Free Spirit.

You can never go wrong with a Free Spirit product! Great visual handouts with accompanying CD.

Wiseman, R. (2009). *Owning Up curriculum: Empowering adolescents to confront social cruelty, bullying, and injustice.* Champaign, IL: Research Press.

Activities and discussion points for adolescents. Comes with a CD to assist the leader with ready-to-use handouts.

CONFLICT RESOLUTION

Barsky, A. (2000). *Conflict resolution for the helping professions* (2nd ed.). New York, NY: Oxford University Press.

An international approach to viewing approaches to resolving conflict for helping professionals and those in supervisory positions.

Riestenberg, N. (2012). *Circle in the square: Building community and repairing harm in school.* St. Paul, MN: Living Justice Press.

A life-long advocate for safe schools, Riestenberg gives a step-by-step guide to creating effective restorative justice circles in school settings. While perhaps more appropriate for high school settings than elementary, it could provide a framework for use in elementary schools with modification.

Weinhold, B., & Weinhold, J. (2009). *Conflict resolution: The partnership way.* Denver, CO: Love.

A sourcebook for individuals in all positions who are faced with resolving conflict among their respective clientele. Helps the individual to understand the basis of conflicts and how to identify ways to get beyond being "stuck."

Zimmerman, J., & Coyle, V. (2009). *The way of the council* (2nd ed.). Viroqua, WI: Bramble Books.

Helps the reader learn the whys and hows of solving problems through the Native American council way. An essential companion to Reistenberg's (2012) book on restorative and remediative efforts in schools.

FOR EDUCATORS AND RELATED SUPERVISORY PERSONNEL

Anderson, S. (2011). *No more bystanders = no more bullies: Activating action in educational professionals.* Thousand Oaks, CA: Corwin.

A proposed model for others based on the Safe Schools Team approach. An effort to increase the number of peer interventions though decreasing the benign neglect of bystanders.

DeWitt, P. (2012). *Dignity for all: Safeguarding LGBT students.* Thousand Oaks, CA: Corwin.

Understanding the mechanics of preventing and intervening in incidents of bullying directed toward one of the most targeted groups of students in schools and society.

Hinduja, S., & Patchin, J. (2009). *Bullying beyond the schoolyard: Preventing and responding to cyberbullying*. Thousand Oaks, CA: Corwin.

Two of the leaders in researching cyberbullying offer their suggestions for responding and preventing it.

Klein, J. (2012). *The bully society: School shootings and the crisis of bullying in American schools*. New York, NY: New York University Press.

An often disturbing book on the links between bullying in American culture and the extreme violence and havoc it sometime wreaks in schools.

Losey, B. (2011). *Bullying, suicide, and homicide: Understanding, assessing, and preventing threats to self and others for victims of bullying*. New York, NY: Routledge.

For helping adults in supervisory positions identify those behaviors that may be indicative of those who are bullied resorting to revenge tactics.

McNamara, B. (2013). *Bullying and students with disabilities: Strategies and techniques to create a safe learning environment for all*. Thousand Oaks, CA: Corwin.

Perhaps as many as 80 percent of students with special needs have reported being bullied in the school setting.

Newman, K., Fox, C., Harding, D., Mehta, J., & Roth, W. (2004). *Rampage: The social roots of school shootings*. New York, NY: Basic Books.

A companion to the Losey (2011) book to further increase supervisory personnel's understanding of the origins of revenge

Patchin, J., & Hinduja, S. (Eds.). (2012). *Cyberbullying prevention and response: Expert perspectives*. New York, NY: Routledge.

A collection of some of the biggest names in contemporary cyberbullying research and prevention provide suggestions for understanding and addressing the issue.

Steiner-Adair, C. (2013). *The big disconnect: Protecting childhood and family relationships in the digital age*. New York, NY: Harper.

A fabulous read about the impact of social networking on all aspects of our lives, particularly as it relates to parenting and communication with our kids.

Strauss, S. (2012). *Sexual harassment and bullying: A guide to keeping kids safe and holding schools accountable*. Lanham, MD: Rowman & Littlefield.

Sexual intimidation in schools places supervisory personnel at risk for legal action and kids in the path of long-term psychological damage.

FOR PARENTS

The following books are perfect accompaniments to my second book, *Working With Parents of Bullies and Victims* (2008).

Benson, P., Galbraith, J., & Espeland, P. (2012). *What kids need to succeed: Proven, practical ways to raise good kids*. Minneapolis, MN: Free Spirit.

Forty developmental assets to help parents and their kids build on family support, school strengths, resistance and resilience skills, and increase self-esteem for all involved.

Horne, A., Stoddard, J., & Bell, C. (2008). *A parent's guide to understanding and responding to bullying: The Bully Busters approach.* Champaign, IL: Research Press.

Another excellent manual from Arthur Horne, this one designed to help parents work with their children who have been identified as behaving in a bullying manner.

Wiseman, R. (2013). *Masterminds & wingmen: Helping our boys cope with schoolyard power, locker-room tests, girlfriends, and the new rules of boy world.* New York, NY: Harmony Books.

It was a toss-up as to whether or not to put this resource in this section or the educators' section. Both need to understand the challenges faced by today's young males and why "being a guy" isn't as easy as it used to be.

UNDERSTANDING LIFE AS A TARGET

Asanti, I., & Kamau, A. (Eds.). (2012). *Letters to my bully.* Sherman Oaks, CA: Glover Lane Press.

A collection of poems, essays, and letters from those who have been victimized by others to express their thoughts and emotions. A good starting point for in-class discussions. Caveat: Some of the material is raw.

Hall, M., & Jones, C. (Ed.). (2011). *Dear bully: 70 authors tell their stories.* New York, NY: Harper Teen.

This book, along with Asanti and Kamau's (2012) book, is another resource to help adults understand what life is like in the crosshairs of a bully.

Meyer, S., Meyer, J., Sperber, E., & Alexander, H. (2013). *Bullying under attack: True stories written by teen victims, bullies & bystanders.* Deerfield Beach, FL: Health Communications.

An anthology of writings from those on both sides of the issue, along with those who chose to stand by and not become involved.

References

This list includes references cited in the manuscript, plus others read as background but not needed in the final text. All links were accurate at the time of sourcing, but owners of those links may have updated them, making the originals inactive. In some instances, online dates may be different from print dates. Every effort has been made to include relevant sources as a courtesy to the reader who may want to explore a specific topic in greater detail.

Abramson, L. Y., Seligman, M. E. P., & Teasdale, J. D. (1978). Learned helplessness in humans: Critique and reformulation. *Journal of Abnormal Psychology, 87*(1), 49–74.

Ad Council. (2015). "Be more than a bystander" campaign developed by the Ad Council and DDB New York debuts new PSAs for National Bullying Prevention Month [Press release]. Retrieved from http://www.adcouncil.org/News-Events/Press-Releases/Be-More-Than-a-Bystander-campaign-developed-by-the-Ad-Council-and-DDB-New-York-debuts-new-PSAs-for-National-Bullying-Prevention-Month

Albert Ellis Institute. (2014). What is REBT? The Albert Ellis institute. Retrieved from http://albertellis.org/

Alexander, K., & Alexander, M. (2009). *American public school law* (7th ed.). Belmont, CA: Wadsworth.

Allen, S. (2014, March 12). More laws needed? Proposed bullying legislation spurs debate. Lakeland (FL) *The Ledger*. Retrieved from http://www.ledgerdata.com/bullying/#day-four

Allen, S., & Pleasant, M. (2013, September 10). Lakeland girl commits suicide after 1½ years of being bullied. Lakeland (FL) *The Ledger*. Retrieved from http://www.theledger.com/article/20130910/news/130919963

Alsaker, F. D., & Valkanover, S. (2001). Early diagnosis and prevention of victimization in kindergarten. In J. Juvonen & S. Graham (Eds.), *Peer harassment in school: The plight of the vulnerable and victimized* (pp. 175–195). New York, NY: Guilford Press.

Amerding, T. (2014). Teen cyberbullying grows with "anonymous" social chat apps. CSO online. Retrieved from http://www.csoonline.com/article/750184/teen-cyberbullying grows-with-anonymous-social-chat-apps

American Civil Liberties Union [ACLU] of Minnesota. (2014, March 25). ACLU-MN settles Facebook case with Minnewaska district. Retrieved from https://www.aclu.org/news/aclu-mn-settles-facebook-case-minnewaska-school-district

American Psychiatric Association. (2013). *Diagnostic and statistical manual of mental disorders* (5th ed.). Washington, DC: Author.

American Psychological Association. (n.d.). Individuals with disabilities act (IDEA). Retrieved from http://www.apa.org/about/gr/issues/disability/idea.aspx

Anderson, C. M., & Kincaid, D. (2005). Applying behavior analysis to school violence and discipline problems: Schoolwide positive behavior support. *The Behavior Analyst, 28*(1), 49.

Anderson, C. S. (1982). The search for school climate: A review of the research. *Review of Educational Research, 52*(3), 368–420.

Apodaca, T. R., & Miller, W. R. (2003). A meta-analysis of the effectiveness of bibliotherapy for alcohol problems. *Journal of Clinical Psychology, 59*(3), 289–304.

Arseneault, L., Bowes, L., & Shakoor, S. (2010). Bullying victimization in youths and mental health problems: "Much ado about nothing"? *Psychological Medicine, 40,* 717–729. doi: 10.1017/S0033291709991383

Associated Press. (2014, February 17). Cyberbullying victims fight back in lawsuits. *Education Week.* Retrieved from http://www.edweek.org/ew/articles/2012/05/09/30cyberbully.h31.html

Baker, O. E., & Bugay, A. (2011). Peer victimization and depressive symptoms: The mediation role of loneliness. *Social and Behavioral Sciences, 30,* 1303–1307. doi: 10.1016/j.sbspro.2011.10.253

Bandura, A. (1973). *Aggression: A social learning analysis.* Englewood Cliffs, NJ: Prentice-Hall.

Bandura, A. (1999). Moral disengagement in the perpetration of inhumanities. *Personality and Social Psychology Review, 3*(3), 193–209.

Bandura, A., Barbaranelli, C., Caprara, G. V., & Pastorelli, C. (1996). Mechanisms of moral disengagement in the exercise of moral agency. *Journal of Personality and Social Psychology, 71*(2), 364.

Bandura, A., Ross, D., & Ross, S. A. (1961). Transmission of aggression through imitation of aggressive models. *Journal of Abnormal and Social Psychology, 63*(3), 575–582. doi:10.1037/h0045925

Barsky, A. (2000). *Conflict resolution for the helping professions* (2nd ed.). New York, NY: Oxford University Press.

Bazelon, E. (2012, March 7). A big win: The landmark settlement in a Minnesota bullying case and how it could help gay students everywhere. *Slate.* Retrieved from http://www.slate.com/articles/news_and_politics/bulle/2012/03/the_anoka_hennepin_settlement_a_big_win_in_the_fight_against_gay_bashing_bullies_.html

Bazelon, E. (2013). *Sticks and stones: Defeating the culture of bullying and rediscovering the power of character and empathy.* New York, NY: Random House.

Beck, A., & Weishaar, M. (2011). Cognitive therapy. In R. Corsini & D. Wedding (Eds.), *Current psychotherapies* (9th ed.). Belmont, CA: Brooks/Cole.

Bellware, K. (2015, March 15). Anonymous message app Yik Yak faces backlash from an entire city. *The Huffington Post.* Retrieved from http://www.huffingtonpost.com/2014/03/10/yik-yak-app_n_4921365.html

Bennett, J. (2010, October 5). Is the "bullying epidemic" a media myth? *Newsweek.* Retrieved from http://www.newsweek.com/bullying-epidemic-media-myth-73847

Benzmiller, H. (2013). The cyber-samaritans: Exploring criminal liability for the innocent bystanders of cyberbullying. *Northwestern University Law Review, 107*(2), 927–962.

Berg, B. (2005). Cognitive-behavioral interventions for bullies, victims, and bystanders. In L. Gallo-Lopez & C. E. Schaefer (Eds.), *Play therapy with adolescents* (pp. 267–286). Lanham, MD: Rowman & Littlefield.

Berger, K. S. (2007). Update on bullying at school: Science forgotten? *Developmental Review, 27*(1), 90–126. doi:10.1016/j.dr.2006.08.002

Bichao, S. (2014, March 17). Central Jersey schools grade their efforts tackling bullies. *My Central Jersey*. Retrieved from http://www.mycentraljersey.com/Central%20Jersey%20schools%20grade%20their%20efforts%20tackling%20bullies.%20/

Bichao, S. (2014, March 18). Parents of bullies allowed to be sued by two Hunterdon school districts. *My Central Jersey*. Retrieved from http://www.mycentraljersey.com/article/20140317/NJNEWS/303170054/

Bilchik, S. (1998). *Guide for implementing the balanced and restorative justice model*. Washington, DC: US Department of Justice Office of Juvenile Justice and Delinquency Prevention.

Bilodeau, L. (1994). *The anger workbook*. Center City, MN: Hazeldon.

Blad, E. (2014, January 15). Feds call for school discipline to be more evenhanded. *Education Week*. Retrieved from http://www.edweek.org/ew/articles/2014/01/15/17discipline.h33.html

Blake, C. (2014, March 21). School will allow boy to bring My Little Pony backpack. *USA Today*. Retrieved from http://www.usatoday.com/story/news/nation/2014/03/21/my-little-pony-backpack-banned-school-north-carolina/6685403/

Bogart, L. M., Elliott, M. N., Klein, D. J., Tortolero, S. R., Mrug, S., Peskin, M. F., . . . Schuster, M. A. (2014). Peer victimization in fifth grade and health in tenth grade. *Pediatrics, 133*(3), 440–447. doi:10.1542/peds.2013-3510

Bollmer, J. M., Milich, R., Harris, M. J., & Maras, M. A. (2005). A friend in need: The role of friendship quality as a protective factor in peer victimization and bullying. *Journal of Interpersonal Violence, 20*(6), 701–712. doi:10.117/0886260504272897

Borba, M. (2001). *Building moral intelligence: The seven essential virtues that teach kids to do the right thing*. San Francisco, CA: Jossey-Bass.

Boulton, M. (1997). Teachers' views on bullying definitions, attitudes and abilities to cope. *British Journal of Educational Psychology, 67*, 223–233.

Boulton, M. J., & Hawker, D. S. (1997). Non-physical forms of bullying among school pupils: A cause for concern. *Health Education, 97*(2), 61–64.

Bowes, L., Arseneault, L., Maughan, B., Taylor, A., Caspi, A., & Moffitt, T. E. (2009). School, neighborhood, and family factors are associated with children's bullying involvement: A nationally representative longitudinal study. *Journal of the American Academy of Child and Adolescent Psychiatry, 48*(5), 545–553. doi:10.1097/CHI.0b013e31819cb017

boyd, d. m., & Ellison, N. B. (2007). Social network sites: Definition, history, and scholarship. *Journal of Computer-Mediated Communication, 13*(1), 210–230. doi:10.1111/j.1083-6101.2007.00393.x

Bradshaw, C. P. (2015). Translating research to practice in bullying prevention. *American Psychologist, 70*(4), 322–332. doi:10.1037/a0039114

Braff, D. (2011, June 22). Movies may cause special effects on the body. *Chicago Tribune*. Retrieved from http://articles.chicagotribune.com/2011-06-22/

health/sc-health-0622-movies-impact-on-body-20110622_1_horror-films-intense-movies-birgit-wolz

Branson, C. E., & Dewey, C. G. (2009). A comparison of self and peer reports in the assessment of middle school bullying. *Journal of Applied School Psychology, 25*(1), 5–27. doi:10.1080/15377900802484133

Breiding, M. J., Basile, K. C., Smith, S. G., Black, M. C., & Mahendra, R. R. (2015). *Intimate partner violence surveillance: Uniform definitions and recommended data elements, version 2.0.* Atlanta, GA: National Center for Injury Prevention and Control, Centers for Disease Control and Prevention.

Briggs, C. A., & Pehrsson, D. E. (2008). Use of bibliotherapy in the treatment of grief and loss: A guide to current counseling practices. *Adultspan Journal, 7*(1), 32–42.

Bruneau, L., Bubenzer, D. L., & McGlothlin, J. M. (2010). Revisioning the self: A phenomenological investigation into self-help reading. *Journal of Humanistic Counseling, Education and Development, 49*(2), 217–230.

Bullying or Harassing Behavior in Public Schools Prohibited, Miss. Code Ann. § 37-11-67 (2013).

Burgess, J., & McLoughlin, C. (2012). Investigating cyberbullying: Emerging research and e-safety strategies within families and communities. *Communities, Children and Families Australia,* 6(1), 3–12.

Burke, K. S. (2013). *An inventory and examination of restorative justice practices for youth in Illinois.* Chicago: Illinois Criminal Justice Information Authority.

Bystanders: Turning Onlookers Into Bully-Prevention Agents. (n.d.). Intervention Central. Retrieved from http://www.interventioncentral.org/behavioral-interventions/bully-prevention/bystanders-turning-onlookers-bully-prevention-agents

Calefati, J. (2012, October 3). Bullying in N.J. schools spikes over previous school year, new stats show. *The Times.* Retrieved from http://www.nj.com/news/index.ssf/2012/10/bullying_in_nj_schools_spikes.html

Campbell, M. A. (2005). Cyber bullying: An old problem in a new guise? *Australian Journal of Guidance and Counselling, 15*(1), 68–76.

Caravita, S. C. S., Blasio, P. D., & Salmivalli, C. (2010). Early adolescents' participation in bullying: Is theory of mind involved? *Journal of Early Adolescence, 30*(1), 138–170. doi:10.1177/0272431609342983

Card, N. A., Stucky, B. D., Sawalani, G. M., & Little, T. D. (2008). Direct and indirect aggression during childhood and adolescence: A meta-analytic review of gender differences, intercorrelations, and relations to maladjustment. *Child Development, 79*(5), 1185–1229.

Carter, B. B., & Spencer, V. G. (2006). The fear factor: Bullying and students with disabilities. *International Journal of Special Education, 21*(1), 11–23.

Casebeer, C. M. (2012). School bullying: Why quick fixes do not prevent school failure. *Preventing School Failure: Alternative Education for Children and Youth, 56*(3), 165–171. doi:10.1080/1045988X.2011.633283

Cenkseven Onder, F., & Yurtal, F. (2008). An investigation of the family characteristics of bullies, victims, and positively behaving adolescents. *Education Sciences: Theory and Practice, 8*(3), 821–832.

Centers for Disease Control and Prevention. (2006). *Principles of epidemiology in public practice: An introduction to applied epidemiology and biostatistics* (3rd ed.). Retrieved from http://www.cdc.gov/ophss/csels/dsepd/SS1978/SS1978.pdf

Child Welfare Information Gateway. (n.d.). State statutes. Retrieved from https://www.childwelfare.gov/topics/systemwide/laws-policies/state/

Christensen, J. (2013, February 28). Our unhealthy love of reality TV bullying. *CNN Health.* Retrieved from http://www.cnn.com/2013/02/28/health/reality-tv-bullies/

Clark, M. (2013, November 4). 49 States now have anti-bullying laws. How's that working out? Governing. Retrieved from http://www.governing.com/news/headlines/49-States-Now-Have-Anti-Bullying-Laws-Hows-that-Working-Out.html

Clark, T., Orman, S., & Schulz, K. (2011). Free to be mean: Balancing hateful student behavior and the first amendment. *National School Board Association.* Retrieved from https://secure.nsba.org/storefront/detail.aspx?id=1324

Cohen, J. (2006). Social, emotional, ethical, and academic education: Creating a climate for learning, participation in democracy, and well-being. *Harvard Educational Review, 76*(2), 201–237.

Colarossi, L. G., & Eccles, J. S. (2005). Differential effects of support providers on adolescents' mental health. *Social Work Research, 27*(1), 19–30.

Coloroso, B. (2003). *The bully, the bullied, and the bystander: From preschool to high school—how parents and teachers can help break the cycle of violence.* New York, NY: HarperCollins.

Colvert. C. (2014). Movie review: In your face, Themistokles! *Star-Tribune,* pp. E1, E6.

Compete Analytics. (2015, March 16). Compete.com. Retrieved from https://www.compete.com/

Conners-Burrow, N. A., Johnson, D. L., Whiteside-Mansell, L., McKelvey, L., & Gargus, R. A. (2009). Adults matter: Protecting children from the negative impacts of bullying. *Psychology in the Schools, 46*(7), 593–604. doi:10.1002/pits.20400

Connolly, I., & O'Moore, M. (2003). Personality and family relations of children who bully. *Personality and Individual Differences, 35*(3), 559–567. doi:10.1016/S0191-8869(02)00218-0

Cook, C. R., Williams, K. R., Guerra, N. G., Kim, T. E., & Sadek, S. (2010). Predictors of bullying and victimization in childhood and adolescence: A meta-analytic investigation. *School Psychology Quarterly, 25*(2), 65–83. doi:10.1037/a0020149

Copeland, W. E, Wolke, D., Angold, A., & Costello, E. J. (2013). Impact of bullying in childhood on adult health, wealth, crime, and social outcomes. *Psychological Science, 24*(10), 1958.

Corey, M., & Corey, G. (2016). *Becoming a helper* (7th ed.). Belmont, CA: Brooks/Cole.

Cormier, S., Nurius, P., & Osborn, C. (2009). *Interviewing and change strategies for helpers: Fundamental skills and cognitive-behavioral interventions* (6th ed.).Belmont, CA: Brooks/Cole.

Cornell, D. G., Sheras, P. L., & Cole, J. C. M. (2006). Assessment of bullying. In S. R. Jimerson & M. J. Furlong (Eds.), *The handbook of school violence and school safety: From research to practice* (pp. 191–209). New York, NY: Routledge.

Corsini, R. (2008). Introduction. In R. Corsini & D. Wedding (Eds.), *Current psychotherapies* (pp. 1–14). Belmont, CA: Brooks/Cole.

Corsini, R., & Wedding, D. (Eds.). (2011). *Current psychotherapies* (9th ed.). Belmont, CA: Brooks/Cole.

Corvo, K., & deLara, E. (2010). Towards an integrated theory of relational violence: Is bullying a risk factor for domestic violence? *Aggression and Violent Behavior, 15*(3), 181–190. doi:10.1016/j.avb.2009.12.001

Cossa, M. (2006). How rude! Using sociodrama in the investigation of bullying and harassing behavior and in teaching civility in educational communities. *Journal of Group Psychotherapy, Psychodrama & Sociometry, 58*(4), 182–194.

Coughlin, P. (2013, October 16). The only way to combat America's bullying epidemic. *Fox News*. Retrieved from http://www.foxnews.com/opinion/2013/10/16/only-way-to-combat-america-bullying-epidemic/

Covey, S. (2004). *The 7 habits of highly effective people: Powerful lessons in personal change*. New York, NY: Free Press.

Creed, T., Reisweber, J., & Beck, A. (2011). *Cognitive therapy for adolescents in school settings*. New York, NY: Guilford Press.

Creston, N. (2013, October 16). Girls charged for cyber-bullying girl who committed suicide. *NPR News*. Retrieved from http://www.npr.org/templates/story/story.php?storyId=235570927

Crick, N. R. (1996). The role of overt aggression, relational aggression, and prosocial behavior in the prediction of children's future social adjustment. *Child Development, 67*(5), 2317–2327.

Crick, N. R. (1997). Engagement in gender normative versus nonnormative forms of aggression: Links to social–psychological adjustment. *Developmental Psychology, 33*(4), 610–617. doi:10.1037/0012-1649.33.4.610

Crick, N. R., & Bigbee, M. A. (1998). Relational and overt forms of peer victimization: A multi-informant approach. *Journal of Consulting and Clinical Psychology, 66*(2), 337–347. doi:10.1037/0022-006X.66.2.337

Crick, N. R., Casas, J. F., & Mosher, M. (1997). Relational and overt aggression in preschool. *Developmental Psychology, 33*(4), 579–588. doi:10.1037/0012-1649.33.4.579

Crick, N. R., & Dodge, K. A. (1996). Social information-processing mechanisms in reactive and proactive aggression. *Child Development, 67*(3), 993–1002.

Crick, N. R., & Grotpeter, J. K. (1995). Relational aggression, gender, and social psychological adjustment. *Child Development, 66*(3), 710–722.

Crick, N. R., Grotpeter, J. K., & Bigbee, M. A. (2002). Relationally and physically aggressive children's intent attributions and feelings of distress for relational and instrumental peer provocations. *Child Development, 73*(4), 1134–1142.

Crick, N., Nelson, D. Morales, J., Cullerton-Sen, C., Casas, J., & Hickman, S. (2001). Relational victimization in childhood and adolescence: I hurt you through the grapevine. In J. Juvonen & S. Graham (Eds.), *Peer harassment in school: The plight of the vulnerable and victimized* (pp. 196–214). New York, NY: Guilford Press.

Crick, N., & Rose, A. (2001). Toward a gender-balanced approach to the study of social-emotional development: A look at relational aggression. In P. Miller & E. Scholnick (Eds.), *Toward a feminist developmental psychology*. New York, NY: Routledge.

Crothers, L. M., Kolbert, J. B., & Barker, W. F. (2006). Middle school students' preferences for anti-bullying interventions. *School Psychology International, 27*(4), 475–487.

Culhane, J. G. (2013). Bullying, litigation, and populations: The limited effects of Title IX. *Western New England Law Review, 35*(2), 323–351. Retrieved from http://digitalcommons.law.wne.edu/lawreview/vol35/iss2/2/

Curtner-Smith, M. E., Smith, P. K., & Porter, M. (2010). Family level intervention with bullies and victims. In E. Vernberg & B. Biggs (Eds.), *Preventing and treating bullying and victimization* (pp. 75–106). Oxford University Press.

Cyber Bullying [sic]: Statistics and Tips. (n.d.). i-Safe. Retrieved from http://www.isafe.org/outreach/media/media_cyber_bullying

Daly, K., & Immarigeon, R. (1998). The past, present, and future of restorative justice: Some critical reflections. *Contemporary Justice Review, 1*(1) 21–45.

David-Ferdon, C., & Hertz, M. F. (2009). *Electronic media and youth violence: A CDC issue brief for researchers*. Atlanta, GA: Centers for Disease Control and Prevention.

Davidson, L. M., & Demaray, M. K. (2007, September). Social support as a moderator between victimization and internalizing-externalizing distress from bullying. *School Psychology Review, 36*(3), 383. Retrieved from http://go.galegroup.com/ps/i.do?id=GALE%7CA169311419&v=2.1&u=mnamsumank&it=r&p=PPRF&sw=w

Deggans, E. (2012, June 19). Facing up to bullies, everywhere but on reality TV. *NPR*. Retrieved from http://www.npr.org/2012/06/20/155358188/facing-up-to-bullies-everywhere-but-on-reality-tv

Derzon, J. (2006). How effective are school-based violence prevention programs in preventing and reducing violence and other antisocial behaviors? Meta-analysis. In S. R. Jimerson & M. J. Furlong (Eds.), *The handbook of school violence and school safety: From research to practice* (pp. 429-441). New York, NY: Routledge.

Detrixhe, J. (2010). Souls in jeopardy: Questions and innovations for bibliotherapy with fiction. *Journal of Humanistic Counseling, Education and Development, 49*(1), 58–72.

Dewar, G. (2009). Teaching empathy: Evidence based tips for fostering empathy in children. Parenting Science. Retrieved from http://www.parentingscience.com/teaching-empathy-tips.html

DiBlasio, N. (2011, September 11). More bullying cases have parents turning to courts. *USA Today*. Retrieved from http://usatoday30.usatoday.com/news/education/story/2011-09-11/bullying-lawsuits-parents-self-defense-courts/50363256/1

Digiuseppe, R., & Bernard, M. E. (2006). REBT assessment and treatment with children. In A. Ellis & M. E. Bernard (Eds.), *Rational emotive behavioral approaches to childhood disorders: Theory, practice and research* (pp. 85–114). Springeronline.com. doi:10.1007/b137389

DioGuardi, R. J., & Theodore, L. A. (2006). Understanding and addressing peer victimization among students. In S. R. Jimerson & M. J. Furlong (Eds.), *The handbook of school violence and school safety: From research to practice* (pp. 339–352). New York, NY: Routledge.

Dodge, K. A., Murphy, R. R., & Buchsbaum, K. (1984). The assessment of intention-cue detention skills in children: Implications for developmental psychopathology. *Child Development, 55*, 166–173.

Dolan, M. (2004). Psychopathic personality in young people. *Advances in Psychiatric Treatment, 10*, 466–473.

Doll, B., & Swearer, S. M. (2006). Cognitive-behavioral interventions for participants in bullying and coercion. In R. B. Mennuti, A. Freeman, R. W. Christner (Eds.), *Cognitive-behavioral interventions in educational settings: A handbook for practice* (pp. 183–201). New York, NY: Taylor & Francis Group.

Downey, G., Irwin, L., Ramsay, M., & Ayduk, O. (2004). Rejection sensitivity and girls' aggression. In M. Moretti, C. Odgers, & M. Jackson, M. (Eds.), *Girls and aggression: Contributing factors and intervention principles* (pp. 7–26). New York, NY: Kluwer Academic/Plenum.

Drew, N. (2010). *No kidding about bullying: 125 ready-to-use activities to help kids manage anger, resolve conflicts, build empathy, and get along*. Minneapolis, MN: Free Spirit.

Dryden, W., & DiGiuseppe, R, Neenan, M. (2010). *A primer on rational-emotive behavior therapy*. Champaign, IL: Research Press.

Dubreuil, J., & McNiff, E. (2010, October 15). Bullied to death in America's schools. *ABC News*. Retrieved from http://abcnews.go.com/2020/TheLaw/school-bullying-epidemic-turning-deadly/story?id=11880841

Eder, D. (1993). "Go get ya a French!" Romantic and sexual teasing among adolescent girls. In D. Tannen (Ed.), *Gender and conversational interaction* (pp. 17–31). New York, NY: Oxford University Press.

Edmondson, D. (1988, April). Bullies. *Parents*, 100–106.

Education for All Handicapped Children Act, U.S.C. 94-142 (1975).

Egan, G. (2014). *The skilled helper: A problem-management and opportunity development approach to helping* (10th ed.). Belmont, CA: Brooks/Cole.

Elias, M. (2013). The school-to-prison pipeline. *Teaching Tolerance, 14*. Retrieved by http://www.tolerance.org/magazine/number-43-spring-2013/school-to-prison

Elliott, M. (Ed.). (1991). *Bullying: A practical guide to coping for schools.* Harlow, England: Longman.

Ellis, A. (1962). *Reason and emotion in psychotherapy*. Secaucus, NJ: Citadel Press.

Ellis, A. (2011). Rational emotive behavior therapy. In D. Corsini & R. Wedding (Eds.), *Current psychotherapies* (9th ed.). Belmont, CA: Brooks/Cole.

Ellis, A., & Bernard, M. E. (Eds.). (2006). *Rational emotive behavioral approaches to childhood disorders*. New York, NY: Springer Science and Business Media.

Enumeration: A tool for advocates. (2009). Gay, Lesbian & Straight Education Network. Retrieved from http://www.nclrights.org/wp-content/uploads/2013/07/inclusion.pdf

Erdely, S. R. (2012, February 16). One town's war on gay teens. *Rolling Stone, 1150*, 50–57.

Eron, L. (2000). A psychological perspective. In V. Van Hasselt & M. Hersen (Eds.), *Aggression and violence: An introductory text*. Needham Heights, MA: Allyn & Bacon.

Espelage, D. L. (2003). Assessment and treatment of bullying. In L. Vandecreek (Ed.), *Innovations in clinical practice: Focus on children and adolescents* (pp. 83–95). Sarasota, FL: Professional Resource Press.

Espelage, D. L., & De La Rue (2012). School bullying: Its nature and ecology. *International Journal of Adolescent Medicine and Health, 24*(1), 3–10. doi:10.1515/ijamh.2012.002

Espelage, D. L., Mebane, S., & Adams, R. (2004). Empathy, caring, and bullying: Toward an understanding of complex associations. In D. Espelage & S. Swearer (Eds.), *Bullying in American schools: A social-ecological perspective on prevention and intervention* (pp. 37–61). Mahwah, NJ: Lawrence Erlbaum.

Espelage, D. L., & Swearer, S. M. (2003). Research on school bullying and victimization: What have we learned and where do we go from here? *School Psychology Review, 32*(3), 365–383.

Espelage, D., & Swearer, S. (Eds.). (2004). *Bullying in American schools: A social-ecological perspective on prevention and intervention*. Mahwah, NJ: Lawrence Erlbaum.

Estevez, E., Murgui, S., & Musitu, G. (2009). Psychological adjustment in bullies and victims of school violence. *European Journal of Psychology of Education, 24*(4), 473–483. doi:10.1007/BF03178762

Evatt, N. (2011, November 2). Reality TV causes bullying? "Real housewives" star says yes. *The Huffington Post*. Retrieved from http://www.huffingtonpost.com/2011/11/02/real-housewives-star-bullying_n_1071482.html

Fanner, D., & Urquhart, C. (2008). Bibliotherapy for mental health service users Part 1: A systematic review. *Health Information & Libraries Journal, 25*(4), 237–252.

Farmer, T. W., Lane, K. L., Lee, D. L., Hamm, J. V., & Lambert, K. (2012). The social functions of antisocial behavior: Considerations for school violence prevention strategies for students with disabilities. *Behavioral Disorders, 37*(3), 149–162.

Farrington, D., & Ttofi, M. (2009). *School-based programs to reduce bullying and victimization.* Oslo, Norway: Campbell Systemic Reviews.

Farrington, D., & Ttofi, M. (2011). Bullying as a predictor of offending, violence and later life outcomes. *Criminal Behaviour and Mental Health, 21*(2), 90–98.

Federal Laws. (2014, March 31). Stopbullying.gov. Retrieved from http://www.stopbullying.gov/laws/federal/

Feindler, E. L., & Weisner, S. (2006). Youth anger management treatments for school violence prevention. In S. R. Jimerson & M. J. Furlong (Eds.), *The handbook of school violence and school safety: From research to practice* (pp. 353–363). New York, NY: Routledge.

Felson, R. (2000). A social psychological approach to interpersonal violence. In V. Van Hasselt & M. Hersen (Eds.). *Aggression and violence: An introductory text.* Needham Heights, MA: Allyn & Bacon.

Ferguson, S., Greenbaum, S., McColm, R., Wilkinson, S., Byrd, T. L., Van, W. A., National School Safety Center (U.S.), . . . National Educational Service (U.S.). (1988). Set straight on bullies. Bloomington, IN: National Educational Service.

Ferriss, S. (2011a, January 8). New federal guidelines aimed at stopping explosion in harsh school discipline. The Center for Public Integrity. Retrieved from http://www.publicintegrity.org/2014/01/08/14084/new-federal-guidelines-aimed-stopping-explosion-harsh-school-discipline

Ferriss, S. (2011b, October 6). New report cites disproportionate punishment for Black students. The Center for Public Integrity. Retrieved from http://www.publicintegrity.org/2011/10/06/6884/new-report-cites-disproportionate-punishment-black-students

Feshbach, N. D. (1969). Sex differences in children's modes of aggressive responses toward outsiders. *Merrill-Palmer Quarterly of Behavior and Development, 15*(3), 249–258.

Feuerborn, L., & Chinn, D. (2012). Teacher perceptions of student needs and implications for positive behavior supports. *Behavioral Disorders, 37*(4), 219–231.

Fisher, H. L., Moffitt, T. E., Houts, R. M., Belsky, D. W., Arseneault, L., & Caspi, A. (2012). Bullying victimisation and risk of self harm in early adolescence: Longitudinal cohort study. *BMJ: British Medical Journal, 344*(7855), 1–9.

Fitzgerald, P. D., & Van Schoiack Edstrom, L. (2006). Second step: A violence prevention curriculum. In S. R. Jimerson & M. J. Furlong (Eds.), *The handbook of school violence and school safety: From research to practice* (pp. 383–394). New York, NY: Routledge.

Flam, L. (2014, January 27). Parents fight cyberbullying with lawsuit. Retrieved from http://www.today.com/parents/parents-fight-cyberbullying-lawsuit-2D11999975

Flannery, M. E. (2015, January 5). The school to prison pipeline: Time to shut it down. *NEA Today*, 42–45. Retrieved from http://neatoday.org/2015/01/05/school-prison-pipeline-time-shut/

Flaspohler, P. D., Elfstrom, J. L., Vanderzee, K. L., Sink, H. E., & Birchmeier, Z. (2009). Stand by me: The effects of peer and teacher support in mitigating the impact of bullying on quality of life. *Psychology in the Schools, 46*, 636–649. doi:10.1002/pits.20404

Forliti, A. (2012, March 6). ACLU sues Minnewaska schools, Pope Co. sheriff's officer over student Facebook incident. *Star Tribune*. Retrieved from http://www.startribune.com/141646423.html

Fox, J. A., Elliott, D. S., Kerlikowske, R. G., Newman, S. A., & Cristeson, W. (2003). *Bullying prevention is crime prevention*. Retrieved from http://www.pluk.org/Pubs/Bullying2.pdf

French, D., Jansen, E., & Pidada, S. (2002). United States and Indonesian children's and adolescents' reports of relational aggression by disliked peers. *Child Development, 73*(4), 1143–1150.

Funke, K., & Hymel, S. (2002, February). *The assessment of empathy in children identified as bullies*. Poster session presented at the annual meeting of the National Association of School Psychologists, Chicago, Illinois.

Galen, B. R., & Underwood, M. K. (1997). A developmental investigation of social aggression among children. *Developmental Psychology, 33*(4), 589–600. doi:10.1037/0012-1649.33.4.589

Gasser, L., & Keller, M. (2009). Are the competent the morally good? Perspective taking and moral motivation of children involved in bullying. *Social Development, 18*(4), 798–816. doi:10.1111/j.1467-9507.2008.00516.x

Gavrielides, T. (2011). Restorative practices: From the early societies to the 1970s. *Internet Journal of Criminology*, 1–20. Retrieved from http://www.internetjournalofcriminology.com/Gavrielides_Restorative_Practices_IJC_November_2011.pdf

Gaysynsky, A. (2011, September 7). New Jersey's anti-bullying law gets bullied by critics [Web log]. Retrieved from http://www.lawline.com/Blog/Post.php?post_id=872

Geiger, T. C., Zimmer-Gembeck, M. J., & Crick, N. R. (2004). The science of relational aggression: Can we guide intervention? In M. M. Moretti, C. Odgers, & M. Jackson (Eds.), *Girls and aggression: Contributing factors and intervention strategies* (pp. 27–40). New York: Kluwer.

George, H., Kincaid, D., & Pollard-Sage, J. (2008). Primary-tier interventions and supports. *Handbook of positive behavior support* (pp. 375–394). doi:10.1007/978-0-387-09632-2_16

Georgia Anti-Bullying Law, Ga. Code Ann. §20-2-751.4 (2006).

Geurs, K., & Shay, G. (Producer), & Geurs, K. (Director). (1997). Pooh's grand adventure: The search for Christopher Robin [Motion picture]. United States: Walt Disney Television Animation.

Gibilisco, S. (2012). Holographic telepresence. *WhatIs.Com*. Retrieved from http://whatis.techtarget.com/definition/holographic-telepresence

Gini, G. (2006). Bullying as a social process: The role of group membership in students' perception of inter-group aggression at school. *Journal of School Psychology, 44*(1), 51–65. doi:10.1016/j.jsp.2005.12.002

Gini, G. (2008). Associations between bullying behaviour, psychosomatic complaints, emotional and behavioural problems. *Journal of Paediatrics and Child Health, 44*(9), 492–497. doi:10.1111/j.1440-1754.2007.01155.x

Gini, G., Albiero, P., Benelli, B., & Altoe, G. (2007). Does empathy predict adolescents' bullying and defending behavior? *Aggressive Behavior, 33*(5), 467–476. doi:10.1002/ab.2024

Gini, G., & Pozzoli, T. (2013). Bullied children and psychosomatic problems: A meta-analysis. *Pediatrics, 132*(4), 720–729. doi:10.1542/peds.2013-0614

Gini, G., Pozzoli, T., & Hauser, M. (2011). Bullies have enhanced moral competence to judge relative to victims, but lack moral compassion. *Personality and Individual Differences, 50*(5), 603–608. doi:10.1016/j.paid.2010.12.002

Gini, G., Pozzoli, T., & Hymel, S. (2013) Moral disengagement among children and youth: A meta-analytic review of links to aggressive behavior. *Aggressive Behavior, 40*, 56–68.

Goble, G. (2012, September 6). The history of social networking. *Digital Trends*. Retrieved from http://www.digitaltrends.com/features/the-history-of-social-networking/

Goethem, A. J., Scholte, R. J., & Wiers, R. W. (2010). Explicit- and implicit bullying attitudes in relation to bullying behavior. *Journal of Abnormal Child Psychology, 38*(6), 829–842. doi:10.1007/s10802-010-9405-2

Gonzalez, J. E., Nelson, J. R., Gutkin, T. B., Saunders, A., Galloway, A. S., & Shwery, C. (2004). Rational emotive therapy with children and adolescents: A meta-analysis. *Journal of Emotional and Behavioral Disorders, 12*(4), 222–235.

Goodman-Scott, E. (2013). Maximizing school counselors' efforts by implementing school-wide positive behavioral interventions and supports: A case study from the field. *Professional School Counseling, 17*(1), 111–119.

Goodman-Scott, E., Doyle, B., & Brott, P. (2013) An action research project to determine the utility of bully prevention in positive behavior support for elementary school bullying prevention. *Professional School Counseling, 17*(1), 120–129.

Gottfredson, G. D., Gottfredson, D. C., Payne, A. A., & Gottfredson, N. C. (2005). School climate predictors of school disorder: Results from a national study of delinquency prevention in schools. *Journal of Research in Crime and Delinquency, 42*(4), 412–444.

Graham, S. (n.d.). Bullying: A module for teachers. American Psychological Association. Retrieved from http://www.apa.org/education/k12/bullying.aspx

Greenbaum, S. (1989). *Set straight on bullies*. National School Safety Center. Malibu, CA: National School Safety Center.

Greenberg, M. T., & Kusche, C. A. (2006). Building social and emotional competence: The PATHS curriculum. In S. R. Jimerson & M. J. Furlong (Eds.), *The handbook of school violence and school safety: From research to practice* (pp. 395–412). New York, NY: Routledge.

Greif, J. L., & Furlong, M. J. (2006). The assessment of school bullying: Using theory to inform practice. *Journal of School Violence, 5*(3), 33–50. doi:10.1300/J202v05n03_04

Grisham, L. (2014, March 14). School bans 9-year-old boy's My Little Pony backpack. *USA Today*. Retrieved from http://www.usatoday.com/story/news/nation-now/2014/03/18/my-little-pony-backpack-banned-school-north-carolina/6565425/

Grossman, D., & DeGaetano, G. (1999). *Stop teaching our kids to kill: A call to action against TV, movie, and video game violence*. New York, NY: Crown.

Grossman, L. (2006, December 27). You—yes, you—are TIME's person of the year. *TIME*, 25.

Gudjonson, G. H., Sigurdsson, J., & Sigfusdottir, I. (2010). Interrogation and false confessions among adolescents: Differences between bullies and victims. *Journal of Psychiatry & Law, 38*(1/2), 57–76.

Hagans, K., & Powers, K. (n.d.). *Multitiered systems of support: Recommendations for elimination of barriers to implementation with fidelity in California*. California State University, Long Beach. Retrieved from http://www.cde.ca.gov/sp/se/cc/documents/mtss.pdf

Hallford, A., Borntrager, C., & Davis, J. L. (2006). Evaluation of a bullying prevention program. *Journal of Research in Childhood Education, 21*(1), 91–101.

Hamburger, M., Basile, K., & Vivolos, A. (2011). *Measuring bullying victimization, perpetration, and bystander experiences: A compendium of assessment tools.* Atlanta, GA: Centers for Disease Control and Prevention, National Center for Injury Prevention and Control.

Hankerson, M. (2014, March 14). Wake sheriff's office still investigating 11-year-old's apparent suicide attempt. *Observer*. Retrieved from http://www.newsobserver.com/2014/03/14/3702347/wake-sheriffs-office-still-investigating.html

Harassment, Intimidation, and Bullying Policy to be Adopted by School Districts: Contents and Notice, N.J. Stat. Ann. § 18A:37 (2011).

Harper, J. (2011, September 2). What's wrong with the "anti-bullying bill of rights." *The Huffington Post*. Retrieved from http://www.huffingtonpost.com/janice-harper/new-jersey-anti-bullying-bill-of-rights_b_945613.html

Harry, B., Hart, J. E., Klingner, J., & Cramer, E. (2009). Response to Kauffman, Mock, & Simpson, (2007): Problems related to underservice of students with emotional or behavioral disorders. *Behavioral Disorders, 34*(3), 164–171.

Haynie, D., Nansel, T., Eitel, P., Crump, A., Saylor, K., Yu, K., & Simons-Morton, B. (2001). Bullies, victims, and bully/victims: Distinct groups of at-risk youth. *Journal of Early Adolescence, 21*(1), 29-49.

Hazler, R. (1996). *Breaking the cycle of violence: Interventions for bullying and victimization.* Washington, DC: Accelerated Development.

Hazler, R. J., & Carney, J. V. (2006). Critical characteristics of effective bullying prevention programs. In S. R. Jimerson & M. J. Furlong (Eds.), *The handbook of school violence and school safety: From research to practice* (pp. 275–290). New York, NY: Routledge.

Hazler, R. J., Carney, J. V., Green, S., Powell, R., & Scott Jolly, L. (1997). Areas of expert agreement on identification of school bullies and victims. *School Psychology International, 18*(1), 5–14.

Hazler, R. J., Hoover, J. H., & Oliver, R. (1992). What kids say about bullying. *The Executive Educator, 14* (11), 20–22.

Heitzeg, N. A. (2009). Education or incarceration: Zero tolerance policies and the school to prison pipeline. In *Forum on Public Policy Online, 2009*(2). Oxford Round Table.

Hemphill, S. A., Kotevski, A., Herrenkohl, T. I., Bond, L., Kim, M. J., Toumbourou, J. W., & Catalano, R. F. (2011). Longitudinal consequences of adolescent bullying perpetration and victimisation: A study of students in Victoria, Australia. *Criminal Behaviour and Mental Health, 21*(2), 107–116. doi:10.1002/cbm.802

Henington, C., Hughes, J., Cavell, T., & Thompson, B. (1998). The role of relational aggression in identifying aggressive boys and girls. *Journal of School Psychology, 36*(4), 457–477.

Hertz, M. F. &, David-Ferdon C.(2008). *Electronic Media and Youth Violence: A CDC Issue Brief for Educators and Caregivers.* Atlanta (GA): Centers for Disease Control.

Higdon, M. (2011). To lynch a child: Bullying and gender nonconformity in our nation's schools. *Indiana Law Journal, 86*(3), 827–878.

Hildebrand Clubbs, B. (2013, February 18). No you can't say whatever you want. *The Chronicle of Higher Education*. Retrieved from http://chronicle.com/article/No-You-Cant-Say-Whatever-You/137283/

Hinduja, S., & Patchin, J. W. (2008). Cyberbullying: An exploratory analysis of factors related to offending and victimization. *Deviant Behavior, 29*(2), 129–156. doi:10.1080/01639620701457816

Hinduja, S., & Patchin, J. (2009). *Bullying beyond the schoolyard: Preventing and responding to cyberbullying.* Thousand Oaks, CA: Corwin.
Hinduja, S., & Patchin, J. W. (2010). Bullying, cyberbullying, and suicide. *Archives of Suicide Research, 14*(3), 206–221. doi:10.1080/13811118.2010.494133
Hinduja, S., Patchin, J. W. (2015). State cyberbullying laws: A brief review of state cyberbullying laws and policies. Cyberbullying Research Center. Retrieved from http://www.cyberbullying.us/Bullying-and-Cyberbullying-Laws.pdf
Hirsch, L., Lowen, C. (Producers), & Hirsch, L. (Director). (2011). *Bully* [Motion picture]. United States: Anchor Bay Entertainment.
Hirschstein, M., & Frey, K. S. (2006). Promoting behavior and beliefs that reduce bullying: The steps to respect program. In S. R. Jimerson & M. J. Furlong (Eds.), *The handbook of school violence and school safety: From research to practice* (pp. 309–323). New York, NY: Routledge.
History of Restorative Justice. (n.d.). Colorado Springs, CO: Restorative Mediation Project. Retrieved from http://www.restorativemediation.org/Concept/history-of-restorative-justice.html
Hoffman, M. (2000). *Empathy and moral development: Implications for caring and justice.* Cambridge, United Kingdom: Cambridge University Press.
Hoffman, S. (2014). Zero benefit estimating the effect of zero tolerance discipline polices on racial disparities in school discipline. *Educational Policy, 28*(1), 69–95.
Hojat, M. (2009). Ten approaches for enhancing empathy in health and human services cultures. *Journal of Health and Human Services Administration, 31*(4), 412–450.
Holt, M. K., & Espelage, D. L. (2007). Perceived social support among bullies, victims, and bully-victims. *Journal of Youth and Adolescence, 36*(8), 984–994.
Hong, J. S., & Espelage, D. L. (2012). A review of research on bullying and peer victimization in school: An ecological system analysis. *Aggression and Violent Behavior, 17*(4), 311–322.
Hook, M. (2014). Discipline and special ed student. *Hook Law Center News, 21*(7), 1–4.
Hoover, J. H., & Hazler, R. J. (1991). Bullies and victims. *Elementary School Guidance & Counseling, 25*(3), 212–219.
Hoover, J. H., Oliver, R., & Hazler, R. J. (1992). Bullying: Perceptions of adolescent victims in the midwestern USA. *School Psychology International, 13*(1), 5–16.
How to beat America's bullying "epidemic." (n.d.) Latitude News. Retrieved from http://www.latitudenews.com/story/how-to-beat-americas-bullying-epidemic/
How to connect forgiveness and accountability. (2014, April 6). Leadership Freak. Retrieved from https://leadershipfreak.wordpress.com/2014/04/14/how-to-connect-forgiveness-and-accountability/
Hu, W. (2011, August 30). Bullying law puts New Jersey schools on spot. *The New York Times.* Retrieved from http://www.nytimes.com/2011/08/31/nyregion/bullying-law-puts-new-jersey-schools-on-spot.html?pagewanted=all
Huesmann, L. R., Eron, L. D., Lefkowitz, M. M., & Walder, L. O. (1984). Stability of aggression over time and generations. *Developmental Psychology, 20*(6), 1120–1134. doi:10.1037/0012-1649.20.6.1120
Huesmann, L. R., Eron, L. D., & Yarmel, P. W. (1987). Intellectual functioning and aggression. *Journal of Personality and Social Psychology, 52*(1), 232.
Hunt, R. (1993). Neurobiological patterns of aggression. *Journal of Emotional and Behavioral Problems, 2*(1), 14–19.
Hutchins, D. E., & Vaught, C. C. (1997). *Helping relationships and strategies.* Pacific Grove, CA: Brooks.
Hyde, J. S. (1984). How large are gender differences in aggression? A developmental meta-analysis. *Developmental Psychology, 20*(4), 722–736.

Individuals With Disabilities Education Act, 20 U.S.C §1400 (1990).
Ivey, A., Ivey, M., & Zalaquett, C. (2014). *Intentional interviewing and counseling: Facilitating client development in a multicultural society* (8th ed.). Belmont, CA: Brooks/Cole.
Jack, R. E., Garrod, O. G. B., & Schyns, P. G. (2014). Dynamic facial expressions of emotion transmit an evolving hierarchy of signals over time. *Current Biology, 24*(2), 187–192. doi:10.1016/j.cub.2013.11.064
Jacobs, A. K. (2008). Components of evidence-based interventions for bullying and peer victimization. In R. G. Steele, T. D. Elkin, & M. C. Roberts (Eds.), *Evidence-based therapies for children and adolescents: Bridging science and practice* (pp. 261–279). New York, NY: Springer.
Jacobson, R. B. (2010). Narrating characters: The making of a school bully. *Interchange, 41*(3), 255–283. doi:10.1007/s10780-010-9126-z
Jeong, S., & Lee, B. H. (2013). Multilevel examination of peer victimization and bullying preventions in schools. *Journal of Criminology, 2013,* 1–10. doi:10.1155/2013/735397A
Johari Window. (n.d.) Retrieved from https://www2.usgs.gov/humancapital/documents/JohariWindow.pdf
Julka, M. J., & Lewis, S. R. (2008, January). The doctrine of "deliberate indifference." Legal Comment. Retrieved from https://www.wasbmemberservices.org/websites/legal/File/legal-comments/C200801.pdf
July 2015 Web Server Survey. (2015, July 22). *Netcraft.Com.* Retrieved from http://news.netcraft.com/archives/2015/07/22/july-2015-web-server-survey.html
Juvonen, J., & Graham, S. (Eds.). (2001). *Peer harassment in school: The plight of the vulnerable and victimized.* New York, NY: Guilford Press.
Juvonen, J., Graham, S., & Schuster, M. A. (2003). Bullying among young adolescents: The strong, the weak, and the troubled. *Pediatrics, 112*(6), 1231–1237.
Kalman, I. (2013, December 31). Fear of "blaming victims" perpetuates bullying epidemic [Web log post]. Retrieved from https://www.psychologytoday.com/blog/resilience-bullying/201401/fear-blaming-victims-perpetuates-bullying-epidemic
Kelman, B. M. (2013, May 12). Study: Black students suspended more often than others. *USA Today.* Retrieved from http://www.usatoday.com/story/news/nation/2013/05/12/black-student-suspensions/2151423/
Keltner, D., Capps, L., Kring, A. M., Young, R. C., & Heerey, E. A. (2001). Just teasing: A conceptual analysis and empirical review. *Psychological bulletin, 127*(2), 229.
Key components in state anti-bullying laws. (2014, March 31). Stopbullying.gov. Retrieved from http://www.stopbullying.gov/laws/key-components/
Kids' suspensions renew debate over zero tolerance. (2013, February 19). *Education Week.* Retrieved from http://www.edweek.org/ew/articles/2013/02/18/594257
Kim, B. S., Green, J. L. G., & Klein, E. F. (2006). Using storybooks to promote multicultural sensitivity in elementary school children. *Journal of Multicultural Counseling and Development, 34*(4), 223–234.
Kirves, L., & Sajaniemi, N. (2012). Bullying in early educational settings. *Early Child Development and Care, 182*(3–4), 383–400. doi:10.1080/03004430.2011.646724
Klein, J. (2006). Cultural capital and high school bullies: How social inequality impacts school violence. *Men and Masculinities, 9*(1), 53–75. doi:10.1177/1097184X04271387
Klein, J., Cornell, D., & Konold, T. (2012). Relationships between bullying, school climate, and student risk behaviors. *School Psychology Quarterly, 27*(3), 154–169. Retrieved from http://doi.org/10.1037/a0029350

Klomek, B. A., Marrocco, F., Kleinman, M., Schonfeld, I. S., & Gould. (2007). Bullying, depression, and suicidality in adolescents. *American Academy of Child and Adolescent Psychiatry, 46*(1), 40–49. doi:10.1097/01.chi.0000242237.84925.18

Knefel, M. (2013a, September 13). When high school students are treated like prisoners. *Rolling Stone*. Retrieved by http://www.rollingstone.com/politics/news/when-high-school- students-are-treated-like-prisoners-20130912

Knefel, M. (2013b, November 7). The school-to-prison pipeline: A nationwide problem for equal rights. *Rolling Stone*. Retrieved by http://www.rollingstone.com/music/news/the-school-to-prison-pipeline-a-nationwide-problem-for-equal-rights-20131107

Kochenderfer-Ladd, B., & Skinner, K. (2002). Children's coping strategies: Moderators of the effects of peer victimization? *Developmental Psychology, 38*(2), 267–278. doi:10.1037/0012-1649.38.2.267

Kooran, J. (2014, March 25). ACLU-MN settles Facebook case with Minnewaska school district. ACLU-Minnesota [Press release]. Retrieved from https://www.aclu.org/technology-and-liberty/aclu-mn-settles-facebook-case-minnewaska-school-district

Kosciw, J. G., Greytak, E. A., Bartkiewicz, M. J., Boesen, M. J., & Palmer, N. A. (2012). *The 2011 national school climate survey: The experiences of lesbian, gay, bisexual, and transgender youth in our nation's schools.* New York, NY: GLSEN.

Kowalski, R. M., & Limber, S. P. (2007). Electronic bullying among middle school students. *Journal of Adolescent Health, 41*(6), S22–S30. doi:10.1016/j.jadohealth.2007.08.017

Kremer, P. K. (2010). *Quality of teacher-student relationships: Moderator of the effects of peer victimization* (Doctoral dissertation, Arizona State University). Retrieved from http://repository.asu.edu/attachments/56082/content/Kremer_asu_0010E_10106.pdf

Kruger, J., Gordon, C. L., & Kuban, J. (2006). Intentions in teasing: When "just kidding" just isn't good enough. *Journal of Personality and Social Psychology, 90*(3), 412.

Kumpulainen, K., & Rasanen, E. (2000). Children involved in bullying at elementary school age: Their psychiatric symptoms and deviance in adolescence. *Child Abuse & Neglect*, 24(12), 1567–1577. doi:10.1016/S0145-2134(00)00210-6

Kuntsche, E., Pickett, W., Overpeck, M., Craig, W., Boyce, W., & de Matos, M. G. (2006). Television viewing and forms of bullying among adolescents from eight countries. *Journal of Adolescent Health, 39*(6), 908–915.

Lagerspetz, K. M., & Björkqvist, K. (1994). Indirect aggression in boys and girls. In L. R. Huesmann (Ed.), *Aggressive Behavior: Current Perspectives* (pp. 131–150). New York, NY: Springer Press.

Lagerspetz, K. M., Björkqvist, K., Berts, M., & King, E. (1982). Group aggression among school children in three schools. *Scandinavian Journal of Psychology, 23*, 45–52.

Lake, V. E. (2004). Profile of an aggressor: Childhood bullies evolve into violent youths. *Early Child Development and Care, 174*(6), 527–537. doi:10.1080/0300443042000187040 http://www.edweek.org/ew/articles/2012/05/09/30cyberbully.h31.html

Lee, K. (n.d.). What to do when your child is a bully. *About.com*. Retrieved from http://childparenting.about.com/od/socialdevelopment/a/What-To-Do-When-Your-Child-Is-A-Bully.htm. Leadership Conference on Civil and Human Rights. http://www.civilrights.org

Leff, S., Power, T., & Goldstein, A. (2004). Outcome measures to assess the effectiveness of bullying-prevention programs in the schools. In D. Espelage & S. Swearer (Eds.), *Bullying in American schools: A social-ecological perspective on prevention and intervention*. Mahwah, NJ: Lawrence Erlbaum.

Lerner, N. (2014, March 8). The problems with Ask.fm. *The Huffington Post*. Retrieved from http://www.huffingtonpost.com/natasha-lerner/askfm-bullying_b_4148961.html

Levy, P. (2013, October 7). Anoka-Hennepin schools take aim at cyberbullying. *Star Tribune*. Retrieved from http://www.startribune.com/lifestyle/kids-health/226611561.html

Limber, S. P. (2006). The Olweus bullying prevention program: An overview of its implementation and research basis. In S. R. Jimerson & M. J. Furlong (Eds.), *The handbook of school violence and school safety: From research to practice* (pp. 293–307). New York, NY: Routledge.

Limber, S. P., Olweus, D., Ph.D., & Luxenberg, H. (2013). *Bullying in U.S. schools: 2012 status report*. Hazelden Foundation. Retrieved from http://www.clemson.edu/olweus/Reports/OBPPBullyinginUSSchools2012Report.pdf?nclick_check=1

Linder, R., Crick, N. R., & Collins, W. A. (2002). Relational aggression and victimization in young adults' romantic relationships: Association with perceptions of parent, peer, and romantic relationship quality. *Social Development, 11*, 69–86. doi:10.1111/1467-9507.00187

Loeber, R., & Hay, D. (1997). Key issues in the development of aggression and violence from childhood to early adulthood. *Annual Review of Psychology, 48*, 371–410. doi:10.1146/annurev.psych.48.1.371

Lomas, J., Stough, C., Hansen, K., & Downey, L. A. (2012). Brief report: Emotional intelligence, victimisation and bullying in adolescents. *Journal of Adolescence, 35*(1), 207–211. doi:10.1016/j.adolescence.2011.03.002

Losen, D. J., & Gillespie, J. (2012, August). Opportunities suspended: The disparate impact of disciplinary exclusion from school. UCLA: The Civil Rights Project / Proyecto Derechos Civiles. Retrieved from http://escholarship.org/uc/item/3g36n0c3

Low, S., Van Ryzin, M. J., Brown, E. C., Smith, B. H., & Haggerty, K. P. (2014). Engagement matters: Lessons from assessing classroom implementation of steps to respect: A bullying prevention program over a one-year period. *Prevention Science: The Official Journal of the Society for Prevention Research, 15*(2), 165–176. doi:10.1007/s11121-012-0359-1

Luft, J., & Ingham, H. (1961). The Johari Window: A graphic model of awareness in interpersonal relations. *Human Relations Training News, 5*(9), 6–7.

Luk, J. W., Wang, J., & Simons-Morton, B. G. (2012). The co-occurrence of substance use and bullying behaviors among U.S. adolescents: Understanding demographic characteristics and social influences. *Journal of Adolescence, 35*(5), 1351–1360. doi:10.1016/j.adolescence.2012.05.003

Lush, T. (2013, September 13). Florida girl was bullied for months before suicide. *The Big Story*. Retrieved from http://bigstory.ap.org/article/florida-girl-was-bullied-months-suicide

Ma, L., Phelps, E., Lerner, J. V., & Lerner, R. M. (2009). The development of academic competence among adolescents who bully and who are bullied. *Journal of Applied Developmental Psychology, 30*(5), 628–644. doi:10.1016/j.appdev.2009.07.006

Maccoby, E. E., & Jacklin, C. N. (Eds.). (1974). *The psychology of sex differences* (Vol. 1). Stanford, CA: Stanford University Press.

Macklem, G. (2003). *Bullying and teasing: Social power in children's groups*. New York, NY: Kluwer Academic/Plenum.

Make every day bullying prevention day. (2012, October 12). Retrieved from http://bullyingepidemic.com/wp-content/uploads/2012/10/2012-0930-Blumen-Media-1-Sheet-1.5-Press-Quality.pdf

Malti, T., & Latzko, B. (2010). Children's moral emotions and moral cognition: Towards an integrative perspective. *New Directions for Child and Adolescent Development, 2010*(129), 1–10. doi:10.1002/cd.272

Marini, Z. A., Dane, A. V., Bosacki, S. L., & YLC-CURA. (2006). Direct and indirect bully-victims: Differential psychosocial risk factors associated with adolescents involved in bullying and victimization. *Aggressive Behavior, 32*(6), 551–569. doi:10.1002/ab.20155

Massachusetts senate passes anti-bullying legislation. (2014, March 20). *The Rainbow Times*. Retrieved from http://www.therainbowtimesmass.com/2014/03/20/massachusetts-senate-passes-anti-bullying-legislation/

McGlone, P. (2014, March 5). NJ schools starts releasing anti-bullying grades. *The Times*. Retrieved from http://www.nj.com/education/2014/03/nj_schools_required_to_post_self- determined_anti-bullying_grades.html

Mendelevich, A. (2014, April 24). Del Campo Saatchi & Saatchi presents first campaign for VH1. *Saatchi & Saatchi*. Retrieved from http://saatchi.com/en-us/news/del-campo-saatchi-saatchi-presents-first-campaign-for-vh1/

Mendler, A. (1992). *What do I do when? How to achieve discipline with discipline in the classroom*. Bloomington, IN: National Education Service.

Merrell, K. W., & Isava, D. M. (2008). How effective are school bullying programs? A meta-analysis of intervention research. *School Psychology Quarterly, 23*(1), 26–42. doi:10.1037/1045-3830.23.1.26

Messitt, M. (2014). *Exposed*.(No.46) Southern Poverty Law Center. Retrieved from http://www.tolerance.org/magazine/number-46-spring-2014/feature/exposed

Michaels, L. (Producer), & Waters, M. (Director). (2004). *Mean girls* [Motion picture]. United States: Paramount Pictures.

Milgram, S. (1963). Behavioral study of obedience. *Journal of Abnormal and Social Psychology, 67*(4), 371.

Miller, P., & Scholnick, E. (2001). *Toward a feminist developmental psychology*. New York, NY: Routledge.

Minnesota girl alleges school privacy invasion. (2012, March 10). CNN US. Retrieved from http://www.cnn.com/2012/03/10/us/minnesota-student-privacy/

Monks, C. P., Smith, P. K., Naylor, P., Barter, C., Ireland, J. L., & Coyne, I. (2009). Bullying in different contexts: Commonalities, differences and the role of theory. *Aggression and Violent Behavior, 14*(2), 146–156. doi:10.1016/j.avb.2009.01.004

Montana anti-bullying laws & polices. Stopbullying.gov. Retrieved from http://www.stopbullying.gov/laws/montana.html

Moretti, M., Odgers, C., Jackson, M. (2004). *Girls and aggression: Contributing factors and intervention principles*. New York, NY: Kluwer Academic/Plenum.

Mounts, N. S. (1997). What about girls? Are they really not aggressive? *Human Development and Family Life Bulletin: A Review of Research and Practice, 3*(2).

Mueller, M. (2014, March 25). Bullies beware: Groundbreaking ruling allows schools to sue students who harass peers. New Jersey On Line LLC. Retrieved from http://www.nj.com/news/index.ssf/2014/03/bullies_beware_groundbreaking_ruling_allows_schools_to_sue_students_who_harass_peers.html

Nansel, T. R., Overpeck, M., Pilla, R. S., Ruan, J. W., Simons-Morton, B., & Scheidt, P. (2001). Bully behaviors among us youth prevalence and association with psychosocial adjustment. *Journal of the American Medical Association, 285*(16), 2094–2100.

Nash, L. (2012). New Jersey's anti-bullying fix: A solution or the creation of an even greater first amendment problem? *BYU Law Review, 2012*(3). 1039–1069. Retrieved from http://digitalcommons.law.byu.edu/cgi/viewcontent.cgi?article=2674&context=lawreview

National Association of School Psychologists. (2001). *Zero tolerance and alternative strategies: A fact sheet for educators and policymakers* [Fact sheet]. *NASP Resources.* Retrieved from http://www.nasponline.org/resources/factsheets/zt_fs.aspx

National Center for Injury Prevention and Control (2008, September 25). Center for Disease Control and Prevention. Psychological/emotional abuse. Retrieved from http://www.cdc.gov/ncipc/pub-res/ipv_surveillance/11_section34.htm

Neil, M. (2014, March 31). Parents of 11 students can be named as defendants in school-bullying suit, judge rules. *ABA Journal.* Retrieved from http://www.abajournal.com/news/article/parents_of_problem_students_can_be_named_as_defendants_in_school-bullying

Nesdale, D., Durkin, K., Maass, A., Kiesner, J., & Griffiths, J. A. (2008). Effects of group norms on children's intentions to bully. *Social Development, 17*(4), 889–907. doi:10.1111/j.1467-9507.2008.00475.x

Nese, R. N. T., Horner, R. H., Dickey, C. R., Stiller, B., & Tomlanovich, A. (2014). Decreasing bullying behaviors in middle school: Expect respect. *School Psychology Quarterly: The Official Journal of the Division of School Psychology, American Psychological Association, 29*(3), 272–286. doi:10.1037/spq0000070

Newman, K., Fox, C., Harding, D., Mehta, J., & Roth, W. (2004). *Rampage: The social roots of school shootings.* New York, NY: Basic Books.

Noon, A. (2015, February). Lawmakers consider making cyberbullying a crime. *Bozeman Daily Chronicle.* Retrieved from http://www.bozemandailychronicle.com/ap_news/montana/lawmakers-to-consider-making-cyberbullying-a-crime/article_4197fe1c-32ac-5ca6-9351-61220193c5c8.html

Norgard, H. (2014). Pushing schools around: New Jersey's antibullying bill of rights act. *Seton Hall Law Review, 44*(1), 305–338. Retrieved from http://scholarship.shu.edu/cgi/viewcontent.cgi?article=1496&context=shlr

O'Brennan, L. M., Bradshaw, C. P., & Sawyer, A. L. (2009). Examining developmental differences in the social-emotional problems among frequent bullies, victims, and bully/victims. *Psychology in the Schools, 46*(2), 100–115.

O'Brennan, L. M., Waasdorp, T. E., & Bradshaw, C. P. (2014). Strengthening bullying prevention through school staff connectedness. *Journal of Educational Psychology, 106*(3), 870–880. doi:10.1037/a0035957

Ojeda, A. E. (Ed.). (2008). *The trauma of psychological torture.* Westport, CT: Praeger.

Okun, B., & Kantrowitz, R. (2015). *Effective helping: Interviewing and counseling techniques* (8th ed.). Stamford, CT: Cengage Learning.

Oliver, R., Oaks, I., & Hoover, J. (1994). Family issues and interventions in bullying and victim relationships. *The School Counselor, 41*(3), 199–202.

Olweus, D. (1978). *Aggression in the schools: Bullies and whipping boys.* Washington, DC: Hemisphere Press: Wiley.

Olweus, D. (1993). *Bullying at school: What we know and what we can do*. Malden, MA: Blackwell.
Olweus, D. (1996). Bully/victim problems at school: Facts and effective intervention. *Reclaiming Children and Youth*, Spring, 15–22.
Olweus, D. (2001). Peer harassment: A critical analysis and some important issues. In J. Juvonen & S. Graham, (Eds.), *Peer harassment in school*, (pp. 3–20). New York, NY: Guilford.
Olweus, D. (2003, March). A profile of bullying at school. *Education Leadership*. Retrieved from http://www.lhsenglish.com/uploads/7/9/0/8/7908073/olweus_profile_of_ bullying.pdf
O'Moore, M. (1987, August). The CDCC's teacher bursaries scheme: European teachers' seminar on "bullying in schools." In M. Vorbeck (Chair), Symposium conducted at the meeting of the Council for Cultural Cooperation, Stavanger, Norway.
Online Etymology Dictionary. (2014). Retrieved from http://www.etymonline.com/index.php?term=discipline&allowed_in_frame=0
Overmier, J. B. (2002). On learned helplessness. *Integrative Physiological & Behavioral Science, 37*(1), 4–8.
Packer, M. (1985). Hermeneutic inquiry in the study of human conduct. *American Psychologist, 40* (10), 1081–1093.
Patel, K. (2011). *The bullying epidemic: The guide to arm you for the fight*. Available from https://www.goodreads.com/book/show/13318539-the-bullying-epidemic-the-guide-to-arm-you-for-the-fight
Paul, A. M. (2012, March 17). Your brain on fiction. *The New York Times*. Retrieved from http://www.nytimes.com/2012/03/18/opinion/sunday/the-neuroscience-of-your-brain-on-fiction.html?_r=0
PBIS World. (2012). *The PBIS world.com book*. Available at http://www.pbisworld.com/
Peck. S. (2012). *STAND TALL teacher's manual & DVD: Grades 4–6 lessons that teach respect and prevent bullying*. Thousand Oaks, CA: Corwin.
Pellegrini, A. D., & Bartini, M. (2000). A longitudinal study of bullying, victimization, and peer affiliation during the transition from primary school to middle school. *American Educational Research Journal, 37*(3), 699–725. doi:10.3102/00028312037003699.
People for the American Way. (n.d.). Big Bullies Update. Retrieved from http://www.pfaw.org/rww-in-focus/updated-big-bullies-right-wings-anti-anti-bullying-strategies
Perez, S. (2013, August). In wake of teen suicides, Ask.fm faces a "MySpace" problem. *Tech Crunch*. Retrieved from http://techcrunch.com/2013/08/12/in-wake-of-teen-suicides-ask-fm-faces-a-myspace-problem/
Perez, S. (2014, March). Amid bullying and threats of violence, anonymous social app Yik Yak shuts off access to US middle and high school students. *Tech Crunch*. Retrieved from http://techcrunch.com/2014/03/13/amid-vicious-bullying-threats-of-violence-anonymous-social-app-yik-yak-shuts-off-access-to-u-s-middle-high-school-students/
Perry, B. E. (Ed.). (1952). *Aesopica: A series of texts relating to Aesop or ascribed to him*. Urbana: University of Illinois Press.
Peskin, M. F., Tortolero, S. R., & Markham, C. M. (2006). Bullying and victimization among Black and Hispanic adolescents. *Adolescence, 41*(163), 467–484.
Peterson, J. S., & Ray, K. E. (2006). Bullying and the gifted: Victims, perpetrators, prevalence, and effects. *Gifted Child Quarterly, 50*(2), 148–168.

Phoenix, J., & Honda, M. (2012, August 28). Our children face a bullying epidemic. *USA Today*. Retrieved from http://usatoday30.usatoday.com/news/opinion/forum/story/2012-08-28/joaquin-phoenix-bullying-epidemic/57379318/1

Polanin, J. R., Espelage, D. L., & Pigott, T. D. (2012). A meta-analysis of school-based bullying prevention programs' effects on bystander intervention behavior. *School Psychology Review, 41*(1), 47–65.

Pollastri, A. R., Esteben, C. V., & O'Donnell, E. H. (2010). Self-esteem in pure bullies and bully/victims: A longitudinal analysis. *Journal of Interpersonal Violence, 25*(8), 1489–1502. doi:10.1177/0886260509354579

Pontzer, D. (2010). A theoretical test of bullying behavior: Parenting, personality, and the bully/victim relationship. *Journal of Family Violence, 25*(3), 259–273. doi:10.1007/s10896-009-9289-5

Post, T. (2012, April 4). Minn. student's Facebook incident could help form schools' guidelines. *MPR News*. Retrieved from http://www.mprnews.org/story/2012/04/04/school-facebook-policy

Pozzoli, T., Gini, G., & Vieno, A. (2012). Individual and class moral disengagement in bullying among elementary school children. *Aggressive Behavior, 38*(5), 378–388. doi: 10.1002/ab.21442

Protalinski, E. (2012, September 14). US judge rules school violated First Amendment by demanding Facebook password from 12-year-old girl. *The Next Web*. Retrieved from http://thenextweb.com/facebook/2012/09/14/us-judge-rules-school-district- demanded-facebook-password-12-year-old-girl/

Quantcast. (2015, March 16). Retrieved from https://www.quantcast.com/

Radcliffe-Brown, A. R. (1940). On joking relationships. *Africa, 13*(3), 195–210.

Ragatz, L. L., Anderson, R. J., Fremouw, W., & Schwartz, R. (2011). Criminal thinking patterns, aggression styles, and the psychopathic traits of late high school bullies and bully-victims. *Aggressive Behavior, 37*(2), 145–160. doi:10.1002/ab.20377

Renda, J., Vassallo, S., & Edwards, B. (2011). Bullying in early adolescence and its association with anti-social behaviour, criminality and violence 6 and 10 years later. *Criminal Behaviour & Mental Health, 21*(2), 117–127. doi:10.1002/cmb.v21.2issuestoc

Riestenberg, N. (2012). *Circle in the square: Building community and repairing harm in school.* St. Paul, MN: Living Justice Press.

Rigby, K. (2005). Why do some children bully at school? The contributions of negative attitudes towards victims and the perceived expectations of friends, parents and teachers. *School Psychology International, 26*(2), 147–161. doi:10.1177/0143034305052910

Rigby, K. (2006). What we can learn from evaluated studies of school-based programs to reduce bullying in schools. In S. R. Jimerson & M. J. Furlong (Eds.), *The handbook of school violence and school safety: From research to practice* (pp. 325–337). New York, NY: Routledge.

Rigby, K. (2012). Bullying in schools: Addressing desires, not only behaviours. *Educational Psychology Review, 24*(2), 339–348. doi:10.1007/s10648-012-9196-9

Rigby, K., & Smith, P. (2011). Is school bullying really on the rise? *Social Psychology of Education, 14*(4), 441–455. doi:10.1007/s11218-011-9158-y

Riordan, R. J., & Wilson, L. S. (1989). Bibliotherapy: Does it work? *Journal of Counseling & Development, 67*(9), 506–508.

Roberts, W. (2006). *Bullying from both sides.* Thousand Oaks, CA: Corwin.

Roberts, W. (2008). *Working with parents of bullies and victims.* Thousand Oaks, CA: Corwin.

Robinson, B. A. (n.d.). The "Golden Rule" (a.k.a. Ethics of Reciprocity): Passages from various religious texts. Religious Tolerance. Retrieved from http://www.religioustolerance.org/reciproc2.htm

Robinson, E. H., Rotter, J. C., Fey, M. A., & Vogel, K. R. (1992). *Helping children cope with fears and stress.* Retrieved from http://files.eric.ed.gov/fulltext/ED482770.pdf

Rogers, C. R. (1951). *Client-centered counseling.* London, England: Constable.

Rosado, L. (2000). *Kids are different: How knowledge of adolescent development theory can aid decision-making in court.* American Bar Association Juvenile Justice Center. Washington, DC.

Rosenberg, L. (2011, March 16). Right wing gins up hysteria over Obama's initiative to curb bullying. *Media Matters for America.* Retrieved from http://mediamatters.org/research/2011/03/16/right-wing-gins-up-hysteria-over-obamas-initiat/177643

Ross, D. (1996). *Childhood bullying and teasing: What school personnel, other professionals and parents can do.* Alexandria, VA: American Counseling Association.

Ross, D. M. (2002). Bullying. In J. Sandoval (Ed.), *Handbook of crisis counseling, intervention, and prevention in the schools* (pp. 105–134). Mahwah NJ: Lawrence Erlbaum.

Ross, S. W., & Horner, R. H. (2009). Bully prevention in positive behavior support. *Journal of Applied Behavior Analysis, 42*(4), 747–759. doi:10.1901/jaba.2009.42-747

Rothon, C., Head, J., Klineberg, E., & Stansfeld, S. (2011). Can social support protect bullied adolescents from adverse outcomes? A prospective study on the effects of bullying on the educational achievement and mental health of adolescents at secondary schools in East London. *Journal of Adolescence, 34*(3), 579–588.

R. S. & S. S. v. Minnewaska Area School District No. 2149, 0:12-cv-00588-MJD-LIB (Pope County 2014)

R. S. & S. S. v. Minnewaska Area School District No. 2149, Complaint 0:12-cv-00588-MJD-LIB (Pope County 2014)

R. S. & S. S. v. Minnewaska Area School District No. 2149, Memorandum of law and order Civ. No. 12-588-MJD-LIB (Pope County 2014)

Sacco, D., Silbaugh, K., Corredor, F., Casey, J., & Doherty, D. (2012). *An overview of state anti-bullying legislation and other related laws.* Cambridge, MA: Kinder and Braver World Project, Harvard University.

Salmivalli, C. (2010). Bullying and the peer group: A review. *Aggression and Violent Behavior, 15*(2), 112–120. doi:10.1016/j.avb.2009.08.007

Samuels, C. A. (2013, August 27). Tensions accompany growth of PBIS discipline model. *Education Week.* Retrieved from http://www.edweek.org/ew/articles/2013/08/28/2pbis_ep.h33.html

Samuels, C. A. (2014, May 7). Autism issues complicate educators' anti-bullying efforts. *Education Week, 33*(30), 16.

Sarle, D. (2013). Ask.fm responds to cyberbullying allegations. ArticSetup. Retrieved from http://www.arcticstartup.com/2013/05/13/ask-fm-responds-to- cyberbullying-allegations

Sauter, D. A., Eisner, F., Edman, P., & Scott, S. K. (2010). Cross-cultural recognition of basic emotions through nonverbal emotional vocalizations. *Proceedings of the National Academy of Sciences of the United States of America, 107*(6), 2408–2412. doi:10.1073/pnas.0908239106

Schenck v. United States, 249 U.S. 47 (1919). Cornell University Law School. Retrieved from https://www.law.cornell.edu/supremecourt/text/249/47

Scholte, R. J., Engels, R. E., Overbeek, G., De Kemp, R. T., & Haselager, G. T. (2007). Stability in bullying and victimization and its association with social adjustment in childhood and adolescence. *Journal of Abnormal Child Psychology, 35*(2), 217–228. doi:10.1007/s10802-006-9074-3

School board policy; prohibiting intimidation and bullying, Minnesota Statutes–121A.0695. (2005).

School bullying: Legal protections for vulnerable youth need to be more fully assessed. Testimony before the Committee on Health, Education, Labor and Pensions, U.S. Senate. United States Government Accountability Office (2012) (Testimony of Linda M. Calbom).

School bullying: Overall victimization declines, NCES reports, Asian students most bullied. (2011, November 11). *The Huffington Post*. Retrieved from http://www.huffingtonpost.com/2011/11/04/school-bullying-overall-v_n_1076986.html

School Bullying Prevention Act, 79 Del. Laws, c.41 Title 14 § 4112D (2014).

Schwarz, A. (2011). School discipline study raises fresh questions. *The New York Times*, p. A14.

Schwartz, D., Gorman, A., Dodge, K., Bates, J., & Pettit, G. (2008). Friendships with peers who are low or high in aggression as moderators of the link between peer victimization and declines in academic functioning. *Journal of Abnormal Child Psychology, 36*(5), 719–730.

Schwartz, K. (2013, January 30). Empathy: The key to social and emotional learning. *KQED Mind/Shift* [Blog post]. Retrieved from http://blogs.kqed.org/mindshift/2013/01/empathy-the-key-to-social-and-emotional-learning/

Schwartz, K. (2013, May 9). How do you teach empathy Harvard pilots game simulation. *KQED Mind/Shift* [Blog post]. Retrieved from http://blogs.kqed.org/mindshift/2013/05/how-do-you-teach-empathy-harvard-pilots-game-simulation/

Scott, J., & Borgman, J. Zits. *Zits.com*. Retrieved from http://zitscomics.com/

Seeds, P. M., Harkness, K. L., & Quilty, L. C. (2010). Parental maltreatment, bullying, and adolescent depression: Evidence for the mediating role of perceived social support. *Journal of Clinical Child & Adolescent Psychology, 39*(5), 681–692.

Seifert, D. (2013). Social question and answer site Formspring to shut down on March 31. *The Verge*. Retrieved from http://www.theverge.com/2013/3/15/4110196/social-question-answer-site-formspring-shut-down-march-31st

Seligman, M. E., & Maier, S. F. (1967). Failure to escape traumatic shock. *Journal of Experimental Psychology, 74*(1), 1.

Shah, N. (2012, April 11). Special education students a focus in *Bully*. *Education Week* [Web log post]. Retrieved from http://blogs.edweek.org/edweek/speced/2012/04/special_education_students_a_f.html

Shah, N. (2013a, January 4). Discipline policies shift with views on what works. *Education Week*. Retrieved from http://www.edweek.org/ew/articles/2013/01/10/16policies.h32.html?intc=EW-QC13-TOC

Shah, N. (2013b, March 6). Pediatricians criticize harsh discipline codes. *Education Week*. Retrieved from http://www.edweek.org/ew/articles/2013/03/06/23brief-2.h32.html

Shah, N. (2013c, June 11). Bullying seen persisting, despite some progress. *Education Week*. Retrieved from http://www.edweek.org/ew/articles/2013/06/12/35bully.h32.html

Shah, N., & McNeil, M. (2014, January 4). Suspension, expulsion data cast harsh light on some schools. *Education Week*. Retrieved from http://www.edweek.org/ew/articles/2013/01/10/16ocr.h32.html

Shapiro, J. (2008). Walking a mile in their patients' shoes: Empathy and othering in medical students' education. *Philosophy, Ethics, and Humanities in Medicine* (Vol. 3). doi:10.1186/1747-5341-3-10

Shapiro, J., Morrison, E. H., & Boker, J. R. (2004). Teaching empathy to first year medical students: Evaluation of an elective literature and medicine course. *Education for Health: Change in Learning & Practice, 17*(1), 73–84. doi:10.1080/13576280310001656196

Sharf, R. (2016). *Theories of psychotherapy and counseling: Concepts and cases* (6th ed.). Boston, MA: Cengage.

Sharp, S., & Smith, P. (2002). Understanding bullying. In S. Sharp, & P. Smith, (Eds.), *Tackling bullying in your school: A practical handbook for teachers*. New York, NY: Routledge.

Sharp, S., & Smith, P. K. (Eds.). (2002). *Tackling bullying in your school: A practical handbook for teachers*. New York, NY: Routledge.

Sijtsema, J. J., Veenstra, R., Lindenberg, S., & Salmivalli, C. (2009). Empirical test of bullies' status goals: Assessing direct goals, aggression, and prestige. *Aggressive Behavior, 35*(1), 57–67. doi:10.1002/ab.20282

Simmons, R. (2002). *Odd girl out: The hidden culture of aggression in girls*. New York, NY: Harcourt.

Sizer, B. B. (n.d.). What to do when your child is a bully. *PBS Parents*. Retrieved from http://www.pbs.org/parents/education/going-to-school/social/what-to-do-when-your-child-is-a-bully/

Sklare, G. (2014). *Brief counseling that works: A solution-focused therapy approach for school counselors and other mental health professionals* (3rd ed.). Thousand Oaks, CA: Corwin.

Smith, P., & Morita, Y. (1999). Introduction. In P. K. Smith, Y. Morita, J. Junger-Tas, D. Olweus, R. Catalano, & P. Slee (Eds.), *The nature of school bullying: A cross-national perspective*. London, England: Routledge.

Smith, P. K., & Sharp, S. (Eds.) (1994). *School bullying: Insights and perspectives*. New York, NY: Routledge.

Smith, S. (2013). Cyberbullying in schools: Chapter 157 updates the law on suspension for online conduct. *McGeorge Law Review, 44*(3), 591–599.

Smokowski, P. R., & Kopasz, K. H. (2005). Bullying in school: An overview of types, effects, family characteristics, and intervention strategies. *Children & Schools, 27*, 101–110.

Snyder, J., Schrepferman, L., Oeser, J., Patterson, G., Stoolmiller, M., Johnson, K., & Snyder, A. (2005). Deviancy training and association with deviant peers in young children: Occurrence and contribution to early-onset conduct problems. *Development and Psychopathology, 17*(2), 397–413.

Sprague, J. R., & Horner, R. H. (2006). Schoolwide positive behavioral supports. In S. R. Jimerson & M. J. Furlong (Eds.), *The handbook of school violence and school safety: From research to practice* (pp. 413–427). New York, NY: Routledge.

Spriggs, A. L., Iannotti, R. J., Nansel, T. R., & Haynie, D. L. (2007). Adolescent bullying involvement and perceived family, peer and school relations: Commonalities and differences across race/ethnicity. *Journal of Adolescent Health, 41* (3), 283–293.

Stadler, C., Feifel, J., Rohrmann, S., Vermeiren, R., & Poustka, F. (2010). Peer-victimization and mental health problems in adolescents: Are parental and school support protective? *Child Psychiatry & Human Development*, *41*(4), 371–386.

Steiner-Adair, C. (2013, November 18). What to do when your child is a bully [Web log post]. *The Wall Street Journal.* Retrieved from http://blogs.wsj.com/speakeasy/2013/11/18/what-to-do-if-your-child-is-a-bully/

Stevens, V. V., de Bourdeaudhuij, I. I., & van Oost, P. P. (2002). Relationship of the family environment to children's involvement in bully/victim problems at school. *Journal of Youth & Adolescence, 31*(6), 419.

Stiller, B., Nese, R., Tomlanovich, A., Horner, R., & Ross, S. (2013). *Bullying and harassment prevention in positive behavior support: Expect respect.* Eugene: University of Oregon.

Stormont, M., Reinke, W., & Herman, K. (2011). Teachers' knowledge of evidence-based interventions and available school resources for children with emotional and behavioral problems. *Journal of Behavioral Education, 20*(2), 138–147. doi:10.1007/s10864-011-9122-0

Stuart-Cassel, V., Springer, J., & EMT Associates. (2011). *Analysis of state bullying laws and policies.* Washington, DC: U.S. Department of Education, Office of Planning, Evaluation and Policy Development, Policy and Program Studies Service.

Stuewig, J., Tangney, J. P., Heigel, C., Harty, L., & McCloskey, L. (2010). Shaming, blaming, and maiming: Functional links among the moral emotions, externalization of blame, and aggression. *Journal of Research in Personality, 44*(1), 91–102. doi:10.1016/j.jrp.2009.12.005

Sue, D. W., & Sue, D. (2013). *Counseling the culturally diverse: Theory and practice* (6th ed.). Hoboken, N.J.: John Wiley & Sons.

Sugai, G., & Horner, R. R. (2006). A promising approach for expanding and sustaining school-wide positive behavior support. *School Psychology Review, 35*(2), 245–259.

Sugai, G., & Simonsen, B. (2012). Positive behavioral interventions and supports: History, defining features, and misconceptions. Center for PBIS & Center for Positive Behavioral Interventions and Supports, University of Connecticut. Retrieved from http://idahotc.com/Portals/6/Docs/2015/Tier_1/articles/PBIS_history.features.misconceptions.pdf

Swearer, S. M., Espelage, D. L., Vaillancourt, T., & Hymel, S. (2010). What can be done about school bullying? Linking research to educational practice. *Educational Researcher, 39*(1), 38-47. doi:10.3102/0013189X09357622

Swearer, S. M., Peugh, J., Espelage, D. L., Siebecker, A. B., & Kingsbury, W. L. (2006). A socioecological model for bullying prevention and intervention in early adolescence: An exploratory examination. In S. R. Jimerson & M. J. Furlong (Eds.), *The handbook of school violence and school safety: From research to practice* (pp. 257–273). New York, NY: Routledge.

Swearer, S. M., Song, S. Y., Cary, P. T., Eagle, J. W., & Mickelson, W. T. (2001). Psychosocial correlates in bullying and victimization: The relationship between depression, anxiety, and bully/victim status. *Journal of Emotional Abuse, 2*(2–3), 95–121.

Szalavitz, M. (2010, April 17). How not to raise a bully: The early roots of empathy. *Time.* Retrieved from http://content.time.com/time/health/article/0,8599,1982190,00.html

Talking to our children about racism & diversity. (n.d.). Leadership Conference Education Fund Children's Campaign. Retrieved from http://www.civilrights.org/publications/reports/talking_to_our_children/

Talwani, S. (2015, February). Montana legislature hears about anti-cyberbullying bill. Retrieved from http://www.krtv.com/story/28078259/montana-legislature-hearing.html

Tannen, D. (Ed.). (1993). *Gender and conversational interaction*. New York, NY: Oxford University Press.

Teske, S.C. (2011) A study of zero tolerance policies in schools: A multi-integrated systems approach to improve outcomes for adolescents. *Journal of Child and Adolescent Psychiatric Nursing, 24*, pp. 88–97 © 2011 Wiley Periodicals, Inc

The bullying epidemic. (n.d.). Black Entertainment Television. Retrieved from http://www.bet.com/topics/t/the-bullying-epidemic.html

The Colorado Trust. (2008). *Bullying prevention resource guide for schools, families and community partners*. Retrieved from http://www.bullyingprevention.org/repository/Best%20Practices%20PDFs/BP-Prevention.Intervention.pdf

The size of the World Wide Web (The Internet). (2015, March 18). WorldWideWebSize. Com. Retrieved from http://www.worldwidewebsize.com/

Thornberg, R., Rosenqvist, R., & Johansson, P. (2012). Older teenagers' explanations of bullying. *Child & Youth Care Forum, 41*(4), 327–342. doi:10.1007/s10566-012-9171-0

Tomasello, M., & Vaish, A. (2013). Origins of human cooperation and morality. *Annual Review of Psychology, 64*, 231.

Top 15 most popular social networking sites. (2015, March). eBizMBA.com. Retrieved from http://www.ebizmba.com/articles/social-networking-websites

Trainor, S. H. (2012). School district liability for peer bullying and harassment: Federal initiatives, plaintiffs' complaints, and current legal standards. *National School Board Association*. Retrieved from https://secure.nsba.org/storefront/detail.aspx?id=1363

Trawick-Smith, J. (1988). "Let's say you're the baby, OK?" Play leadership and following behavior of young children. *Young Children, 43*(5), 51–59.

Ttofi, M. M., & Farrington, D. P. (2008a). Bullying: Short-term and long-term effects, and the importance of defiance theory in explanation and prevention. *Victims & Offenders, 3*(2–3), 289–312. doi:10.1080/15564880802143397

Ttofi, M. M., & Farrington, D. P. (2008b). Reintegrative shaming theory, moral emotions and bullying. *Aggressive Behavior,34*(4), 352–368. doi:10.1002/ab.20257

Ttofi, M. M., & Farrington, D. P. (2009). What works in preventing bullying: Effective elements of anti-bullying programmes. *Journal of Aggression, Conflict and Peace Research, 1*(1), 13–24. doi:10.1108/17596599200900003

Ttofi, M. M., & Farrington, D. P. (2011). Effectiveness of school-based programs to reduce bullying: A systematic and meta-analytic review. *Journal of Experimental Criminology, 7*(1), 27–56. doi:10.1007/s11292-010-9109-1

Ttofi, M. M., & Farrington, D. P. (2012a). Bullying prevention programs: The importance of peer intervention, disciplinary methods and age variations. *Journal of Experimental Criminology, 8*(4), 443–462. doi:10.1007/s11292-012-9161-0

Ttofi, M. M., & Farrington, D. P. (2012b). Risk and protective factors, longitudinal research, and bullying prevention. *Evidence-based bullying prevention programs for children and youth* (pp. 85–98) San Francisco, CA: Jossey-Bass.

Ttofi, M. M., Farrington, D. P., & Losel, F. (2012). School bullying as a predictor of violence later in life: A systematic review and meta-analysis of prospective longitudinal studies. *Aggression and Violent Behavior, 17*(5), 405–418. doi:10.1016/j.avb.2012.05.002

Ttofi, M. M., Farrington, D. P., Lösel, F., & Loeber, R. (2011). The predictive efficiency of school bullying versus later offending: A systematic/meta-analytic review of longitudinal studies. *Criminal Behaviour & Mental Health, 21*(2), 80–89. doi:10.1002/cbm.808

Umbreit, M. (2003). Talking circles. *Center for Restorative Justice and Peacemaking: University of Minnesota*. Retrieved from http://www.cehd.umn.edu/ssw/RJP/Projects/Victim-Offender-Dialogue/Peacemaking_Healing_Circles/Talking_Circles.pdf

U.S. Department of Education. (2011.) *Analysis of State Bullying Laws and Policies*. Retrieved from http://www2.ed.gov/rschstat/eval/bullying/state-bullying-laws/state-bullying-laws.pdf

U.S. Department of Education. (2014a). *Directory of federal school climate and discipline resources*. Washington, DC: Author.

U.S. Department of Education. (2014b). *Guiding principles: A resource guide for improving school climate and discipline*. Washington, DC: Author.

U.S. Department of Education Office of Special Education Programs Technical Assistance Center on Positive Behavioral Interventions and Supports. (n.d.). *Positive behavioral interventions and supports-OSEP*. Washington, DC: Author.

U.S. Department of Health and Human Services. (n.d.). What is cyberbullying? *Stopbullying.gov*. Retrieved from http://www.stopbullying.gov/cyberbullying/what-is-it/index.html

U.S. Government Accountability Office. (2012). School bullying: Extent of legal protections for vulnerable groups needs to be more fully assessed. Retrieved from http://www.gao.gov/assets/600/591202.pdf

Valencia, N. (2014, March 10). Yik Yak chat app stirring up trouble in high schools. *CNN Tech*. Retrieved from http://www.cnn.com/2014/03/07/tech/yik-yak-app-high-school-problems/

Valinsky, J. (2013). The real story behind Snapchat leaked, the site publishing screenshots of your embarrassing snaps. *Observer.com*. Retrieved from http://betabeat.com/2013/05/snapchat-leaked-creator/

van Dijck, J. V. (2013). *The culture of connectivity: A critical history of social media*. New York: Oxford University Press.

Van Hasselt, V., & Hersen, M. (Eds.). (2000). *Aggression and violence: An introductory text*. Needham Heights, MA: Allyn & Bacon.

Veenstra, R., Lindenberg, S., Oldehinkel, A. J., De Winter, A. F., Verhulst, F. C., & Ormel, J. (2005). Bullying and victimization in elementary schools: A comparison of bullies, victims, bully/victim, and uninvolved preadolescents. *Developmental Psychology*, *41*(4), 672–682. doi:10.1037/0012-1649.41.4.672

Verdick, E., & Lisovskis, M. (2003). *How to take the grrrr out of anger*. Minneapolis, MN: Free Spirit.

Vernberg, E., & Biggs, B. (Eds.). (2010). *Preventing and treating bullying and victimization*. New York, NY: Oxford University Press.

Vlachou, M., Andreou, E., Botsoglou, K., & Didaskalou, E. (2011). Bully/victim problems among preschool children: A review of current research evidence. *Educational Psychology Review*, *23*(3), 329–358. doi:10.1007/s10648-011-9153-z

Völlink, T., Bolman, C. A., Dehue, F., & Jacobs, N. C. (2013). Coping with cyberbullying: Differences between victims, bully-victims and children not involved in bullying. *Journal of Community & Applied Social Psychology*, *23*(1), 7–24. doi:10.1002/casp.2142

Vreeman, R. C., & Carroll, A. E. (2007). A systematic review of school-based interventions to prevent bullying. *Archives of Pediatrics & Adolescent Medicine*, *161*(1), 78–88.

Wallace, K. (2013, October 16). Parents, beware of bullying on sites you've never seen. *CNN.com*. Retrieved from http://www.cnn.com/2013/10/10/living/parents-new-apps-bullying/

Wedding, D., & Niemiec, R. M. (2003). The clinical use of films in psychotherapy. *Journal of Clinical Psychology, 59*(2), 207–215.
Weiner, M. T., & Miller, M. (2006). Deaf children and bullying: Directions for future research. *American Annals of the Deaf, 151*(1), 61–70.
What if your child is the one showing bullying behavior? (2015). PACER Center. Retrieved from http://www.pacer.org/parent/php/php-c109.pdf
What to do if your child exhibits bullying behavior. (2012). Anti-Defamation League. Retrieved from http://www.adl.org/assets/pdf/education-outreach/What-to-Do-if-Your-Child-Exhibits-Bullying-Behavior.pdf
Wilf, R. (2012). Disparities in school move students of color toward prison: New data show youth of color disproportionately suspended and expelled from school. Center For American Progress. Retrieved from https://www.americanprogress.org/issues/race/news/2012/03/13/11350/disparities-in-school-discipline-move-students-of-color-toward-prison/
Willard, N. E. (2007). *Cyberbullying and cyberthreats: Responding to the challenge of online social aggression, threats, and distress.* Champaign, IL: Research Press.
Williams, K. R., & Guerra, N. G. (2007). Prevalence and predictors of Internet bullying. *Journal of Adolescent Health, 41*(6), S14–S21. doi:10.1016/j.jadohealth.2007.08.018
Wilmot, W., & Hocker, J. (2011). *Interpersonal conflict* (8th ed.). New York, NY: McGraw-Hill.
WiredSafety.org. (n.d.). What is cyberbullying, exactly? Stop cyberbullying. Retrieved from http://stopcyberbullying.org/index2.html
Wiseman, R. (2002). *Queen bees & wannabes: Helping your daughter survive cliques, gossip, boyfriends, and other realities of adolescence.* New York, NY: Crown.
Wiseman, R. (2013). *Masterminds & wingmen: Helping our boys cope with schoolyard power, locker-room tests, girlfriends, and the new rules of boy world.* New York, NY: Harmony Books.
Wubbolding, R., Brickell, J., Imhof, L., Kim, R., Lojk, L., & Al-Rashidi, B. (2004). Reality therapy: A global perspective. *International Journal for the Advancement of Counselling, 26*(3), 219–228.
Yancey, V. (2012, February 13). Youth are turning in to reality TV bullies (RTVB). *Examiner.com.* Retrieved from http://www.examiner.com/article/youth-are-turning-into-reality-tv-bullies-rtvb
Yarm, M. (2014). Hot apps: The race to be the next Snapchat. *Rolling Stone,* 24.
Ybarra, M. L., Diener-West, M., & Leaf, P. J. (2007). Examining the overlap in Internet harassment and school bullying: Implications for school intervention. *Journal of Adolescent Health, 41*(6), S42–S50. doi:10.1016/j.jadohealth.2007.09.004
Yeung, R., & Leadbeater, B. (2010). Adults make a difference: The protective effects of parent and teacher emotional support on emotional and behavioral problems of peer-victimized adolescents. *Journal of Community Psychology, 38*(1), 80–98. doi:10.1002/jcop.20353
Yik Yak. (2014, March). *CrunchBase.* Retrieved from https://www.crunchbase.com/organization/yik-yak
Young, M. (2013). *Learning the art of helping: Building blocks and techniques* (5th ed.) Boston, MA: Pearson.
Yuen, L. (2009, September 2). Teachers put on leave after bullying supposed gay student. *MPR News.* Retrieved from http://www.mprnews.org/story/2009/09/02/teachers-accused-of-mocking-student-on-leave
Zhao, E. (2011, September 2). New Jersey's anti-bullying law, toughest in country, garners praise and criticism. *The Huffington Post.* Retrieved from http://www.huffingtonpost.com/2011/09/02/new-jerseys-anti-bullying_n_946625.html
Zimmerman, J., & Coyle, V. (2009). *The way of the council* (2nd ed.). Viroqua, WI: Bramble Books.

Index

A-B-C model, 137 (figure)–138
Accountability
  of bullying child, 213, 223
  strings of, 18
Adulthood, bullying continuing into, 12, 37
Affective empathy, 114, 118
Affirmative duty to act, 195
After School, 16
Agents of bullying, 32
  sample dialog of logic of, 128–130
  sample dialog of logic of, reflection on, 130–134
Age/size of bully, relevance of, 11–12
Aggression
  as learned behavior, 19
  behavioralized, 30–31
  direct, 31
  indirect, 31
  interpersonal, 31
  masked, 40
  on reality television, 11
  retaliatory, 17
  See also Relational aggression; Violence
Aggressor-target interaction, 5–6
American Academy of Pediatrics, 64
American Civil Liberties Union (ACLU), 181
Amorality, 119
Anderson, R. J., 37
Anger
  as idiosyncratic, 165
  defining, 160
  prompts for intervention, 160–161
  prompts for intervention, answers in response to, 161–162
  underestimating, 159–162
Anger management, 162–165
  Johari window and, 163 (figure)–164 (figure), 163 (note 1)
  Johari window and sample dialogue, 166–168
Ask.fm, 16, 178
Ayduk, O., 41

Bad Samaritan rules, 195–198
  applying to adults, 197–198
  applying to minors, 196–197
Bandura, A, 153
Barbaranelli, C., 153
Bazelon, E., 103
Beck, A., 150
Behavioral inertia, 73, 162–163
Behavioralized aggression, 30–31
Behavioral manifestation of bullying, 29–31
  aggression, 30–31
  physical abuse, 30
  shunning/exclusion from peer activities, 30
  spoken/written insults/intimidations, 30
Benign neglect, 35
Benzmiller, H., 195
Berger, K. S., 28
Best fit strategy, 145
Best practice legislation, 55
Bibliomedia therapy, 235–242
  defining, 235
  effect on the brain, 234–236
  empathy and, 235, 238–239
  guidelines for, 236–239
  sample discussion, 239–242
  sample discussion, reflection on, 242
Bibliotherapy, defining, 234. *See also* Bibliomedia therapy

Bilodeau, L., 160
Blame *vs.* responsibility, 214
Blind spot of self-awareness, 164
Bonding, 115
Borba, M., 153, 154
Boys/men, aggression by, 31, 42
Braff, D., 235
Brott, P., 68
Bully (film), 239–242
Bully, defining, 9. *See also* Bullying
Bullycreep, 21–22, 38
Bullying
  as hyperendemic, 38
  as peer activity, 13
  covert *vs.* overt, 11
  definition of, 9
  definition of, common, 28–29, 49–50
  definition of, new and comprehensive, 31–35
  dysfunctional family life and, 12–13
  historical/stereotypical factors in, 11–13
  insecurities and, 11
  intellectual/academic problems and, 12
  misconceptions about, 21–27
  physical size/age of bully and, 11–12
  poor attitude toward school and, 12
  reactive *vs.* proactive response to, 3–4
  reasons kids bully, 13–15
  recalcitrance in reacting to, 4–5
  relevant behaviors associated with, 10–11
  self-esteem and, 11, 32, 35, 152–153
  trouble with the law and, 12
  See also Aggression; Covert/indirect bullying; Power; Psychology of domination
Bully-target continuum, 3
Bully-target dyad, 3
Bully-victim, 24n2, 33, 46
Bumpers/spacers, 147
Burn it off technique, 149–150
Bystanders, 116–117
  empathy and, 113
  fear of intervening by, 192–194
  lack of skills for intervening by, 193
  penalties for failing to act, 195
  penalties for failing to act, applying to adults, 197–198
  penalties for failing to act, applying to minors, 196–197
  psychological impact of bullying on, 33, 35
  STAND TALL program to turn into upstanders, 116–117, 194–195
Caprara, G. V., 153
Center for Civil Rights Remedies, 244–245
Centers for Disease Control and Prevention (CDC), 60
Challenge/confrontation, 133–134
Cheater words/phrases, 88–89
Children with special needs, suspensions and, 246–249
Choice therapy, 134
Christensen, J., 26
Christie, F., 218 (note 1)
Cinematherapy, 235
Civil discourse/behavior, basis of, 27
Civil law, on bullying, 18
Client-centered approach, 82 (note 2)
Close-ended questions, 161
Cognitive behavioral therapy, 150
Cognitive empathy, 114, 117–119, 120
Cognitive shift, 131
Coloroso, B., 115, 116–117, 193, 204
Columbine High School shooting, 55
Commonality, feeling of, 114
Communication/relational connection with bully, 91–97
  first contact, 91–93
  first contact, discovery and boundaries, 92–94
  first contact, reflection on, 93–94
  first contact, setting for, 91–92
  role of trust in, 94–96
  tips for, 96–97
Comparison behaviors, 238
Conduct disorder, 24
Confidentiality, 188
Conflict avoidance, 148
Conflict resolution, resources for, 282
Confrontation/challenge, 133–134
Connectivity, as synonymous to communication, 174–175. *See also* Cyber bullying
Conscience
  defining, 154
  moral intelligence virtues and, 155
Consistency of prevention policy, 61
Constructive Behavioral Change (CBC) plan, 227–231
  components of, 228
  sample plan, 228–230
Context of negative behavior, 25
Continuum, bullying, 3
Cormier, S., 82 (note 2)
Corsini, R., 146 (note 2)
Counting, as impulse behavior control technique, 147

Covert/indirect bullying
cyberbullying as, 12
defining, 32, 33
gender and, 11, 12, 31, 32, 33
overt/direct bullying *vs.*, 11
psychological bullying as, 11, 12
See also Overt/direct bullying
Covey, S., 78
Crick, N. R., 28, 29, 40
Criminal law, on bullying, 18
Cultural capitol, 30
Cultural differences
in concepts of time, 81
in nonverbal communication, 79 (note 1)
Curriculum, resources for, 280–282
Curtner-Smith, M. E., 113–114
Cyberbullying, 173–190
as covert bullying, 12
as peer activity, 13
authority over online accounts, 181–183
defining, 9
interventions for, 183–189
intervention tips for, 189 (figure)
legal jurisdiction over, 178–180
psychological aspect of, 17, 36
reasons to engage in, 14
sample dialog, 183–187
sample dialog, refection on, 187–189
scope of problem, 173–174
state legislation on, 56, 56 (note 7)
types of, 175 (figure)
Cyberstalking, 175 (figure)
Decisions, process-oriented, 17

Defamation, 179
Defensive posture, 80
DeGaetano, G., 233, 234
De La Rue, **[no initial in biblio--with Espelage]**, 12 (note 1)
Deliberate indifference standard, 179–180
Denigration, 175 (figure)
Department of Education (DoE), 53–54, 248
analysis of state statutes, 54–56
key findings of analysis of state statutes, 56
recommendations for prevention, 56–58
Department of Justice (DoJ), 247, 248
Depression, 17, 19
Desensitization to violence, 233
Detrixhe, J., 235
Developmental behavior, abnormal, 23
Direct aggression, 31
Disagreement, as not bullying, 25–27

Discipline
incremental process of, 211
punishment *vs.*, 196
Dislike of person or group, as not bullying, 27
Documentation
of bullying behavior, 211
of interventions, 225–227
sample incident report, 220 (figure)–221
Domination. *See* Psychology of domination
Double bind, 213, 213 (note 2)
Downey, G., 41
Doyle, B., 68
Drew, N., 165, 166–167
Due diligence, 226
Duty to warn, 182 (note 13)
Dysfunctional family, relevance to bullying, 12–13

Education for All Handicapped Children, 246
Educators, resources for, 282–283
Effective empathy, reinforcing, 119–122
Egan, G., 82 (note 2)
Ellis, A., 136
Emotional abuse, 36–37
Emotionally hardened, 119
Emotions, moral, 152
Empathy
affective, 114, 118
applying toward others, 122–124
bibliomedia therapy and, 235, 238–239
cognitive, 114, 120
cognitive/kindness, reinforcing, 117–119
defining, 113–114, 154
effective, reinforcing, 119–122
encouraging, 213–214
lack of, as factor in bullying, 11, 113
logic of bullying and, 128–134
moral intelligence virtues and, 154–155
possibility of teaching to others, 115
sample dialogue, 124–126
sample dialogue, reflection on, 127
sympathy *vs.*, 114–115
teaching by concept, 115–117
Emphatic hesitant, 119
Encouragement skills, 83–84, 213–214
Enumerated groups, 58–60
CDC report on, 60
defining, 52, 58
DoE on expansion of protection to, 57
examples of, 52, 58–59
GAO report on, 59–60

Environmental saturation of violence theory, 233, 234
Epidemic, media view on bullying as, 38
Equity of power, talking circles and, 106
Espelage, D. L., 12 (note 1), 21, 113
Ethic of reciprocity, 213 (note 3)–214 (note 3)
Exclusion/shunning, 43, 45, 175 (figure)
Expulsion, of non-White children, 64

Facebook, 16, 176
  authority over online accounts, 181–183
  See also Social media
Fairness
  defining, 154
  moral intelligence virtues and, 156
False situation, 99
Fiction, use in bibliotherapy, 235
Fiduciary responsibility, 195
Films
  stereotypes/myths in, 238, 238 (note 2)
  violence in, 233
  See also Bibliomedia therapy
First Amendment rights, 181–182
Fisher, H. L., 18–19
Flaming, 175 (figure)
Fluency of speech, 80
Focus, as Intervener skill, 78
Forced apologies
  appropriateness of, 100
  as not restorative justice, 101
  defining, 99
  example of, 99–100
Formspring (social media site), 178
Free speech, 181–182
Fremouw, W., 37
Funke, K., 113

Galen, B. R., 40–41
Garrod, O. G. B., 119 (note 2)
Gender
  covert/indirect bullying and, 11, 12, 31, 32, 33, 42
  relational aggression as gender neutral, 42–43
  sexual identity and, 42–43
  sexual orientation and, 59, 60
Geofencing, 177
Geography of Problem Solving (GPS), 104 (note 1), 218
Gillespie, J., 244–245
Gini, G., 153
Girls/women
  covert *vs.* overt bullying by, 11, 12, 31, 32, 33
  physical aggression by, 42
  rejection sensitivity and, 41
  romantic dispute as reason for aggression, 45
Glasser, W., 134
Golden Rule, 213–214
Goldstein, A., 29
Gonzalez, J. E., 150
Goodman-Scott, E., 68
Gould, M. S., 19
Government Accountability Office (GAO), 59–60
Grossman, D., 233, 234
Grotpeter, J. K., 28, 29
Groupthink, 16

Harassment, 52, 175 (figure)
Harty, L., 157
Haynie, D., 28
Hazler, R., 10
Healing circles. *See* Talking circles
Heigel, C., 157
Helplessness, 18, 19
Higdon, M., 54–55
Hinduja, S., 174
Hoffman, S., 245
Hold harmless shield, 195
Hong, J. S., 21
Hostile environment, 52, 56
Huesmann, L. R., 37
Human development, relational aggression and, 44–45, 46
Humiliated fury, 157
Hymel, S., 113, 153
Hyperendemic, bullying as, 38
Hypervigilance, 36, 41

Ideation. *See* Suicide/ideation
Identity theft/impersonation, 175 (figure)
Impulse, defining, 136
Impulse behavior
  burn it off technique and, 149–150
  counting technique and, 147
  leaving the scene technique and, 148
  rational-emotive behavioral therapy for, 118, 136–140
  Stop. Think. Then Act. approach to, 140–146
  techniques for first mindset thinking, 146–150

triggers and, 147–148
walk away technique and, 148–149
In-depth questions, 161
Indirect aggression, 31
Individual education plan (IEP), 247–248
Individuals With Disabilities Education Act, 246
Ingham, H., 163 (note 1)
Innuendo, 218
Insecurities, relevance to bullying, 11
Institution, defining, 10
Intellectual and academic problems, 12
Intentional interviewing, defining, 82
Intentional interviewing microskills, 82–89
cheater words/phrases, 88–89
encouragement, 83–84
interpretation, 86–89, 87 (diagram)
observation, 82–83
paraphrasing, 84, 85
questioning, 83
reflection, 84–85
summarizing, 86
Internet, role models of bullies on, 14. *See also* social media
Interpersonal communication, 77
Interpersonal relationship, defining, 32, 34
Interpersonal *vs.* relational aggression, 31
Interpretation skills, 86–89, 87 (diagram)
Interpretive summary, 86
Intervener, defining, 76–77. *See also* Communication/relational connection with bully; Intervener skills
Intervener skills, 76–89
intentional interviewing, 82–89
listening, 78
nonverbal communication/behavior, 79–81
patience, 76, 77
tolerance, 76, 77
Interventions
behavioral outcomes goals of, 221
Constructive Behavioral Change and, 227–231
defining, 77
documenting, 220 (figure)–221, 225–227
goals of, 211, 212
Level 2 sample dialog, 222–224
Level 2 sample dialog, documentation of, 226–227
Level 2 sample dialog, proposed interventions for, 228–230
Level 2 sample dialog, reflection on, 225
levels of, 222
policy/practice for successful, 61–62
purposes of, 218
rules for, 97 (figure)
See also see Bibliomedia therapy; Intervener; Investigation; Supervisory personnel
Interviewing. *See* Intentional interviewing
Intonation, 80
Investigation, 219–221
critical questions for, 219
defining, 219
documentation of first, 220
See also Intervention
Invitation of trust, 120
Irrational thinking, 138
Irwin, L., 41
Ivey, A., 82

Jack, R. D., 119 (note 2)
Johari window, 163 (note 1)
advantages of using, 171
sample dialogue, review of information, 168–171
sample window, 163 (figure)–164 (figure)
Juvonen, J., 46

Keywords, during reflection, 85
Kindness
defining, 154
moral intelligence virtues and, 155–156
Kinesics, 79–80
Klein, J., 30
Kleinman, M., 19
Klomek, B. A., 19
Kopasz, K. H., 15 (note 2)
Kowalski, R. M., 173
Kumpulainen, K., 37

Labeling, 9, 24–25
Language of equity, 132
Law and bullying
civil law, 18
criminal law, 18
deliberate indifference standard, 179–180
enumerated groups and, 58–60
legal definitions of what constitutes bullying, 51–52
legal jurisdiction over cyberbullying, 178–180
need for best legislation model, 55
problems with efforts to legislate prevention, 49–51
reasonable person standard and, 52–54

state statutes, DoE analysis of, 54–56
state statutes, DoE recommendations for prevention, 56–58
state statutes, key findings of DoE analysis of, 56
successful intervention, policy and practice for, 61–62
unintended consequences of law, 52
zero tolerance and, 15, 54 (note 5), 62–65, 103
See also Restorative justice
Learned behaviors, relevance to bullying, 10–11
Learned helplessness, 19
Leaving the field, 148
Leff, S., 29
Libel, 179
Life as target, resources for, 284
Limber, S. P., 173
Listening skills, 78
Losen, D. J., 244–245
Luft, J., 163 (note 1)

Macklem, G., 28, 44, 46
Magic Question, 156–157
Malicious website, 175 (figure)
Marrocco, F., 19
Masked aggression, 40
McCloskey, L., 157
Mean girl persona, 31
Mebane, S., 113
Media. *See* Bibliomedia therapy; Films; Reality television; Social media; Television
Mediation, purpose of, 100
Message decoding, 22
Metacommunication
defining, 77
themes of, 87 (diagram)
trust and, 120
Milgram, S., 153 (note 1)
Misdirected passionate energy, 149
Misery index, 35–37
Mobbing, 16 (note 3)
Moral disengagement, 153
Moral emotions, 152
Moral intelligence, 154–155
Morality, bullying prevention and, 152–157
cognition and moral intelligence, 153–154
leads embedding moral intelligence virtues, 154–156
Magic Question and, 156–157
shaming and, 157
Mounts, N. S., 41–42
MySpace, 176

Natural affective empathy, 119
Negative emotions, 121–122, 121 (note 3)
Negative schemas, 137
Negligence, 198
Neutrality, 76–77, 96
Nonverbal communication/behavior, 79–81
cultural concept of time and, 81
cultural differences in, 79 (note 1)
environmental effects on, 81
kinesics in, 79–80
paralinguistics in, 80
proxemics in, 80

Objectification, 11
Observation skills, 82–83
Observers of bullying, 35. *See also* Bystanders
Olweus, D., 28, 29, 33, 49, 50
Open-ended questions, 161
Organization, defining, 10
Outing, 175 (figure)
Overt/direct bullying
as psychological, 15–16
defining, 32, 33
gender and, 11, 12, 31, 32, 33
vs. covert/indirect bullying, 11
See also Covert/indirect bullying
Ownership to the action, 123

Paralinguistics, 80
Paraphrasing skills, 84, 85
Parental engagement, 201–216
receptive to intervention, 201–204
resistant to intervention, 206–210
skeptical about intervention, 204–206
tips for, 204, 206, 210, 212–214, 215
what parents need to know, 210–212
Parents
justification of bullying behavior by, 21
resources for, 283–284
Part-value, of program/video, 74
Pastorelli, C., 153
Patchin, J. W., 174
Patience, 131, 134, 209
Patterns of negative behavior, 25
Paul, A. M., 235
Peck, S., 117
Peer group attack, 16
Perceptual flaws, 133
Persona, 120

Personal space, 80
Physical comfort zone, 80
Policy, prevention
environmental climate and, 65–66
equity/continuous improvement and, 67
expectations/consequences and, 66
new Guiding Principles for, 65–67
zero tolerance and, 15, 54 (note 5), 62–65, 103
Polling, 175 (figure)
Porter, M., 114
Positive Behavioral Interventions and Supports (PBIS) **[same as next entry?]**, 67–68
Positive Behavioral Interventions Strategies (PBIS), 131
Positive reinforcement, 131
Power
bullying as, 10, 14–15, 28, 34–35
equity of power, talking circles and, 106
inequity of, effect on teasing, 22
trust and, 120
Power, T., 29
Power spectrum, 23
Pozzoli, T., 153
Prevention policy, uniformity of, 61–62
Primary agent in bullying, 24
Privacy, 92
Private educational institutions, bullying law and, 53
Process-oriented decisions, 17
Protalinski, E., 183
Provocative victim, 41, 106
Proxemics, 80
Psychological bullying
as covert bullying, 11, 12
depth of, 15–16
types of, 36
Psychological illness, bullying as not, 24–25
Psychological torture, 36–37
Psychology of domination, 13–15
bullying as display of power, 14–15
examples of role models on television/Internet, 13–14
small chance of getting caught, 14
Punishment *vs.* discipline, 196
Pure bully, 24 (note 2)
Push-until-pushed-back behavior, 23

Questions
close-ended, 161
critical, for investigation, 219
intentional interviewing and, 83
Magic Question, 156–157
open-ended, 161

Racial discrimination, 34, 64, 244–245
Ragatz, L. L., 37
Ramsay, M., 41
Rasanen, E., 37
Rate of speaking, 80
Rational-emotive behavioral therapy (REBT), 118, 136–140
A-B-C model of, 137 (figure)–138
activating event and, 137 (figure), 139 (figure)
belief system and, 137 (figure), 138, 139 (figure)
consequence and, 137 (figure), 140 (figure)
example of, 138–140
Rational thinking, 138
Reality television
role models of bullies on, 13, 14, 26
violence and aggression on, 11
Reasonable cause, 180
Reasonableness of prevention policy, 61
Reasonable person standard, 52–54
Reciprocity, 213 (note 3)–214 (note 3)
Recognition of thought process, 114
Reflection, 84–85
Reflective synopsis, 85
Rejection sensitivity, 41
Relational aggression, 28, 35, 40–47
as gender neutral, 42–43
defining, 32, 40–42
examples of, 45–46
human development and, 44–45
interpersonal aggression *vs.*, 31
social media as venue for, 45
Respect, 154, 155
Responsibility *vs.* blame, 214
Restorative justice, 106–107
applying elements of, 103–111
as restorative/remediative efforts, 106–108
concept behind, 103–104
forced apologies as not, 101
guidelines, 108
sample dialog, 108–110
sample dialog, reflection on, 111
talking circle approach, 104–106
Retaliatory aggression, 17
Revenge of the Nerds (film), 238 (note 2)
Revictimization, 99
Riestenberg, N., 105, 113

Riordan, R. J., 234
Rogers, C., 82 (note 2)
Role models, 213
  on Internet, 14
  on reality television, 13, 14, 26
  supervisory personnel as, 25–26
Role play, 122
Rumors, 43, 44, 45, 218
Rumr (social media site), 177

Safe and Supportive Minnesota Schools Act, 54 (note 4)
Samaritan laws, 195
Schemas, 137
Schonfeld, I. S., 19
Schools
  bullying and poor attitude toward, 12
  safety of, 246
  violence in, 55, 246, 246 (note 1)
School-to-prison pipeline, 64, 65, 245–246
Schwartz, R., 37
Schyns, P. G., 119 (note 2)
Secondary agent in bullying, 24
Secret (social media site), 177
Self-awareness, blind spot of, 164
Self-control, 154, 155
Self-disclosure, 132
Self-esteem, 11, 32, 35, 152–153
Self-harming behavior, 16–19, 55
  suicide/ideation, 4, 17, 19, 178
Self-help reading, 234
Seligman, Martin E. P., 19
Sensate skills, 84–85
Sense of privacy, 92
Sexual discrimination, 34
Sexual identity, 42–43
Sexual orientation, 59, 60
Shame-rage, 157
Shaming, 157
Sharp, S. **[spelled Sharpe on p. 29]**, 29
Show of force message, 81
Shunning/exclusion, 43, 45, 175 (figure)
Silence, 132–133
Simmons, R., 40
Single-incident negative interactions
  bullying as, 33–34
  bullying as not, 25
Size/age of bully, relevance of, 11–12
Skills. *See* Intervener skills
Smith, P., 29
Smith, P. K., 113–114
Smokowski, P. R., 15 (note 2)
Snapchat, 177
Social media
  as power venue for bullies, 15
  as psychological torment venue, 16, 36
  as relational aggression torment venue, 45
  new technology and, 174, 176
  potential for misuse, 176–178
  top network sites, 176 (figure)
  Softened sense of empathic abilities, 117–118
  See also Cyberbullying; Empathy
Solution equation, 210
Spacers/bumpers, 147
STAND TALL program, 117, 194–195
Stereotypes/myths, in film, 238, 238 (note 2)
StopBullying.gov, 193
Stop. Think. Then Act. (STTA), 140–146, 162
  sample dialogue, 141–145
  sample dialogue, reflection on, 145–146
Strings of accountability, 18
Structural educational session, 111
Stuewig, J., 157
Sue, D., 79 (note 1)
Sue, D. W., 79 (note 1)
Suicide/ideation, 4, 17, 19, 178
Supervisory personnel
  as role models, 25–26
  benign neglect by, 35
  defining, 10
  deliberate indifference standard and, 179–180
  professional discretion of, 221
  resources for, 282–283
  See also Intervener skills; Interventions
Suspensions, defining, 66
Suspensions, problems with
  children with special needs, 246–249
  disportionality, 64, 244–245
  disportionality, federal intervention to address, 248
  removal of bully from education setting, 248–249
  school-to-prison pipeline, 64, 65, 245–246
Swearer, S. M., 46
Sweet and sour approach, 225
Symbolic gains, 30
Sympathy, empathy *vs.*, 114–115
Synopsis, reflective, 85
Szalavitz, M., 113, 115, 116 (note 1

Talking circles, 103, 106
Talking piece, 104 (note 1)
Talk therapy, 74
Tangible gains, 30
Tangney, J. P., 157
Target-agent in bullying, 24
Targets of bullying, 32
Tattling, 27
Taunting, 22, 22 (note 1)
Teasing, bullying as not, 22
Technology. *See* Cyberbullying
Television
  affect on bullying, 10–11
  role models of bullies on, 13–14
  See also Reality television
Temperaments. *See* Patience; Tolerance
Terbin, I., 178
Terminology issues, 9–10
Themes, during reflection, 85
Tiered interventions, 66, 67–69
Time issues, 81, 91, 134
Tipping point, 206
Tolerance, 209
  defining, 154
  moral intelligence virtues and, 156
Training
  in bullying prevention for school staff, 58
  in restorative approach, 104
  STAND TALL program, 117, 194–195
Triggers, 147, 162
Trust, 94–96
  communication/relational connection and, 94–96
  parents resistant to change and, 209
  power and, 120
Twitter, 16

Underwood, M. K., 40–41
Upstanders, 193. *See also* Bystanders

Verbal intimidation, 11
Vicarious victimization, 14–15, 15 (note 2), 32, 33, 34–35
Vieno, A., 153
Violence
  environmental saturation of violence theory, 233, 234
  in media, 11, 233
  in schools, 55, 246, 246 (note 1)
Volume, of voice, 80

Whisper (social media site), 177
Wilson, L. S., 234
Wiseman, R., 31, 40
Wolz, B., 235
Worldview, 131

Yik Yak, 16, 177–178
YouTube, 14, 176
role models of bullies on, 14

Zero tolerance, 15, 54 (note 5), 62–65, 103

Printed in the USA
CPSIA information can be obtained
at www.ICGtesting.com
JSHW062352070824
67754JS00005B/12

9 781506 3338